INDUSTRIALIZATION AND DEVELOPMENT

Edited by
Tom Hewitt, Hazel Johnson
and David Wield
for an Open University Course Team

OXFORD UNIVERSITY PRESS

in association with

 The Open University

This book has been printed on paper produced from pulps bleached without use of chlorine gases and produced in Sweden from wood from continuously farmed forests. The paper mill concerned, Papyrus Nymölla AB, is producing bleached pulp in which dioxin contaminants do not occur.

Published in the United Kingdom by Oxford University Press, Oxford
in association with
The Open University, Milton Keynes

Oxford University Press, Walton Street, Oxford OX2 6DP

Oxford New York
Athens Auckland Bangkok Bombay
Calcutta Cape Town Dar es Salaam Delhi
Florence Hong Kong Istanbul Karachi
Kuala Lumpur Madras Madrid Melbourne
Mexico City Nairobi Paris Singapore
Taipei Tokyo Toronto
and associated companies in
Berlin Ibadan

Oxford is a trade mark of Oxford University Press

The Open University, Walton Hall, Milton Keynes MK7 6AA

First published in the United Kingdom 1992
Paperback edition reprinted 1994

British Library Cataloguing in Publication Data
Data available

ISBN 0–19–877332–3
ISBN 0–19–877333–1 (Pbk)

Library of Congress Cataloging in Publication Data
Data available

ISBN 0–19–877332–3
ISBN 0–19–877333–1 (Pbk)

Printed in Great Britain by the Alden Press, Oxford

CONTENTS

THE OPEN UNIVERSITY
U208 *THIRD WORLD DEVELOPMENT*
COURSE TEAM AND AUTHORS

Tom Hewitt, Lecturer in Development Studies, The Open University (Course Team Chair 1991–92)

Ben Crow, Lecturer in Development Studies, The Open University (Course Team Chair 1989–90)

Tim Allen, Lecturer in Development Studies, The Open University

Paul Auerbach, Reader in Economics, Kingston Polytechnic (Part Assessor)

Carolyn Baxter, Course Manager, The Open University

Henry Bernstein, Senior Lecturer in Agricultural and Rural Development, Institute of Development Policy and Management, University of Manchester

Krishna Bharadwaj, Professor, Centre for Economic Studies and Development, Jawaharlal Nehru University, New Delhi, India

Suzanne Brown, Course Manager, The Open University

Janet Bujra, Lecturer in Sociology, Department of Social and Economic Studies, University of Bradford

David Cleary, Research Officer, Centre of Latin American Studies, University of Sussex

Kate Crehan, Associate Professor, New School for Social Research, New York, USA

Sue Dobson, Graphic Artist, The Open University

Harry Dodd, Print Production Controller, The Open University

Kath Doggett, Project Control, The Open University

Joshua Doriye, Professor, Institute of Finance and Management, Dar es Salaam, Tanzania

Chris Edwards, Senior Lecturer in Economics, School of Development Studies, University of East Anglia

Diane Elson, Lecturer in Development Economics, University of Manchester (Part Assessor)

Sheila Farrant, Tutor Counsellor and Assistant Staff Tutor, The Open University, Cambridge (Course Reader)

Jo Field, Project Control, The Open University

Jayati Ghosh, Associate Professor, Centre for Economic Studies and Development, Jawaharlal Nehru University, New Delhi, India

Heather Gibson, Lecturer in Economics, University of Kent at Canterbur

Garry Hammond, Senior Editor, The Open University

Barbara Harriss, Lecturer in Agricultural Economics and Governing Body Fellow, Wolfson College, University of Oxford

John Harriss, Director, Centre for Development Studies, London School of Economics (Part Assessor)

Pamela Higgins, Graphic Designer, The Open University

Caryl Hunter-Brown, Liaison Librarian, The Open University

Gillian Iossif, Lecturer in Statistics, The Open University

Rhys Jenkins, Reader in Economics, School of Development Studies, University of East Anglia

Hazel Johnson, Lecturer in Development Studies, The Open University

Sabrina Kassam, Research Assistant, The Open University

Andrew Kilminster, Lecturer in Economics, School of Business Studies, Oxford Polytechnic

Patti Langton, Producer, BBC

Christina Lay, Course Manager, The Open University

Anthony McGrew, Lecturer in Government, Social Science Faculty, The Open University

Maureen Mackintosh, Reader in Economics, Kingston Polytechnic

Mahmood Mamdani, Professor, Centre for Basic Research, Kampala, Uganda

Charlotte Martin, Teacher and Open University Tutor (Course Reader)

Mahmood Messkoub, Lecturer in Economics, University of Leeds

Richard Middleton, Staff Tutor in Arts, The Open University, Newcastle

Alistair Morgan, Lecturer in Institute of Educational Technology, The Open University

Eleanor Morris, Producer, BBC

Ray Munns, Cartographer, The Open University

Kathy Newman, Secretary, The Open University

Hilary Owen, Lecturer, Department of Hispanic Studies, University of Belfast

Debbie Payne, Secretary, The Open University

Ruth Pearson, Lecturer in Economics, School of Development Studies, University of East Anglia

Richard Pinder, Training consultant, Sheffield (Course Reader)

David Potter, Professor of Government, The Open University

Janice Robertson, Editor, The Open University

Carol Russell, Editor, The Open University

Vivian von Schelling, Lecturer in Development Studies, Polytechnic of East London

Gita Sen, Fellow (Professor), Centre for Development Studies, Kerala, India

Meg Sheffield, Senior Producer, BBC

Paul Smith, Lecturer in Environmental Studies, The Open University

Ines Smyth, Senior Lecturer, Institute of Social Studies, The Hague, Netherlands; Research Associate, Department of Applied Social Studies and Social Research, University of Oxford

Hilary Standing, Lecturer in Social Anthropology, School of African and Asian Studies, University of Sussex (Part Assessor)

John Taylor, Head of Centre for Chinese Studies, South Bank Polytechnic (Course Reader)

Alan Thomas, Senior Lecturer in Systems, The Open University

Steven Treagust, Research Assistant, The Open University

David Treece, Lecturer in Brazilian Studies, Kings College, University of London

Euclid Tsakalotos, Lecturer in Economics, University of Kent at Canterbury

Gordon White, Professorial Fellow, Institute of Development Studies, University of Sussex

David Wield, Senior Lecturer in Technology Strategy and Development, The Open University

Gordon Wilson, Staff Tutor in Technology, The Open University, Leeds

Philip Woodhouse, Lecturer in Agricultural and Rural Development, Institute of Development Policy and Management, University of Manchester

Peter Worsley, Emeritus Professor, University of Manchester (External Assessor)

Marc Wuyts, Professor of Applied Quantitative Economics, Institute of Social Studies, The Hague, Netherlands

The Course Team would like to acknowledge the financial support of Oxfam and the European Community in the preparation of U208 *Third World Development*.

Countries and major cities of the world

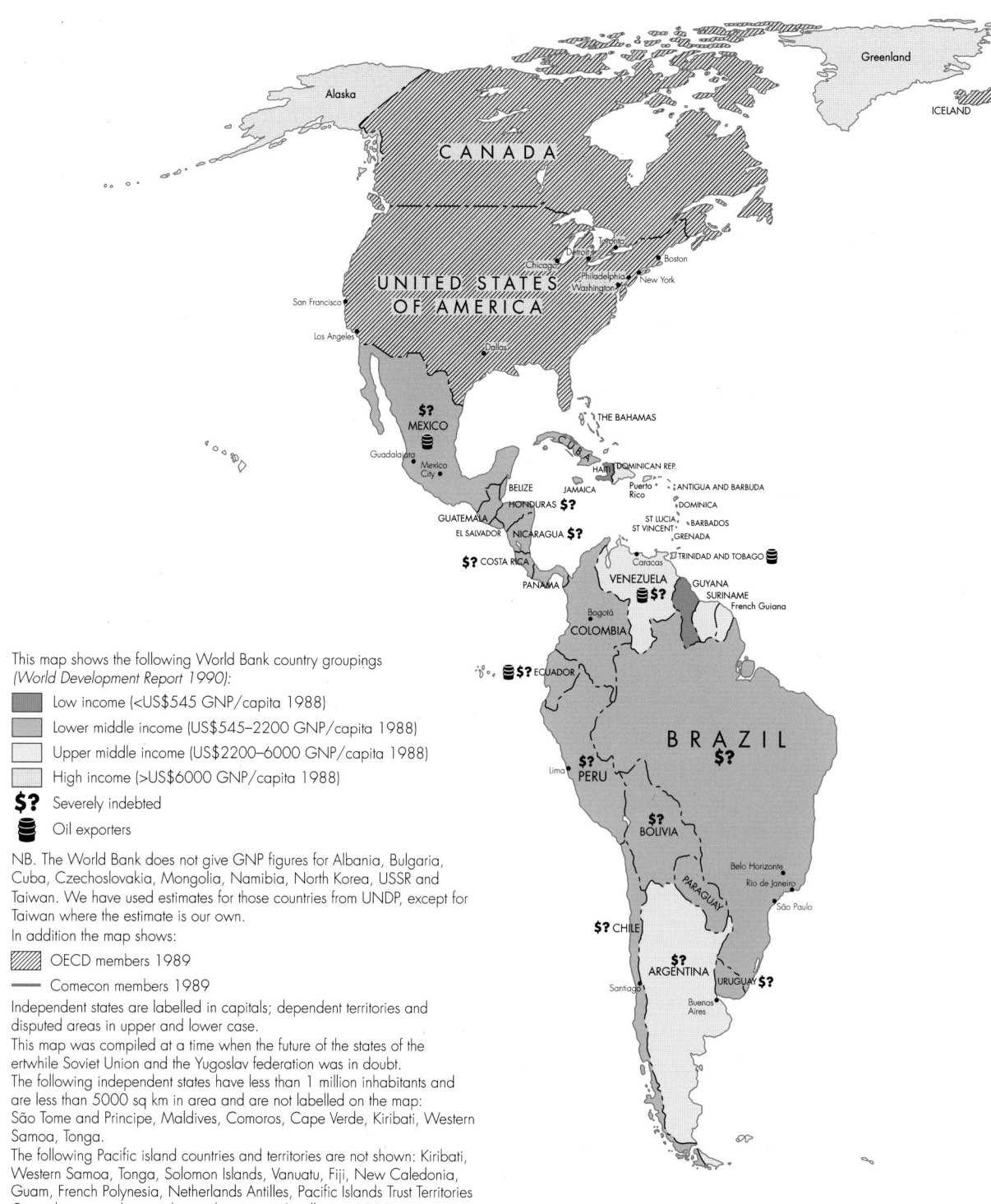

This map shows the following World Bank country groupings (*World Development Report 1990*):

- ▨ Low income (<US$545 GNP/capita 1988)
- ▨ Lower middle income (US$545–2200 GNP/capita 1988)
- ▨ Upper middle income (US$2200–6000 GNP/capita 1988)
- ▨ High income (>US$6000 GNP/capita 1988)
- **$?** Severely indebted
- ▤ Oil exporters

NB. The World Bank does not give GNP figures for Albania, Bulgaria, Cuba, Czechoslovakia, Mongolia, Namibia, North Korea, USSR and Taiwan. We have used estimates for those countries from UNDP, except for Taiwan where the estimate is our own.

In addition the map shows:

- ▨ OECD members 1989
- —— Comecon members 1989

Independent states are labelled in capitals; dependent territories and disputed areas in upper and lower case.

This map was compiled at a time when the future of the states of the erstwhile Soviet Union and the Yugoslav federation was in doubt.

The following independent states have less than 1 million inhabitants and are less than 5000 sq km in area and are not labelled on the map: São Tome and Principe, Maldives, Comoros, Cape Verde, Kiribati, Western Samoa, Tonga.

The following Pacific island countries and territories are not shown: Kiribati, Western Samoa, Tonga, Solomon Islands, Vanuatu, Fiji, New Caledonia, Guam, French Polynesia, Netherlands Antilles, Pacific Islands Trust Territories

Cities shown are those with population over 3 million in 1985.

ix

INTRODUCTION

**TOM HEWITT, HAZEL JOHNSON AND
DAVE WIELD**

Why study industrialization?

Industrialization is at the centre of development. Since the industrial revolution in Britain, industrialization has been perhaps the single most profound change to the social and economic make-up of societies. Eastern European regimes and the Soviet Union underwent the process with a single-minded determination. Japan has industrialized with startling speed and with important consequences for the world economy. Many developing countries have been industrializing at a rapid pace.

These have not been isolated events. Industrialization in one society has repercussions for many others. We only have to look at the origins of clothes, consumer durables and car components to recognize the complex and dispersed nature of industrial production. This worldwide growth of industry may raise many contradictory images:

- the consumerism of the West

- the role of cheap Third World labour in producing exports for First World markets

- urbanization and the growth of shanty towns in many Third World cities

- employment with poor working conditions

- unemployment and under-employment

- uneven access to technology and technical know-how

- environmental pollution.

But no-one, whatever their views on industrialization and its side effects, would say that it is irrelevant to the study of development. This book explores the significance of industrialization for developing countries today.

Is industrial production important for development?

Just as the British and later industrial revolutions gave, 'for the first time the real possibility of ending material want and suffering among human beings' (Kitching, 1982), so industrialization has often been seen as the most important means of developing the Third World. This view has been hotly debated.

Is it necessary?

There are strongly held views for and against the idea that industrialization is a prerequisite for economic development. On one side, industrialization is central to increasing productive capacities and productivity. These processes are generally associated with growth in scale, specialization and mechanization. Some Third World countries, like Brazil and other newly industrializing countries (NICs) of South East and East Asia, have industrialized rapidly along these lines. Even so, some argue that this model is irrelevant for most Third World countries, and would support types of economic development that use small-scale technology in agriculture and industry to provide more employment.

Industry or agriculture?

Development strategies involve debate, and decisions, about the relative roles and organization of industry and agriculture. Increasing output in agriculture has usually involved increasing productivity through machines and other industrial inputs. Developing agricultural production either requires industrial imports, or a national process of industrialization to reduce a country's import dependence. Strong arguments have been made that industry should be the driving force for more general economic development and that, to achieve rapid and lasting economic growth, investment in industrial production should be given priority over agriculture. Others have argued that this has gone too far, to the detriment of existing resources (land and people) in agriculture.

Quality of life

Industrialization concerns questions about how people live and work and thus about quality of life in the Third World. It enables an increasing range and quality of goods to be produced and is a major source of employment. At the same time it can uproot and transform whole communities.

Some questions

To argue that industrialization is important for development is not to accept all its ramifications. Many questions have been raised on the basis of recent history. For example:

- Has not the experience of Soviet block countries shown once and for all that rapid industrialization in the latter part of the twentieth century caused more harm than benefit?

- Do not well-publicized industrial disasters such as Chernobyl and Bhopal prove that industrialization has risks we could do without?

- Would not developing countries be better off spending limited resources on agriculture and leaving the already industrialized countries to supply the world with manufactures?

- Is not the world already inundated with the products of industry?

Criteria for evaluating industrialization

To examine whether or not industrialization is a 'good' or a 'bad' thing we need criteria to enable us to evaluate its process and effects. How do we select such criteria? For example, choosing economic growth as a criterion would present us with a different picture from using, say, environmental impact. But neither would give us a complete picture, nor a wholly positive or negative assessment. There are many other criteria we could use — the generation of wealth, the distribution of wealth, the different impact on women and men, the development of technological capabilities, generating employment and skills, cultural change and the impact on urban and rural communities, the financial costs of industrialization and debt generation — to name only a few.

How we select criteria depends in part on what we want to find out. For example, this book shows that looking at industrialization from a gender perspective raises different issues and questions from those raised by straightforward economic criteria. Selecting criteria also depends on the theoretical framework being used. Some theories emphasize certain issues and problems while playing down the role of others.

Costs and benefits of industrialization

There has generally been a strong belief that development is messy but necessary; that industrialization is a difficult part of development, but is essential to meet people's basic needs. This belief, which has been current for many years, is based on an assumption that the Third World had to follow in the footsteps of the West. This, in turn, meant industrialization, warts and all. There were negative side-effects but they were a small price to pay for development. But in the light of experiences of industrialization in the late 20th century, in developed and developing countries alike, we are now beginning to question whether the side-effects really are marginal or whether they are too big a price to pay. Thus, as well as examining industrialization as a process, this book explores negative as well as positive outcomes.

What are the possible negative side-effects of industrialization? Amongst them we might include:

- alienation (a breakdown of social networks and relationships) and the increasing insertion of market criteria into daily life

- rapid urbanization with attendant poverty, poor housing, crumbling infrastructure, poor health and low access to education

- environmental degradation through industrial pollution of the air and waterways.

There is no clear-cut argument about the costs and benefits of industrialization. Their relative weights vary over time and from place to place. But many now consider the side-effects to be such central concerns that the formerly accepted path of development through industrialization has been strongly questioned.

Certainly the environmental consequences of industrialization are now beginning to be taken seriously in the design and production of some products, particularly in those contexts where such investments can be afforded and are profitable in the long term. In some instances, new environmental regulations are having a significant impact on technological innovation, as in car emission and recycling technologies. Companies taking a lead in building more environmentally friendly products are doing so because they think they will gain competitive advantage in the long term.

Thus, although the study of industrialization is important, we need to be able to assess its costs and benefits. Again, to do this we need theoretical frameworks that help us explain how industrialization takes place and to evaluate its consequences from different perspectives. Frameworks are needed that assess all the outcomes and not just the production of commodities and the generation of wealth. They are also needed to differentiate between different types of industrial production and their appropriateness for different contexts and groups of people.

What do we mean by industrial production?

There are three ways of defining industrial production (or industry) in current usage.

The first defines industry as 'not agriculture'. It is a residual definition based on industry as the production of all material goods not grown directly on the land.

The second definition, much used for statistical purposes, is a sectoral definition: industry comprises the mining, manufacturing and energy sectors of the economy. Mining is that sector extracting minerals, energy is that producing energy. Manufacturing is more diverse and cannot be defined so neatly; it is the making of finished articles from raw materials by hand or using tools or machines. In this sectoral definition it is defined in terms of the kind of output, not how goods are made. For example, it would include sandals made in households for sale as well as sandals produced on a large scale in factories, even though production methods and scale are different. Nevertheless, this sectoral definition can be useful, because it does tell us what goods are actually being produced.

The sectoral approach divides manufacturing into a number of quasi-independent sectors according to an international standard classification:

> food products
> drink and tobacco
> textiles
> clothing and footwear
> wood products and furniture
> paper and printing
> chemical and petroleum products
> bricks, glass and cement
> basic metals
> metal products
> electrical machinery
> transport equipment
> others.

Figure 1 Types of industrial production.
(a) Agriculture: a large estate in Brazil. (b) Mining:
plant and rail head at Carajás iron ore mine in
Brazil. (c) Manufacturing: South Korean textile
worker. (d) Construction; building spillway pillars at
the Xavantes hydro-electric scheme on the
Paranpanema River in Brazil. (e) Energy: Tucurui
hydro-electric project in Brazil.

(a)

(b)

(c)

(d)

(e)

For most sectoral categories, the products are self-evident. For some, however, this breakdown is becoming increasingly inadequate. This applies particularly to metal products, electrical machinery and transport equipment. These are sectors where product diversification and innovation has been most intensive in recent decades. The most common example, is the confusion over the categorization of products based on information technology.

The third definition of industry is based on the nature of the production process and is more satisfactory than the other two for understanding industrialization. This definition sees industry as a particular way of organizing production and assumes there is a constant process of technical and social change which continually increases society's capacity to produce a wide range of goods.

There are limitations with definitions. For example, the first definition does not encompass the idea of industrialized agriculture. The second fails to distinguish scale or method of production. The choice of definition therefore has important implications for what we study.

Although the use of more than one definition can be legitimate and helpful, the third definition is the most useful for the focus of this book because it allows us to analyse industrialization dynamically as a process of social and technical change. We now look at two different ways this definition can be used.

Industrial production processes

Industry can be defined as a particular way of producing things. Industrial production processes are characterized by:

- complex techniques and sophisticated machinery usually associated with large-scale production

- a wide range of raw materials, often already processed through the use of complex technologies and which, therefore, have linkages with other forms of production

- a relatively complex division of labour by task within units of production, usually called 'technical divisions of labour'

- a diverse range of skills within the workforce

- the use of technology rather than people to provide energy.

This 'industrial way of doing things' can be contrasted with craft production. For example, in India, millions of handloom weavers work in their own households to produce textile cloth to customers' orders. At the other extreme, India has many large textile factories with different types of machinery, complex systems of organization, and workers doing many different tasks and producing a range of industrial products for the domestic and external markets. The contrast is not always so stark. In between craft and industrial production there are a variety of forms of organization.

Industrial production processes not only involve more than just technical conditions such as techniques of production, machines and skills. They also involve social organization: who does what, and under what conditions. One example of this is the gender division of labour in an electrical factory in Brazil (Figure 2).

The process of industrialization

Another way of looking at industrial production is as a process of industrialization. This includes understanding how industry spreads and what social modifications are involved. It therefore involves considering wider social and economic conditions within which particular industrial production processes develop, and the extent to which such processes have become so widespread as to create what would be called a fully industrialized society.

The industrial revolution in Britain was the first example of generalized industrial forms of production and accompanying social transformation:

> "... the first historical instance of the breakthrough from an agrarian handicraft economy to one dominated by industry and machine manufacture. The industrial revolution ... transformed in the space of two lifetimes the life of western man [sic], the nature of his society and his relationship to other peoples of the world."
>
> (Landes, 1969, p.1)

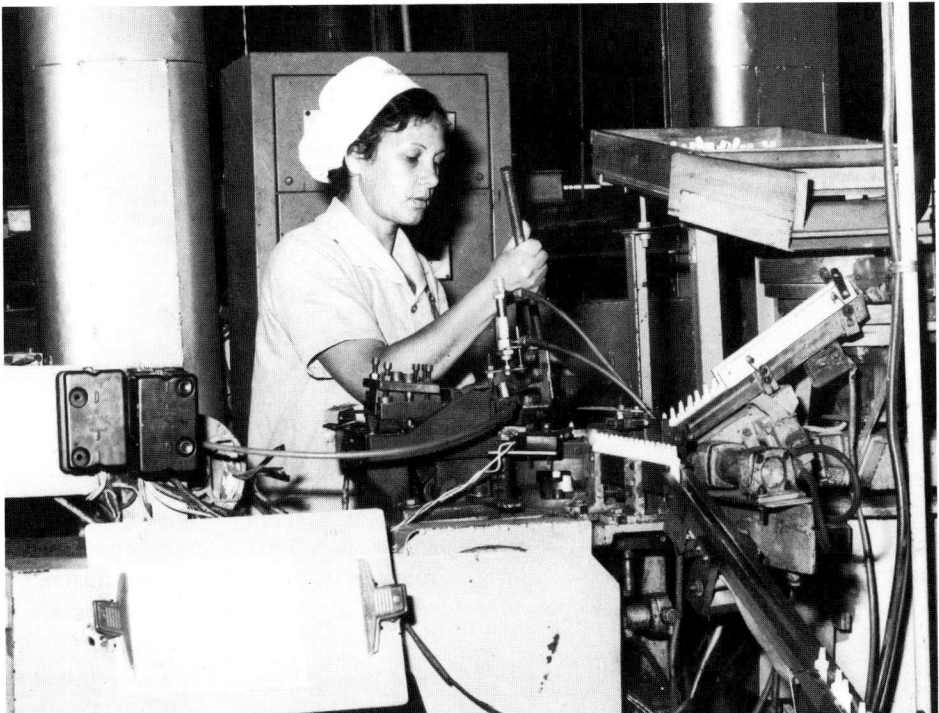

Figure 2 "*In many factories, particularly those in the electrical industry, 'women's work' is associated with sitting down or remaining in one place, a clear and quiet environment, and the use of hand tools. In this automotive parts factory a woman is tending a machine which assembles parts into a finished product. She is responsible for keeping the machine stocked with each of the components, checking on the quality of the product and keeping the machine running. She is using an iron bar to unjam the flow of components. In spite of the noise involved, remaining on foot and moving around the machine, and getting dust, grease, and talcum powder on her arms, she is still considered to be doing 'women's work'. In this factory, 'men's work' means operating less automated machines, or setting and maintenance work. In different factories, different elements are used to create the division between male and female work and workers.*" (Humphrey 1987, p.103)

Using the two approaches

Understanding industrialization requires both micro and macro levels of analysis. For example, analysing the significance of multinational investment in the Third World requires examining both the particular production processes it establishes and their effects on industrialization in the country as a whole.

While these two levels of analysis are not easily isolated from each other because industrialization as a total process includes and subsumes the establishment of industrial production processes, there are important distinctions. Industrial production processes can be established without setting in motion a wider process of industrialization. For example, many former British colonies contained important extractive industries such as copper mining in Zambia and rubber extraction in Malaysia. Others had complex agricultural industries, such as sisal in Tanzania and sugar in Guyana. These were established without stimulating the development of other industries in these countries. Although they reinforced the spread of industry in Britain and elsewhere, they were not part of a national industrialization process.

Industrialization and development

We have already said that understanding industrialization requires the study of theory. This book examines industrialization through two theoretical perspectives that have been dominant in studies of development over the last three decades:

- *structuralism* — linked to more protective policies to nurture the growth of industry
- *neo-liberalism* — linked to more market oriented policies.

These two macro theories of economic development can be directly related to strategies or models of industrialization.

Structuralists would argue for state intervention in industrialization, be this regulation of trade tariffs or direct production by state companies. Neo-liberals, on the other hand, argue that the market left to its own devices is a far more efficient arbiter of economic development.

Structuralists argue the importance of greater self-reliance of developing countries, whereas neo-liberals put emphasis on integration in the world economy. Self-reliance leads to policies of *import substitution industrialization* where goods formerly imported will be produced locally. This can only be achieved, structuralists argue, if local production is protected from outside competition, at least in its initial or 'infant industry' phase. Integration into the world economy, by contrast, implies an emphasis on *export-oriented industrialization*. Neo-liberals argue that exports can only compete with world market prices if production is unfettered by price controls such as trade tariffs.

This is only a caricature of the two approaches. But their competing elements (state versus market, self-reliance versus integration, import substitution versus export orientation and protection versus the free market) have been influential in interpreting the experiences of developing countries. The industrial strategies of Brazil and South Korea, which are examined in detail in this book, have been held up as examples of the two approaches.

Such competing interpretations of development do not exist in a historical vacuum. Theories and their policy prescriptions have been influential at different times. Two points should be stressed:

1   The dominance of a particular theoretical approach at any one time is frequently a reaction to, or a development from, the dominant ideas which preceded it. For example, the dominance of neo-liberal thinking in the 1980s was a reaction to the influence of structuralism in the previous 20–30 years.

2   The influence of a particular economic theory cannot be dissociated from the historical period in which its policy prescriptions are applied. Even since the 1960s, the world economy has passed through several phases. In the 1960s, output and trade grew at unprecedented rates. This created favourable conditions for the use of structuralist policies as sketched above. But this expansion was stopped in its tracks with the oil crisis of 1973. It pushed up again in the late 1970s and then settled down into a prolonged recession throughout the 1980s. In these two decades the conditions for industrialization in many developing countries became less favourable and ways out of deepening recession were sought in neo-liberal policies.

In short, policy prescriptions are partly reflections of changing international conditions. The strategy that worked in one period may not necessarily work in the following one. Some 'learning' from one period to another obviously takes place in how development theories evolve or how one paradigm is replaced by another but, as the development economist Hans Singer points out:

> "… the development actors as well as the development thinkers seem to base their actions and thoughts on experiences of the last-but-one decade or a last-but-one phase, only to be overwhelmed by the inappropriateness of such action and thought in the face of new events and new problems. Is it perhaps a case of a problem for every solution, rather than a solution for every problem?"
>
> (Singer, 1989, p.3).

The message is perhaps that there is a need for some humility and circumspection when we are thinking and arguing about the options for future development.

What this book is about

This book has three main aims:

- to explain the process of industrialization in developing countries at a global level and through case studies

- to provide ways of understanding this process through applying development theories

- to explore issues and outcomes resulting from industrialization using different perspectives.

The first two are the focus of Section 1 of the book and the third is addressed in Section 2.

Section 1 first presents an analysis of global industrialization since the second world war (Chapter 1). The international debt crisis of the 1980s has dramatically changed the conditions for Third World industrialization. Debt is arguably the major impediment to breaking out of the global recession. This is the subject of Chapter 2. Chapters 3 and 4 examine the industrialization experiences of Brazil and South Korea. These two countries were picked for special attention, firstly because they are industrialized and secondly because econo-

mists have treated them as prime examples of the two different theories in the book. Following the case studies, Chapter 5 discusses the theoretical frameworks of structuralism and neo-liberalism, while Chapter 6 uses them to interpret the Brazilian and South Korean experiences.

While Section 1 treats industrialization as given, Section 2 adopts a more critical approach. Industrialization is a social process which impinges directly on people's lives. This occurs in many different ways:

- through technological change

- through changes in gender relations

- through cultural change

- through environmental change.

These issues are often ignored in mainstream development theory but are of fundamental importance in raising new questions about industrialization. Dealing with these issues allows us to examine some of the consequences of industrialization, as well as giving us fresh perspectives on industrialization which do not fit easily into mainstream economic theory.

PART I

Heavy industry in South Korea

INDUSTRIALIZATION AND THE GLOBAL ECONOMY

RHYS JENKINS

A glance at the distribution of world industry will immediately reveal the gap between the developed world and the Third World. The developed capitalist countries, with a sixth of the world's population, account for 64% of the world's manufacturing industry and consume more than half the world's energy. The Third World, with almost four-fifths of the world's people, produces only 14% of its manufactures and consume only a quarter of world energy (World Bank, 1990; UNIDO, 1990).

This division between an industrial centre and a less developed hinterland has characterized the world economy for over two hundred years, since the first industrial revolution in Britain in the late eighteenth century. For some writers, this was seen as a mutually beneficial relationship whereby different countries specialized in producing those commodities which they were relatively good at producing, and everyone gained. Others however have emphasized the unequal relationship between centre and periphery by which the industrial countries were able to obtain the lion's share of the benefits from international trade. For them this international division of labour was associated with colonialism and neo-colonialism which blocked the industrialization of the periphery. These two competing views have been at the centre of debates on how to industrialize for at least 150 years.

The emergence of the Third World, as colonies in Africa and Asia gained their independence after The Second World War, led to concerted efforts at industrialization in the periphery. Nevertheless, as the figures quoted above indicate, industrial production continues to be highly concentrated in the traditional industrial centres. Political independence has not transformed the international division of labour. At the same time, rapid industrial development has occurred in certain newly industrializing countries (NICs), two of which, Brazil and South Korea, will be considered in more detail in Chapters 3 and 4.

This raises a number of questions.

Q What are the obstacles to rapid industrial growth which have made it so difficult for the Third World to narrow the gap with the developed countries?

Q Are there international conditions which tend to favour or discourage industrial development in Third World countries?

Q Does the lateness of their industrialization create problems or advantages for Third World countries which attempt to industrialize?

Although international conditions do not determine the rate or nature of industrialization in less developed countries (LDCs), they do set certain parameters within which countries are forced to operate. In some periods, international conditions are particularly conducive to industrial development in the Third World, in others less so.

There are several ways in which the international economy conditions the industrialization process in Third World countries.

- *The overall level of economic activity*, which is linked to world economic conditions, determines the growth of industrial production in LDCs. The growth of industrial exports is influenced by the growth of world trade, by access to markets in developed countries and by the extent of protectionist measures.

- *The availability of capital for investment*, either in the form of direct foreign investment (DFI) or through loans, is also determined by international economic conditions. As the recent experience of the debt crisis shows, lack of international capital can seriously compromise industrial development.

- *Technological change* affects the competitive position of different countries. Developments in transport and communications tend to reduce the cost of doing business over large distances. This lessens the advantage of producing near the final market. Changes in production technology can affect the comparative advantage of different production sites for particular products. The speed of technological change in some industries can also make it possible for an LDC to narrow the 'technological gap' between it and the developed countries, and to achieve international competitiveness.

- *Changes in organization* in manufacturing companies, both company-wide and at the level of production plants, can influence the prospects for industrialization in LDCs. These are often linked to technological developments. For example, the introduction of Japanese management practices such as 'just in time' supply of components, which is facilitated by computerized stock control, can make a significant impact on the relative advantages of different locations for suppliers.

This chapter outlines the international context of Third World industrialization. In Section 1.1 we look at the very rapid growth of world industry and trade in manufactures since the Second World War, before looking in more detail at shifts in the geographic distribution of industry between different parts of the world in Section 1.2. Section 1.3 explores the growing internationalization of production and the way in which manufacturing operations scattered around the world have come to be increasingly integrated within a global manufacturing system. Section 1.4 considers the changing nature of technology and the labour process at an international level in the post-war period. In Section 1.5 we discuss the problem of 'de-industrialization' that is allegedly occurring within the advanced Western nations. Section 1.6 takes a critical look at two interpretations which attempt to explain the various trends in the international industrial economy. The concluding section of the chapter considers future prospects for industrialization.

1.1 The growth of world trade and industry

The period since the Second World War can be usefully divided into two sub-periods, up to the early 1970s and from the early seventies to the present. The first period, often referred to as the long boom, saw the fastest growth of industrial production that the world has ever experienced. Between 1948 and 1973, world industrial production grew at an average of over 6% a year. To give some idea of the speed of this process, it is worth remembering that during the Industrial Revolution, between 1780 and 1830, world industrial output grew at only 2.6% a year, less than half as fast as in the post-war period (Beenstock, 1984).

The 1970s and 1980s however were characterized by much lower rates of industrial growth particularly after the oil price rises of 1973. Even so, these were only low compared to the achievements of the 1950s and 1960s, and were quite respectable by historical standards (see Figure 1.1).

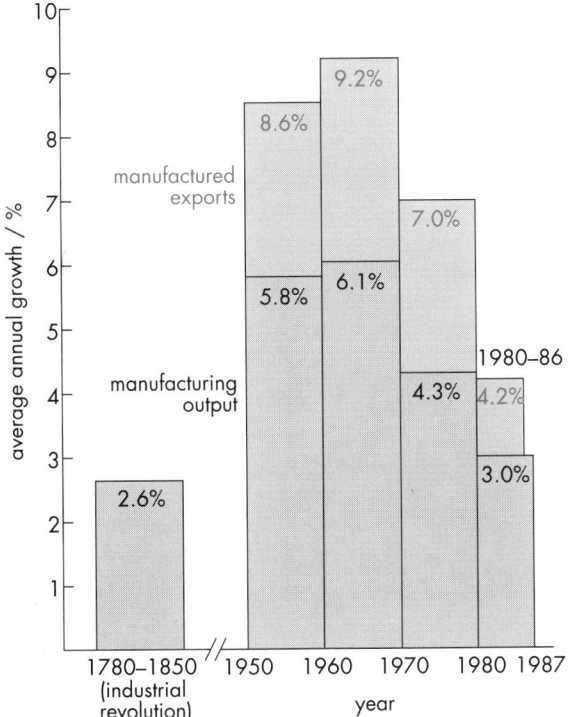

Figure 1.1   Growth of world manufacturing and trade. [Data source: United Nations]

In the advanced industrial countries reconstruction after the Second World War gave a boost to the growth of manufacturing. Subsequently growth was based on absorbing labour from other sectors, particularly agriculture. As these sources of labour supply were exhausted with the shrinking of the agricultural sector, many countries resorted to the use of immigrant labour. One model was the *Gastarbeiter* (or guest worker) system used in West Germany to bring in workers from southern Europe on a temporary basis. Other European countries such as France and Britain encouraged migrant workers from colonies or former colonies to provide cheap labour in industry and services. By 1972 there were over seven million migrant workers in Western Europe.

However by the late 1960s there were growing signs of problems facing industrial production in the advanced capitalist countries. Although productivity in industry was still growing, increases in output per employee were not sufficient to keep

up with increases in real wages. The rate of return on capital invested in industry therefore declined. There was a sharp fall in the rate of growth of industrial production in 1970 and 1971, and although output grew rapidly in 1972 and 1973, the slowdown was confirmed during the remainder of the decade.

> **Real wages:** The real money value of wages when adjusted for inflation

It is clear that the extremely favourable conditions for industrial accumulation, which were established in the aftermath of the Second World War, were being eroded by this time, even before the first oil price shock in 1973. The effect of the oil price increases was merely to intensify the emerging crisis by bringing to an end the cheap energy which had underpinned Western industrialization for many decades.

If industrial production grew fast during the boom, international trade in manufactured goods grew even faster.

Q Look again at Figure 1.1 How much faster than production did manufactured exports grow? For example, 1950–60 exports expanded at $(8.6 - 5.8)\% = 2.8\%$.

In the advanced capitalist countries, economic growth in the 1950s and 1960s was accompanied by a rapid increase in trade in manufactured goods. But the increased trade took place mainly among the advanced capitalist countries, and not with the Third World. By the early 1970s three-quarters of world trade in manufactured goods was between developed countries (Gordon, 1989).

The growth of international trade was facilitated by the international system set up after the Second World War, known as the Bretton Woods System (see Chapter 11 of *Allen & Thomas, 1992* and Chapter 2 in this volume). This established the role of the US dollar as the key reserve currency and a system of fixed exchange rates under the tutelage of the International Monetary Fund (IMF). It was designed to avoid problems of international monetary instability which had done so much to disrupt the international economy

---

Box 1.1   The General Agreements on Tariffs and Trade (GATT)

GATT was created in 1947 with 'the primary objective of making substantial reductions of tariffs and other barriers to trade ... and the elimination of discriminatory treatment in international commerce'. Since then it has organized numerous rounds of trade negotiations of which the best known have been the Kennedy Round (1964–67), the Tokyo Round (1973–79) and most recently the Uruguay Round (from 1986). Currently there are about a hundred countries participating in GATT, accounting for the bulk of international trade.

GATT rules are designed to facilitate the growth of international trade through liberalization and non-discrimination. Until the Uruguay Round which, included trade in agricultural products and services, GATT was mainly concerned with trade in manufactured goods.

A major exception to the GATT emphasis on freeing trade has been the special agreements negotiated for textiles and textile products. The first of these was the Long Term Arrangement Regarding International Trade in Cotton Textiles between 1962 and 1973. Since 1974, the trade has been controlled under four successive Multifibre Agreements, whose coverage has been extended at each renegotiation. These have been designed to limit the growth of Third World textile exports in order to protect producers in the developed countries.

---

during the inter-war period. At the same time the Geneva-based General Agreement on Tariffs and Trade (GATT) was charged with liberalizing the international trading system which it did through a number of trade rounds during which reciprocal tariff reductions were negotiated (see Box1.1).

It was not surprising that the GATT negotiations tended to favour the developed countries, given that almost three-quarters of world trade in manufactured goods was between them. The area of international trade in which Third World countries had the greatest interest, textiles and textile products, was made an exception to the general GATT rules and subject to strict quotas under the Multifibre Agreements.

Nevertheless, despite these restrictions, some Third World countries — particularly Hong Kong, Singapore, South Korea, Taiwan, Brazil and Mexico — were able to take advantage of the growth of international trade and increase their exports of manufactured goods to the developed countries in the sixties and early seventies (OECD, 1988).

The growth of world trade decelerated sharply with the international economic crisis after 1973. The trend towards more liberal trading arrangements (with the exception of textiles) which characterized the 1950s and 1960s went into reverse. Protectionism reappeared in the developed countries in new guises with euphemistic titles such as 'voluntary export restraints' and 'orderly marketing agreements'. This has come to be known as 'the new protectionism' (see Box 1.2), and although initially introduced in Europe and North America against Japanese imports, has come to be increasingly applied to newly industrializing countries as well.

Since the early seventies, with the slow down in world trade and the emergence of the new protectionism, there has been a slight decline in the relative significance of trade amongst developed countries. Although this has not reversed the growth of industrial exports from the NICs, the changing international environment has meant that establishing and increasing such exports has become much more difficult.

1.2 Geographical shifts in industrial production

The post-war distribution of world industry

Up until the late 1920s, a small group of industrial countries in Western Europe, North America and Japan accounted for over 90% of the world's industrial production and had done so since the nineteenth century. In the 1930s and during the Second World War, the growth of the centrally planned economies in the USSR and Eastern Europe, and the industrialization of some Third World countries, particularly India and some of the Latin American states, reduced the share of the advanced capitalist countries. By the late 1940s it was just under 80%. Nevertheless the traditional picture of an international division of labour between a core of countries manufacturing industrial goods and a periphery which produced raw materials, remained largely true.

The USA's dominant position in world industry in the aftermath of the Second World War was clear. The US economy accounted for well over half the industrial production by the industrialized countries and its output was seven times that of the UK, the second largest industrial power at the time.

As in the inter-war period, a significant proportion of international trade in manufactures consisted of exports from the industrialized countries to the agricultural periphery. Exports to countries outside the core accounted for over a third of all trade in manufactures. These trade flows continued to be structured by colonial or neo-colonial links with Britain and France trading mainly with their colonies and the USA trading mainly with Latin America.

The core industrial countries

As can be seen from Figure 1.2, the *relative* share of the advanced capitalist countries in world industrial production has declined continuously in the post-war period. Moreover this decline, which as noted above had started in the 1930s, accelerated during the 1960s and 1970s, so that by the 1980s little more than 60% of world production came from the traditional industrial centres.

The most marked decline has taken place in the United Kingdom and the United States. Between them these two countries accounted for more than half the world's industrial output in 1948, but by the 1980s this had fallen to less than a third. The clear leadership which the USA enjoyed within the group of industrial nations has also become much less marked. In 1948, the USA produced ten times as much as West Germany. But by the mid-1960s, it produced only four times as much as West Germany, which was by then in second place. Japan overtook West Germany in the late 1970s and by the late 1980s it was catching up with the USA. So within the core countries there has been a considerable *deconcentration* of industrial production, away from the USA and the

---

Box 1.2   The new protectionism

Under GATT rules, the use of quotas and other forms of restriction on the quantity of goods which can be imported into a country are frowned upon. Taxes on imports (tariffs) are a more acceptable form of protection but these should be kept low. The GATT trade rounds were mainly concerned with cutting tariffs.

In the 1970s and 1980s however, with the slowdown in the world economy and growing competition from imports, particularly from Japan and the NICs, the developed countries have increasingly resorted to new forms of import restrictions. Because of GATT rules, these have often involved 'voluntary' agreements between the importing and exporting countries to limit the level of exports. For instance in Britain an agreement was reached with the Japanese motor manufacturers to limit exports of cars from Japan to 11% of the British market.

Developed countries have also made increasing use of a number of 'escape clauses' which exist under GATT rules. These permit countries to restrict imports in the case of substantial damage or potential damage to domestic industry, to impose countervailing duties on exports which are subsidized and to take action against dumping (i.e. selling at below cost) by other countries. These measures which cover a growing proportion of world trade have come to be known as 'the new protectionism'.

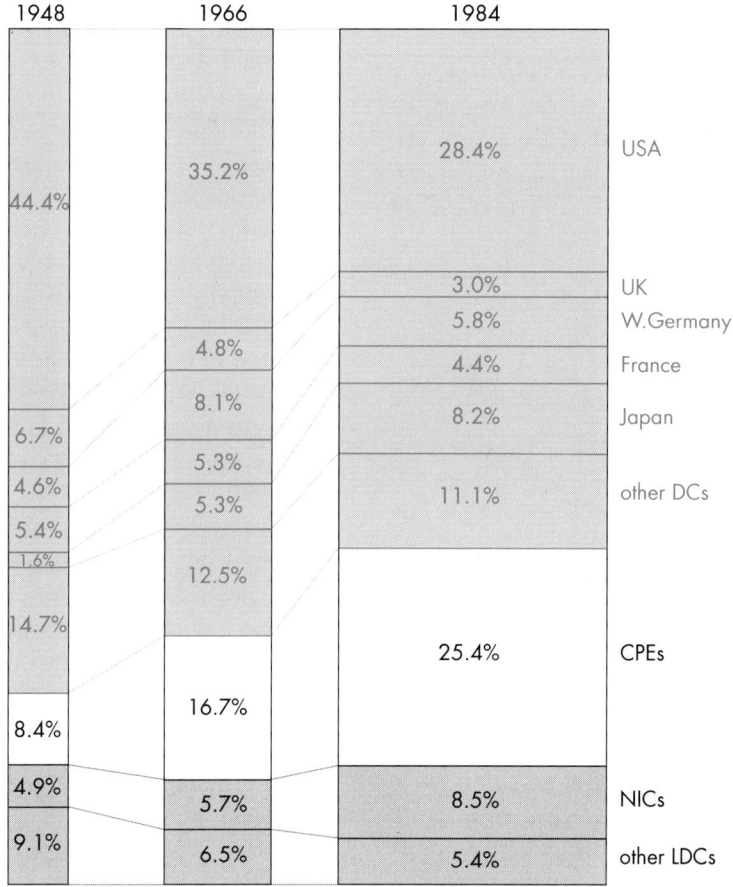

Figure 1.2   The global distribution of industry. [Data source: Gordon, 1989]

UK. This has been accompanied by increasing international competition.

Although the share of the advanced capitalist countries in world production declined throughout the post-war period, we should not lose sight of the fact that this was a relative decline. In absolute terms industrial production was growing, and growing extremely fast by historical standards, particularly in the 1950s and 1960s. This was especially true of Japan and of Western Europe (excluding the UK) where the formation of the EEC in 1958 stimulated trade amongst the European countries.

Centrally planned economies

The most striking change in the geographical distribution of industrial production which can be seen from Figure 1.2 is the sharp increase in

the share of the centrally planned economies (CPEs) which rose three-fold from just over 8% in 1948 to over a quarter by the mid-1980s. Unlike the advanced capitalist countries where industrial growth slowed down considerably during the 1970s, the CPEs continued to grow into the 1980s at only slightly lower rates than in the 1960s.

Trade played a much less important role in industrial development within these countries and their share of world trade in manufactured goods declined in the 1960s and 1970s. Their development therefore had relatively little impact on the Third World's industrialization except in the case of a small number of socialist Third World countries such as Cuba and Vietnam which became members of the Council for Mutual Economic Assistance (COMECON).

The Third World

Industrialization in the Third World is not a completely new phenomenon. In some countries it dates back to the early part of the twentieth century. Two world wars and the Great Depression, which disrupted international trade and the supply of manufactured goods from the industrial countries, boosted industrialization in some parts of the Third World. Nevertheless, at the end of the Second World War most of the Third World, apart from Latin America, was still under the control of the colonial powers and remained predominantly agricultural.

In Latin America, industrialization had occurred in the 1930s in response to the drastic fall in the region's agricultural and mineral export earnings and the need for tighter control on imports. After the Second World War it became a central feature of development strategy advocated by the influential United Nations Economic Commission for Latin America (ECLA). Not surprisingly, after the experience of the Depression 'export pessimism' reigned and the prospects for increasing exports to the industrialized countries seemed bleak. If the Latin American economies were to grow, it was argued, they would have to produce manufactured goods.

With decolonization, newly independent countries in Africa and Asia took a similar view, and industrialization spread. Specialization in agriculture and raw materials was identified with colonialism and backwardness; industrialization with increased economic activity, productivity and increased standards of living. The need for political independence to be accompanied by economic independence provided a further impetus to industrialization.

However the initial optimism concerning both the possibilities and potential results of industrialization proved exaggerated. The technological lead of the advanced industrialized countries meant that the new industries being set up in the Third World had to be protected from competition from imports. It also meant that they were unable to compete in world markets with manufactured goods from developed countries, so that exports which had played such an important part in the

Industrial Revolution in Britain, did not play a leading role. This form of industrialization — replacing imported manufactured goods with locally produced goods — came to be known as *import substitution*.

One obstacle to industrialization was the small size of the domestic market in most Third World countries. Many countries had relatively small populations and most people lacked the purchasing power to provide a substantial market, particularly in the countryside. The use of imported technology also meant that industrial employment grew relatively slowly so that most people remained in non-industrial employment with low income levels. In the 1960s a number of countries attempted to form regional groups which would expand their domestic markets but these were generally not successful.

The setting up of a modern industrial sector did not come cheaply. Although import substitution could begin with relatively simple, labour-intensive industries, governments soon found it necessary to move on to more complex and more capital-intensive activities. Rapid industrial growth therefore came to require heavy investment. It also needed a trained, well educated labour force to provide the human input into industrialization, as well as the physical infrastructure in the form of roads and power generation.

The result of these obstacles was that new industries set up in the Third World often remained high-cost and inefficient. Industrial employment grew slowly and income distribution was highly unequal. Moreover, in many cases the foreign companies which had previously exported to Third World markets, 'hopped the tariff' and set up their own subsidiaries in the Third World to supply the local market.

Despite these obstacles, in the early 1960s a small number of Third World countries began successfully to produce industrial goods for export. Amongst the first to do so were the East Asian NICs; Hong Kong, Taiwan, South Korea and Singapore. With the exception of Hong Kong, these had all undergone some import-substituting industrialization in the 1950s, but shifted the balance towards export promotion in the 1960s.

In the late 1960s a number of other Third World countries began to give more emphasis to export promotion, without abandoning the policy of import substitution and the protection given to domestic producers. In particular, a number of Latin American countries, including Brazil, as well as other Asian countries began giving incentives to manufactured exports at this time.

As Figure 1.3 indicates, the Third World's share of world industrial production remained roughly constant at about 10% until the late 1960s. It then showed an upward trend until 1980, increasing to more than 13%. Finally in the 1980s the share levelled off or even declined slightly after 1982 under the impact of the debt crisis.

There is a similar pattern in the share of Third World countries in exports of manufactured goods with an even more pronounced increase in share in the 1970s than for production. Unlike the case of production, the Third World's share of manufactured exports continued to increase even after 1982, and, as a result, exceeded its share of world industrial production for the first time in 1983. This no doubt reflected the increased pressure on debtor countries to expand exports in order to service their debts, despite the relatively slow growth of world trade.

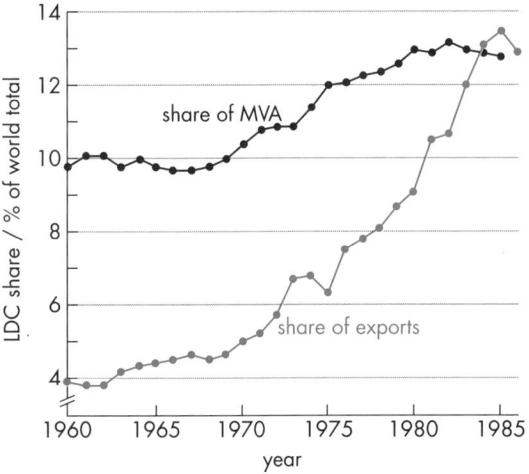

Figure 1.3   LDC share in world manufacturing value-added (MVA) and manufactured exports.

> **Manufacturing value added (MVA):**
> MVA is the value of sales minus the value of purchases of material inputs in manufacturing. It is used as a measure of manufacturing activity because it avoids double counting raw material values where there are intermediate products. For example, in the car industry, totalling the sales value of components and finished cars would over-estimate the total manufacturing activity because the value of the steel, tyre rubber, etc. would be counted several times.

Not only has industrial production increased significantly in the Third World in the post-war period, but the structure of industry has become much more complex. It is no longer based on a few simple sectors such as food processing and textiles and clothing, but has extended to include consumer durable goods such as cars and televisions, intermediate goods for further processing, like steel and petrochemical products, and capital goods such as ships and machinery. These products are produced in a number of Third World countries and are increasingly being exported from some of them to the developed countries.

This industrial expansion has not been even across the whole of the Third World. It has been largely concentrated in a small group of newly industrializing countries in Asia (Hong Kong, Singapore, South Korea and Taiwan) and Latin America (Brazil and Mexico). These together accounted for the whole of the increase in the Third World's share of industrial output between the mid-1960s and the mid-1980s. The NICs also accounted for the entire increase in its share of manufactured exports during this period (OECD, 1988). In other words, the share of Third World countries other than the NICs in world industrial production and in manufactured exports has actually fallen since the mid-1960s (see Figure 1.2).

As a result of this industrial growth, by 1980 Brazil and Mexico were amongst the ten largest industrial producers in the world, while Taiwan, Hong Kong, South Korea and Brazil were amongst the twenty largest exporters of manufactured goods (Dicken, 1986). At the other end of the scale however, this industrial expansion has largely bypassed the least developed countries and particularly the Sub-Saharan African countries. The obstacles to industrialization are particularly acute here. There are low levels of income and, therefore, savings, small markets and relatively low skill and educational levels.

Although industrial production rose in absolute terms, the share of low income developing countries in industrial production of market economies (i.e. other than CPEs) fell from 7.5% in 1965 to 6.9% twenty years later, while their share of manufactured exports went down from 2.3% to 2.1% (World Bank, 1987). The share of the developing countries of Sub-Saharan Africa in global manufacturing production has consistently remained at less than 0.5% of the total (UNIDO, 1990).

Regional blocs

The growth of protectionist pressures (see Box 1.2) and increasing trade conflict between the United States, the EEC and Japan, has led to the possibility that industrial production and trade will increasingly be organized within regional blocs. The exact form which this might take is unclear.

One possibility is that the formation of the single European market in 1992 might lead to the creation of 'fortress Europe', with the market being closed to outside suppliers. On the other hand the transition from centrally planned economies in Eastern Europe also opens up the possibility of these countries developing closer links with the EEC.

There is also talk of the emergence of the Pacific rim (including Japan, South Korea, Taiwan and

Figure 1.4   A cotton factory in Mali. Cotton is one of Mali's few exports.

the West Coast of the USA) as the new industrial growth area in the twenty-first century. A shift in the centre of gravity of the world industrial economy from the North Atlantic to the Pacific could have major implications for future industrial development both in Europe and in parts of the Third World.

Finally a free trade area has already been created between the United States and Canada which it is proposed to extend to Mexico. The US has also attempted to tie the countries of the Caribbean and Central America politically and economically more closely to itself. Thus a third possible trend may be the emergence of a more cohesive regional bloc in the Western Hemisphere.

At present all these are open possibilities but it is impossible to predict the shape which the world economy will take in the early 21st century. What we can be certain of is that the outcome will play an important part in determining the prospects and shape of industrialization in the Third World in the future.

Summary

The post-war period has seen major shifts in the distribution of industrial production. The share of the traditional industrial centres has declined continuously while that of the CPEs and, since the late 1960s, the Third World, has increased.

The pattern of trade in manufactures has also changed considerably first with the growth of trade amongst developed countries in the 1950s and 1960s and then with the rapid growth of Third World exports.

There have been important changes within the group of advanced countries with the decline of the USA and UK and the rise of Japan. As a result the concentration of industrial production within the industrialized countries has been reduced and competition has increased.

Much of the growth of industrial production and exports within the Third World has been concentrated within a small group of NICs, while the least developed countries have become increasingly marginalized in terms of industrial production and trade.

1.3 Globalization of production

In the last section we looked at the geographic changes in the distribution of industrial activity. But industrial production has changed in other ways too during the past thirty or forty years. In particular there has been a tremendous *globalization of production* reflected in the control of manufacturing activities in different countries by *transnational corporations* (TNCs), increasing *interpenetration* of markets, and the growing use of international subcontracting.

Growth of TNCs and foreign investment

Although the TNCs can be traced back to the late nineteenth century, the golden age of the TNC came after The Second World War. At first it was identified very much as an American phenomenon as large US corporations (such as Ford, ITT, National Cash Register and Goodyear) expanded into the United Kingdom and Western Europe. Since the 1960s however, European and Japanese firms have been expanding more rapidly overseas than their US rivals and in the 1980s they increasingly penetrated into the United States.

Direct foreign investment associated with TNCs grew rapidly until the 1980s, more rapidly indeed than international trade. However in recent years this has slowed down as new forms of international investment which do not involve majority shareholdings, such as joint ventures, licence agreements and management contracts, have increased in importance.

Traditionally TNC activities in the Third World were concentrated in agriculture, mining and oil extraction. From the 1950s however there was an increasing shift towards manufacturing activities (Jenkins, 1987). This change was closely linked to the import substituting industrialization strategies discussed in the last section. When firms from the industrialized countries found their traditional export markets being threatened by protectionist policies in the Third World they engaged in 'tariff hopping', that is, setting up manufacturing operations behind the newly erected tariff walls. Indeed many countries offered specific incentives to foreign firms to set up in manufacturing — what was sometimes referred to as 'industrialization by invitation'.

In the late 1960s, a new type of foreign investment in manufacturing began to emerge in some Third World countries, with the relocation of certain industrial processes and products to the periphery, with the output being exported back to the industrialized countries. A number of countries encouraged this process by setting up free trade zones (FTZs) or export processing zones (EPZs), as described in Box 1.3.

The first EPZ in the Third World was set up in Kandla in India in 1965, quickly followed by Taiwan, the Philippines, the Dominican Republic and the US–Mexican border. They grew in number rapidly in the 1970s and 1980s. The countries offering such zones increased from 9 in 1971 to 25 in 1975 and had reached 52 by 1985 (Fröbel, Heinrichs & Kreye, 1986). It was estimated that by the mid-1980s a total of 173 zones around the world employed 1.8 million workers.

Internationalization of the production process

The globalization of production in the post-war period has not only involved the growth of foreign investment and TNC activities. It has also changed the composition of the products which we buy. Today it is often difficult to identify the national origin of many products. The same product may be produced in a number of different countries with exactly the same characteristics. Even more to the point, a finished product may be assembled from components produced in a large number of different countries, thus producing a truly multinational product.

Cars

Take the case of the car industry. In the 1960s the Ford Cortina was a British car. It is true that it was produced by the UK affiliate of an US multinational, but in all other respects it was a British product, designed in Britain for the British market and assembled here with British parts and components.

Contrast this with the Escort produced by the same company in Britain in the 1980s (see Figure 1.6). This uses parts and components from fourteen countries other than Britain. Moreover it was designed for the international

---

Box 1.3   Export processing zones and free trade zones

The World Bank gives a detailed definition of Export Processing Zones, distinguishing them from Free Trade Zones, as follows:

'The export processing zone (EPZ) is a relatively recent variant of the widely used free trade zone (FTZ) — a designated area, usually in or next to a port area, to and from which unrestricted trade is permitted with the rest of the world. Merchandise may be moved in and out of FTZs free of customs, stored in warehouses for varying periods and repackaged as needed. Goods imported from the FTZ into the host country pay the requisite duty; their prior storage in FTZ warehouses permits rapid delivery to order, meanwhile saving interest on customs payments.

'EPZs, more specifically, also provide buildings and services for manufacturing, i.e., transformation of imported raw and intermediate mater-

ials into finished products, usually for exports but sometimes partly for domestic sale subject to the normal duty. The EPZ is thus a specialized industrial estate located physically and/or administratively outside the customs barrier, oriented to export production. Its facilities serve as a showcase to attract investors and as a convenience for their getting established, and are usually associated with other incentives.' (Quoted in OECD, 1984).

What this quotation fails to point out is that often firms in EPZs are not only exempt from customs duties, but may also be exempted from other government legislation such as labour laws and domestic taxes. In other words they are 'enclaves' within which firms, which are mainly foreign, enjoy special privileges which do not apply to the country as a whole.

Figure 1.5   Export docks in Kaohsing free trade zone in Taiwan.

market and produced at a number of different locations within Ford's global operations. The only sense in which one can talk of the Escort as a British car is that final assembly takes place in the UK.

The car industry is not unique in this regard. Computers, televisions and even clothes may involve inputs from different countries.

How has this change come about? With the growth of TNCs a lot of international production takes place between affiliates of the same company. Thus some of the parts used to assemble the Escort in Britain will have been imported from Ford subsidiaries elsewhere in Europe. This is known as intra-firm trade and it has been estimated that almost a third of all international trade takes this form (Jenkins, 1987).

This is important because it suggests that many decisions about which countries produce what products on the international market are not decided by impersonal market forces. Rather they are administrative decisions taken in the headquarters of major corporations about what to produce where.

Although in the case of Ford, parts and components were supplied mainly from other industrialized countries, this is not always the case. Indeed, one of the characteristics of the last quarter century of industrialization is the way in which manufacturing in Third World countries has come to be increasingly integrated into the global manufacturing system. This is reflected in the marked increase in exports of manufactures from Third World countries to the industrial core since the mid-1960s.

Washing machines

Japanese companies have been particularly active in integrating production in East Asia. Take for example the Matsushita Company which has a joint venture with a local firm in Malaysia producing washing machines for the local market, re-export to Japan and exports to third countries. The outer case, control unit and drive shaft are made in Japan, the motor comes from Matsushita's subsidiary in Taiwan, the condenser from the firm's subsidiary in Thailand and the valve magnet from South Korea, with other components supplied by local suppliers in Malaysia. This is not the end of the story because most of these components are themselves assembled from parts from different countries e.g. the motor from Taiwan includes parts from Japan and Canada as well as those produced locally (UNIDO, 1990).

The growth of world-wide sourcing also has significant implications for industrial workers in developed and developing countries alike. The labour market has become increasingly international in the sense that workers in different countries compete against each other for jobs. This reduces the bargaining power of labour *vis-à-vis* capital because of the latter's much greater international mobility.

Summary

In the past thirty or forty years manufacturing production has become increasingly global in nature. This has been reflected in the increasing

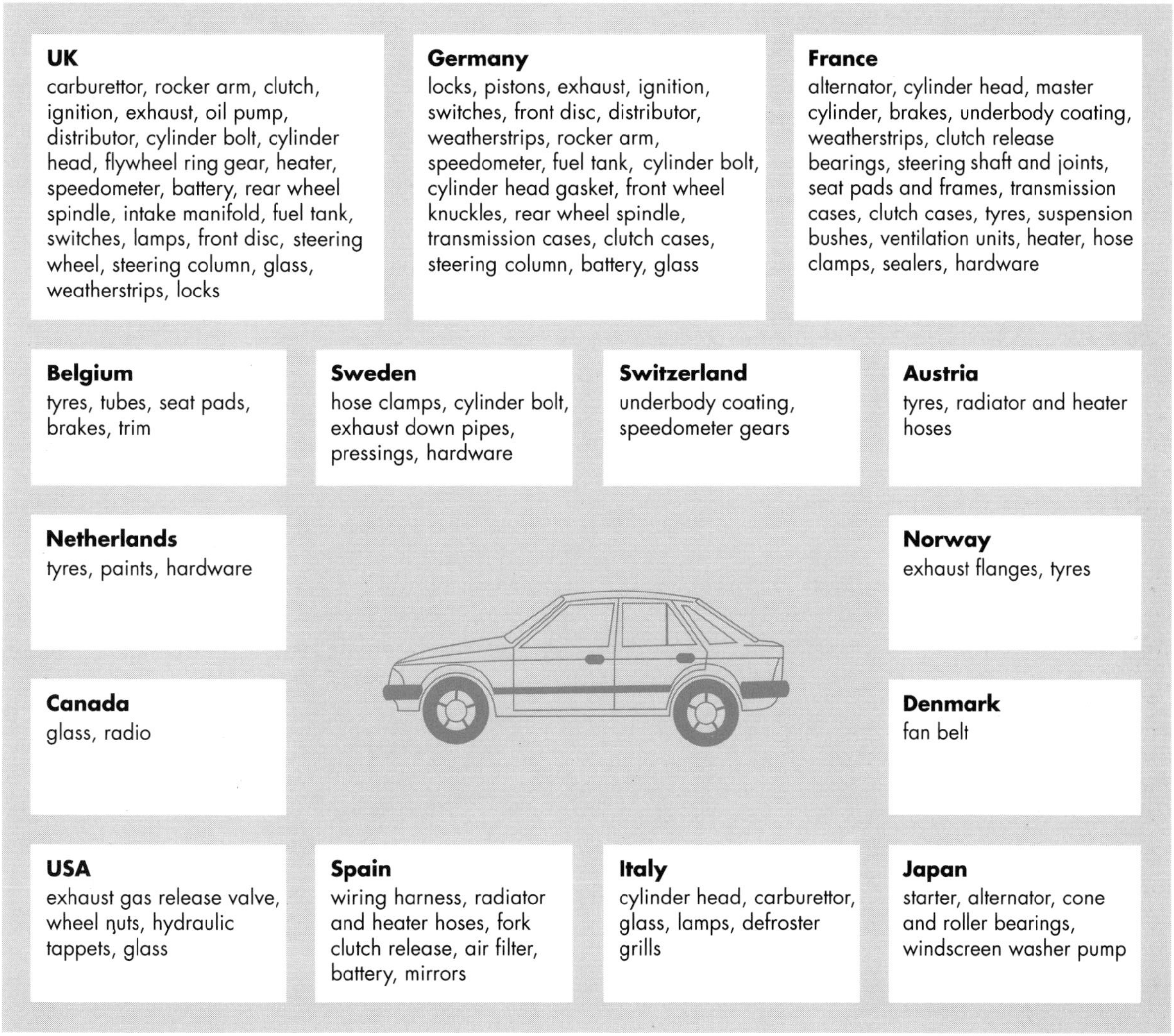

UK
carburettor, rocker arm, clutch, ignition, exhaust, oil pump, distributor, cylinder bolt, cylinder head, flywheel ring gear, heater, speedometer, battery, rear wheel spindle, intake manifold, fuel tank, switches, lamps, front disc, steering wheel, steering column, glass, weatherstrips, locks

Germany
locks, pistons, exhaust, ignition, switches, front disc, distributor, weatherstrips, rocker arm, speedometer, fuel tank, cylinder bolt, cylinder head gasket, front wheel knuckles, rear wheel spindle, transmission cases, clutch cases, steering column, battery, glass

France
alternator, cylinder head, master cylinder, brakes, underbody coating, weatherstrips, clutch release bearings, steering shaft and joints, seat pads and frames, transmission cases, clutch cases, tyres, suspension bushes, ventilation units, heater, hose clamps, sealers, hardware

Belgium
tyres, tubes, seat pads, brakes, trim

Sweden
hose clamps, cylinder bolt, exhaust down pipes, pressings, hardware

Switzerland
underbody coating, speedometer gears

Austria
tyres, radiator and heater hoses

Netherlands
tyres, paints, hardware

Norway
exhaust flanges, tyres

Canada
glass, radio

Denmark
fan belt

USA
exhaust gas release valve, wheel nuts, hydraulic tappets, glass

Spain
wiring harness, radiator and heater hoses, fork clutch release, air filter, battery, mirrors

Italy
cylinder head, carburettor, glass, lamps, defroster grills

Japan
starter, alternator, cone and roller bearings, windscreen washer pump

Figure 1.6   Sources of Ford Escort components. [Data source: Dicken, 1986]

ownership and control of production overseas by TNCs, the growth of export processing zones and the increasingly international nature of industrial products and processes. This globalization of production has implications for labour as workers in different countries increasingly compete against each other for jobs and bargain with the same employers.

1.4 Technological change and the labour process

Fordism/mass production

There have been major changes in technology and the labour process internationally during the last three or four decades. These are summarized in Table 1.1. The years after the Second World War saw the spread of 'Fordist' production methods from the United States to other advanced industrial countries and Eastern Europe. Fordism is characterized by assembly line production involving a high degree of division of labour which simplifies the tasks of workers to routine operations requiring minimal skill or training. The pace of work is controlled by the machine through the speed of the line, rather than being under the control of individual workers. The worker is effectively reduced to an adjunct of the machine.

Of course Fordist production was not universal but it was particularly characteristic of some of the key growth industries of the post-war period such as cars, 'white goods' (such as fridges), and televisions.

Fordist production was not without its problems. It tended to be highly inflexible, although not

Figure 1.7   Original Fordism — testing Model T chassis at Ford's Highland Park factory, USA, circa 1914.

perhaps to the degree suggested by the original Henry Ford's dictum 'They can have any colour they like so long as it's black'. It required long runs of standardized products in order to justify the large-scale investment in highly specific machinery. It also tended to dehumanize work and contributed to worker alienation and the possibility of forms of worker resistance which reduced productivity. The very inflexibility of production led to firms carrying large inventories of parts on a 'just in case' basis, which tied up working capital and further increased costs.

Post-Fordism/flexible specialization

There have been important technological changes in international industry since the 1970s based particularly on the introduction and diffusion of microelectronic systems in production, greatly increasing flexibility. In the car industry, for example, it is now possible to produce a number of different models and variants on the same assembly line.

At the same time there have been important changes in the organization of industrial pro-

Figure 1.8   Car assembly line at the Vauxhall plant in Luton, UK (1976).

duction. Attention has been particularly focussed on the Japanese *kanban* or 'just-in-time' system, whereby inventories are cut to a minimum through arranging for suppliers to deliver

Table 1.1   Fordist and post-Fordist models

	Fordism/mass production	Post-Fordism/flexible production
Size of firm/plant	large (corporation)	scope for small and large
Technology	specialized dedicated machinery	general purpose machinery
Labour	narrowly trained	broadly trained
	conception and execution separated	conception and execution integrated
	fragmented and routine tasks	multiskilled and varied tasks
	narrow job classification	broad job classification
Management	hierarchical and formal	flat hierarchy, informal
Output	high volume	large and small batch, single units
	limited range of standard products	varied/customized products
Competitive behaviour	strategy to control market	fast adaptation to change, innovation
Institutional framework	centralized	decentralized
	national/multinational Keynesianism	local institutions which fuse competition and cooperation

[Source: Schmitz, 1989]

on a daily basis or even several times a day. Not surprisingly, given the phenomenal industrial performance of Japan, attempts have been made to emulate the Japanese model in the other industrialized countries. A new model of industrial relations involving greater job security, more flexible working conditions (no demarcations) and the use of quality control circles through which workers make suggestions for improvements in production, has also formed part of the Japanese package.

The implications of these changes are subject to considerable debate. For some the new trend is towards 'flexible specialization' in which production will come to be based on decentralized production in relatively small units, with subcontracting arrangements. For these the mass production factories which characterized Fordism are industrial dinosaurs. Such developments are seen as opening up possibilities for Third World producers.

A less optimistic view as far as the prospects for industrialization in the Third World is concerned emphasizes the increased importance of agglomeration tendencies arising from the emphasis on 'just-in-time'. Producers will increasingly want their suppliers to locate near to their own factories in order to guarantee delivery times. Thus those Third World producers who are able

That's an independent small-scale unit. He is supposed to supply us with all our spares and components.

Figure 1.9   A cartoon by R K Laxman in The Times of India.

to establish themselves as suppliers on the basis of low-cost labour may become increasingly marginal.

1.5   De-industrialization in developed countries

There has been a lot of talk about 'de-industrialization' in Britain in recent years. The term carries with it connotations of empty factories and closed down shipyards. The general feeling is that de-industrialization is a problem and not something to be welcomed.

Q What do we mean when we refer to de-industrialization? How significant is it?

The common sense meaning of de-industrialization is a decline in the importance of industry within the economy. But how do we measure this decline? Should we look at the numbers employed or the industrial output? Are we concerned with absolute decline or with relative decline compared with other sectors? As with most definitions, it depends on the questions that we are trying to answer.

Clearly the concern with de-industrialization in recent years has not been the result of falling industrial production in the advanced industrialized countries, because as we have seen in earlier sections production has continued to increase (although the rate of increase has fallen). Figure 1.10 summarizes trends in the other variables in major industrial countries in recent years.

The upper graph in Figure 1.10 shows the share of manufacturing in total output (GDP) and in employment in six major developed countries and in the OECD as a whole. The figures for the UK for instance show that between 1960 and the late 1980s, the proportion of the country's output

Gross domestic product (GDP): A measure of the output of goods and services in the economy of a country. It includes production by foreign companies and earnings by foreign workers in the country

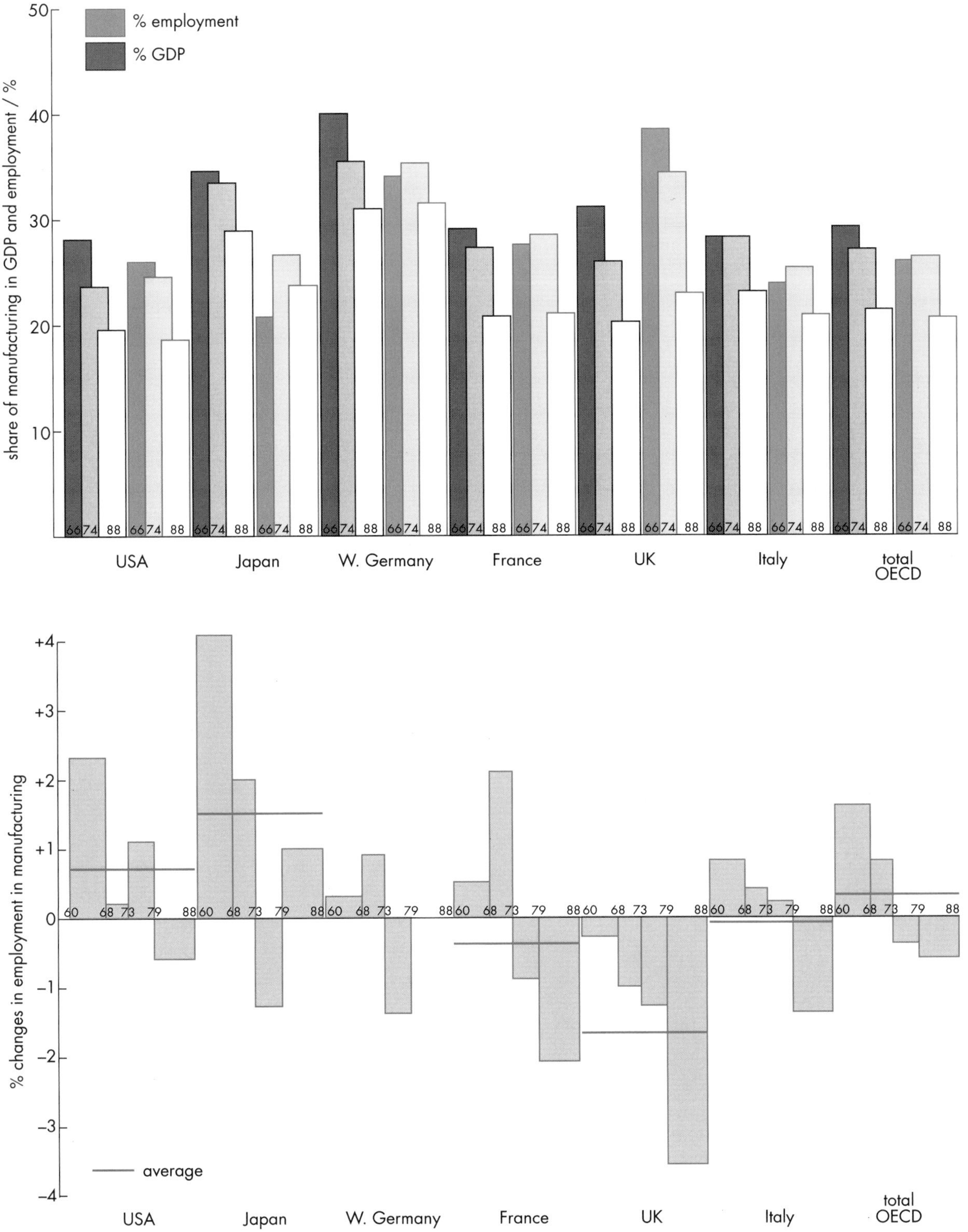

Figure 1.10   De-industrialization in the major OECD countries.

which was accounted for by the manufacturing sector fell from just under a third (32.1%) to just over a fifth (20.7%). Similarly the number of jobs in manufacturing fell from almost two-fifths (38.4%) of the total to less than a quarter (23.6%).

From what you know about Britain in this period what factors might have caused this decline?

Note that this was not an uniquely British phenomenon. The figure shows the same pattern in all the other major industrial countries, since at least the early 1970s.

Look at Figure 1.10 again and see what differences you can see between the British pattern and that of other countries in terms of the scale and timing of de-industrialization.

The lower graph in Figure 1.10 shows changes in the absolute numbers employed in manufacturing in the major developed countries. Again

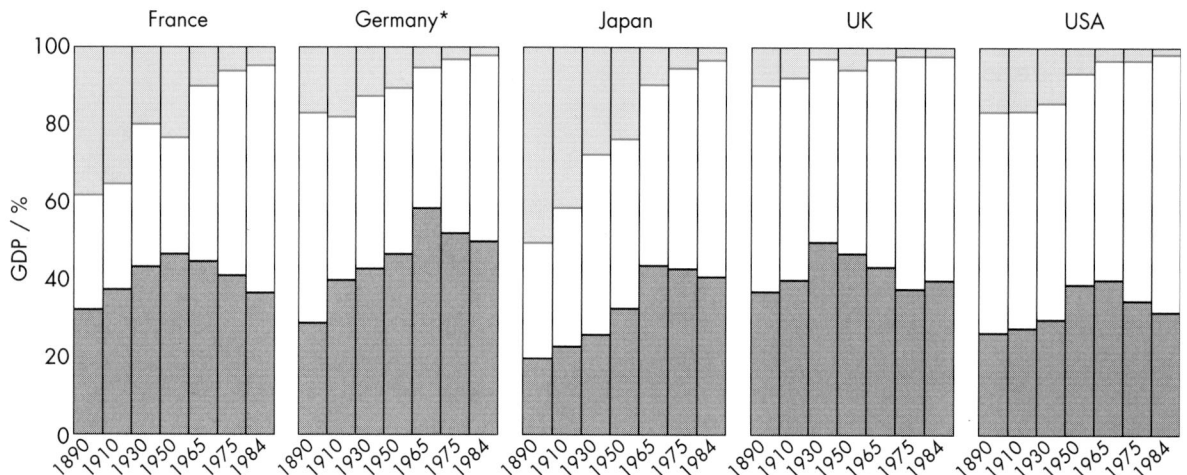

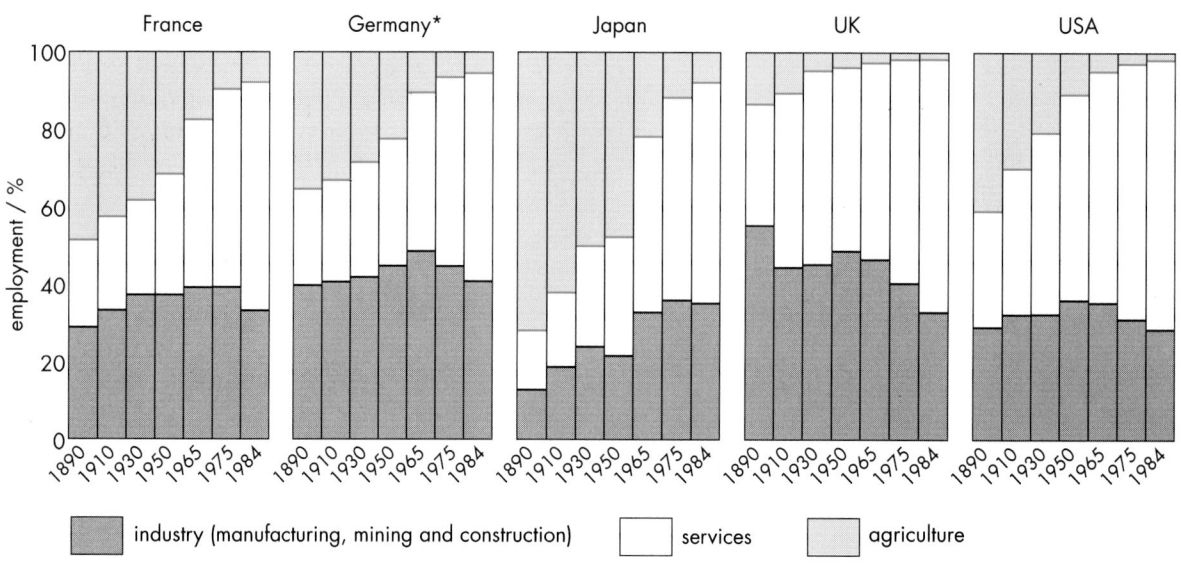

industry (manufacturing, mining and construction)   services   agriculture

*Data from 1950 onwards refers to W. Germany only

*Figure 1.11   Sectoral shares in employment and GDP from the 19th century to present.
[Data source: World Bank, 1987]*

the British case stands out as being an early and extreme case of de-industrialization. The number of people employed in manufacturing has fallen since the early sixties at an accelerating rate. Manufacturing employment in the OECD countries as a whole was lower in 1988 than in 1973 and in the 1980s all the major OECD countries, apart from Japan, have experienced an absolute reduction in the number employed in manufacturing.

Whether or not this is seen as a problem, depends on why such a change has taken place. There is considerable evidence that as economies develop over time, gradual shifts take place in the sectoral shares of output and employment. At early stages of development there is a shift away from agriculture towards industrial and service activities, as the relative importance of agricultural products (food in particular) declines in people's consumption and manufactured goods and services become more important.

This trend is borne out by studies of the historical experience of the now advanced countries (see Figure 1.11). The figure also shows that at higher levels of income, the share of manufacturing in GDP and employment tends to decline, and that of services tends to increase. Amongst competing explanations of the causes of de-industrialization I will discuss two.

Changes in international specialization

The first is that de-industrialization can result from a change in the pattern of international specialization. A country which is initially a net exporter of manufactured goods which discovers a natural resource is likely to experience a degree of de-industrialization. Production of this new sector will increase rapidly and the share of other sectors including manufacturing is reduced. Can you think of an example of this process taking place?

The obvious one of course is the discovery of North Sea oil. This changed Britain from being a net importer to being a net exporter of oil and was associated with a reduction in the share of manufacturing industry in output and employment.

Like the relative decline in industry associated with economic maturity, this type of de-industrialization is not necessarily negative, and simply reflects changing patterns of comparative advantage. Thus it could be argued that Britain was forced to expand the manufacturing sector after the Second World War in order to generate a massive manufactured export surplus to pay for the food and raw materials which the country needed to import. With the development of the oil industry, the country simply did not need such a large industrial sector.

Lack of competitiveness in manufacturing

The second possible way in which international factors may lead to de-industrialization is through a lack of competitiveness of manufacturing industry. This is the case which really underlies the concern over de-industrialization (Box 1.4). A country which is becoming less competitive in manufacturing will see its share of world exports of manufactures decline and imports increase. Declining employment in the manufacturing sector will not be offset by increased labour absorption elsewhere in the economy. The slow growth of domestic manufacturing will lead it to fall further behind its competitors as productivity increases lag, and a vicious circle of industrial and economic decline is set in motion, with rising unemployment and a deteriorating balance of payments. This may be further aggravated as local manufacturers cut back on investment or invest increasingly overseas.

This concern over de-industrialization is based on the assumption that industrial production is of particular benefit to an economy. This is usually explained in terms of the greater potential which exists for increased productivity and economies of scale in industry, and the notion that the overall pace of economic growth depends fundamentally on industrial performance.

While this may have been the case in the past, the question has been raised of whether industry is becoming less central to economic development than it was in the nineteenth and the first half of the twentieth century?

Box 1.4   Concern over de-industrialization

In the advanced industrialized countries concern has been expressed over the problem of de-industrialization in recent years. As long ago as 1975 in Britain, the then Secretary for Industry, Tony Benn, raised the problem in the following terms:

'The trend to contraction of British manufacturing industry which we are now suffering has gathered force in the last four years. If this trend is allowed to continue, we will have closed down 15% of our entire manufacturing capacity and nearly 2 million industrial workers will have been made redundant between 1970 and 1980.'

(Quoted in Singh, 1977)

But the problem was giving concern not only in Britain and not only amongst those on the left. In 1980 the influential US business magazine *Business Week* was alarmed about the situation in the United States:

'The US economy must undergo a fundamental change if it is to retain a measure of economic viability let alone leadership in the remaining 20 years of this century. The goal must be nothing less than the re-industrialization of America. A conscious effort to rebuild America's productive capacity is the only real alternative to the precipitous loss of competitiveness of the last 15 years, of which this year's wave of plant closings across the continent is only the most vivid manifestation'.

(Business Week, 30 June 1980.)

Summary

For almost twenty years now, there is evidence that in the major industrial countries there has been a process of de-industrialization in the sense of falling shares of manufacturing in employment and GDP.

We have discussed two possible causes of de-industrialization:

specialization — changes in a country's comparative advantage in international trade

lack of competitiveness — loss of export markets and increased import penetration

The relative importance of each of these factors in explaining the de-industrialization which we have observed since the early 1970s will come up again in the next section.

1.6 Explaining international industrial change

So far in this chapter we have identified a number of features of international industrial development in the post-war period.

These include:

- a cycle of rapid and then slower growth of industrial production and trade

- geographical shifts in the distribution of industrial production and trade between and within blocs

- the increasingly global nature of manufacturing

- changes in technology and the organization of production

- a process of de-industrialization in the core industrial countries.

Although we have looked at each of these in isolation, they are in many ways interrelated. In this section therefore we shall look at some of the ways in which these trends fit together to make up the broader picture. In particular we shall look at the link between the growth of Third World industry and de-industrialization in the West. Is de-industrialization in the developed countries a result of Third World industrial growth? Do these changes open up new opportunities for industrialization in the South?

A new international division of labour?

A common view is that a new international division of labour has emerged within the world economy since the 1960s. The distinction between an industrial centre and a primary product producing periphery which characterized the colonial international division of labour no longer holds.

There is less agreement over the causes of this change. Some see it as a result of the adoption of 'outward oriented' (i.e. export-led) policies by many Third World countries at this time. Others seek a more systemic explanation, arguing for instance that certain long term tendencies in the development of capitalism led to a new trend for industrial production to be relocated to low wage areas from the mid-1960s (Fröbel, Heinrichs & Kreye, 1980). The development of a world-wide reservoir of potential labour available at low wages combined with certain technological developments, such as the decomposition of tasks and the deskilling of the labour process, made it possible for firms to employ workers with a minimum of training at Third World production sites. Developments in the fields of transport and communications such as containerization, jet transport, international direct dialling, telexes etc. made it possible for dispersed production operations to be co-ordinated from a single centre as never before.

In short, firms from the advanced industrialized countries seek to maximize profits by relocating production. This export of capital has led to a reduction in industrial investment within the advanced industrial countries and increasing levels of unemployment. For some writers this is merely a temporary problem arising from a mismatch between existing skills and new job opportunities which will disappear once a new equilibrium is reached with the Third World countries enjoying a greater share of world industrial output (Beenstock, 1984). Other more radical writers, however, see these trends leading to a weakening of the working class in the core countries, and a questioning of the social-democratic consensus of the post-war period (Fröbel, Heinrichs & Kreye, 1980). They argue that this results from

(i) the difficulty that a capitalist state faces in taxing firms because of their greater international mobility

(ii) the growing cost of state expenditure because of increased unemployment .

What makes the idea of a new international division of labour appealing is the way in which it brings together a number of the trends which we have observed in earlier sections, particularly changes in the geographical distribution of production, the globalization of manufacturing, technological change and de-industrialization in the West. But there are a number of problems with these views.

Has industrial production relocated?

Contrary to the claims concerning a new international division of labour, the share of the Third World in industrial production has increased relatively slowly, and was concentrated in the decade of the 1970s. There was little increase between 1960 and 1969, a sharp increase from 1969 to 1975 followed by a slower increase from 1975 to 1980 and stagnation between 1980 and 1985 (look back to Figure 1.2).

A change in the geographical distribution of production is not in any case necessarily evidence of industrial relocation in the sense meant by Fröbel *et al*. It can just be the relative decline of manufacturing share in developed countries as industrial growth increases in Third World countries.

Has the direction of trade in manufactures changed?

A more relevant indicator of changes in the international division of labour is the direction of trade in manufactures. Although the increase in the Third World's share of manufactured exports has been more pronounced than in the case of output, it has been concentrated in a very small number of countries (see Section 1.2). This is hardly consistent with the view that there has been a massive relocation to the Third World as a whole.

Taking a longer term perspective on trade in manufactures, the increase in the share of the Third World since the early 1960s has only re-established its share to the levels reached in the mid-1930s (Gordon, 1989). The only clear indicator that supports the relocation thesis is that whereas in the 1930s two-thirds of Third World manufactured exports went to other Third World countries and only a third to the developed world, by the 1980s the proportions had been reversed.

Does LDC competition cause de-industrialization?
To what extent can increased imports from LDCs be held responsible for de-industrialization in the advanced industrialized countries? In aggregate, the level of Third World imports into developed country markets has been very limited. As Table 1.2 shows, less than 3% of the manufactured

Table 1.2   Developed countries' consumption of imports from the Third World, as % of consumption

	LDC imports
EEC	2.83%
USA and Canada	3.42%
Japan	1.43%
Average	2.83%

[Source: UNCTAD, 1988]

goods sold in the major developed country markets come from the Third World. This is not to deny that in certain industries such as clothing or footwear, there has been a significant impact, but overall it is difficult to attribute a major process of de-industrialization to such low levels of imports.

In fact studies have shown that increases in productivity (output per employee) are a much more important source of job losses in most developed countries than increased imports (Greenaway, 1983). The major exception to this generalization is the UK, where in recent years job losses as a result of trade exceeded the loss through increases in productivity. But even in the British case, it was the change in its trade with other developed countries which led to job losses (UNIDO, 1986).

Table 1.3 shows the net effect, on employment, of trade in manufactures with the Third World (taking account of both exports to, and imports from the South). For the United Kingdom in 1975 there was a net gain of more than half a million jobs. In other words the extra jobs created through exporting manufactures to LDCs were considerably greater than those lost as a result of competition from imports from the Third World. The same was true of all the other major industrial countries in the three years shown.

Comparing the figures in the first and third column of Table 1.3, we can also see that except for West Germany and the United Kingdom, trade in manufactures between developed and less developed countries created more employment in 1983 than in 1975. Far from changes in the international division of labour leading to job losses in the industrialized countries in this period, in four of the six countries additional jobs were being created as a result of North–South trade in manufactures.

Table 1.3   Increases in employment in developed countries, as a result of trade with the Third World

	Increases in employment level / person years		
	1975	1980	1983
West Germany	437 000	321 000	294 000
France	352 000	376 000	449 000
Italy	338 000	456 000	550 000
Japan	1 389 000	2 135 000	2 099 000
UK	557 000	319 000	249 000
US	307 000	616 000	669 000

[Source: UNIDO, 1986]

Have there been shifts in investment?

Has there been a massive shift in investment by TNCs towards Third World countries in recent years to take advantage of low cost labour? Again there are grounds for scepticism. The bulk of direct foreign investment (DFI) in manufacturing by the major industrialized countries, apart from Japan is in other developed countries. Figure 1.12 shows that in the mid-1980s less than a fifth of direct foreign investment from Western European countries and North America was located in the Third World. Furthermore, comparing the figures in the Table for the mid-1970s with the mid-1980s, we can see that the trend in recent years has been for the share of the Third World to decline rather than to increase.

Moreover the bulk of DFI in manufacturing goes to supply the domestic market of the host country, despite the publicity given to individual examples of export-oriented projects. In the late seventies (the last year for which data have been published), US manufacturing subsidiaries in developing countries made more than four-fifths of the total sales in the local market, while less than a tenth were exported back to the United States and to other countries respectively (UNCTC, 1985).

As in the case of exports of manufactures, the number of countries which have been preferred locations for TNC investment have been relatively few with eight countries accounting for more than half of the total stock of DFI in the Third World during the 1980s (Jenkins, 1987). These countries tend to be relatively developed Third World countries and investment is not attracted to countries with the cheapest labour. For example very little manufacturing investment takes place in Sub-Saharan Africa. Moreover concentration in a small number of countries has been on the increase.

Summary

We have seen that there is a commonly held view that rapid industrial growth in less developed countries and relocation of industry from the developed world have led to a new international division of labour. It has also been argued that

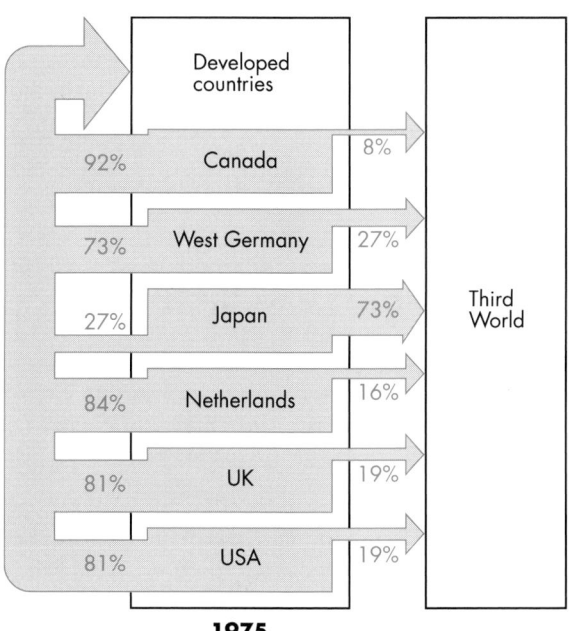
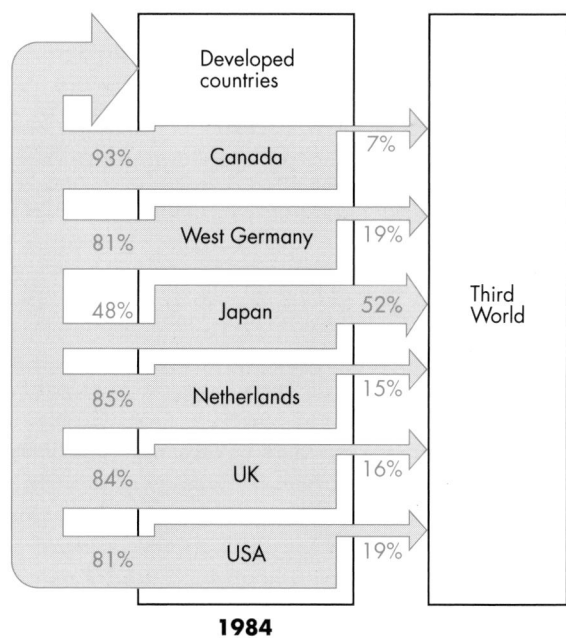

	1975			1984	
Canada	92%	8%		93%	7%
West Germany	73%	27%		81%	19%
Japan	27%	73%		48%	52%
Netherlands	84%	16%		85%	15%
UK	81%	19%		84%	16%
USA	81%	19%		81%	19%

Figure 1.12   Direct foreign investment from a few of the developed countries in 1975 and 1984. The green arrows show how much of the investment from each country went to other developed countries and how much went to the Third World. [Data source: UNCTC, 1988]

this has been a major factor leading to de-industrialization and rising unemployment in the industrialized countries.

This view has been questioned on a number of empirical grounds. I have shown that changes in the distribution of industrial activity and the direction of world trade in manufactures have been relatively limited and that direct foreign investment continues to be concentrated in the developed countries. I have also shown the limited extent of competition from LDC imports in the developed countries. This indicates that de-industrialization cannot be attributed to increasing Third World competition. It also suggests that de-industrialization has not led to major new export opportunities in the developed world for LDCs as some have hoped.

1.7 Future prospects for industrialization

In analysing the international context for industrialization in the post-war period it is useful to distinguish between certain long-term tendencies and cyclical movements. Amongst the long-term trends, the following seem to be of particular significance:

- 'shrinking' of the world economy through improvements in transport and communications

- globalization of production through the internationalization of capital

- changing shares of industry in employment with changes in levels of development

- changes in technology and the labour process as a result of the microelectronics revolution.

The post-war era consists of two main periods within a long-term cycle: the years up to about 1970 and the period from about 1970 to the present. Many writers see this as the latest of a number of long waves of growth and decline which have characterized capitalism since the Industrial Revolution.

The main cyclical characteristics of the period can be seen in a number of aspects:

- changes in the rate of growth of industrial production

- changes in the rate of growth of international trade

- changes in the rate of profit

- a switch from trade liberalization to growing protectionism.

These features of changing world economic conditions have given rise to opportunities and constraints for industrialization in the Third World and have influenced the international distribution of industrial activity.

Trade growth in the 1960s and 1970s

In the period up to 1970, world industry and trade grew rapidly. The growth in trade in manufactures was mainly amongst developed countries, encouraged by increasing trade liberalization. Conditions for industrialization in Third World countries were relatively favourable. Fast rates of growth increased the demand for manufactured goods domestically, while trade liberalization, although primarily benefiting the industrialized countries, offered the opportunity for a small number of Third World countries to begin exporting manufactured goods.

By the late 1960s, however, the long boom was running out of steam and the rate of profit in the advanced industrial countries fell, inflation accelerated and the rate of growth began to falter. The economic crisis intensified in the 1970s with the breakdown of the Bretton Woods system and the increased price of oil in 1973. Governments in the developed countries adopted deflationary measures in an attempt to bring inflation under control and the rate of growth fell sharply.

Faced with falling profitability and increased competition, firms in the developed countries were forced to restructure. Such restructuring can take a number of forms including take-overs and mergers, the introduction of new technology, rationalization, and geographical decentralization. Again, decentralization can involve various processes: subcontracting and outworking within developed countries as well as industrial relocation to the Third World.

Why then did the 1970s see a more pronounced increase in the Third World's share of industrial production and trade than the 1960s? Basically what happened was that although the rate of growth of manufacturing fell in the Third World, it fell less sharply than in the developed countries, allowing the Third World to increase its share. The fundamental reason for this is that the economies of the Third World continued to grow after 1973. Whereas the developed countries slowed down their economies to correct the balance of payments deficits which emerged as a result of the oil price increases, the Third World countries borrowed in order to keep on growing (Chapter 2 explains how they were able to do this). Thus although the 1970s were less favourable for industrial growth than the sixties in terms of the growth of trade and markets, they were more favourable in terms of the availability and terms of finance on offer.

Figure 1.13   Shopfloor of Philips factory in Singapore — assembling cassette recorders.

Figure 1.14   Textile factory in Taipei, Taiwan.

Industrial relocation to Third World countries

Although industrial relocation to low-wage countries was by no means the only possible response to falling profitability in the West, it was important in some industries such as electronics and clothing. In assembly industries like these, manufacturers were able to separate labour-intensive routine operations requiring manual skills from capital-intensive operations requiring a highly educated workforce. In consumer electronics, some high-technology electronics (computer components) and clothing (where fashions change), not only are the product life cycles relatively short, but also it was difficult and costly to automate assembly operations, making such investment in the developed countries uneconomic when compared with relocation to the Third World.

Although it is more common to regard industrial production in the developed countries as an 'engine of growth' for Third World countries through its effect on demand for their exports, it is also possible that crisis in the West can offer new opportunities for Third World producers.

Debt in the 1980s

Since the main basis of the rapid increase in the share of LDCs in world industrial production was credit which enabled the Third World to postpone adjustment, it is not surprising that once the bubble burst, the share of manufacturing production stagnated again in the 1980s (see Chapter 2). The possibilities for industrial growth became highly unfavourable. Not only was finance no longer available for industrialization, but the net outflow of resources from the Third World required a painful process of adjustment, which led to severe recession and, particularly in Latin America, to falling industrial output and employment in a number of countries. As was seen earlier, developed countries increasingly resorted to protectionist measures against cheap imports so that many LDCs found themselves in a Catch 22 situation, required to generate export surpluses in order to service their foreign debts while at the same time being denied access to Western markets which they needed in order to earn foreign exchange.

Prospects for the 1990s

The immediate prospects for Third World industrialization appear rather bleak. The debt problem is far from being resolved and a sustained economic expansion which would be necessary to bring about renewed industrial growth is certainly not around the corner, particularly in Latin America and Sub-Saharan Africa. Even if the world economy were to move into a new expansionary phase of the long-term cycle sometime before the end of the century, the experience of the long boom suggests that this would not lead to major shifts in the distribution of world industry.

This is reinforced by the analysis of likely trends in technology. It is predicted that the consolidation of microelectronics-based production and the diffusion of Japanese management practices will tend to reduce the scope for industrial relocation to take advantage of cheap labour. As outlined in Section 1.4, 'just in time' supply of components, along with the requirement for a highly trained multiskilled workforce who can understand and operate complex general-purpose machinery, may make the developed countries more attractive for manufacturing investment.

The picture, however, is not necessarily one of uniform gloom. The last three decades have seen increasing differentiation within the Third World with the emergence of the high-income oil-producing countries of OPEC and the growth of the NICs. In the 1990s some countries are likely to continue to be particularly favoured locations for industrial production.

This trend will be reinforced if particular regional blocs are consolidated. Mexico, if it is able to develop a special relationship with the United States is one such country, which has already received priority in debt negotiations. In Europe, the breakup of communist rule in Eastern Europe and the turn to market economies, together with the substantial opportunities for investment that may, emerge, makes it the most likely candidate for integration as a new European periphery. In the Far East, links with Japan which have been important in the rapid development of South Korea and Taiwan may be extended to other countries.

However this scenario leaves most of the Third World, particularly Latin America, Africa and South Asia out in the cold. Some countries such as Brazil, India and China are large enough to have the possibility of industrializing outside these regional blocs, but for the rest the future is at best uncertain. The possibility of increasing South–South co-operation is one avenue that is open to them, but the diversity of conditions, the large distances involved and the lack of both appropriate physical and institutional infrastructure all militate against this. Also, past experience with regional integration schemes amongst groups of Third World countries have not been encouraging.

Some conclusions

At the beginning of this chapter, a number of questions were raised concerning Third World industrialization in an international context. Are we now any nearer to being able to answer these questions?

Obstacles to the growth of industry

We have discussed a number of internal obstacles to industrialization in the Third World such as the low level of income which limits the size of the domestic market, the low level of investment which makes it difficult to set up modern industry, the lack of local technological capabilities, and the absence of a skilled labour force. These are all major obstacles at low levels of development and tend to become less of a problem as the process of industrialization proceeds. Rapid industrial growth in the NICs show that under certain circumstances, these obstacles can be overcome.

International conditions

We have also seen the way in which in some periods international conditions favour industrialization and in others pose an obstacle. On the whole rapid growth of world trade and production have in the post-war period been favourable to industrialization, while stagnation and protectionism have been associated with a slowdown in industrial growth. One should be careful about generalizing this however. In the 1930s the Great Depression gave a substantial boost to industrialization in Latin America (see Chapter 3).

International conditions can also operate in favour of industrialization in certain parts of the world rather than others. We have just seen how in the 1990s the formation of regional blocs may affect the prospects of different parts of the Third World. Some of the most successful NICs may have benefited from being in a strategic geopolitical position during the Cold War. We shall see later how important a factor this was in the case of South Korea (see Chapter 4).

Late industrialization

The problems of industrialization in the Third World cannot be divorced from the fact that it happened much later than in Europe and North America. Industry must be built up in competition with existing industrial capacity. When Britain and other European countries industrialized they were able to expand at the expense of handicrafts at home and abroad. The conquest of foreign markets is much more difficult for latecomers and even the domestic market has to be protected, at least initially, against the superior productive powers of the developed world.

But lateness is not necessarily a disadvantage. LDCs are in a position to take advantage of technological developments elsewhere. Under some conditions it may be possible for them to close the gap relative to the developed countries. But although international conditions set the parameters within which Third World industrialization develops, they do not determine where and when industrialization will occur. To answer this question one must return to a more detailed analysis of specific case studies.

Summary of Chapter 1

After the Second World War, world industrial production grew at over 5% a year. Continuing, but slower growth in the 1970s and 1980s was accompanied by trade agreements and protectionist measures on the part of the developed countries, which to some extent has hindered growth in the newly industrializing countries.

The post-war period has seen major shifts in the distribution of industrial production and in the pattern of trade. The share of the traditional industrial centres has declined continuously while that of the centrally planned economies and, since the late 1960s, the Third World, has increased. Within the Third World, most of the growth in industrial production and exports has been in a few countries, while the least developed countries have become increasingly marginalized.

Manufacturing production has become increasingly global in nature. This has been reflected in the increasing ownership and control of production overseas by transnational corporations, the growth of export processing zones and the increasingly international nature of industrial products and processes. This globalization of production has implications for labour, as workers in different countries increasingly compete against each other for jobs and bargain with the same employers.

There have been major changes in technology and in the labour process during this period. Assembly line mass production which spread in the 1940s and 1950s later began to be replaced by flexible automated manufacturing systems, with accompanying changes in industrial management practice.

Over the last two decades, there has been evidence of de-industrialization (a reduction in the proportion of employment in, and production by, manufacturing industry) in the industrial centres. Possible causes of this are specialization and lack of competitiveness, but not, as is often thought, increasing production in the Third World. The developed countries still trade and invest more with other developed countries than with the Third World. Some of the newly industrializing countries also have to contend with an increasing burden of debt.

Debt, changing industrial technology and other problems associated with late industrialization make the prospects for industrialization in the Third World seem bleak. But late industrializers may be able to take advantage of technical changes.

THE INTERNATIONAL DEBT CRISIS: CAUSES, CONSEQUENCES AND SOLUTIONS

HEATHER D GIBSON AND EUCLID TSAKALOTOS

By the end of the 1980s, the total debt of developing countries was over US $1 100 billion. As a direct result of this huge debt, the drive towards industrialization and economic restructuring for long-term development came to a halt in many countries. Instead, there ensued a desperate struggle to find resources to meet the short-term goal of debt repayment. As well as shaking the world financial system, the 'debt crisis' has also had serious repercussions for social and economic development in most of the Third World.

In this chapter, we want to examine and discuss the nature of this crisis for less developed countries (LDCs), its causes and possible solutions to it. To do this we need to look at the *history* of events leading up to and following the crisis, and address the following questions:

> **Q** What is the debt crisis and what factors contributed to causing it?

> **Q** Was the debt crisis just the result of the unfortunate combination of unfavourable economic circumstances in the 1970s or are there deeper, more fundamental causes?

> **Q** What effect has the debt crisis had on the people and the economies of LDCs?

To delve deeper into the fundamental causes of the debt crisis and to enable us to choose between competing explanations, we need to introduce some *theoretical* concepts. A key feature of the period leading up to the debt crisis was that it was associated with much less government intervention and a greater role for markets. To assess the success of this move we need to look at the way in which markets work.

> **Q** What are markets good at? To what extent are interventions in markets necessary and why?

More specifically, we want to introduce some theoretical concepts which will allow us to understand the problem of the international monetary system.

> **Q** What is the international monetary system set up to do and does it work?

The ultimate aim of this mixture of theory and history is to allow us to think about what might constitute a solution to the debt crisis, and remove what is a major obstacle to development.

Throughout the chapter, there are three main themes which persistently recur. Firstly, we emphasize the relationship between *debt, growth and development*. Whilst the build-up of debt can lead to a virtuous circle of growth and development, this has not, on the whole, been the experience of LDCs in the 1980s. Rather the volume of debt is now so large that it is severely restricting growth and development.

Secondly, we want to assess the balance which should be struck between allowing *private markets* to work unhindered and *government intervention*. As we have noted, the 1970s were a period when markets were given much more space. This experience, however, has not been altogether successful and we suggest that a move toward more official organization of the international monetary system may be required for the 1990s.

Our final theme is the *interdependence* which exists in the world economy between LDCs and industrial countries. By industrial countries we mean the developed countries which are the major lenders. We use the term loosely to distinguish them from (LDCs). The debt crisis has had a profound effect on LDCs in terms of reduced living standards. However, industrial countries have also been affected. Reduced demand for industrial country goods has affected growth and employment in these countries. Whilst this interdependence is being increasingly recognized, we shall see that this does not imply that conflicts of interest do not still arise.

The chapter is organized into four sections. In Section 2.1, we outline the main characteristics of the debt crisis and the build-up of debt. Section 2.2 examines the causes of the crisis. In particular, we look at the international monetary system, the role of the banks and the conduct of economic policy in LDCs themselves. Section 2.3 provides an analysis of the consequences of the crisis. We describe how the crisis has been managed and examine the effect this has had on LDCs in the 1980s. Finally, Section 2.4 discusses solutions to the crisis.

2.1 Characteristics of the crisis and the debt build-up

What is the debt crisis?

The debt crisis became big news in August 1982 when Mexico announced that it was not in a position to continue to repay its debt. This was the first sign that the issue of debt would dominate development and the international economy throughout the 1980s.

Figure 2.1   Headline from Sunday Times *5 September 1982; cartoon: Ingram Pinn.*

Figure 2.2 shows what has happened to total debt of LDCs as defined by the World Bank. From 1970 to 1988, the total debt stock increased some seventeen-fold. Although this figure shows an extraordinary increase in debt, it is not immediately clear why this should constitute a 'crisis'. In order to see the seriousness of the situation we need to make some important distinctions about the nature of the debt and explain why the debt is such a burden. Box 2.1 gives a number of such distinctions and measurements which are widely used in academic writings and newspaper articles on the debt crisis. We, however, only concentrate on a few of these.

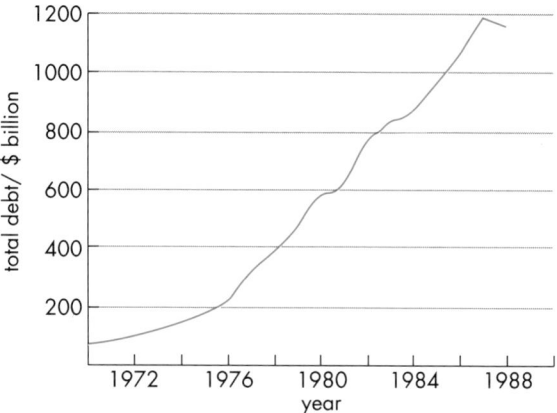

Figure 2.2   Total debt of less developed countries (US$ billion).

BOX 2.1 Glossary of debt terms and measures

Debt/GNP ratio: Debt as a percentage of Gross National Product (GNP). This gives us an indication of the volume of debt relative to the strength of the economy.

Debt per capita: Volume of debt per member of the population.

Debt service ratio: Interest plus original sum borrowed (principal) as a percentage of export earnings in any one year. This is a commonly used ratio which shows the debt burden relative to earnings from exports. Ultimately foreign debt has to be repaid in foreign currency and export earnings are the most important source of foreign currency.

Debt/exports ratio: Total debt as a percentage of total exports. This has a similar rationale to the debt service ratio.

Foreign currency debt: Debt denominated in a currency other than that of the debtor country.

Interest payments: Repayments of the cost of debt, rather than the repayment of the original

sum borrowed (see principal payments). It is often referred to as debt servicing.

Maturity of debt: The number of years which the country has to repay the debt. We often distinguish short-term debt (up to one year to maturity) and long-term debt (greater than one year to maturity).

Official debt: Debt which is owed to governments or official international institutions. This is in contrast to private debt which is owed to international banks.

Principal payments: Repayment of the original sum borrowed excluding the interest on that sum.

Public debt: Borrowing by the government, either national, state, or local.

Publicly guaranteed debt: Borrowing by a private or state company, but backed by a government guarantee which allows the company to achieve better terms on the international capital markets (lower interest rates, longer maturities etc.).

First, this debt is denominated in foreign currency and not the domestic currency of the particular debtor country. This has two implications.

- The debt we are dealing with here does not include government debt to its own citizens, such as bonds and treasury bills. Nor does it include private individual's debt denominated in domestic currency, such as mortgages and hire purchase.

- Most of this debt is denominated in dollars, with much smaller amounts in other currencies such as deutschmarks, yen and sterling which means that LDCs have to find foreign currency to repay it.

Figure 2.3.

A second distinction to make is between official and private debt. Official debt is debt which is owed either to other governments (in the main industrial country governments) or to official international institutions (such as the International Monetary Fund and the World Bank). Private debt is debt which is owed to international banks.

This distinction can be important because the terms of repayment of official debt are usually concessional. In other words, interest rates are lower and maturities longer compared to commercial or private debt.

Table 2.1 Concentration of debt in 1982 (% of total debt)

Sub-Saharan Africa	10.8
South and East Asia	26.8
Latin America and the Caribbean	51.3
North Africa and the Middle East	11.1

To what extent is this debt a burden for LDCs? A first approach could be to look at how the debt is geographically spread. Table 2.1 shows that debt is highly concentrated in a small number of countries, the most highly indebted of which are either in Latin America or South East Asia. Does this mean that Latin American and South East Asian countries are among the worst affected by the debt crisis? Not necessarily. We can see why by examining two other indicators, which illuminate different aspects of the debt problem

The first is the debt service ratio (see Box 2.1). This seeks to capture the burden of repayment. The importance of export earnings reminds us of the fact that this debt is in foreign currency and has to be repaid in foreign currency. Export earnings are the main source of foreign currency. Figure 2.4 shows debt service ratios for Brazil and South Korea. Both are countries in areas of high concentration of debt. In 1982 Brazil used 81% of its export earnings for debt repayment, whereas South Korea used only 22%. So clearly the burden of debt is more onerous for Brazil. Note that Brazil's debt service ratio declined sharply after 1982. Unfortunately, this does not necessarily imply that Brazil's debt burden eased. In practice, debt service is calculated using the interest and principal repayments actually made in any one year, not those that were due to be made. Thus the debt service ratio could decline simply because the country

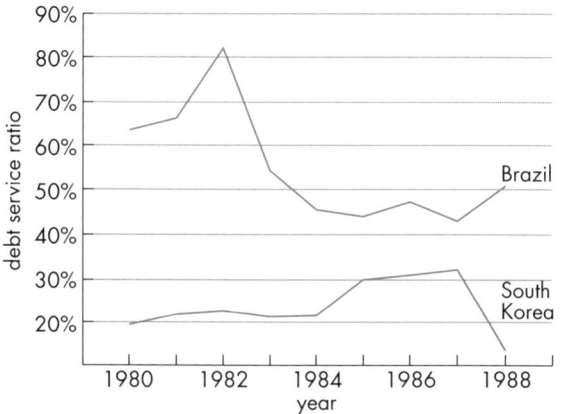

Figure 2.4   Debt service ratios for Brazil and South Korea.

stops repaying its debt. This happened in Brazil in 1982. In spite of this drawback, the debt service ratio is widely used as an indicator of debt burden.

A second indicator which is commonly used is debt as a percentage of gross national product (GNP). Figure 2.5 illustrates the different debt burdens of sub-Saharan Africa and Latin America. African debt might not be high in absolute terms. But, its high debt to GNP ratio shows that debt is a serious problem for African countries. Indeed, since the mid-1980s it has become much higher than the corresponding ratio for Latin American countries.

Thus no one debt indicator is sufficient to highlight all the aspects of the debt crisis and care is needed in interpreting any particular indicator.

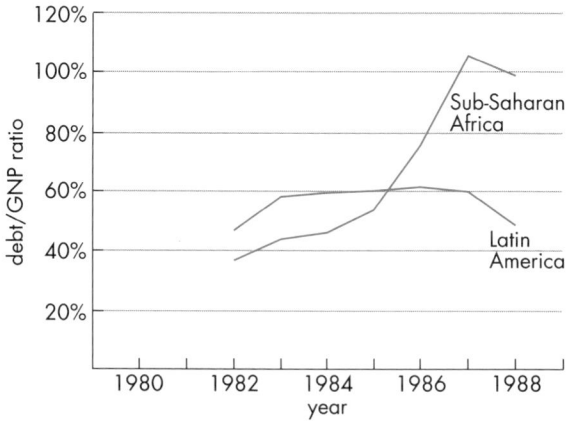

Figure 2.5   Debt/GNP ratios for Latin America and sub-Saharan Africa.

Rather we need a range of indicators whose usefulness will vary according to the nature of the problem faced by particular countries or regions.

How did the debt crisis emerge?

Why did this build-up of debt occur? Moreover, need such borrowing necessarily lead to crisis? To answer these questions, we need to look firstly at why LDCs may need to borrow in foreign currency. Secondly, we need to examine the economic conditions under which debt repayment will be easy and to contrast that with the conditions faced by LDCs in the late 1970s and early 1980s.

For a country to develop, it needs access to finance for investment. There are some well known reasons why such finance may be lacking in LDCs. We can point to two although only in a very simple way given the complex specific conditions of individual countries

Lack of domestic savings

The first problem is the possible inadequacy of savings which can be channelled to investment through financial intermediaries such as banks. Incomes in LDCs are low. The lower personal income, the greater the proportion each person has to spend on basic consumption needs, leaving little scope for saving. In addition, savings may be low because of the underdeveloped nature of LDC financial systems. The financial system is an important medium through which savings are channelled into investment opportunities. It acts to bring together borrowers and savers. In its absence, savers find it difficult to place their funds directly into investment opportunities. LDCs can either try to encourage domestic savings and/or rely on financial inflows from abroad. The latter can take the form of borrowing from abroad, aid or attracting direct foreign investment.

Lack of foreign exchange

In addition to the lack of domestic savings, LDCs face a second problem. They may need access to foreign currency (foreign exchange). Development and industrialization usually require imports of goods and services (such as machinery, capital goods, expertise, etc) which cannot be provided by the domestic economy. These purchases require foreign exchange. Of course, foreign exchange can be earned from exports. But it is rarely enough. A country may have to import more than it exports. This means it has a current account deficit on balance of payments (see Box 2.2). The capital account must cover (or finance) such a deficit. Let's see how this may be done.

Firstly, there is foreign direct investment, as when a foreign company sets up a plant in an LDC. This involves a capital inflow which does not entail debt. Secondly, there is aid. This can take the form of either grants or loans. Although loans create debt, one of their attractions is that they are usually on softer terms (i.e. lower interest rates and longer periods for repayment) than commercial loans.

Finally, there is borrowing from international banks. This is clearly debt since it leads to an obligation to repay in the future. Such borrowing takes place on commercial terms (i.e. there are no soft or concessionary terms).

Dynamics of debt build-up

Up till now, we have been viewing the current and capital accounts in a rather static manner (i.e. at one point in time). But there is clearly a dynamic element as these evolve over time. Let us now examine the dynamics of the debt build-up.

Taking an abstract example, for a country to repay its debt easily, it requires three things:

- low interest rates on its debt
- high export prices
- a high demand for its exports.

The last two ensure that foreign exchange is available for debt repayment. Conversely, a world in which interest rates are high, the price of LDC exports are low, and the demand for such goods is also low, is likely to mean that the country will find it more and more difficult to continue to repay.

Recycling of oil surpluses

We can now look at the history of the 1950s to 1980s to see how the existing debt relationships

---

BOX 2.2   Current and capital accounts of the balance of payments

The balance of payments of a country is the record of all transactions which the country undertakes with other countries over a given period, for example a year. It is usually divided into three main sections: the current account, the capital account and the balance of official financing.

The current account records the import and export of all goods and services. Where payments for imports exceed export earnings, the balance of payments is said to be in deficit. Where imports are less than exports, the balance of payments is said to be in surplus.

The capital account records all capital inflows (import of capital) and outflows (export of capital) in any period. Again the capital account can be either in deficit or surplus.

The balance of official financing records all government intervention in the foreign exchange market.

All these three elements must sum to zero in any given time period. This means that, disregarding the balance of official financing, any deficit on the current account, for example, must be matched by a surplus on the capital account.

To relate this to the debt problem, we can view the period of debt build-up as one where capital inflows (producing a capital account surplus) covered the current account deficit. However, when the debt is due for repayment, capital outflows lead to a capital account deficit which must be covered by a current account surplus. This illustrates an important principle of debt repayment; that heavily indebted countries require at some time in the future to produce a current account surplus. There is an example of Brazil's balance of payments in Chapter 3.

evolved. Most commentators are agreed that a central element in the debt build-up was the rise in oil prices in 1973–74. In LDCs which were not oil producers, this generated an additional demand for foreign exchange (dollars to buy oil). Oil is a necessity for which there are few substitutes in the short term, so these countries' increased import bills caused their current accounts to go further into deficit.

How were their current account deficits financed? There was an important difference between the 1950–69 period and the 1970–89 period. In the 1950s and 1960s aid and foreign direct investment were the main sources of foreign exchange, with borrowing from industrial country governments on concessional terms (official borrowing) also playing a part. In the 1970s, the main source of finance was the private international banks (Stanyer & Whitley, 1981; Stewart & Sengupta, 1982).

Why should this shift make any difference? Recall our earlier distinctions between different capital inflows. The main difference lies in the terms of international borrowing on the private markets. Aid and official borrowing either did not require repayment or were offered on very good terms. Commercial borrowing involves no concessions. LDCs were willing to contract debt on these poorer terms because they had no alternative if they wanted to continue to consume oil. So they faced a large increase in their current account deficits. An additional attraction of private banks as a source of finance was that the loans were not tied to specific purposes as was often the case with aid or official borrowing.

But the increased borrowing from international banks in this period also reflects an increased keenness by banks to lend to some favoured LDCs — those seen as reasonable risks. Middle East oil producers had such huge surpluses on their current accounts in the 1970s, that they could not possibly invest it all in their own countries. So oil-exporting countries deposited the receipts from oil sales with international banks. The banks therefore had plenty of funds available for lending to LDCs. This process became known as the *recycling* of oil surpluses.

The second oil price rise in 1979–80 further increased the current account deficits of non-oil-exporting LDCs. However, there is a central difference between the 1974 and 1979 oil crises. In 1974, the major industrial countries did not react to the oil crisis in a concerted and systematic manner. But by 1979 the desire to combat inflation came to the top of the political and economic agenda of all industrial countries. Their response in terms of reducing demand in (deflating) their economies had serious implications for the dynamics of debt growth in LDCs.

Firstly, this deflation led to decreased demand for exports from LDCs and the prices of raw materials and commodities exported by LDCs fell. The reduced export earnings of many LDCs made it difficult to pay the interest on their debt.

Secondly, interest rates were increasing in this period. This was a policy measure to bring down inflation. Thus LDCs had to make increased interest payments. It has been calculated that the additional costs of interest payments following the rise in interest rates for non–oil LDCs were US$41 billion per annum in 1981 and 1982 (Cline, 1984).

Summary

In answer to how the debt crisis emerged we can state the following:

- LDCs need to borrow foreign currency because domestic savings are low and because they need foreign currency to purchase the imports which will help their industrialization.

- Borrowing to finance industrialization need not result in crisis. However, in the early 1980s, crisis resulted when economic conditions worsened, leading to lower export earnings, higher import bills and higher interest payments on debt. For some observers it is these three factors that led to the debt crisis (Cline, 1984). For others these three changes merely helped to trigger the crisis (Lever & Huhne; Gibson, 1989; Allsop & Joshi, 1986). It is to the deeper and more fundamental causes which we now turn.

2.2 The causes of the debt crisis

What are the underlying causes of the debt crisis? Knowing the causes is of paramount importance to deciding between alternative solutions. We examine here three potential causes: (i) the international monetary system; (ii) the banking system; (iii) the debtors themselves. It is useful to consider these causes separately even though there may be links between them.

Cause 1: the international monetary system

There is an important degree of interdependence in the world economy. For instance, we have already seen the relationship between oil surpluses, the economic policies of industrial countries and the need of LDCs for financial resources. We now investigate how LDCs' financial needs have been dealt with by the international monetary system. One of the central aspects of the debt crisis can be understood as a problem of the world economy, specifically what economists call a recycling problem.

Recycling is taking money from those countries which have current account surpluses (see Box 2.2) and lending this money on to those countries which have current account deficits. This may be done by private banks or by international institutions (see Box. 2.3).

Before examining why recycling is a problem, let us take an example of how recycling might work in theory. Theoretically, there can be no such thing as a balance of payments deficit or surplus in the world economy. At any one time, there will be countries with balance of payments deficits and surpluses but these should in principle cancel each other out.

However, it is important that individual countries should avoid having persistent deficits or persistent surpluses. Why is this so? Let us take the simple case of two countries: the UK which has a deficit and Germany which has a surplus. The UK cannot continue to finance the deficit from its own reserves of foreign currency or by borrowing forever. Eventually its reserves will run out and the debt incurred by borrowing will have to be repaid. At some point the UK has to run a current account surplus. This implies that there are two ways in which adjustment can come about. Firstly, the UK could reduce its GNP. Lower incomes reduce the demand for imports and hence reduce the current account deficit. This has the obvious disadvantage that it implies a lower rate of growth. But there is another solution. Germany (the surplus country) could increase its national income. This would increase its demand for imports from the UK and thereby help to reduce the UK's deficit. The second solution is more favourable to both countries' growth prospects than the first. But critically, it depends on some coordination by the two countries over economic policy issues.

This is, of course, a theoretical example. How has the world economy dealt with the recycling problem in practice? After the Second World War, the international monetary system was organized under the Bretton Woods system (see Box 2.3). Part of the inspiration and political will for a new international monetary order came from what was seen as a lack of coordination of international economic policies and the massive recession between the First and Second World Wars.

The Bretton Woods system set up the International Monetary Fund (IMF) which was responsible, among other things, for resolving the recycling problem. The IMF was responsible for providing finance to countries with current account deficits. In addition, the IMF was supposed to ensure that both deficit and surplus countries undertook measure to reduce their current account deficits and surpluses, as in our example of the UK and Germany. This is known as *symmetric adjustment.*

Figure 2.6   Bretton Woods conference.

BOX 2.3 Bretton Woods: Keynes versus White

The Bretton Woods conference was in July 1944 (at Bretton Woods, New Hampshire, USA; Figure 2.6). Bilateral negotiations had been carried out between the US and the UK since 1941. Although the conference included other wartime allies, UK and US ideas were dominant. The UK was represented by John Maynard Keynes, the US by Harry Dexter White. The differing views put forward by the UK and the US became known as the Keynes plan and the White plan.

Keynes envisaged the establishment of an International Clearing Union which would issue a new international reserve currency known as the 'bancor'. Countries would be able to draw on their reserves of 'bancors' and would be able to borrow additional 'bancors' for financing their balance of payments deficits. Keynes envisaged that deficit countries should have access to large amounts of international finance on an unconditional basis. In this way resources would have to be provided to help weaker deficit countries. The purpose of Keynes' plan was to ensure the automatic recycling of surpluses to deficit countries. To this end, not only did deficit countries have to pay interest on 'bancors' borrowed from the funds,

so surplus countries had to pay a penalty if their 'bancor' balances became excessive. If deficit countries were using 'bancors' to pay for their imports, then surplus countries would be accumulating 'bancor' balances with the International Clearing Union. This penalty imposed on surplus countries was meant to force symmetric adjustment, by ensuring both surplus and deficit countries undertook policies to eliminate balance of payments deficits.

The US, however, thought that this plan made too much finance available to deficit countries. Given that they were providing most of the funds for the new international monetary arrangements, their view prevailed and the White plan was implemented. This plan created a pool of foreign exchange and gold held at the International Monetary Fund (IMF). Deficit countries could have automatic access on a temporary basis to a restricted amount of finance. The more finance required, the greater the conditions attached. The highest level of conditionality is known as an IMF programme, which we discuss in Section 2.3.

(Scammel, 1975; Yeager, 1976; Tew, 1977.)

What can we say in practice about Bretton Woods' ability to deal with the recycling problem?

- Was the volume of funds adequate to the task in hand? Have another look at Box 2.3 which indicates how some economists, such as Keynes, thought that the recycling problem would need an international institution with much larger funds (Figure 2.7). We will come back to this issue later when we discuss what an appropriate international monetary system might look like.

- Did the IMF manage to ensure the intended symmetric adjustment both by deficit and by surplus countries? Some have argued that the inadequacy of funds went hand-in-hand with an inability of the IMF to enforce the type of symmetric adjustment initially envisaged. It was the deficit countries that had to reduce their income. This led to a great deal of resentment. It also reduced the desire for international

Figure 2.7 J M Keynes — a man of action or armchair theorist? (Cartoon courtesy of the executors of the estate of Sir David Low and the Evening Standard).

cooperation. There was no similar pressure on surplus countries to make adjustments.

- Was the system sensitive to the needs of LDCs? As in other areas of economic policy, the form of economic cooperation reflects the realities of economic power. The Bretton Woods system was no exception and the central and most powerful player was the US. As a result the principles enshrined in the system reflected to a large degree the interests of the US. LDCs became increasingly dissatisfied with the minimal role they had in international monetary arrangements. One way of looking at this is to suggest that had LDCs more of a say in setting up the post-war monetary institutions, they would most probably have supported the larger and more ambitious conception of Keynes.

The Bretton Woods system came under increasing stress in the late 1960s and broke down completely in the early 1970s (*Allen & Thomas, 1992,* Chapters 11 and 12). Given some of the limitations of the Bretton Woods system which we have discussed, was its demise a benefit in disguise? The answer to this clearly depends on what replaced it. For what replaced Bretton Woods was not a new system of international monetary cooperation which would have been more sensitive to the needs of the LDCs in terms of a greater LDC role in international monetary institutions and in ensuring that they had plentiful access to funds on soft terms. Rather the 1970s and the early 1980s were characterized by a lack of world cooperation on economic and financial matters, manifested in a decline in the use of IMF funds in the second half of the 1970s. In other words the key problems of world economic management were left to market solutions. Furthermore, this trend towards a more market-oriented solution and a diminishing role for international monetary institutions coincided with a worsening recycling problem because of rising oil prices.

Cause 2: the private international banking system

If there was to be no internationally coordinated response to the enlarged recycling problem of the 1970s, then was the market solution adequate to the task or did it actually exacerbate the problem? The market solution consisted of allowing private international banks to lend to LDCs. In other words, as we have seen, international banks used the current account surpluses of oil-exporting countries to lend to oil-importing deficit countries.

- How did international banks determine how much they should lend?

- Why did international banks lend so much to LDCs?

Credit rationing

Banks discriminate between borrowers using two methods:

Riskier borrowers may have to pay a higher interest rate. With respect to differential interest rates, banks normally charged countries the market rate of interest (LIBOR, see Box 2.4) plus some mark-up known as the spread. If LDCs are divided into various categories (for example, oil-importing LDCs, oil-exporting LDCs etc) some paid larger spreads than others. For example, in 1977, an oil-importing country could expect to pay a spread of around 1.85%. Oil-exporting LDCs, on the other hand, were able to get loans on better terms; spreads were around 1.6%. By 1980, however, many of these differences had been eliminated. Oil-importing LDCs and oil-exporting LDCs were able to borrow on similar terms (Gibson, 1989).

Riskier borrowers will be more limited in the quantity of funds they can borrow. In practising credit rationing, banks had to set country limits. In other words, to decide (i) whether they would lend to a country at all and (ii) if they decided to lend, how much they should lend. Since country limits are not made public by banks we cannot present any concrete examples, but the evidence presented in Section 2.1 on how bank lending was concentrated in particular LDCs suggests that some form of credit rationing was operating. In other words, some countries did not receive bank loans. What about those countries which the banks did lend to? It appears there was little or no credit rationing because those countries received large amounts of funds.

BOX 2.4 Glossary of banking terms

Capital base of a bank: The amount subscribed by the shareholders of the bank. In other words, it is the money which the owners of the bank have raised.

Country limits: The maximum loan a bank would be willing to make to any individual country.

Cross default clause: A clause in a loan agreement which states that if the borrower defaults on one loan, all others loans to the same borrower could be called into default. This is meant to prevent a country from refusing to pay back some loans, while continuing to pay back others.

Fees: Additional payments that developing countries make to banks for each loan the bank gives them. These cover administrative costs as well as contributing to profits. The fee is usually some percentage of the total loan (for example, 2%). Given that loans of $100 million are not unusual, these fees can be large.

Interest-rate spread (or spread): A percentage which each country pays over and above the market rate of interest. These spreads sometimes vary between countries, between loans which have government guarantees and those which do not and so on.

LIBOR (London Interbank Offered Rate): A market interest rate on dollar deposits held in banks in London. It is frequently used as the market interest rate in lending to LDCs.

Rollover loan: A loan in which the interest rate is changed every three or six months in line with movements in LIBOR. Most loans to LDCs fall into this category.

Syndicated loan: A loan in which a number of banks participate. The amounts involved in single loans to LDCs are often very large and no one bank would be prepared to lend all the money.

Overall it appears that banks lent large amounts to a small number of countries. For example, by 1982 the nine largest US banks had lent over twice their combined capital base (see Box 2.4) just to non-oil LDCs. If we look at their loans to Brazil alone, this amounted to some 44% of their capital bases in 1982. (See in particular Cline, 1984). Thus in retrospect, banks appear to have lent too much, in the sense that if some of these countries had defaulted in the early 1980s, many large banks would have failed.

How do we explain the fact that spreads were squeezed and that certain countries, far from being credit-rationed, seem to have had almost unlimited access to bank credit? One reason which has been suggested is that the banks lacked a proper system for credit rating (or country risk analysis). A wide range of methods were adopted and all were subject to various limitations. But this argument on its own seems unconvincing. If an adequate credit rating system was of such importance, why did the banks not try to find a better one or use existing methods more effectively? The banks' role in the international debt crisis can be better explained by the highly competitive nature of the international banking system.

Competition between banks

Table 2.2 shows the number of foreign banks in London and New York, the two main international financial centres in the world. All these banks were competing for business. Indeed, banking magazines such as *Euromoney* used to publish tables of rankings listing who had lent most, how many syndicated loans (see Box 2.4) each bank had participated in, how many syndicated loans each bank had organized, etc. This competitive environment was enhanced by the fact that these markets are not as regulated as domestic banking markets. They are essentially offshore markets. Thus there is little government intervention to moderate competition.

Table 2.2 The number of foreign banks in London and New York

Year	London	New York
1970	163	75
1975	263	127
1980	353	253
1985	399	320

[Data source: Gibson, 1989]

Banks which did not participate in syndicated lending feared that they might lose out to competitors. For example, they feared loss of profits, or loss of market share. Such behaviour tends to promote a herd instinct amongst banks. That is, if some banks are seen to be lending to certain countries others will follow, with little or no analysis of the risks. US regional banks were particularly guilty of this in the late 1970s. These are fairly small banks who were neither able nor willing to invest in country risk analysis (which can often be expensive). Rather they relied on the larger banks' country risk analysis. If they saw larger banks lending to a country, they would take this as a signal that the country was creditworthy. In this way, the banking system as a whole could easily begin to overlend.

Some economists (for example, Guttentag & Herring, 1986) have argued that the banks ignored the possibility of countries defaulting: the probability that a country would default in the 1970s was fairly low, but the banks acted as if it were zero. This 'disaster myopia' meant that while banks may have been unsure about the creditworthiness of a country, competitive forces tended to make them ignore any worries they had. In view of the fact that overseas bank contracts were not easily enforceable, this tendency to overlend proved to be even more problematic.

Response to repayment problems

After 1982 when Mexico and other countries declared themselves unable to meet their debt service commitments, each bank sought to stop lending, not only to developing countries who were seeking rescheduling, but also to others. This action exacerbated the problem. Countries which would have expected to continue to receive new loans now found they could not raise any new money. This frequently forced countries into repayment problems. Nevertheless, such actions were rational for each individual bank, which would not want to continue to lend while others were getting out.

If a company makes a bad investment, it fails. But industrial country governments could not simply allow the banks to bear the 'free market' consequences of their actions. There are significant social costs associated with bank failure. The consequences are not confined to the shareholders and managers of the bank. In a modern economy, banks provide the means of payments, finance for investment and so on. Bank failures have considerable knock-on effects, in falling output and rising unemployment.

So the market solution, through the private banking system, to the problem of recycling in the 1970s has not worked. We have seen how the highly competitive environment led banks to lend what, in retrospect, appears to have been too much. This conclusion brings us back to two of the themes of this chapter. The first is the interdependence of the world economy. The build-up of LDC debt and the subsequent repayment problems faced by many countries threatened the international financial system. Because governments in the industrial countries could not allow banks to fail, the whole crisis had to be highly managed, as we shall see below. The second theme relates to the balance between the role of the market and more interventionist measures. Our analysis suggests that banks are, at least on their own, not well suited to recycling and this theme is taken up again more fully in Section 2.4.

Cause 3: the debtors themselves?

The blame for the debt crisis is often laid at the door of borrowing countries themselves.

- Did they follow inappropriate development policies in the 1950s and 1960s?

- Was there too much or too little state intervention?
- Did inappropriate strategies lead to the misuse of the money borrowed in the 1970s and therefore to difficulty in repayment?

Given the many differences between LDCs, it is difficult to say anything very useful without going into the details of specific cases. The interaction of domestic policies and the factors outside the control of any developing country is likely to be complex and be worth studying in detail. The case studies of Brazil and South Korea illustrate this (Chapters 3 and 4).

What can we say at the very general level? Most commentators (Marcel & Palma, 1987; Stewart & Sengupta, 1982; Allsopp & Joshi, 1986, to name a few) argue that debtor countries attempted to use their loans for investment. For instance, for those developing countries who had access to international banking markets in the 1970s (mostly, middle income countries) per capita economic growth was about 3.1%, as compared to 3.6% in the 1960s. In the lower income LDCs, with no access to international capital markets in the 1970s per capita growth fell to 0.9% as compared with 1.6% in the 1960s (Stewart & Sengupta, 1982, p.18). Moreover those countries who were able to borrow saw an increase in their domestic investment. In Latin America, for example, both GDP and investment growth rates were satisfactory and export growth remained high (See Table 2.3).

Of course there are some well known examples where debt was not used productively. The most often-quoted are the Philippines (under Marcos), Nicaragua (under Somoza) and Zaire (under Mobutu). While luxury consumption, extravagant military expenditure or simply embezzlement and corruption are clearly significant problems, they cannot be generalized to all LDCs. Here we focus on two issues that developing countries had to confront which have an immediate bearing on the problem of debt and are common to a large number of developing countries.

Borrowing and investment

The first has to do with the relationship between borrowing and investment. The quantity of investment undertaken during the debt build-up was high, but what was the quality like? Investment based on borrowing poses particularly difficult issues for LDCs:

(i) The project may have a high social return (infrastructural investment, education etc) but it may not generate enough revenue to repay the loan. If for example the government decides to build a dam, it can tax its citizens to pay for it. A major problem of LDCs is the difficulty of raising adequate tax revenue because of low income, tax evasion and large informal sectors. This does not imply that investments which have large social returns represent mistaken development policies. One could easily argue that the long-run development of any LDC depends exactly on such

Table 2.3 Latin American economies, 1970–81 (annual rates of growth)

	1970/75	1975/79	1979/81
Gross Domestic Product	6.4	5.5	3.6
Government Consumption	6.0	5.5	4.2
Private Consumption	9.3	5.9	3.1
Gross Investment	3.4	5.1	3.1
Exports	9.2	9.8	7.1
Imports	6.4	7.3	7.9

[Data source: Marcel & Palma, 1987]

investment with high social returns. The problem arises if the lenders have short-run horizons and require repayments within a short space of time. (This brings us back to the issues of whether there is enough finance available for this kind of investment so that LDCs need not depend on lenders with short-term horizons.)

(ii) Foreign exchange is needed to repay the loans. Ultimately, investment projects have to generate, either directly or indirectly, greater export revenues. Again a dilemma can exist. Investments in those projects which maximize the availability of foreign exchange in the near future may not necessarily be those which work for the development of a particular LDC in the long run.

Capital flight

The second issue has been the phenomenon of capital flight (Lessard & Williamson, 1987), where private citizens of a country export large amounts of their wealth either legally or illegally to private bank accounts abroad. This occurs either for speculative reasons (for example, a devaluation is anticipated) or because of a lack of political and economic stability in the home country. Measurements of capital flight are probably gross underestimates. Even so, in many countries they are a high proportion of capital inflows (Allsopp & Joshi, 1986). This leads to a number of consequences. The immediate effect of capital flight is to reduce the availability of foreign exchange for imports or to necessitate increased foreign borrowing. If no borrowing is possible then the effects of capital flight will be felt in a reduction in domestic output or investment. Once more we can see the potential for a vicious circle. Lower investment and output may lead to greater difficulties with debt servicing. Such difficulties may lead to greater expectations of financial or political instability which may in turn lead to greater capital flight.

Capital flight has an insidious effect on income distribution in LDCs. Those who can remove their capital get the benefit of the security provided by owning wealth outside their country. The poor on the other hand, who have little or no savings, have to bear the brunt of belt-tightening policies directed to debt repayment.

Summary

We have introduced three potential underlying causes of the 1980s debt crisis:

1 The rise of the debt problem was occurring at precisely the time when international cooperation on monetary issues was in decline. There was no strong coordinated response to the problem of recycling in the 1970s from the international community as a whole, and the regulation of the international financial system broke down.

2 International private banks chose to lend to a relatively small number of what were perceived as low credit risk countries. While banks overlent to these countries, others in need of credit were bypassed since they were considered to be commercial risks. Competitive behaviour between (large and small) banks exacerbated the spate of overlending but, threatened with default in 1982, they withdraw further credit. While developed country governments bailed out the banks for fear of serious repercussions in the world's financial system, debtor countries had to go to the IMF for assistance.

3 LDCs faced two problems which exacerbated the debt crisis. First, the kind of investment projects which LDCs undertook did not always generate foreign exchange. Moreover, loans were often too short-term and investment projects were not given enough time to generate returns. Thus debt repayment was often difficult. Second, capital flight reduced the amount of investment capital available to many LDCs. This resulted either in more borrowing or in less consumption and investment.

Debt problems in LDCs resulted from a combination of the above causes. Resolution of the problems of the debt crisis point to the need for an overhauled international monetary system.

2.3 The management of the debt crisis

Now we are going to examine the response to the crisis by the LDCs themselves, the banks and industrial countries. How has the debt crisis been managed up to now and why has it been managed in the way it has?

The case-by-case approach

Although as we shall see there are a number of ways in which the debt crisis could have been handled, the approach actually adopted in the 1980s came to be known as the 'case-by-case' approach. In other words, each country which is facing debt servicing problems is treated on its own. Indeed it could be argued that the 'case-by-case' approach represented an attempt by those organizing the crisis management to highlight the fact that they saw the debt crisis as a problem specific to certain countries and not a general problem requiring a 'global' solution

Nonetheless, this case-by-case approach should not hide the fact that the management of the crisis was highly organized. Debt servicing problems were not just left to the debtors and the creditors (the international banks) to sort out. Rather industrial country governments via the IMF took an active role in determining the attitude which should be adopted towards the crisis. Why should this be? There are two main reasons:

1   the threat to banking and the international monetary system arising from default on debt repayments

2   the need to coordinate banking activities and ensure that all banks agreed on the package adopted.

In order to understand what rescue operations entail, we have to distinguish between methods of dealing with official debt and private debt (Box 2.1).

Rescheduling official debt

Those countries with debt servicing difficulties on official debt approach the Paris Club. The Paris Club was set up in 1956 by some European governments to deal with LDCs who were having problems in repaying loans granted or guaranteed by official agencies in industrial countries (for example, the export credit guarantee agencies or development agencies). The Paris Club plays no part in rescheduling private debt. A country with debt repayment problems seeks a *rescheduling agreement*. This usually involves agreeing new terms on existing debt such as:

- an extended repayment period

- a reduction of interest payable on the debt

- a grace period during which none of the rescheduled debt is due to be paid

- some debt relief (that is, the cancelling of debt due).

Figure 2.8 '… So you see, the entire future of the international financial system hinges on your capacity for quick recovery and vast economic growth.' (Guardian, 8 February, 1983).

The agreement can involve conditions imposed by the creditor countries. For example an IMF programme may have to be agreed and implemented before debt rescheduling or relief is forthcoming. Indeed, in recent years an IMF programme has been a necessary condition for approaching the Paris Club.

Rescheduling private debt

By contrast, debtors with debt servicing difficulties on private debt owed to the international banks do not have a forum such as the Paris Club to which they can turn. Instead, procedures for gaining a rescheduling agreement are more *ad hoc* and often extremely time consuming. There are several common features involved in a rescheduling agreement of this type.

1 *A bridging loan:* This loan covers the period between the start of the crisis and the disbursement of new money by the IMF and the commercial banks. It is usually used to enable the rescheduling country to continue to repay the interest due on its debt. The bridging loan is usually granted by the US government or the Bank for International Settlements (BIS).

2 *An IMF programme:* The banks have insisted that in the vast majority of cases, countries must agree a package of policies with the IMF before rescheduling can take place. If an IMF agreement is signed, then the IMF normally provides the country with some new money.

3 *Rescheduling terms:* The loans are usually rescheduled at a cost to the country. The banks charge a rescheduling fee. In the early period after the debt crisis the banks also increased the spread over LIBOR on the rescheduled debt. For example, Brazil rescheduled at 2.5% above LIBOR in 1983 compared with 1.5% on new money borrowed before. In return for these increased costs, the banks would postpone repayment of principal. Indeed often a grace period was negotiated during which none of the rescheduled debt had to be repaid.

4 *New money:* The banks would also grant the countries new money on commercially agreed terms.

There were two modifications to this broad approach to private debt in the second half of the 1980s. The first outlined in October 1985 was the so-called Baker plan, named after its proposer James Baker, then US Treasury Secretary. This plan sought to soften the terms of rescheduling for the top fifteen debtors. Baker aimed to persuade banks to lengthen maturities and reduce spreads on rescheduled debt. He also sought to increase new money made available. Whilst he was relatively successful with the former, banks were reluctant to increase their exposure further and success with the latter aim was limited.

The second US debt plan, the Brady plan, was put forward in March 1989. It aimed for small amounts of debt reduction or relief, in other words reducing the volume of debt rather than merely offering better terms for its repayment. Although the overall amounts of debt relief were small, this was the first official recognition that debt reduction was necessary to improve the debt problem. By the end of the decade, a number of countries such as Mexico, the Philippines, Costa Rica and Venezuela had completed negotiations under the Brady plan.

Whatever the long-term implications of this response, it did contribute to achieving the short-term crisis management goal of preserving the international financial system. Critical to the achievement of this goal was preventing LDCs, especially the larger debtors, from defaulting on their debt. Some LDCs owed so much that there was a clear incentive simply to stop repaying the debt, on what has popularly come to be known as the 'can't pay, won't pay' principle.

The Baker and Brady plans attempted to reduce the incentive not to pay by softening rescheduling terms and reducing the volume of debt. Box 2.5 outlines the costs and benefits of default.

Before going on to examine whether there were any alternative approaches to dealing with the debt crisis, we turn to the implications for LDCs of the case-by-case approach actually implemented.

Implications of the case-by-case approach

As we have seen, debt rescheduling did not imply a serious reduction in the debt owed. The most immediate result of the management of the crisis was that LDCs had to find vast resources to pay back both the principal and interest due on their debt. It has been estimated that between 1982 and 1987, this amounted to US$700 billion. This represents a massive and unprecedented transfer of resources from LDCs to industrial countries. A conservative estimate of these transfers is shown in Table 2.4. This measures total interest and principal repayments minus new debt inflows in any given period. Table 2.4 shows that LDCs as a whole have had cumulative net negative transfers

of the order of $20–$30 billion per annum between 1985 and 1987. That is, they are paying substantially more than they have received.

Figure 2.9.

Table 2.4 Net transfers (US$ billion)

Year	LDCs	Highly indebted LDCs
1982	17.80	3.85
1983	7.10	–7.50
1984	–7.30	–17.50
1985	–20.80	–26.10
1986	–30.70	–24.90
1987	–29.00	–20.00

[Data source: World Bank, 1990a]

BOX 2.5 The costs and benefits of default

Eaton and Gersovitz argued that banks should have lent to countries until the costs of defaulting were equal to the benefits. Whilst it appears in retrospect that banks did not follow their advice (in that they overlent), the cost–benefit approach has, nevertheless, focused attention on the issue of the incentive to default.

The costs of defaulting include:

- deprivation of access to international capital markets for some time to come, thus depriving a country of a potential source of finance to aid development

- lack of access to international capital markets for trade credit, making it more difficult for exporters to export and further isolating the country

- the moral costs of nonrepayment

- unfavourable effects on other contracts which the country may wish to enter with foreign agents; for example multinationals may no longer wish to invest in the country since default is likely to increase fears of nationalization and such like

- retaliation by the countries to whom the creditor banks belong; for example, the country may impose sanctions on the defaulter, freeze any assets the defaulter may have and so on.

The benefits of default are much simpler. They are essentially the savings made by not having to repay the existing debt.

(Eaton & Gersovitz, 1981; Allsopp & Joshi, 1986; Cline, 1984)

Of course, the total net transfer of resources from LDCs, including things such as capital flight and repatriated profits, would certainly be much larger than this, and represent an even more distressing picture for LDCs. Unfortunately, it is not very easy to present reliable figures on this. One estimate given is $230–240 billion for all LDCs between 1981 and 1985 (Marcel & Palma 1987).

How have these massive transfers been achieved and at what cost? Most countries have had to follow a similar policy package to achieve debt repayments. Almost all countries who have been involved in debt rescheduling (either official or private) have been required to have in place an IMF programme. Similarly, a number of countries have carried out IMF programmes even although they did not reschedule, or have carried out programmes similar to those of the IMF on their own initiative.

The main elements of an IMF programme are:

- *Devaluation of the exchange rate:* This makes imports more expensive and exports cheaper. It thus aims at improving the balance of payments by cutting imports and increasing exports.

- *Ceilings on domestic credit expansion:* This means control over the money supply. It aims at reducing overall demand in the economy, which in turn should reduce the demand for imports and improve the balance of payments. This is also seen as a way of reducing inflation.

- *Reduction of fiscal (government) deficits:* This aims at reducing overall demand (and thus improving the balance of payments as before). In addition, however, the IMF seeks to reduce the size of government control over the economy.

- *Removal of price subsidies:* This helps to reduce the public deficit and introduces a greater reliance on market forces.

The first two of these policies are the most important since the basic goal is a 'viable balance of payments'. In the 1980s this has implied the need for a current account surplus in order to enable the country to meet its debt repayments.

Box 2.6 provides a discussion of the usual criticisms of IMF programmes. Whatever the theoretical case for and against IMF policies, it is difficult to exaggerate the scale of the adjustment that many countries have had to undergo. National income in 1982 fell by 1% in sub-Saharan Africa and 3.5% in Latin America and the Caribbean. In 1983, national income fell by 3.5% and 4.6% respectively. It has been estimated that for Latin America as a whole, real *per capita* expenditure

Figure 2.10   Demonstration against IMF debt, Mexico 1985.

BOX 2.6 IMF conditionality

The following is an outline of the rationale behind some of the the major points of an IMF programme and of some of the criticisms which have been levelled at IMF programmes.

• *Should there be any conditionality at all?* Most authors are agreed that there should be conditions attached to funds lent by the IMF. These funds are limited and countries would not like to see them used unproductively, for example to build up military strength or for luxury consumption by an élite. However, many would question the way in which conditionality is decided. The voting structure of the IMF is undemocratic. The USA, the UK, Germany, France and Japan in 1983 had 41.2% of total votes . The USA alone, which has just under 20% of the total votes, is effectively able to exercise a veto and can thus control major policy decisions within the IMF, including conditionality.

• *What should be the balance between high and low conditionality funds?* Not all IMF funds are subject to high levels of conditionality. However, the amount available with either no conditions or only low levels of conditionality are small. Over time, moreover, the real size of the unconditional funds has declined. Thus some have argued they should be increased.

• *Should adjustment be more symmetric?* We have already discussed how one country's deficit is another country's surplus. IMF programmes are imposed only on deficit countries. Yet arguably, surplus countries are just as responsible and should be forced to undertake policy changes.

• *Are the IMF objectives desirable?* Whilst ultimately, the IMF hopes to achieve a 'viable current account', usually the targets explicitly mentioned in an IMF agreement include credit expansion and inflation targets. Some have therefore argued that the IMF's attention seems to

have shifted away from the balance of payments to other factors that are merely incidental , such as the size of the government sector and the public deficit. Of course, even if the IMF were to focus explicitly on the balance of payments, there are likely to be differing views on what a 'viable current account' entails.

• *What do IMF programmes say about what the IMF believes is the cause of balance of payments deficits?* The IMF, in focusing on devaluation, domestic monetary growth, public deficits and the like, appears to consider that current account deficits are the result of inappropriate domestic policies. Other economists argue that external factors (for example, a fall in the demand for exports, a fall in the price of exports, world recession) are far more likely causes of current account deficits. The structuralist school, for example, emphasizes these external factors along with domestic supply-side factors within LDCs. Structuralists argue that supply bottlenecks are common and that dependence on imports for development makes it difficult, and indeed undesirable, for programmes to be directed at reducing deficits in the way they are.

• *Are IMF policies appropriate?* The set of policies prescribed by the IMF tends to be monetarist in orientation. That is, adjustment is undertaken via the imposition of monetary growth targets which aim at reducing inflation and overall demand. This leads to falling national income, rising unemployment and frequently fails to improve the balance of payments or the country's prospects. Critics of the IMF (Figure 2.10) have suggested that the long-run effects of IMF programmes are to the detriment of development because of their impact on investment and their inability to correct the fundamental causes of LDC deficits which they see as structural.

(Sources: Spraos, 1984; Killick, 1984)

---

fell by 16.8%. In the Southern cone, the figures are 29.3% for Argentina, 30.6% for Uruguay and 20.2% for Chile. As Wells says :

"… reductions in economic and social welfare of this size have probably rarely if ever

been equalled — even in the depths of the 1930s depression."

(Wells, 1986)

This loss in social welfare was also associated with increases in unemployment and reductions in real wages. Unemployment figures for LDCs are notoriously unreliable (see Chapter 3 of *Allen & Thomas, 1991*), because of the large informal sector, but all the evidence that we do have points to a very serious problem in most debtor countries. Figures for real wages are more reliable. For instance in 1983, real wages fell in Peru and Mexico by 20% and 30% respectively (Marcel & Palma, 1987).

The effects on investment were also serious. Figure 2.11 shows the scale of the problem. Compare investment in Latin America and the Caribbean and Sub-Saharan Africa with investment in South and East Asia. The relatively larger declines in investment in Latin America and the Caribbean and Sub-Saharan Africa resulted from cuts in government spending, financial instability, bankruptcies and declining profitability in the productive sector (Wells, 1986).

On the other hand, the decline in investment has led to the desired goal of reducing imports. Falling investment has reduced the need for imported capital goods, and falling incomes have reduced demand for imported consumables.

So one can argue that the immediate objective of 1980s economic policy in many LDCs, of generating current account surpluses to enable debt repayment, has been achieved. But there are two problems with this strategy. First is the appalling

social and economic costs. There is a growing recognition of what has been called 'the Debt Trap' (see Chapter 11 of *Allen & Thomas, 1991*). As we have seen the debt: income ratio actually increased during the 1980s. The debt trap involves a vicious circle, in that slow growth makes it difficult for a country to work out a strategy for the long-term solution to its debt problem. But the necessity of paying debt is a major component behind that slow growth. Look at the data for 1982 and 1983 in Figure 2.11. There was a dramatic fall in investment in these years for sub-Saharan Africa and Latin America. Investment levels then remained consistently low. Any long-term sustainable solution to the debt crisis needs to take on this basic, and crippling, dilemma faced by developing countries (Figure 2.12).

Secondly, the long-term implications of failing to solve the debt crisis were not restricted to developing countries. As Wells puts it:

> "Just as Latin America's willingness to get into debt in the 1970s helped to stabilize the level of economic activity in the rest of the world, so the fact that this region is now generating surpluses is imparting a significant deflationary twist to world economic activity"
>
> (Wells, 1986)

This brings us back to one of our major themes, that is the interdependence between the fate of industrial countries and LDCs. To take one example, we can look at the effect of the debt crisis on the UK. UK exports to LDCs fell by some 30% between 1980 and 1985: to highly indebted countries, they fell by some 47% (Marcel & Palma, 1987). Thus debt problems in LDCs have had an impact on output and employment in industrial countries.

Summary

1   The debt crisis was managed in a case-by-case approach rather than as a general problem requiring a global solution.

2   Effectively, renegotiation of debt from both private and public sources required LDCs to turn

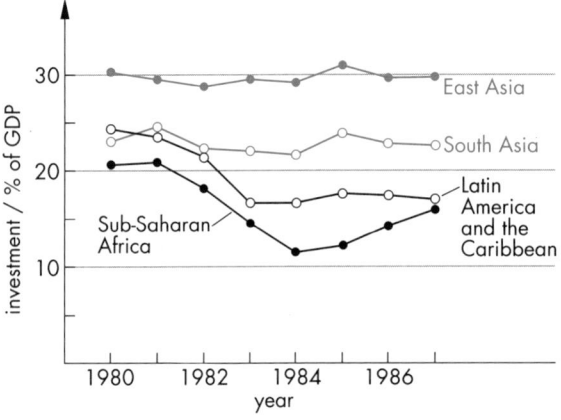

Figure 2.11   Investment in the LDCs in the 1980s (Source: World Bank, 1990).

Figure 2 .12   Bolivian women demonstrating against austerity measures in La Paz, Bolivia, March 1985.

to the IMF. This involved accepting the conditions imposed through IMF programmes.

3   The case-by-case approach resulted in large net transfers of money out of LDCs, and the demolition of social and welfare programmes.

4   The management of the debt crisis has resulted in a vicious circle — the 'debt trap' — which has not alleviated the crisis.

5   To succeed, long-term solutions to the debt crisis for LDCs must prevent serious social consequences such as poverty and unemployment and must prevent economic consequences such as low growth and poor investment.

6   The failure to respond to the debt crisis also has serious implications for the world economy.

7   It follows that any long-run and sustainable solution to the debt crisis needs to be sensitive to the social and economic effects of recession and austerity programmes, as well as the interdependence of the world financial system.

2.4.   Solutions to the debt crisis: looking to the future

The debt crisis which originated in 1982 is still with us in the 1990s. Despite the fact that LDCs paid back some $700 billion between 1982 and 1987, total long-term debt rose from $568 billion to approximately $1000 billion during these years. Moreover, the number of reschedulings on private debt (that is, commercial bank debt) have remained high — twelve in 1986, nineteen in 1987 and ten in 1988. The implications for LDCs, which lie behind these figures, have been very serious. The 1980s was a period in many LDCs of falling living standards, rising unemployment and poverty and slow, if not negative, growth.

Thus a solution to the debt crisis is crucial if LDCs are to reverse the above situation. There are two main sets of questions which arise when discussing solutions to the debt problem.

- *Existing debt:* Should rescheduling continue? Should there be more debt relief?

- *Future finance:* How should recycling problems be handled in the future? Should we allow commercial bank lending to be resumed to LDCs? Should future finance be left to official institutions?

Existing debt

We have discussed the 'case-by-case' approach to debt management that has been employed since 1982 and have noted its negative effects on LDCs. Many argue that the case-by case approach has failed. This is true even of the modifications to the case-by-case approach, the Baker and Brady plans. For instance, the more advanced Brady plan has been subject to the following criticisms:

- It is rather small-scale: the amounts of actual debt relief appear to have been small. There was thus little impact on the overall debt burden in those countries which have negotiated agreements.

- Countries still have to undertake an IMF programme if a successful deal is to be negotiated. The terms of these programmes are unchanged.

- It is not clear that the proposal deals with the issue of new flows of finance to these countries. It is based on the principle that banks should continue to be important providers of development finance, a point we discuss below.

There have, of course, also been other more radical proposals for how to confront the debt problem. The mechanics of how the various schemes would operate are less important than the fact that they share a common concern, which is to reduce the absolute amount of debt. These would obviously benefit highly indebted LDCs and would contribute to stemming the perverse flow of funds from poorer to richer countries. But if the process of industrialization and development is to be restored in LDCs, then something more is needed — not only a radical reduction in debt burden but also the provision of new finance for development. It is to this issue that we now turn.

Future finance: a new international monetary order

To understand why new finance is crucial, recall some of the reasons we gave earlier for why LDCs borrowed in the first place. We argued that LDCs needed access to finance because of inadequate savings or foreign exchange. Since the beginning of the debt crisis, industrial country governments and international institutions such as the IMF and World Bank have been reluctant to engage in a discussion about the best way to provide development finance. Having examined the causes of the debt crisis and some of its consequences, we are now in a better position to judge the claim that development finance is best provided by the private sector. We can suggest three possible reasons why banks are not suited to lending funds to LDCs for development as they did in the 1970s.

1 LDCs require debt at much longer maturities than banks can offer. LDCs have investment projects which often have long gestation periods. That is, the returns from such projects will not materialize for a number of years. The maturities which banks can offer are arguably too short for many such development projects and thus banks may not be suited to long-term lending.

2 Even in the 1970s, there were only a small number of countries, mainly the higher income LDCs, who could get access to bank finance. Thus to entrust the question of development finance to banks would imply depriving a large number of LDCs access to funds.

3 It is not clear that banks can adequately monitor the use to which loans are put. Whilst much of the finance lent by banks in the 1970s was put to potentially productive use, there were some notable exceptions, as we have already shown. Even if there is a large degree of disagreement about what form loan conditions should take, there is fairly widespread agreement that some conditions have to be agreed on. It is not clear that it should be the responsibility of banks to decide on such conditions or seek the means to impose them.

For these reasons, if the aim is to put issues of development back at the top of the agenda, then providing finance via private institutions such as banks may not best promote that aim. As Allsopp and Joshi have argued:

"... the experience of the 1970s and 1980s raises serious questions about the future of development finance. The fashion of *laissez-faire* in this area is relatively recent and contrasts with attitudes in the 1950s and 1960s. Many of the difficulties ... provide a *prima facie* case for public intervention and control. Now that the problems are coming to be appreciated, attitudes to official lending also need to change. It seems inevitable that official flows of one kind or another will have to play a larger role."

(Allsopp & Joshi, 1986)

Thus an alternative solution we should look at is a more organized response to the issue of new financial flows to LDCs from the world community and international institutions. What form might this official international coordination of finance take? International institutions such as the IMF and World Bank already exist, charged with the duty of dealing with issues of balance of payments financing (in the case of the IMF) and longer term development projects (in the case of the World Bank). However, such institutions have lost a lot of credibility particularly with LDCs. It seems that whilst they could take on the roles of providing finance for balance of payments and development needs, there would need to be some fundamental changes to their structure and operation.

Voting rights and a new international economic order.

At present the power structure of the IMF is determined by the contribution each member makes to the IMF's resources. This ensures it is weighted towards industrial countries. Until LDCs feel they have a say in the decision making processes which affect them, it is unlikely that stability of the international monetary system will be achieved. Unfortunately, at present it is difficult to be optimistic for change in this direction. In the 1970s, the issue of a new international economic order, with a greater role for LDCs, was firmly on the agenda in world economic discussion. This resulted from the increasing power and confidence of a number of LDCs and was reflected in such bodies as OPEC, UNCTAD (UN Committee for Trade and Development) and the non-aligned movement. Indeed pressure from LDCs did affect international institutions. For instance, the World Bank in this period was much more sensitive to the needs of LDCs and promoted much wider objectives (such as concern for equality, employment and poverty) than the usual focus on growth. However in the 1980s this process of a greater role for LDCs was reversed, in part reflecting their economic weakness (rising debt, declining commodity prices etc). Whether solutions to the debt crisis and the issue of new finance sensitive to the LDCs' long-term development needs can be found, depends considerably on the LDCs themselves rebuilding the self-confidence they showed in the 1970s and being able to intervene effectively in international financial institutions.

Symmetric adjustment and the volume of funds available.

As we explained in Section 2.2, balance of payments imbalances should be the responsibility of both deficit and surplus countries. During the 1970s and 1980s almost all the costs of adjustment fell on deficit countries. It is those countries which are now having to repay the enormous debts incurred at that time. It is the deficit countries of the 1970s and 1980s which are now having to sacrifice growth and development. A mechanism for ensuring that surplus countries take their share of the responsibility has to be found. Such a process might involve the use of surpluses to finance deficit countries on favourable terms whilst adjustment takes place. This would increase the absolute amount of funds available. This brings us back to the issue of recycling and the need for an international monetary system that can be responsible for international economic relations. Go back to Box 2.3 and compare the wider and more ambitious plans of Keynes with those of White. Those who argue for more symmetric adjustment in the world economy and larger financial resources for such adjustment are effectively trying to resurrect the ideas of Keynes.

The actual mechanics of such a proposal are less important here than the question of whether such a new international financial system is desirable.

The need for change in the terms and conditions imposed on official finance

The ultimate aim of both finance for development and for balance of payments adjustment must be continued growth and development of LDCs. The kind of programmes currently undertaken by the IMF have had large negative effects on growth and development as we saw in Section 2.3. There should be less emphasis in IMF programmes on meeting money supply targets and much more on ensuring that investment continues. As we argued in Section 2.3, the future welfare of LDCs is at present bleak because of the reduction in investment which IMF programmes entail.

Three options

Our discussion of a new international financial system suggests that there are three possible broad options.

- Continue with the current method of dealing with debt and the issue of development finance. This implies a painful and prolonged adjustment period for LDCs before they can return to the international banks for further finance.

- Move to a new international monetary order where issues of finance for adjustment and development are undertaken by reformed official international institutions, with LDCs having a much greater say in the way the world economy is organized.

- Have a hybrid system combining elements of both. This would entail a much greater role for international institutions in the future. They would act as important intermediaries between international banks and LDCs. In particular they would monitor the use LDCs make of funds and act to moderate the negative effects of competition on bank lending whilst at the same time tapping one major source of finance, namely private banks.

You will see that the above three options reflect the major areas of disagreement between economists, and between those in international institutions and LDCs, which we have developed in this chapter. Where should the balance lie between the private and government sectors? To what extent is the world economy interdependent and therefore how important is its management? Finally, in what ways can we best promote a virtuous cycle of growth and development in LDCs, rather than the vicious cycle of debt? The answers to these three questions will determine which option one considers to be most appropriate for the world economy and LDCs in the 1990s.

Summary of Chapter 2

Third World countries needed to borrow foreign currency to finance industrialization. But in the early 1980s, world economic conditions led to lower export earnings, higher import bills and higher interest payments on debt. Although some people see this as the main cause of the debt crisis, there are other underlying causes, which include:

- decline in international cooperation on monetary issues, leading to problems of 'recycling' of oil revenues

- private banks overlending to some countries while bypassing others

- short-term private loans for long-term public investments, coupled with capital flight.

Rather than attempting a global solution, the world financial institutions took a case-by-case approach to the debt problem, mediated by the IMF which imposed conditions such as austerity programmes. This resulted in large net transfers of money out of the less developed countries, aggravating the debt crisis rather than alleviating it.

The world financial system is highly interdependent. Any sustainable solution to the debt crisis has to prevent the social and economic consequences of high debt repayments — poverty, unemployment and low growth — if it is to succeed.

Current measures involve small-scale debt relief and/or rescheduling. Since the 1980s, LDCs have had little say in international financial institutions.

There appear to be three options for the future, favoured by different schools of economic thought.

1 Carry on dealing with debt and development finance as at present, even if this means a prolonged and painful adjustment period for LDCs, during which they will be unable to develop their economies.

2 Change the international financial system so that LDCs have more control and are not at the mercy of the developed countries and private banks.

3 Combine both approaches, giving international institutions a greater role in financing development, while still making use of funds from private banks.

3

BRAZILIAN INDUSTRIALIZATION

TOM HEWITT*

3.1 Introduction

The Brazilian economy is plagued by inflation, a huge foreign debt, declining real wages and an inability to compete effectively on international markets. Wealth and poverty have an uneasy, sometimes explosive, coexistence in a country where income distribution is amongst the most inequitable in the world. Rural and urban poverty are the outward signs of the failure by successive governments (military and civilian) either to implement effective changes in land ownership or to meet minimum standards of social provision for the vast majority. Politically, the country is still recovering from 20 years of military dictatorship. Democracy still lives under the threatening shadows of authoritarianism and landowner interests whose roots stretch back to colonial rule.

Yet Brazil, in terms of the value of GNP, is amongst the ten biggest economies in the world. It has a large industrial base. In 1987, 27% of Brazil's GDP was from industrial production and two-thirds of that was from the manufacturing sector. And manufacturing 'value added' was approximately equal to the rest of Latin America and the Caribbean put together. Industry is also diversified, particularly in 'modern' manufacturing sectors such as machinery and transport equipment, chemicals and electronics. In addi-tion, capital goods production forms a significant part of industrial output (14.7% in 1980). Brazil's inequitable development has been aptly named one of 'unaimed opulence' (Drèze & Sen, 1989). This phrase captures both the substantial wealth of Brazil and its uneven distribution.

Industrialization in Brazil, as anywhere else, has both positive and negative aspects. On the negative side we might pinpoint pollution and rapid urbanization. Environmental damage through emissions into the atmosphere, rivers and the sea has taken its toll over the years. The industrial city of Cubatão near São Paulo is amongst the most polluted places on earth.

The process of industrialization has also exacerbated regional inequality through the concentration of industry in the country's south eastern region (Figure 3.1). Migration to São Paulo on a massive scale has made it the second most populated city in the world, after Mexico City, and its population is projected to reach 25.27 million by the end of this century. But the population size is not as important as poor social conditions (housing, health and education). These are negative, but changeable, outcomes of industrial concentration.

On the positive side, the diverse industrial base gives Brazil a degree of flexibility for development which other less industrialized countries do not have. Industrialization has generated

* The author wishes to acknowledge the work of John Humphrey, who wrote a significant part of Sections 3.3 and 3.4 for a previous Open University Course.

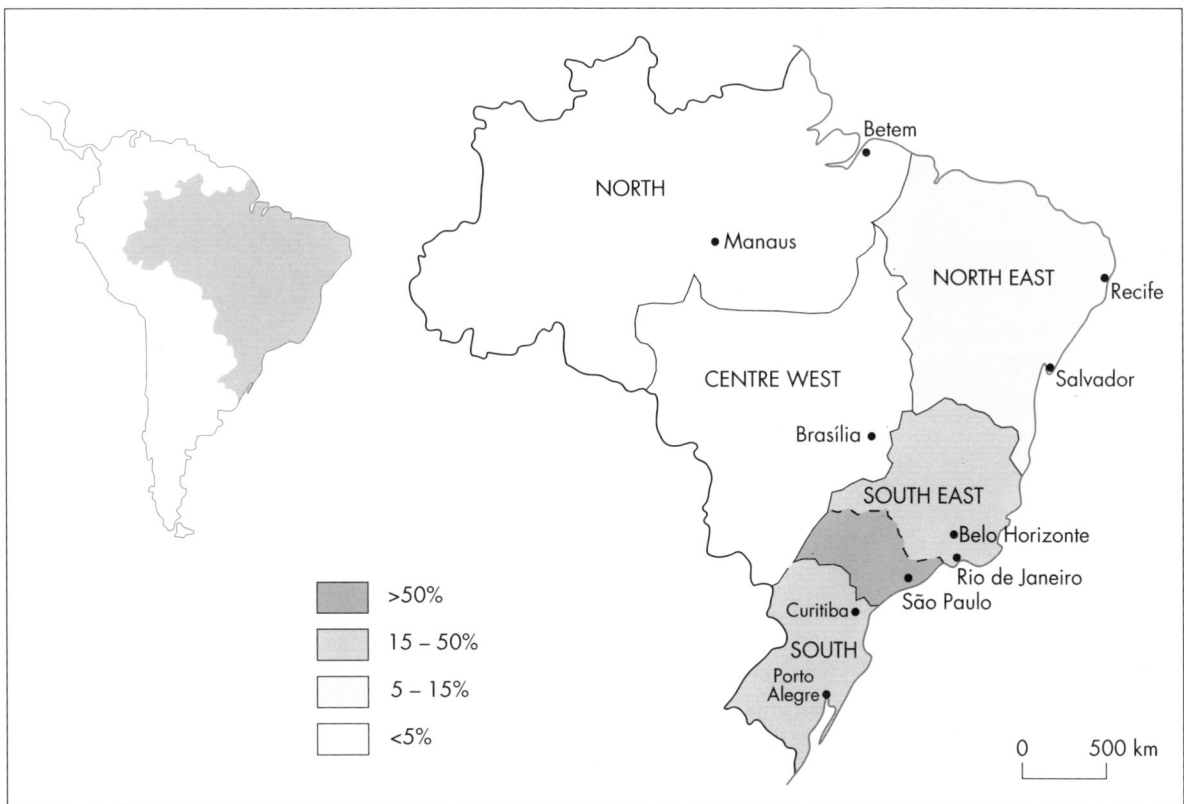

>50%

15 – 50%

5 – 15%

<5%

Figure 3.1

employment opportunities, skill formation, technical and productive capacity unequalled in the rest of Latin America.

Politically, Brazil has suffered many years of authoritarian government. Nevertheless, more democratic movements have made headway in recent years with the trade union movement taking a central role in this process.

This chapter explores three questions.

Q What were the internal and external conditions which allowed Brazil's industrialization.

The process of industrialization neither happens overnight, nor are its outcomes foreseeable in the longer term. Industrialization is mediated by internal political, social and economic forces, and by external (international) conditions which may be more or less favourable to industrialization at different times.

Q What have been the opportunities for and barriers to late industrialization in Brazil?

We will examine Brazil as a case of 'late industrialization' (see Box 3.1). That is, it has shown some of the characteristics of late industrialization, although not always with the success of other economies.

Q Has import substitution industrialization in Brazil been a help or a hindrance to the long-term development of an internationally competitive and sustainable industrialization?

Finally, we will examine Brazil as an example of industrialization through import substitution which requires state intervention and protection of local industries. This approach is associated with 'structuralist' theories of development. In the late 1980s and early 1990s, state intervention in economic matters has become unfashionable. It is believed that free markets are a more efficient

Box 3.1 Late industrializers

Brazil's industrialization spans nearly a century, so how can we call it a late industrializer? The most obvious reply is that Brazil industrialized later than other countries, e.g. the United Kingdom, West Germany and the United States. Alice Amsden, an economist based at Harvard Business School in the US, has developed a more useful definition. She defines late industrializers as: 'Countries which industrialize without the competitive asset of being able to monopolize an original technology'.

What does this mean? Amsden argues that earlier industrializations were based on 'inventions' (the discovery or devising of new products and processes as in the industrial revolution in Britain) or on 'innovations' (the commercial application of inventions as in the US and West Germany). But, she says, late industrializers (including Japan) have relied on borrowing technology and learning. Late industrializers have used advanced technologies previously developed by the earlier industrializers. This, in turn, has meant that different routes to industrialization have been more appropriate (or successful) than those employed by the early industrializers.

Amsden has published several studies of the role of the state in newly industrializing countries, particularly in the East Asian economies such as South Korea which we will be looking at in the next chapter. In this chapter we will see how, in Brazil, late industrialization has implications for industrial strategy and policy making.

Box 3.2 Some reference facts on Brazil

Population (1988): 144.4 million

Area: 8.5 million km^2

Age structure of population (1988)

0–14 years	35.7%
15–64 years	59.8%

GNP per capita: US$2 160

Average annual growth of GNP per capita (1965–88): 3.6%

Average annual rate of inflation:

1965–80	31.5%
1980–88	188.7%

Life expectancy at birth: 65 years

Distribution of GDP:

year	1965	1988
agriculture	19%	9%
industry	33%	43%
(of which Manufacturing	26%	29%)
services	48%	49%

Total external debt: US$114 592

Total debt service (interest payment): 4.5% of GDP, 42% of exports

Urban population:

year	1965	1988
as % of total population	50%	75%
% in cities over 500 000	35%	52%

Income distribution (1983)

2.4% of national total earnings go to the poorest 20% of households

8.1% of national total earnings go to the poorest 40% of households

62.6% of national total earnings go to the richest 20% of households

46.2% of national total earnings go to the richest 10% of households

Adult illiteracy (1985): female 24%; male 22%

(Source: World Bank, 1990)

arbiter of the direction of development than any kind of planned intervention in those markets. Does this mean that Brazil has been getting it all wrong for the past 45 years?

Our approach is largely chronological. Section 3.2 examines the early days in Brazil when Portuguese colonizers set up exports of sugar and coffee based on slave labour. Agricultural exports continued after the abolition of slavery, but by the Second World War the basis for industrialization had been set. In the post-war period (Section 3.3), the pace of industrialization accelerates. Governments shift political and economic power away from the landed elites towards the state and urban, industrial interests. This is an intensive period of import substitution industrialization. Section 3.4 discusses military takeover in 1964 and goes on to examine the so-called 'Brazilian miracle' and the subsequent economic decline

of the late 1970s. Section 3.5 briefly looks at the involvement of the labour movement in Brazil's industrialization. The final section moves to the economic crisis of the 1980s. Here we make an assessment of the questions posed above.

3.2 The early days in Brazil

When they first landed on Brazil's north-eastern coast in the year 1500, the Portuguese found no gold, no silver, no El Dorado, only *pau brasil* (Brazil wood). For want of anything else, the Portuguese exported the wood to Europe to make chemical dyes. At this time, there are thought to have been some 5 million indigenous people in Brazil. Today they make up a tiny proportion of Brazil's total population.

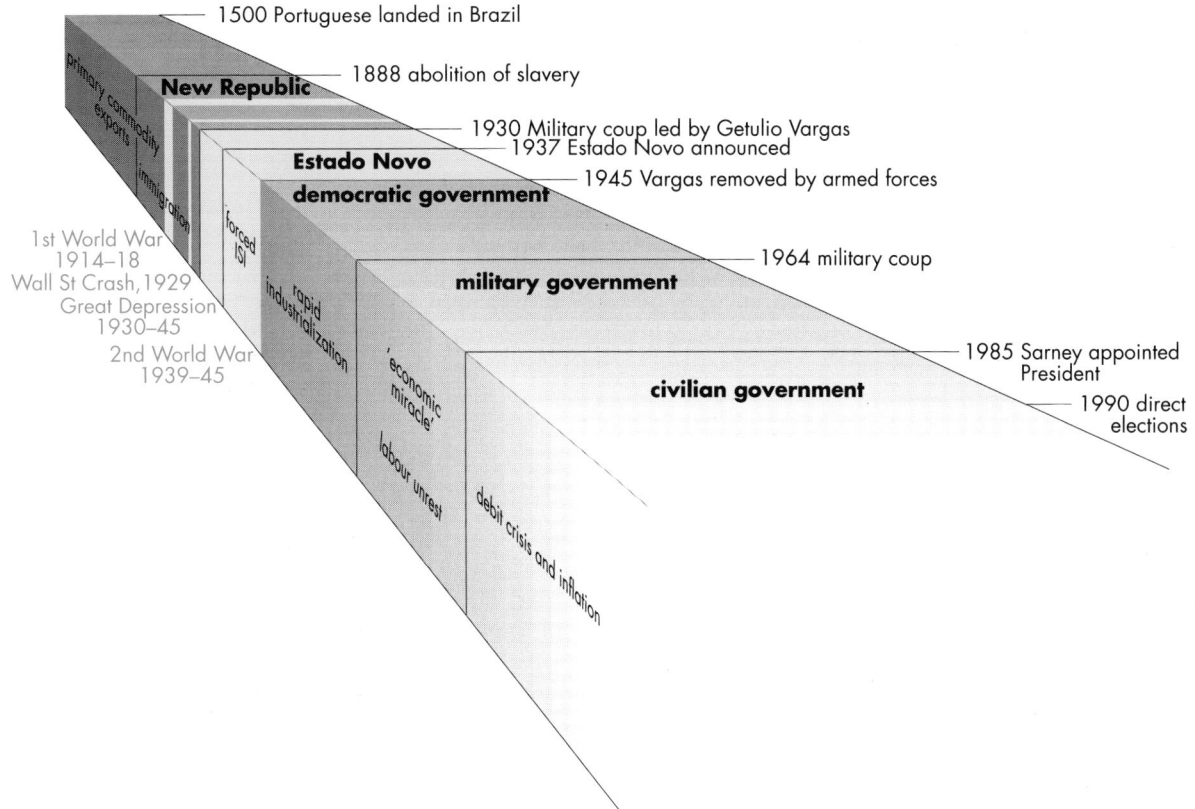

Figure 3.2   An overview of Brazilian history.

Colonization by Europe: slaves, sugar and coffee

Colonization and settlement did not take place until the potential for sugar cane production was realized. Growing sugar consumption in Europe in the 17th century turned this into a booming export. Sugar production in the North East opened up new land and swelled the slave trade from Africa. The slave plantations became a point on a triangle which encompassed Europe, Africa and Latin America (see *Allen & Thomas, 1992*, Figure 8.3). Sugar made a few people very rich, but the boom turned to slump when international sugar prices declined due to increased production in the Caribbean.

The growth and later decline of the sugar industry was not a unique phenomenon of Brazilian development. The cycle of glorious expansion and dramatic decline can be observed in other areas of the economy at different periods. For example, in the eighteenth century, the gold and diamond boom in the state of Minas Gerais (literally 'general mines') attracted migrants from the coast, but this trend reversed once the deposits had been exhausted. In the latter part of the nineteenth century the rubber boom produced a rush to the Amazon and the creation of the city of Manaus, which boasted its own sumptuous Opera House in the middle of the tropical rain forest. But an English landowner and amateur botanist, Henry Wickham, smuggled rubber seeds wrapped in banana leaves out of the country. They were propagated at Kew Gardens and transplanted to the British colony, Malaysia. Amazonian prosperity vanished and the region fell back into obscurity and isolation for over half a century.

An important break with the cycle of expansion and decline came in the South East with the growth of coffee exports in the nineteenth century. The production of coffee was on such a scale and had such ramifications in the fields of transport, commerce and banking that it laid the foundations for a profound change in the South East region of Brazil.

At the end of the last century, the coffee export economy was the country's leading sector. It had implications for the growth of infrastructure, mass immigration and the birth of a labour movement, and how industrial production was to develop. At the turn of the century, coffee was 53% of all exports and by 1929 had reached 73%. With this increase in exports, there was growing investment in railways and port facilities. The city of São Paulo developed as the administrative centre between the coffee growing areas inland and the port of Santos. The 'coffee oligarchy' of landowners in São Paulo state wielded considerable economic and political power.

Two events were to trigger off industrialization — the abolition of slavery and the collapse of coffee exports. Like the sugar boom before it, coffee production was based on large plantations using slave labour. Whilst abolitionists campaigned against slavery, its demise also resulted from the spread of capitalist relations of production. Slaves had become an economic liability, expensive to keep healthy and strong. 'Free' wage labour was a more attractive proposition because as long as there was sufficient supply it was expendable and easily replaceable. Landowners recognized this and fully supported incentives to attract European immigration to Brazil at the turn of the century.

Immigration from Europe

Between 1887 and 1920, there were 1.7 million immigrants into Brazil. In the 1920s, a further half a million arrived from Europe. Immigrants came mainly from the poverty-stricken rural areas of Italy, Portugal and Spain in search of a better life. However, according to reports at the time, conditions were often worse than those they had left. As one workers' newspaper of this time put it, '… the word immigrant is synonymous with slave and misery' (Max Nettlau archives, 1913).

Disillusioned by false promises of land, many workers left the countryside for the cities of São Paulo and Rio de Janeiro, providing between 70% and 80% of the labour for budding industries. This wave of immigration marked the beginning of industrialization in Brazil.

Although the immigrants from Southern Europe were not generally industrial workers, they brought skills and traditions which would strongly influence the course of Brazilian economic and political development. So while many did become wage labourers on the coffee and sugar plantations of the South East, some had sufficient skills to set up small engineering workshops which serviced the mills, and the origins of some of Brazil's largest engineering firms can be traced back to this time. Many also went to work in the docks of Santos.

European traditions of labour militancy became evident in the 1920s. Low wages and poor working conditions were not taken lying down. Strikes and general labour unrest were prevalent. This was the beginning of industrial labour history in Brazil.

Forced import substitution

The second boost to industrialization came from problems in coffee production, combined with a crisis in the world economy.

Since the First World War, Brazilian coffee growers had been over-producing. Price stabilization policies and government stockpiling provided only short-term remedies. With an abundance of land, there was no effective long-term way to curtail the expansion of coffee production. This expansion had been the stimulus for growing infrastructure, particularly in transport and hydroelectric power (in which British capital played a decisive role) and had helped to generate the growth of urban markets. The crisis of over-production was to be compounded by external events which paradoxically provided a further boost to industrialization.

Up to 1945 industrialization was a 'side-effect' of coffee production and exports. But the Great Depression and the Second World War both coincided with periods of accelerated industrialization in Brazil. These events caused what has been termed 'forced import substitution industrialization' (Furtado, 1976). In other words, world events literally cut off the supply of imported goods to Brazil and they had to be produced internally. At the same time exports, particularly coffee, declined dramatically, resulting in scarce foreign exchange.

The collapse in exports and the consequent reduction in capacity to import affected industrialization, as Furtado has noted:

> "It was in connection with the industrialization process that the 1929 crisis constituted a landmark. Until then, the development of the industrial sector had been a reflection of export expansion; from then on, industrialization was induced largely through the structural tensions provoked by the decline or inadequate growth of the export sector."
>
> (Furtado, 1976)

Political changes

The economic effects of crisis were accompanied by political changes which also influenced Brazilian industrialization. Government had been in the hands of an oligarchy based on control over

Figure 3.3   Vargas' balance of power.

Box 3.3   Populism in Latin America

The term 'populism' has been used to describe state ideologies of certain Latin American countries. Populism has been a political strategy used by elites to forge alliances with working classes (particularly urban workers) against an agrarian oligopoly. Thus, this alliance had the promotion of industry and the cooption of workers as its objective. A crucial element of populism is rhetoric aimed directly at winning political support from the (urban) poor. The leader is projected as the the protector of the powerless.

The typical cases of populism in Latin America are the Brazil of Getulio Vargas and the Peronism of Argentina. But the term has been used quite freely since to describe many other manifestations of state power based on popular appeal in nearly all Latin American countries. The presidency of Fernando Collor in Brazil has been described as populist.

Great emphasis is put on the state. However, populism is essentially a political style based on the personal charisma of a leader and personal loyalty to that leader invoked by a system of patronage. Populist ideology is moralist, emotional and anti-intellectual. It presents society as split between the powerful and the powerless but with little notion of the relationship between different classes.

coffee production and exports. But the Wall Street crash of 1929, followed by the Great Depression and its effects on the world economy, as well as labour agitation in the docks of Santos, the cities of São Paulo and Rio and even on the plantations, sparked off a political crisis which resulted in the overthrow of the 'coffee oligarchy' and the landed elites. President Getulio Vargas, a right-wing populist (see Box 3.3), came to power in 1930 backed by a military coup. Compared to the strongly regional interests of landowners, the army was a strong national force. The *Estado Novo* (New State) formed in 1937 was an authoritarian form of government similar to Mussolini's Italy. In the fifteen years that followed profound changes took place in the economic, political and institutional fabric of the nation. The state was centralized and the power of the regional oligarchies neutralized by the use of centrally appointed superintendents.

Under the direction of Vargas, the State began to foster industrialization actively. Aware that coffee exports could never regain their former pre-eminence, Getulio Vargas adopted a policy of diversification. Investment funds withdrawn from coffee production were directed to industry and exchange controls, tariffs and credits to stimulate industrial production were introduced. To create the right conditions for industry, the State took on responsibility for basic inputs, developing energy resources and setting up the country's first integrated steel mill, at Volta Redonda, in 1943.

Figure 3.4   Getulio Vargas announces the Estado Novo.

By the end of the Second World War, Brazil had a much larger industrial base than had been the case in 1929. A comparison of the industrial censuses of 1920 and 1940 shows that in the industrial centre of the country, São Paulo, the number of workers in industry increased by 325%, from 84 000 to 273 000. Simão (1966) records a 42% rise in the number of workers in São Paulo State between 1939 and 1943. Coffee was still the main economic activity, but industry was the rising activity.

In industry, the lion's share of output was in traditional sectors (such as food, textiles, wood and leather). They were 70% of output in 1940. But between 1920 and 1940, the share in industrial output of such industries as metal fabrication, machinery, chemicals and pharmaceuticals grew from 11% to 20.3% (Baer, 1967). These early developments formed the building blocks of Brazil's more rapid industrial development after the Second World War.

Summary

Summarizing Brazilian economic development up to the Second World War, we can say:

- The Brazilian economy has experienced a number of booms and slumps in its history.

- Coffee production was a qualitatively different boom from previous ones. Its extent and the degree to which it fostered the development of finance, commerce and transport created the basis for further development.

- Some industrial development was fostered by the coffee boom, the abolition of slavery and mass immigration of European workers, but industry remained subordinate to the export economy.

- During the Great Depression, export earnings fell. Industry flourished as locally produced goods replaced those which Brazil no longer had the foreign exchange to import.

- Following a crisis in 1930, a new authoritarian government centralized the country's administration and began to develop positive policies of industrial promotion.

3.3 Post-war industrialization and the 'democratic interlude' (1945–64)

Following the end of the Second World War the world economic system was reintegrated under the control of the USA. Brazil, like other Latin American nations which had industrialized through protectionist policies, had to decide how best to continue the process of economic and industrial development. Because Brazilian industry had been developing rapidly since 1930, there was now a substantial market for industrial goods from abroad. A free trade economy would open up this market to imports, but at the expense of local industry. Brazil could no longer export enough raw materials and food to pay for these. So a return to policies of free trade would result in the bankruptcy of many local industrial firms and serious balance of payments problems.

This is precisely what began to happen after the isolation of the war years. The newly elected President Dutra opened up the economy to imports from the US. In less than a year, foreign exchange reserves were reduced from US$708 million to US$92 million. The bulk of this was spent on the import of luxury consumer items rather than inputs for industrial development. This was the beginning of a long-standing relationship with the US.

Economic growth in the 1950s

Economic planners now had to choose between two options:

(i) further development of heavy industry, which would mean a further expansion of the State's role and curtailment of trade with the outside world

(ii) controlled integration and development of industries producing consumer durables for domestic consumption, with the help of foreign companies and investment.

After some vacillation, the government of President Kubitschek (1956–61) opted for a mix of both, promoting a policy of rapid industrial development, with special emphasis on the development of energy and transport. Put forward with the slogan, 'fifty years in five', the aim of the policy was to combine State investment in infrastructure (such as roads, hydro-electric schemes) and some heavy industry (such as steel and oil refining) with private capital investment in new industrial ventures. Foreign companies were given a major role, and massive government incentives were provided. The implantation of new industries was meant to provide the technological leap and impetus that would propel Brazil into the ranks of the developed nations.

In the short term, the *Plano de Metas* (target plan) strategy had some success. There was a construction boom as the government poured money into building roads and the new capital, Brasília, which was itself symbolic of the new age; a town without a rail link, designed around a basic pattern of major roads. Brazil was entering the age of the car, and the target plan was to give priority to road transport. From 1957 to 1961, manufacturing output rose by 62% in real terms, and for consumer durables, growth was even more startling. Between 1955 (just before the target plan strategy was implemented) and the end of Kubitschek's term of office in 1961, motor industry production rose by five and a half times, and electrical equipment (including domestic appliances) by three and a half times. In contrast, the main bases of previous industrialization in Brazil, the food and textile industries, grew by only 46% and 29% respectively in the same period (Singer, 1976).

Figure 3.5   Brasília : Congress and Senate buildings.

Political and economic problems in the early 1960s

This boom was bought at a price, and towards the end of the 1950s there were increasing economic and political problems surrounding the government. Firstly, the rapid industrial growth of the period had not resolved the inflation and balance of payments problems. Inflation was stimulated by the State's borrowing money to cover the budget deficit resulting from its expenditure on infrastructure. The balance of payments was made worse by the need for imports of machinery and raw materials to build and supply the new industries. In addition to this, the balance of payments also suffered from outflows of profits and royalties to foreign companies and from interest payments on debt.

A second major problem for the government was the political conflict over industrialization strategy. The target plan had received support from the labour movement. The political Left had seen industrialization as a chance to create a genuinely national economy. In 1956, coffee still accounted for 69% of all exports. The Left had thought that a balanced internal growth would replace dependence on agricultural exports, creating jobs and increasing wages for the working class. In fact, at the end of the 1950s neither of these two effects appeared to be materializing.

The rapid industrialization programme depended so heavily on foreign capital that the foreign grip on the economy was reinforced, as multinational companies expanded in the heart of the manufacturing sector.

At the same time, the rapid industrialization strategy was not creating jobs in sufficient numbers to resolve the problems of employment and wages. Between 1950 and 1960 the rate of increase in manufacturing jobs had been less than the increase in the number of people either in work or seeking work (the economically active population). This was partly because the new industries were capital intensive and did not create as many jobs as some had anticipated. But the main problem was that, although industrial employment grew, it was outstripped by a massive rural to urban migration. With an increasing surplus of urban labour, by 1961 there were signs of a fall in industrial wages and a fall in the real value of the minimum wage.

From 1962, it appeared that Brazilian industrialization was running into problems that are usually associated with import substitution industrialization (see Box 3.4); namely low-volume high-cost production for a restricted internal market. Inflation soared, profits fell and the government was in a quandary over economic policy.

A period of mounting political unrest ensued. Falling real wages, along with government suggestions for an IMF-linked stabilization policy, fuelled political opposition to the industrializa-

---

Box 3.4   The mechanisms of import substitution industrialization in Brazil

As in the other late-industrializing countries, the main driving forces behind development have been import substitution and the expansion of domestic demand. Brazil's industrial growth has taken place within a protectionist framework that provided 'captive market' opportunities for local manufacturers. A variety of approaches has been used to this end, including import controls and tariff policy, encouraging and screening foreign investment in line with policy objectives, expanding the role of direct State participation in industry, and maintaining an over-valued exchange rate.

At the same time, elements of export promotion have long existed alongside import substitution in Brazilian policy. And, with the increasingly pressing need for foreign currency earnings in the late 1970s and early 1980s, the emphasis shifted to increasing financial resources devoted to export promotion and readjusting the exchange rate.

Among the policy mechanisms which had evolved by the 1970s we can include:

* *Import licensing,* a system under which licenses, needed for most products, are granted only to firms on the registry of importers and exporters maintained by CACEX, the trade department of the Bank of Brazil; applicant companies are required to provide stipulated information on the imports concerned. In addition to import licensing requirements, Brazil prohibits over 5000 tariff categories to be imported into the country except in special cases.

* *Export incentives* in which, in exchange for lower import tariffs and duties, firms undertake to reach export targets.

* *The 'law of similars',* which has been used to limit imports of items regarded as superfluous or as luxuries, or which are already being produced in Brazil. This is essentially a measure of import substitution policy based on various provisions of Brazilian foreign trade regulations.

* *Tariffs*, which the government has had considerable leeway to use as a policy instrument to cope with economic difficulties.

* *Control over industrial ownership*, instrumental in creating an industrial structure characterized by the coexistence of State, foreign and private domestic sectors (see Box 3.5). This has been achieved by large-scale government investment in key industrial sectors, incentives and other promotional activities directed to domestic industry, and by attracting and controlling over investment.

* *Regulation of technology imports,* through registering technology-related agreements and ensuring conformity with Brazilian regulations concerning terms and payments, national participation in relevant projects, etc;

* *Promotion of development in selected industries* through an array of instruments that include financial incentives, direct government participation, import controls and exclusion of foreign participation (see, for example, the case of the computer industry in Box 3.10).

(Source: OECD, 1988)

---

tion strategy. The Right demanded wage controls, cuts in government expenditure and control of the money supply. The Left became increasingly vociferous in its demand for fundamental economic reforms such as redistribution of land in the countryside, nationalization of key sectors and greater control over the multinationals.

This polarization of economic strategies and political forces led to a military coup in 1964. The constitutional president, João Goulart, was deposed by a military junta that was determined to halt what they saw as the threat of communism and a slide into economic chaos. The coup produced not only a change in economic policy, but also a dramatic change in the political framework. The highly centralized decision-making structure of the military government was almost totally immune from pressure from the working class and the peasantry. So the technocrats, drafted into the Ministries of Finance and Planning, had a free hand to develop economic policy.

Summary

In the post-war period, industrialization policy was a key political issue:

- Following the end of the Second World War, attempts to liberalize commerce proved disastrous, and the government reverted to protectionism and support for industry.

- In the 1950s, the State gave a further impetus to industrialization by implanting new industries and by developing the infrastructure.

- Consumer durables production expanded rapidly, and the participation of multinational firms increased. Production was of the import substitution industrialization type.

- Rapid industrialization did not solve balance of payments problems. While industry generated some new jobs, it could not absorb a huge wave of rural to urban migration.

- Increasing polarization over economic policy in the early 1960s led to a military coup in 1964.

3.4 The Brazilian economic 'miracle' (1964–74)

After 1964 came a turning point in Brazil's history. Economically, it was a period of rapid growth and industrial 'deepening'. Politically, it was a period of authoritarianism and the repression of democratic rights. Socially, it was a period of growing inequality.

What was the Brazilian economic miracle?

Before the spectacular emergence of the Asian NICs, Brazil caught world attention because of its extraordinary economic growth rates which averaged an increase in GNP of 10% per year between 1969 and 1974.

In purely economic terms, developments in this period were remarkable (if not actually miraculous). However the social and political costs were substantial. It may be that such substantial economic expansion would not have been possible without the stamp of authoritarianism in that industrial policies were instigated by decree and not by consensus. Internally, there was the development of what one observer called a 'triple alliance' between the state, local capital and foreign capital (Box 3.5). It proved a profitable alliance for all partners (although not for those excluded from the alliance). On the other side of the coin, international conditions were conducive to the rapid growth of industry. It is no coincidence that the miracle occurred at a time when international trade and access to finance was growing at an unprecedented rate (see Chapters 1 and 2).

The features of this period of rapid growth or 'economic miracle', were:

- A *partial* shift from import substitution to an outward looking phase based on the expansion of non-traditional exports.

- An increase in direct state involvement in the economy.

- Increasing integration with the world economy.

What were the visible signs of growth? Between 1969 and 1974, GNP grew at rates over 10% per

Box 3.5   The triple alliance

The Brazilian state has long had a central role in industrial development. Not only has it invested hugely in infrastructural development (sometimes wastefully in the era of 'big development' often crucially as in telecommunications) but it has taken a central role as producer. Thus state firms are dominant in such areas as oil (Petrobras), steel (Sidebras), electricity (Eletrobras) and mining (CVRD). Between 1959 and 1988, the number of state-owned companies grew from 45 to 176 and employed well over half a million workers. During the late 1960s and early 1970s, the military encouraged both private Brazilian firms and foreign firms to invest in industrial production. The resulting combination of state, private and foreign industrial ownership has been called the 'triple alliance'.

year but the industrial sector took a leading role in this, growing at over 13% per year. The rate of inflation dropped from 87% in 1964 to 20% in 1973. The balance of payments was in permanent surplus over the period although the current account ran a permanent deficit which was financed by a growing external debt. Thus, the seeds of future difficulties were being sown. Exports grew consistently and industrialized (as opposed to primary product) exports increased their share in the total from 15% in 1964 to 42% in 1974. There was considerable growth in employment in industry, particularly in the so-called modern sectors such as transport equipment, mechanical, electrical and metalworking sectors where the inflow of direct foreign investment was concentrated. Box 3.6 gives an account of the environmental and social impact of the rapid expansion of the mining industry. Box 3.7 describes the expansion of the auto industry.

How did this happen? The economic miracle has often been interpreted as the result of outward-oriented policies (Balassa, 1980; Krueger, 1974) and a success for free market principles. The World Bank's 1987 *World Development Report* also held up Brazil in this period (along with the Asian NICs) as a good example of export-oriented industrialization. To an extent this was the case. But it was only part of the story. Imports were liberalized through a reduction in tariffs with special emphasis on the import of machinery and other capital goods. Exchange rates were depreciated in a series of mini-devaluations which favoured exporters. In addition, exporters were provided with a range of fiscal and financial incentives. But contrary to the orthodox view that export incentives should be uniform across the economy (if they are to be used at all), they were targeted only at

Figure 3.6   'A day in the life of Brasilino' — foreign investment in Brazil.

Box 3.6 **'Opening' the new frontier — Amazonia**

In the late 1960s, a helicopter owned by US Steel had to make an emergency landing in the Southern Para jungle. It landed on an exposed range of hills, the Serra dos Carajas. One of the passengers was a geologist. He instantly recognized why the hillside supported no vegetation: it was composed of high-grade iron ore. Today, Carajas has become the biggest of Brazil's development projects.

The iron deposits form the core of an integrated development area, including mining, logging, iron and aluminium smelting, agro-industrial smelting, and agro-industrial plantations. There, some 800 000 square kilometres of the Amazonian forest (10% of Brazil's national territory and bigger than the United Kingdom and France together) is being clearcut, bulldozed and mined. In the States of Maranhão and Para, farming communities have had to watch in despair as their houses, crops, orchards and nut trees are bulldozed to make way for steel plants, fuel terminals, and property development. Pig iron smelters are being established, paving the way for a steel belt that will rival the German Ruhr. The forest around is being felled for charcoal. The cleared land is being planted with export crops like black pepper, palm oil, bananas and pineapples. Gold mines and aluminium smelters are mushrooming where once there were trees. Power lines stalk through the forest, carrying power from the giant Tucurui dam to the new industries.

There are estimated to be 18 billion tonnes of iron ore in Carajas. The concession to the area is held by the state Companhia Vale de Rio Doce (CVRD) which established a joint venture with US Steel and then bought out its US partner. The zone is also estimated to contain rich deposits of other minerals: manganese, copper, bauxite, nickel, cassiterite and gold. The region is planned to generate US$17 billion a year in export earnings in the 1990s. Since Minas Gerais supplies all Brazil's domestic mineral needs, all the Carajas production will go down the rail line to the São Luis terminal for export to Europe, North America and Japan. In 1987, 35 million tonnes of iron ore were exported, and the target figure is 40 million tonnes. They are talking now

of doubling the rail line. Even at that rate of extraction, the Carajas iron fields are estimated to have 350–400 years' worth of reserves.

Six trains a day, of 200 wagons each, travel the new 900 km railroad from the Carajas mines to the CVRD terminal at Sao Luis. The rail line, which forms the backbone of the programme, passes through and is transforming 131 municipalities. The iron ore dumped by the trains travels the last half mile by conveyor belt to a pipe hanging over the water into the holds of waiting European ships. The European Community is the largest funder of the iron ore project. The European Iron & Steel Confederation put up a loan of US$600 million, and European banks lent US$450 million. The World Bank contributed a further US$300 million. In return, the European Community has been guaranteed 13.6 million tonnes a year for 15 years, reportedly at 'banana' prices. This amounts to one third of Carajas' production and half of the communities total needs for iron ore imports.

Atop it all is the powerful CVRD company. In addition to the iron fields and rail line, it owns half of the Alumar and Alnorte aluminium smelters.

For poor communities in the area, the development programme offers only dispossession. Many now live in squatter camps by the roadsides. Violence has erupted over land disputes, as land grabbing by the rich and powerful have forced hopes of land reform into the background. The area is in turmoil. Thousands of landless peasants are on the move, looking for new ways of making a living, leaving behind a growing number of women-headed households. Immigrants are streaming in from other parts of Brazil, hoping for a new future in the steel mills, the logging camps and especially the gold fields. As Amazonia becomes the new industrial centre of Brazil, whole communities and ways of life are being transformed. Peasants have no choice but to become industrial workers.

Extract from Oxfam (1991)

Figure 3.7   Opening up the Amazon forest.

manufacturing. The state also played a central role both in production and in orchestrating the pattern of accumulation of the rest of the economy.

The economic miracle, although much more open to the international economy than the previous twenty years, was not so much 'open' as 'less

Figure 3.8   The colours of the Brazilian national flag are green for the forests (the background), yellow for gold (the diamond) and blue for the sky (the globe). The motto reads 'order and progress'.

closed'. The economy was still based on the domestic market and the pattern of accumulation was still based on the rapid expansion of durable consumer goods, growing state investment in production of basic and intermediary goods and of infrastructure.

The rapid expansion of world trade and liquidity in the late 1960s and early 1970s were favourable to the expansion of the Brazilian economy, as they were to other late industrializers such as the Asian NICs (see Chapter 1). From 1967 to 1973, world trade grew at average annual rates of 18%. OECD countries were open to trade while they still enjoyed the post-war boom. They even encouraged imports from their own subsidiaries based in developing countries with special value-added tariffs. With the expansion of trade, there was a considerable growth in direct foreign investment. Unlike other developing countries where foreign firms had a relatively small share of exports, in Brazil foreign corporations accounted for between 43% and 51% of total exports.

The growth in trade and investment was accompanied by a growth in liquidity due in main to the recycling of petrodollars (see Chapter 2). Easy

Figure 3.9 The banking and business district of São Paulo.

Box 3.7 The motor industry

Apart from the exploitation of Brazil's mineral wealth and the industrialization that has accompanied it (see Box 3.6), the motor industry is probably the single most significant sector in the history of the country's industrial development.

The motor industry has been the centrepiece of import substitution strategies since the 1950s, the driving force behind the 'Brazilian Miracle' and the centre of trade union mobilization. It is situated in São Paulo's industrial heartland.

By 1988 the motor industry accounted for 7.4% of GDP. In 1989 it earned US$3.2 billion in foreign sales and supported 4.1 million workers in direct or indirect employment. It is a big consumer of the products of other Brazilian industries, such as steel, glass and plastics.

Development in the 1960s were predicated on the idea that the car was the transport of the future. Major road building programmes were the order of the day. The capital Brasília, which was built around roads and not vice versa, is a clear example of the thinking of planners at the time.

Foreign firms quickly moved into the large protected market. Ford, Volkswagen, General Motors and, later Fiat, all have production plants in Brazil and together amount for 98% of sales. The 1973 oil crisis modified this view of the future of road transport but, ironically, it did not stem the growth of the industry. As can be seen from Figure 3.10, the spectacular growth of the auto industry only decreased with the economic crisis of the 1980s.

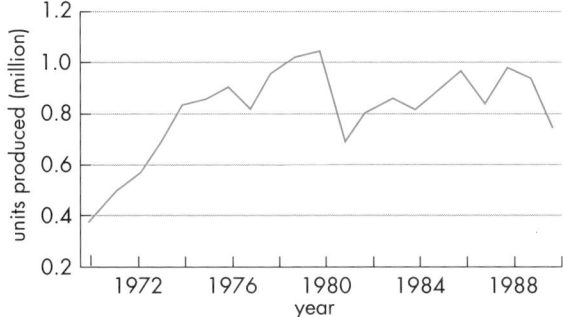

Figure 3.10   Brazilian motor industry production between 1970 and 1990 [Source: Anfavea (Brazilian Association of Autoproducers)].

access to finance at low interest rates made it possible for Brazil to import capital goods needed for industry.

The particular nature of the accumulation process was also demonstrated by the regime of labour use. The economic and political conditions of the 1970s enabled industrial firms to adopt a practice of labour use characterized by intensive exploitation (i.e. extending working hours or employing more people as opposed to productivity increase through greater efficiency) and the use of rapid labour turnover in order to control that labour (see Section 3.5). These practices were based on access to a ready supply of cheap labour (see also Chapter 1). The end of the economic miracle was the beginning of more than a decade of political turbulence and economic crises. Popular opposition to the military government grew and the trade union movement gained in strength. The combined effects of debt service and inflation meant that macroeconomic management turned into short-term crisis management.

The economic miracle and the balance of payments

In the 1970s the Brazilian economy was beset by a mounting series of problems that made the 'miracle' look rather more tarnished. By the end of the decade it looked more like a brief interlude than a solution to the problem of how to develop. As had been the case in previous periods of industrial development, the problems centred on the balance of payments.

The balance of payments is made up of inflows and outflows of goods, services, transfers, and long and short-term capital. It measures the changes in a period of time (usually the calendar year) in the foreign assets and liabilities of a country (see Chapter 2 Box 2.2 for a more detailed explanation). Leaving aside the minor items in the balance of payments account, we can divide it into four areas:

1   *the balance of trade account* (exports less imports = the visible balance)

2   *services*, the inflow and outflow of funds for travel, insurance, and freight; and also inflow and outflow of profits, interest and dividends (known as invisibles)

3   *the long-term capital account* (the inflow and outflow of long-term investment and loans)

4   *the short-term capital account* for short-term funds.

Areas 1 and 2 constitute the current account. Areas 3 and 4 constitute the capital account.

If a country has a net outflow on trade and services (the current account balance) then it must either finance this through investment and borrowing (the capital account) or run a balance of payments deficit. The balance of payments deficit can be financed by running down reserves of gold and currency, or borrowing by the Central Bank.

Table 3.1 shows the development of the Brazilian balance of payments for the years 1969 to 1977. First, compare the figures for years 1969 and 1977.

In 1969 Brazil exported more goods than it imported; a balance of trade surplus of US$318 million. There was a net outflow on the services account of US$630 million, of which US$263 million consisted of outflows of interest, dividends and profits. A relatively small inflow of long-term capital investment (US$189 million) was not enough to balance the current account deficit of US$312 million. But more than US$1 000 million was raised in long-term loans, bringing the total long-term capital account balance, even after some loans were paid back, to US$719 million. Further short-term inflows of capital meant that

Table 3.1 Brazil's balance of payments (in US$ million)

Year	1969	1971	1973	1975	1977
trade	+318	−363	+7	−3 540	+97
of which oil		−363	−853	−3 107	
services	−630	−958	−1 722	−3 162	−4 028
of which interest etc.	−263	−420	−712	−1 713	−2 559
current account balance	−312	−1 321	−1 715	−6 702	−3 931
investment capital	+189	+172	+977	+892	+841
long-term loans	+1 023	+2 037	+4 495	+5 932	+8 231
long-term loan repayments	−493	−850	−1 673	−2 172	−4 053
short-term loans	+178	+486	−197	+1 551	−43
capital account balance	+897	+1 845	+3 602	+6 203	+4 976
balance of payments	+585	+524	+1 887	−499	+1 045

A surplus is indicated by '+' and a deficit by '−'.

the capital account balance was US$897 million. So Brazil's liquid assets were some US$585 million greater at the end of the year than at the beginning.

The situation in 1977 is very different. Although the balance of payments is positive (after three years of heavy deficits), there is a massive deficit on the service account, mainly due to the outflow of interest, profits and dividends. Capital investment is still far too small to offset this, and it is only after the country has borrowed more than US$8 billion that there is enough money to finance the current account deficit and pay back US$4 billion in long-term loans.

Note the following points about Brazilian balance of payments during this period:

1 Oil was clearly a big problem (think back to Chapter 2). Oil imports cost much more in the latter part of the 1970s.

Although oil data are not available for 1977, by then, exports of goods had made up for the oil deficit, assisted by the fact that oil prices had fallen in real terms compared to 1975.

2 The deficit on the service account rose every year, increasing by more than six times in the period as a whole. A good part of this service deficit is attributable to the outflow of interest, profits and dividends, which rose nearly tenfold between 1969 and 1977.

3 The reason for rising service payments can be seen in the capital account. There is a steady net inflow of long-term capital. The table has data only for alternative years, so you cannot add up the total net inflow. The net inflow of long-term capital totalled US$5 400 million in the period. There was also a massive inflow of long-term loans, on which interest had to be paid. In the whole period US$42 billion of new loans were raised and only US$16 billion repaid.

4 The short-term loans are not particularly significant. But note that in 1975 the situation was so desperate that US$1 500 million of short-term loans were needed to finance the current account deficit.

The economy was in a vicious circle. Fresh long-term loans were raised to finance service payments on loans and repayments of old loans. Even with the trade account in surplus in 1977, net long-term loans of US$4 billion were raised. Was there any solution to this predicament? In the long-term a solution would have been to run down foreign investment and long-term loans. The loans were the main problem.

In the course of the 1970s the Brazilian economy ran into problems because oil prices were rising. In 1974 and 1975, increasing imports were needed to continue the growth of the economic miracle. This, combined with the outflow of profits, dividends and interest from earlier loans created a balance of payments problem that led to more and more borrowing. For a number of years, until 1980, Brazil merely carried on borrowing; hoping that another miracle, such as the discovery of vast oil deposits, would provide a solution. The real miracle was, perhaps, that Brazil kept on growing until 1980 and managed to hold off the international financial community.

By 1980, the total external debt had reached nearly US$60 billion. In the latter part of the 1970s, interest rates on foreign loans had risen (making the service deficit even larger) and the time periods over which loans were made had shortened, thus making repayment of loans more frequent. How could Brazil ever hope to repay even part of this massive deficit? The answer is, of course, to make such a surplus on the trade account that it pays for all the service deficit and still leaves some exchange inflow to finance a run-down of foreign debt. With oil imports running at US$4 billion this would not be easy.

In 1980 the government was forced to abandon its policy of 'growth at any price'. Despite the growing financial and political crisis at the end of the 1970s, it is important to register that the structure of Brazilian manufacturing had been transformed. This is shown clearly in Table 3.2.

By 1980, the share of capital goods (machinery for example) in the total output had risen to 14.7%. The share of durable consumer goods (such as cars and TVs) and intermediate goods (such as steel and other industrial inputs) had also risen from previous decades. These increases were accompanied by a relative decline in non-durable goods (foodstuffs for example). In short, the years following the Second World War witnessed a thorough transformation of the Brazilian economy.

Other structural characteristics of the economy, however, did not change. Agriculture has remained an important part of the economy. Alongside industrial diversification, there was concentration of land ownership in rural areas. Increasingly larger areas of land were owned by fewer people. The social consequences of this are described in Box 3.8.

Brazilian politics since the economic miracle

One of the reasons for the military regime's economic success was its single-minded pursuit of growth, unfettered by political opposition. Control of the working class, co-operation with foreign capital and willingness to expand the State sector were all ingredients of the recipe for rapid industrialization. However, just as the economic strategy of the regime came unstuck in the 1970s, so too did its political strategy. There were two main reasons for this. Firstly, the military themselves were unsure about what political form they wished to impose. Secondly, economic difficulties led to opposition from within the ranks of the regime's own supporters.

Table 3.2   Structure of manufacturing production

	1949	1970	1980
Non-durable consumer goods	72.8%	45.0%	34.4%
Intermediate goods	20.4%	34.4%	37.4%
Consumer durable goods	2.5%	9.3%	13.5%
Capital goods	4.3%	11.3%	14.7%
Total	100.0%	100.0%	100.0%

[Source: OECD, 1988]

Box 3.8 People without land and land without people

The Brazilian economic miracle was based on rapid industrial expansion. Rural–urban migration over the last 30 years has been encouraged by the pull of industrial employment and by the push of changes in the countryside. Agricultural modernization rapidly changed the patterns of land use and ownership.

In 1950, 19.2% of rural workers owned no land. By 1975 this had risen to 36%. Each year the production of basic foodstuffs such as cassava, beans and corn by small farmers is being displaced by concentration of land ownership for large plantations of export crops such as soya, sugar cane, cacao, coffee and oranges. As a result, during the 1970s, around 15 million people migrated to Brazil's urban centres. Even so, by the mid-1980s an estimated 12 million rural people were landless. Changing agricultural practices (i.e. agro-industrial development) are only part of the problem. The real issue is land ownership. In Brazil, 2.8 million square kilometres of agricultural land lies idle. The 18 biggest landowners in Brazil own 180 000 square kilometres — an area bigger than the Republic of Ireland, Holland and Switzerland put together.

After a congress of rural labour unions in 1985 which demanded the redistribution of idle lands to the landless, the civilian government of José Sarnay attempted to implement a land reform programme. It was to concede some of this unused land to 1.4 million families. The reaction from the landowners was rapid and violent as they formed the Democratic Rural Union (UDR) to 'defend their land'. The powerful political lobby of the UDR ensured that the reform did not take place.

Land conflict has long been a feature of the Brazilian countryside. Between 1964 and 1985, 1 125 people have died or disappeared in land conflicts. But in the 1980s the problem intensified: from 1980–85, there were 279 deaths and from 1985–89, deaths totalled 488 in nearly 3000 different disputes over land. In the 1980s, rural workers have formed this Landless Workers' Movement both to defend themselves against violence and to stake claims to unused land. The movement has had some successes but the killings continue.

(Sources: Oxfam, 1991; Ribeiro *et al.*, 1991).

Figure 3.11   Rural workers invading idle land in 1986.

When the military took power in 1964 they did so with the intention of 'purifying' the government and, at some point in the future, returning the nation to democracy. However, some currents in the military favoured a more overt authoritarian stance, and these gained power in the five years following the coup. By 1969 the regime was authoritarian and centralized. Congress was a rubber-stamp convention and the President had almost absolute power. The period of maximum centralization of power and minimum legal constraints on the security forces ran from 1969 to 1973.

By 1973, a burgeoning guerilla movement and popular opposition to the military had been violently put down. For the less authoritarian factions within the armed forces, the uncontrolled power of largely autonomous units of the security apparatus, over which the central government had limited authority, now posed a greater threat. In order to rein in the security forces, the new government became more responsive to civilian groups which could demand greater respect for the rule of law, such as the Catholic Church, the press and the Bar Association. It was within this context that liberal political opposition to the government began to grow. Such opposition was further stimulated by the impact of the 1973–4 oil crisis on the Brazilian economy.

During the period of the economic miracle, the government had gained the support of businessmen and the middle classes. The accumulation of wealth for these groups had risen markedly. But when economic conditions began to worsen and the government began to apply corrective measures, the business community became very anxious about policy-making. As a leading industrialist expressed it in 1977:

> "In the golden years of the Brazilian economy, from 1972 to 1974 for example, the businessman did not talk about politics and was not interested in the subject, but not because there was or there was not censorship, but just because the economy was going well ... The lack of interest in political questions was seen not only in public pronouncements but also in private conversations among businessmen. Political discussion only started in effect when economic perspectives for the near future were lacking, which was the consequence of a very hesitant and ill-defined economic, financial and industrial policy."

(Luis Eulálio Bueno Vidigal Filho, President of the Auto Component Employers' Union)

In 1977 the government faced a rising tide of criticism from industry, expressed in the newspapers, on which censorship had been relaxed. Industrialists feared that the 'tough decisions' needed to stabilize the economy would fall on them, rather than on finance or the State sector. Many Brazilian businessmen viewed the expansion of the State and foreign enterprise sectors with great concern.

In the general climate of political discussion and criticism, the working class, too, took the opportunity to raise its voice. Some of the more representative unions began to demand better wages and more freedom. In May 1978 a series of strikes and stoppages spread through the main industrial centre, São Paulo, and in the following year the labour movement created its own political party (see Section 3.5). The new President, General Figueiredo, took office in March 1979 with a commitment to continue the political liberalization process and democratize the country, but he faced considerable opposition from conservative and radical forces in the military. Both were determined to see that the regime's plans for continuation of the same power group within a manipulated democratic system would be defeated. With party reform, the postponement and modification of elections and intense political mobilization and debate, Brazil entered the 1980s with political as well as economic uncertainty (see Section 3.6).

Summary

* After plunging the country into deep recession, the military government and its development technocrats were responsible for five economic miracle years between 1969 and 1974. The miracle was based on an alliance between state, local and multinational capital.

- The economic miracle years were characterized by a partial shift from import substitution to outward orientation, with some liberalization of trade and increasing integration with the world economy.

- From 1974, the Brazilian economy began to suffer from higher oil prices and the massive imports needed to sustain the industrialization of the economic miracle. Debt repayment also began to catch up with it and loans taken out at the beginning of the miracle period needed to be repaid.

- By 1977 the government was facing strong criticism from industry and from a much-strengthened trade union movement.

3.5 The labour movement in Brazilian industrialization

Who were the people involved in Brazil's industrialization and who generated the value created by the economic miracle? Wage earners in formal industrial employment are by no means the majority in Brazil. Subsistence farming, petty commodity production and so-called 'informal' sector activities outweigh the 'formal' industrial sector. Similarly, industrial wage earners are poor, but poverty levels are generally worse in these other areas of economic activity. Nevertheless, the relatively strong position of industrial wage earners has been demonstrated by the labour movement's interventions over the years.

Through trade unions, industrial workers have long played an important part in the development of industry and in the country's political history. In Section 3.2 we discussed how an industrial working class formed in Brazil between the turn of the century and the 1930s, as a result of mass migrations from Europe. This immigrant labour was militant, as attested by the considerable labour unrest during the 1920s. After a brief spell under the sway of ideas emanating from European anarcho-syndicalists, the 1930s saw the emergence of the Communist Party as a strong influence in the labour movement.

'Populist' trade unions

Another important current developed in the 1940s, in the form of populist trade unions, encouraged by Getulio Vargas (see Box 3.3). To prevent the labour movement from gaining strength, Vargas incorporated it into the State. He was a wily politician. On the one hand, Vargas used labour as a source of political support by granting many favourable terms. For example, Brazil's extensive and positive labour legislation stems from this time. He used this support to create a balance of power against the landed oligarchy which had ruled Brazil up to the 1930s. On the other hand, by incorporating labour into the state (the Ministry of Labour was instrumental in this), Vargas was able to stifle the development of an autonomous trades union movement. Vargas' political career was a constant juggling act between left and right. He even founded two political parties of opposite ideologies to play the two sides off against each other and to maintain his position of power. It was for these reasons that the Vargas regime has been labelled both 'corporatist' (vertical integration of society under the state) and 'populist'. Note that this meaning of populism is different from that current in the development literature of the 1990s (*Allen & Thomas, 1992*, Chapter 6).

Overriding these political concerns, Vargas needed the political support of labour in order to counter the deep mistrust of industrialization held by landowners. Much of the industrialization of the Vargas period was in state-owned industries and the majority of trade unions represented in the Ministry of Labour were from this state sector.

Repression and persecution

The corporatist model was inherited by the military in 1964 and turned to their own ends. From 1964 to 1969 there was a progressively severe persecution of the trade union movement until it was silenced. Around 150 labour leaders were imprisoned and deported. Until 1975 there was hardly a murmur from the labour movement. Its political head had been removed and the 'rank and file', which had never really been represented by its leadership in the Vargas era, lost all channels to voice their grievances. Thus the military were able to make political appointments out of trade union leaders. These were the so-called *pelegos* or 'yellow unions' whose leaders were little more than lackeys for the military. More significantly, the military were able to use existing legislation (combined with force) to discipline and control labour.

The 'economic miracle', as described in the previous section, was in part fuelled by a huge wage squeeze on industrial employees. This 'policy' is well documented in the case of the car workers (Humphrey, 1982). Immediately after the coup of 1964, the government imposed strict controls on trade unions. Strikes were made illegal and the military introduced laws which allowed the government to determine wages. For three years after the coup, nominal wage increases were well below the rate of inflation (Box 3.9).

Union militancy in the 1970s

A combination of the denial of workers' rights, declining wages and the persecution of labour militants bred a militancy from below, from the shop floor, which was to erupt in waves of general strikes in the late 1970s. This upsurge in labour militancy, although easy to understand in retrospect, came as a complete surprise to Brazilians at the time. Those involved were a new working class which had grown up during the military government and who, until this moment, had been silent. Unlike the trades union movement in

Figure 3.12   Lula, metalworkers union leader.

the 1940s and 1950s, which was centred in the state-owned sector, this new working class was from the private industrial sector which had been built up by the military, that is, in the auto and auto-parts sector, electrical goods and capital goods sectors.

The metalworkers union of São Paulo, representing car workers and led by Luis Ignacio da Silva (Lula) was at the forefront of this industrial action. This action began from the shopfloor

---

Box 3.9   Real and nominal wages

Nominal (or money) wages are wages in money form as received by a worker in her or his pay pay packet. A nominal wage rate is £1 per hour or £40 per week. But, when prices are changing, what is important is not the amount of cash a worker receives but how much that cash will buy. This is what 'real wages' refers to. The real wage represents the amount of goods and services that a money wage can buy. For example, if a worker earns £100 per week in July 1990, but inflation is running the rate of 20% per year, then by July 1991 the goods the worker bought for £100 a year earlier would cost £120. If the worker's wages in money terms remained the same, then she or he would only be able to buy 100/120ths (83.3%) of what had been bought a year before. So a nominal wage of £100 in 1991 would be equivalent to real wage (in 1990 pounds) of only £83.30. In other words, in one year the worker's real wages would have fallen by 16.7%. In practice, money wages will also rise, but by more or less than the rate of inflation, leading to higher or lower real wages.

workers of a Saab-Scania plant who went on strike. Lula was asked to come and legitimize the strike. Within hours, most of the industrial belt of São Paulo was out on strike. At the height of the strikes, workers from the banking and construction sectors, from agriculture and from transport sectors were all involved in industrial action. Industrial action lasted for 10 days in which 14 years of pent-up anger burst out.

While the initial industrial action was centred on wage demands and working conditions, the movement rapidly became political. In 1979, the *Partido Trabalhista* (PT or Workers Party) was formed. In its early days, this political party was interested only in industrial workers and made no alliances with other groups such as the church, populist politicians or the (then banned) Communist Party. Subsequently, this position has changed.

Shortly afterwards a new national trade union organization called CUT (*Central Unica dos Trabalhadores*) was formed. The political agenda of CUT was to obtain freedom of organization and the right to strike and to dismantle the corporatist structure of trade unions, allowing for autonomy from the State.

Apart from the obvious message from wage workers that they would no longer tolerate low pay and repression, the significance of labour militancy in the late 1970s goes further. It marked the beginning of the end of the military government.

Summary

The urban working class has played an important role in Brazil's industrial development, which can be summarized as follows:

- Labour activism goes back to the beginning of the century when ideas imported by European migrants were influential.

- This activism was diffused and 'harnessed' by the populist politics of Getulio Vargas.

- After 1964, the military suppressed any political voice from the trade unions and consciously exerted a downward pressure on industrial wages.

- The waves of strikes in the late 1970s heralded the birth of a new trade union movement based in private sector industry. It was also the start of a new political party of the left in Brazil.

3.6 From military to civilian rule and deepening economic crisis (1980s)

A combination of political turbulence and macroeconomic crisis brought on by debt and inflation dominated the 1980s, particularly from the middle of the decade onwards. In order to understand the difficulties faced by the industrial sector, it is essential to know about the political context of this decade. First we will examine the events surrounding the end of military rule and the subsequent civilian government. Then we will look at the industrial situation in the late 1980s. At this time, internal political and economic crisis, combined with changed international circumstances, militated against a repeat of the kind of growth witnessed during the 'miracle' years.

While some newly industrializing countries such as South Korea (see next chapter) were able to gain industrial strength during the 1980s, Brazil was not so successful. Short-term considerations such as inflation and debt certainly played their part. But the 1980s was a decade in which longerterm structural difficulties of Brazilian industry came into clear view.

The end of military government

Popular discontent in the late 1970s both in the form of labour unrest and strikes (as we saw in the last section) and through mass demonstrations demanding an 'amnesty' for all political prisoners and exiles marked the last breath of the economic miracle and the beginning of the end of the military government.

As thousands of Brazilians began to return from exile, the new government of General Figueiredo was being pushed towards democratization, or *abertura* (opening), of the country. The military were not going to give up power easily. Social unrest and strikes continued into the 1980s and the army continued to subdue them with characteristic force and violence.

At the turn of the decade, nonetheless, the military allowed the formation of five new political parties. Despite allegations that the military were merely trying to divide the opposition, the elections for state governors in 1982 returned opposition majorities in Brazil's three richest states: São Paulo, Minas Gerais and Rio de Janeiro.

Slowly but surely, Brazil was becoming a more open society. Press censorship was lifted. Critical theatre and music was again staged openly. New independent newspapers and magazines could be found on the newstands. Perhaps most significantly, ordinary people began to lose their fear of speaking up openly and critically about their rulers and bosses, an act which in previous years would have meant persecution, imprisonment or death.

In this political sea-change which the military could barely control, the economy was going from bad to worse. Inflation, which in 1979 was already 40% per year, rose to 220% by 1985. In 1983, the price of milk rose 152%, meat rose by 225%, soya oil rose by 374% and beans rose by 574%. In fact, between 1980 and 1988 the average annual inflation was 188%. As one observer put it: 'the cooking pots of the poor remained empty and the refrigerators of the middle classes were no longer so full' (Ribeiro *et al.*, 1991). In desperation and frustration, citizens took to sacking shops and supermarkets.

The response of industrialists to the growing economic crisis was to invest in financial markets. Speculation was more profitable than production. As a result GNP per capita fell by 13% between 1980 and 1983, industrial production stagnated, industrial unemployment grew by 13% and real wages fell by 25.5%. In 1984, Brazil's external debt had reached US$100 billion. The threat of debt default in 1982 following Mexico's lead (see Chapter 2) forced the IMF to reschedule Brazil's debt, that is, to concede more lending in order that the Brazilian government could pay interest on previous borrowing.

By the end of 1985 and at the end of his term of office, Figueiredo could not conceal his relief at standing down. His parting comment to the Brazilian people was, "I want you to forget me".

Civilian government and the neglect of human development

With the last of the Generals leaving government, Brazilians began a hugely popular campaign for direct presidential elections (*diretas já*). In an unprecedented show of public support, a million people took to the streets of São Paulo and Rio de Janeiro one day in April 1984. Despite such demonstrations, the country's first civilian president in 21 years, Tancredo Neves, was chosen by the government's 'electoral college'. Tancredo was a popular choice under the circumstances and so his untimely death before taking office was a blow to the nation.

Automatically, the Vice-President, José Sarnay, took office. Sarnay was a member of the military party (PDS) and was chosen as Vice-President as a political compromise on the part of opposition parties. He was a reluctant leader and during his term of office never gained strong support. Nevertheless, the economic situation of the country demanded some form of action.

Figure 3.13   President Sarnay — biting off more than be could chew.

Attempts to control inflation

Sarnay's most significant move as president was his government's attempt to control inflation. In February 1986 he launched the Cruzado Plan (also known as the Inflation Zero Plan). Overnight, all prices and wages were frozen. Automatically, inflation was reduced to zero and the national currency, *cruzeiros*, was devalued by 1 000%. Prices of all consumer goods were published in the press and the public were urged to report anyone exceeding these prices. With glee, consumers made 'citizens arrests' of supermarket owners who were overcharging. For a while, this 'heterodox' shock to the economy worked, but not for long. Supplies of goods began to dry up as suppliers could no longer maintain profit margins. Ranchers drove their cattle over the border to Paraguay where prices for beef were higher. Intermediate goods producers refused to supply end producers. Towards the end of the year the economy began to grind to a halt as the business community blocked the success of the plan. Inflation indices began first to creep up and then, out of control again, shot up.

Trying to control the economy (debt and inflation) was an important aspect of government policy in the 1980s. But some commentators were sceptical. First, there were few successes. Second, the fight against inflation was also a mask behind which other pressing social problems could be hidden such as agrarian reform and income distribution. This becomes quite apparent if we examine Brazil's record of social development. Brazil failed to achieve satisfactory human development despite high incomes, rapid growth and substantial government spending on the social sectors.

Neglect of human development

Brazil had a per capita GNP of $2 020 in 1987. Except for 1980–87, when its per capita GDP grew at just over 1% a year, Brazil's growth has been quite high, with average annual growth of GDP per capita hovering around 3% in the 1950s and 1960s and rising to 6.4% in the 1970s.

Despite relatively high GNP per capita growth rates, Brazil's human development record has been far from impressive. According to the United Nations (UNDP, 1990), the under-five mortality rate was still 85 per 1 000 in 1988, almost twice Sri Lanka's and only slightly lower than Burma's, countries with per capita incomes amounting, respectively, to a fifth and a tenth of Brazil's. Life expectancy was 65 years in 1987, and the male and female literacy rates respectively were 79% and 76% in 1985.

These national averages hide significant regional differences. In the poorer North East, for example, infant mortality rates were more than twice those in the rest of Brazil in 1986 (116 compared with 52), life expectancy at birth in 1978 was only 49 years compared with 64 in the rest of Brazil, and child malnutrition was twice the national average.

There are two important reasons for such poor human development in Brazil. One is the extreme inequality of income distribution. The other is the inefficient targeting of public resources. The distribution of income in Brazil, as shown in Box 3.2, is among the worst in the world.

As indicated earlier, well structured policies can compensate for a poor distribution of income and

Figure 3.14   Poverty and wealth in Rio de Janeiro — homeless camp outside the Brazil's state bank.

improve the human condition. This has not happened in Brazil because public resources did not reach the poor or improve the basic dimensions of human development. Substantial public subsidies were provided for 'private' goods, usually consumed by the better-off sections of society, while 'public' goods and services likely to have the widest impact on human welfare are neglected.

In health, preventive programmes such as immunization, prenatal care and vector-borne disease control are estimated to be about five times more cost-effective than curative programmes in reducing mortality. But an estimated 78% of all public spending on health goes to largely curative, high-cost hospital care, mainly in urban areas and especially in the urban South. This is in sharp contrast with the 87% of public health expenditure that Brazil allocated to preventive care in 1949, a share that fell steadily to 41% in 1961 and to a low of 15% in 1982 before rising to 22% in 1986.

Inequalities in education

More than a quarter of all public spending on education went to higher education in 1983, and only half to primary education. Total public spending per student in higher education, where the benefits accrue overwhelmingly to higher-income groups, was about 18 times that in secondary and primary education. Of all children in Brazil, 13% come from households receiving less than one legal minimum wage, but they account

for only 1% of higher education enrolment. Children from households earning more than ten times the minimum wage account for 48% of the enrolment but constitute only 11% of all children in the country. That is not the only inequity in the system. Spending per pupil is lower in municipal than in state schools, lower in rural than in urban schools and lower in schools in the North East than elsewhere (UNDP, 1990).

Industry in the 1980s

Given the combination of big political changes which occurred in the course of the 1980s and a macroeconomic crisis of debt and inflation, it might be expected that industry would suffer.

According to Wilson Suzigan (1989), Brazilian industry in the 1980s had reached a turning point. In a state of crisis, it was not clear whether it could weather the storm or not. Industry had the following characteristics.

- First, the structure of industry had been diversifying, trying to follow the pattern found in the advanced capitalist countries (look back to Table 3.2). Pursuing this objective, however, through high and permanent protectionism, resulted in some industries remaining inefficient. This, in turn, prejudiced international competitiveness. There is also a wide divergence between sectors in terms of 'modernity', capabilities, competitiveness, etc.

- Second, a reduction in industrial investment in the 1980s (both public and private) was the principle obstacle to industrial growth. This was due to uncertainty over macro-economic policies and inflation with the latter encouraging speculative financial investment rather than productive investment.

This pattern of growth and investment has accentuated technological heterogeneity both in equipment and technological capacity. In general terms, industry was technologically backward by international standards, particularly in nationally owned private firms. This resulted in low productivity and low product quality. Sectors such as aircraft and steel, which are

Figure 3.15   I've no change'.

technologically advanced and internationally competitive coexist with others, such as textiles, that are 15–20 years out of date.

Where Brazilian industry is internationally competitive, this is still based on a combination of low wages and fiscal policy rather than

---

Box 3.10   A success story against the odds: the computer industry

One of the most controversial aspects of industrial development in Brazil in recent years is the case of the computer industry. Controversy in industry usually revolves around the negative aspects: poor working conditions, low wages, environmental damage and so on. In the case of the computer industry, the controversy was centred on the notion that Brazil could not (should not) enter a high-tech industry from scratch and expect to survive.

The start of the industry was the creation of a 'reserved market' for Brazilian-owned firms in the mid 1970s. That is, only firms which were 100% Brazilian-owned could produce in certain areas of the computer market (essentially small and medium sized computers and their peripherals).

Until the late 1970s, Brazil's computer industry was in the hands of foreign firms which either imported finished products or carried out the final assembly of goods locally. By the mid 1980s, this situation had changed almost out of all recognition. The number of firms operating in the nationally-owned computer and peripherals market increased 4 in 1977 to 310 in 1986. Employment in these firms grew from just 4 000 in 1979 to over 40 000 in 1986. The computer industry was responsible for 40% of the US$8 billion total sales of electronics equipment in Brazil in 1986. This represents the largest electronics market segment in Brazil, superseding that of consumer electronics and telecommunications. Within computer production, it is the national firms which have undergone the fastest growth in output; 300% between 1981 and 1986. Indeed, by 1986, national firms had passed a watershed by attaining 51% of the total computer market.

The reserved market was the 'infant industry' argument with an added twist. In the auto industry, foreign firms such as Ford and Volkswagen were the main import substituting agents. But in the computer industry Brazilian firms (and consumers) were sealed off from outside competition and products. In this unusual situation, a number of advantages accrued in the space of only a decade:

1   There was a huge increase in electronics-related skills and know-how, reflected in the research and development (R&D) intensity of firms relative to their locally based foreign counterparts and in the rapidly growing number of engineering and technical jobs.

2   Some firms, particularly those linked to national banks, were able to become innovative in specialized markets such as bank automation equipment.

3   There was a remarkable increase in the bargaining power of national firms. They were able to bargain from a position of strength with foreign corporations who were willing to transfer technology on terms which had previously been refused.

4   There were rapid 'externalities'; that is, a large number of supplier firms sprung up to produce intermediate inputs for the industry.

The reserved market was not an unmitigated success. Amongst its limitations we may include:

* Compared to international standards, users were forced to use lower quality products although this did not always imply a lack of competitiveness.

* Product prices were higher than international standards although the trend in local prices was always downwards.

* There was an undue emphasis on the producer sector and not enough to the users.

Optimism for the future of the industry is marred not so much by the strategy adopted or the performance of the industry itself but by the environment in which it operated through the 1980s — specifically, the lack of overall industrial strategy into which the computer industry could be plugged and, second, the general economic crisis of the Brazilian economy.

on productivity gains, quality improvements and technological improvement (but see Box 3.10). For example a productivity increase of 14% between 1980 and 1987 in São Paulo industry compares poorly to increases of 70.5% (in Japan) and 34% (in the USA and West Germany) in the same period.

What is of interest to us is that the most recent changes in Brazilian industry, changes which were still taking place at the beginning of the 1990s, are a clear reflection of the combination of internal political forces and their impact on economic and industrial policy and changes in the international economy.

The result has been a rapid and widespread enforcement of market-led reforms which, if carried through, represent a dismantling of the protectionist measures of the preceding decades and are in line with the internationally prevailing market ideology of neo-liberalism.

In reality things are not that simple. The industrial policy priority in the 1990s is how to pull Brazil out of the crisis which it has been facing for the last decade. Part of this is to solve the economic difficulties of debt and inflation. In addition, however, decades of import substitution policies at a time where technological capabilities are, increasingly, defining a country's international competitiveness have their own price. As one observer puts it:

> "... countries such as Brazil, in which the behaviour of economic agents and the practice of industrial policy is rooted in decades of experience with import substitution industrialization, face particular problems in adapting to the requirements of restructuring their economies on the basis of exploiting new technologies"
>
> (Carvalho, 1990)

Given the vested interests in import substitution this is no easy task.

> "Brazil has grown into an industrial power largely because of four decades of protectionism, state support of local industry and import substitution. Protection had created a politically powerful constituency that opposes liberalization. The nationalists say that Brazilian capitalism would not survive if it had to compete, unprotected, with unshackled transnationals."
>
> (cited in Gwynne, 1990)

Figure 3.16   Democracy'.

Summary

The 1980s, as for many economies, was a difficult decade for Brazil. Political transition from dictatorship to democracy combined with economic crisis internally and big changes in the international economic climate. While other late industrializers such as South Korea and Taiwan may have been able to weather the storm, Brazil stumbled from one crisis to another. Debt and inflation on a scale never imagined before rocked the economy. This section has argued that:

- *Politically* there was a transition from an intolerant military government which had maintained power for 21 years to a more democratic but fragile civilian government which took office in 1985. This raised hopes (for a better life) and also expectations that a civilian government could deliver. After so long in the wings, democracy was a little rusty. Not only was the newly formed government having to steer its way through severe economic crisis of debt and inflation, it was also in search of a political identity.

- *Socially*, the combined effects of years of neglect of social welfare, of inflation and of cuts in government expenditure in basic services made life even harder for Brazil's poor.

- *Economically*, the 1980s were dominated by short-term crisis management of spiralling debt and inflation. As a result, the real economic growth area was in financial speculation.

- *Industrially*, a declining share of industrial output was one indication that industrialization would not continue at the pace it did during the military years. Given the state of the economy, it was difficult to consolidate the economic gains made in the previous decades. However, short-term crisis management (devaluations, price and wage freezes, etc.) concealed a structural weakness of Brazil's industrial base; it could no longer rely on import substitution as an engine for industrial growth.

The crisis of the 1980s was seen by many not as a short-term problem but as a crisis of a development model which could no longer be sustained. Entrenched vested interests in the state (landowners, the military, business and finance) and of many Brazilian industrialists (who had benefited from the years of protection from foreign competition) hung on tenaciously to their positions. This ensured that the model of import substitution was a difficult one to break. But effectively in the 1980s there was no coherent industrial policy to keep Brazil's industrial machine going.

3.7 Conclusions

Let us return to the questions posed at the beginning of this chapter.

The conditions that allowed Brazil's industrialization

Brazil's industrialization, by historical standards (that is, compared with Europe and the USA) has been rapid. Nevertheless, it was many years before the phase of rapid industrial growth that the conditions for it were set. By the end of the 19th century, there was considerable accumulation of wealth from coffee production which provided the basis for industrial expansion in São Paulo. Industrialization was 'forced' during the First World War, when the international trade in consumer goods was halted.

After this, the picture became much more complex. There was a purposeful drive to industrialize, based on state encouragement and state ownership of industry. Industrialization was as much a political decision as an economic imperative. The type of industrialization, based on the substitution of imports, was very much in line with the structuralist view of development which was prevalent in the post-war period. The structuralist perspective is taken up in detail in Chapter 5.

Despite Brazil's inward-looking industrial strategy, international conditions have been crucial at all stages of the country's industrial development. The period immediately after the Second World War was a time of expanding North American overseas investment. U.S. multinationals were very willing to invest production facilities in Brazil behind protective barriers in order to gain access to a large and expanding domestic market. The Brazilian government encouraged such direct foreign investment, particularly in the so-called 'modern' industries such as autos, chemicals and engineering.

By the time the military came to power in 1964, there was, therefore, a substantial industrial base. Without this, the 'economic miracle' could not have occurred. But it seems that the miracle also sowed the seeds of the subsequent and growing economic crisis.

Opportunities and barriers for late industrialization

Brazil's industries have relied on technologies 'borrowed' from the OECD countries. As such, it can be viewed as a 'late industrializer' (as defined in Box 3.1). This has had both advantages and disadvantages. Brazil has not been the economic success story of Japan or even South Korea (see Chapter 4) and yet it has exploited some of the advantages of later industrialization.

There is a commonplace notion that infant industries do not grow up. In other words, protecting industry from international competition produces inefficiency which is eventually passed on to consumers in the form of higher prices. This is the view attributable to neo-liberal thinking (see Chapter 5).

The key question here is whether Brazilian industry has been able to learn how to use borrowed technology and, thereby, build up a competitive industrial base. The issue of technological learning is taken up in detail in Chapter 7, but we can point to a few instances from the Brazilian experience. Perhaps the most impressive is the way that Brazil has built up a highly diversified industrial base encompassing most branches of industry and relatively self-sustaining in that it can produce consumer, intermediate and capital goods. This has been achieved in industry owned by foreign capital (e.g. the car industry), to some extent in industry owned by local private capital (e.g. the computer industry and some parts of engineering) and in state-owned industry (such as steel and petrochemicals).

However, it appears that the learning has been limited too, for two reasons. Firstly, international standards of products and processes have advanced at an accelerated rate in the last two decades. Secondly, it appears that under this new international regime of competitiveness, Brazilian import substituting industries are having trouble competing in international markets.

Did import substitution help in the long term?

This leads to the final question of whether import substitution industrialization in developing countries has been a help or a hindrance in building up a competitive industrial base. The evidence from Brazil seems to give contradictory signals.

First, the historical development of industry shows that it took active intervention on the part of the state (protection of locally based industry, direct involvement in production, etc.) to develop industry at such a fast rate.

Second, the crisis of the 1980s was partly based on the inability of industry in general to be internationally competitive (as indicated by its export record). In other words, the big push to industrialize appears to have produced a fragile industrial structure which is not yet capable or mature enough to be internationally competitive. Only time will tell if this will change.

Part of the answer lies in the competing and often contradictory views about industrial development. Since the Second World War, Brazil has been caught between nationalism and internationalism (both politically and economically). Nationalists have vigorously pursued policies of import substitution industrialization, based on notions of national sovereignty and national capability. Internationalists, by contrast, have always pushed to make the Brazilian economy more open to unrestricted foreign investment and free trade.

It is this tension between these two currents of thought which has produced Brazil's particular model of development. Although easy to state with hindsight, the Brazilian economy has probably suffered from lack of consistency in the area of industrial policy. This became most apparent in the 1980s when there was a complete absence of any coherent industrial policy in the country.

Summary of Chapter 3

Brazil has succeeded in building a large industrial base, but at the cost of soaring inflation, huge foreign debts and poverty for the majority of the population.

Brazil's industrial development started in the late 19th century, on the back of colonization by Europe and trade in coffee. European immigrants became the industrial labour force and founded the labour movement. The Second World War forced further independent development of Brazilian industry, because imports were unavailable.

After the Second World War, the economy was opened up to US imports. But the economic effects of this led the Brazilian government to reintroduce protectionist measures. In the 1950s, they opted for a mixed strategy of State investment in infrastructure, import controls and foreign investment in industry. The strategy led to rapid industrial growth, but with continuing balance of payments problems. Polarization over economic policy led to a military coup in 1964.

The 1960s saw a deep economic recession. But this was followed by five years of spectacular industrial growth, based on foreign capital combined with State control. However, in 1974 this came to an end as higher oil prices, massive imports and accumulating foreign debt plunged the economy into crisis again.

Throughout the 1960s there was increasing persecution of the trade union movement and wages were forced down. However, opposition to the government rallied in the 1970s and began to demand political change.

In the 1980s, the military government faced growing opposition as debt and inflation spiralled. In 1985 a civilian government took over raising hopes for improved living standards. But social inequalities continued into the 1990s, and Brazil's industrial base was not strong enough to lift the country out of its economic difficulties.

4

INDUSTRIALIZATION IN SOUTH KOREA

CHRIS EDWARDS

4.1 The South Korean 'miracle'

The previous chapter looked at industrialization in Brazil. In this chapter we shift to the other side of the world to tell quite a different story, the story of South Korea. In tales of industrialization and development, South Korea is often lumped with Brazil, along with a handful of other less developed countries with high industrialization rates. One key reason for considering Brazil and South Korea together has been their growth as 'late industrializers'. But Brazil and South Korea have very different stories.

Firstly, South Korea's record of industrial and economic growth has been outstanding since the 1960s, even compared to that of Brazil. Since 1950, South Korea's growth rates for total output have been more than twice as fast as that of all LDCs, and for manufacturing output about three times as fast (see Figure 4.1).

Secondly, South Korea's spectacular growth record has been backed up by a considerable improvement in living standards. South Korea's average per capita income in 1988 of US$3 600 was less than a fifth of that in the USA. But on average, a South Korean born in 1960 could expect to live to the age of 53 whereas one born in 1988 could expect to live to 70, only six years less than in the USA. Almost all South Korean children go through elementary school. Over a third

of South Koreans of the relevant age group receive some higher education compared with 60% in the USA and only 22% in the UK. Furthermore income distribution in South Korea is more equal than that in most LDCs. Thus not only has South Korea grown fast, but it has also achieved an impressive improvement in 'social indicators'.

Thirdly, South Korea moved towards an export-oriented industrialization strategy in the 1960s. This was relatively early in comparison with Brazil, which did not do so until the 1970s.

This chapter focuses on South Korea, with the following question in mind:

> **Q** Why has the industrialization process in South Korea been so rapid, and what industrialization strategies were used?

To isolate significant reasons for this process requires an understanding of the history of South Korean industrialization. One lesson you learned from the story of Brazil is that industrialization does not happen overnight. Even 'rapid' and 'late' industrialization is a relatively long process. In South Korea's case, it stretches over at least the whole of the twentieth century. So we need to look at strategies for industrialization over the whole of this time. There has been a series of profound structural transformations in South Korean society this century. We shall look at these over four periods.

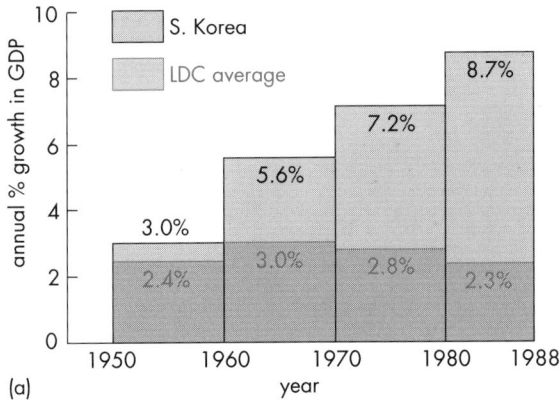

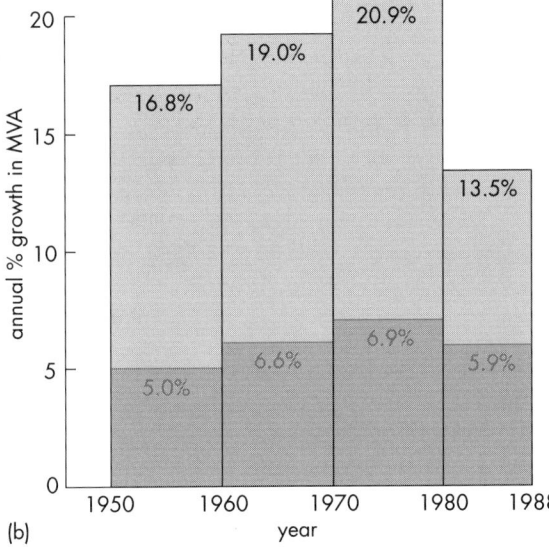

Figure 4.1   *Growth in South Korea compared to other LDCs [Sources: Van Liemt, 1988; World Bank, 1990].*

(a) *Colonialism (1910–45):* Many people know that large parts of Africa were colonized by Britain and France from the 1880s to the 1960s, that Britain colonized most of South Asia and that much earlier Spain and Portugal divided Latin America between them. Fewer people know that Korea was colonized by Japan for the first half of the twentieth century.

(b) *The Korean War and its legacy (1945–60):* You will probably have heard of the Korean War. But do you know why the war began and why Korea is divided, or what happened afterwards and how that influenced South Korea's industrialization and growth?

(c) *The economic miracle (1961–79):* How did rapid export-oriented industrialization and economic growth emerge and continue? To answer this we need to look at and assess some of the reasons put forward to explain the 'economic miracle'.

(d) *Riding the storm (the 1980s):* Unlike Brazil and many other less developed countries, South Korea's growth hiccup at the beginning of the 1980s was soon shaken off and the country continued its high growth trajectory.

South Korea's outstanding growth record has been achieved in the face of what might seem to be considerable odds. South Korea is a relatively small country in terms of area (99 000 square kilometres) with one of the highest population densities in the world, at just over 400 per square kilometre; considerably greater than the UK's 233, although less than Bangladesh's 756. But, unlike Bangladesh, South Korea is mostly

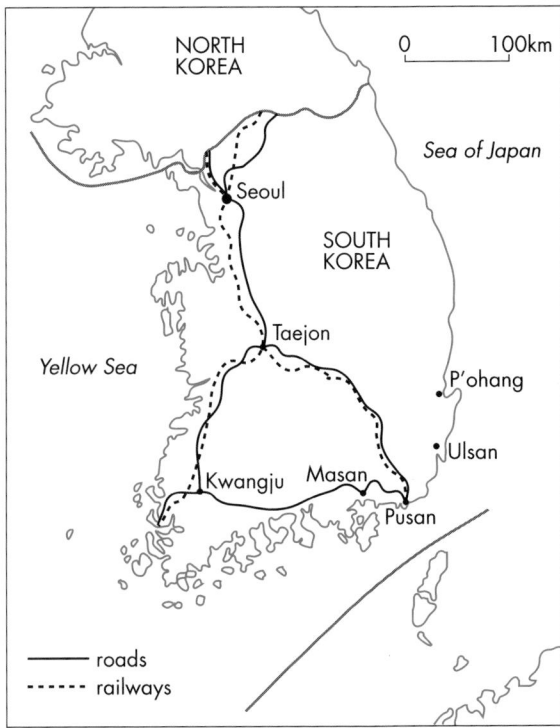

Figure 4.2   *South Korea.*

mountainous with less than a quarter of the land suitable for cultivation. The odds would also seem to have been stacked against South Korea inasmuch as it has few mineral reserves.

In 1954, these odds seemed insurmountable. The Korean War had ended the previous year, leaving both South and North Korea devastated. Well over a million South Koreans had been killed in the war, and more than half of manufacturing capacity, the rail network and electricity generating capacity had been destroyed. The average annual income of the 22 million people in the South was less than US$100, and housing conditions were miserable. And yet, by the end of the 1980s, the average income of the 43 million South Koreans was about US$4 000. Even after allowing for the increased cost of living over these four decades, the average income at the end of the 1980s was at least eight times what it had been in the early 1950s.

Given this record, it is not surprising that South Korea has been widely labelled as an economic 'success' story. Nor is it surprising that many economists have tried to use this successful case of late industrialization as a development model to be copied by other less developed countries. However, there are at least two major and opposed views about why South Korea is a 'development model'. In the introduction to this book there is a brief outline of two ways of industrializing; import substitution and export orientation. South Korea is an excellent example for us to examine, because there is great controversy about why it has been such a successful industrializer. The view of the South Korean economy from the political right is that its outstanding success has been

---

Box 4.1   Some reference facts on South Korea

Population (1988):   42.01m

Area: 99 000 km²

Age structure of population (1988):

0–14 years	27.3%
15–64 years	67.9%

GNP per capita: US$3 600

Average annual growth of GNP per capita (1965–88):   6.8%

Average annual rate of inflation

| 1965–80 | 18.7%, |
| 1980–88 | 5.0% |

Life expectancy at birth :   70

Distribution of GDP (%):

	1965	1988
Agriculture	38%	11%
Industry	25%	43%
(of which manufacturing	18%	32)%
Services	37%	46%

Total external debt : US$37 156 million

Total debt service (interest payments):
4.8% of GDP, 11.5% of exports

Urban population:

	1960	1965	1980	1988
urban population as % of South Korean total		32		69
% in cities over 500 000	61		77	

South Korea is divided administratively into nine provinces and the two special cities of Seoul (the capital) and Pusan. In 1985, Seoul, which is only 35 km from the frontier with North Korea, contained more than a quarter of the total population while about 8–9% lived in Pusan.

Conscription: One legacy of the Korean War (1950–53) is that there is still conscription. All young men have to do military training for three years and thereafter for 50–80 hours a year until the age of 35.

Language: Korean, based on an alphabet of 28 letters.

Climate: Continental, with extremes of temperature; very hot (average daily maximum of 31°C) in August and very cold (average daily minimum of -9°C) in January.

Currency: The *won*. Approximate average exchange rates in 1988 were W1 100 (1 100 won) to the pound and W671 to the US dollar.

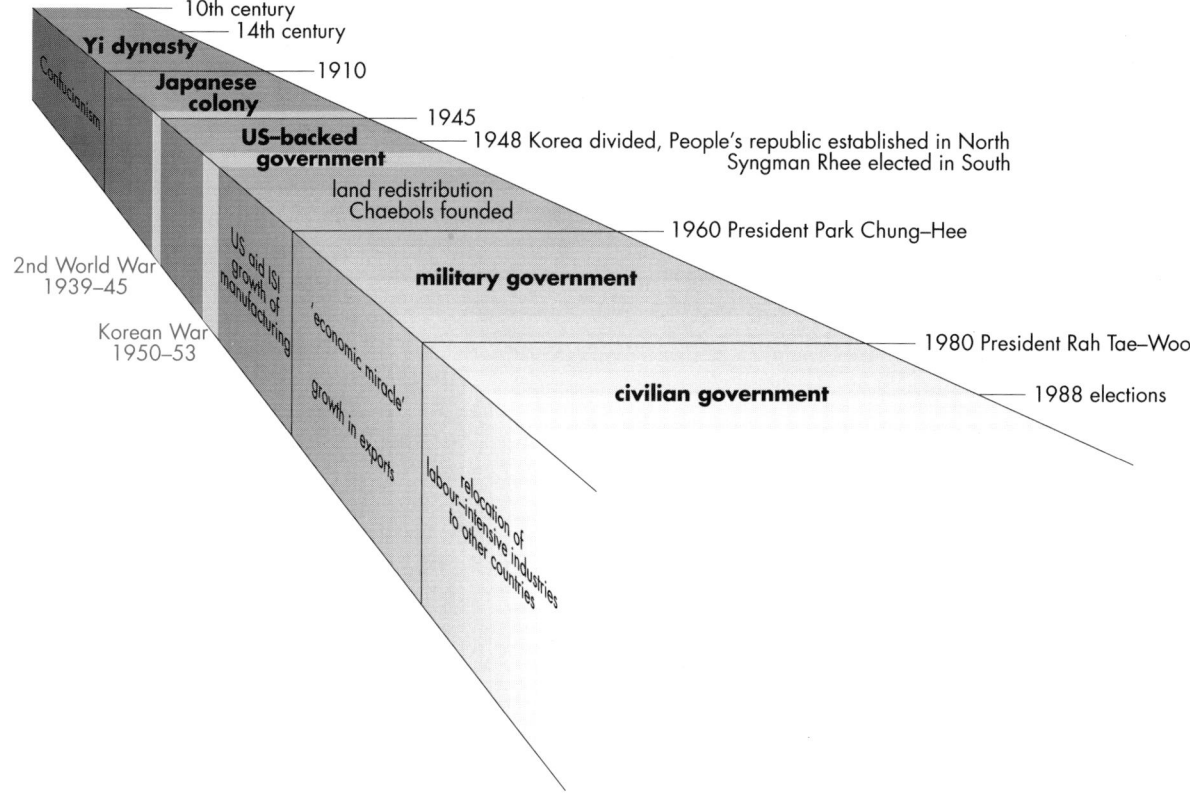

Figure 4.3   Reference dates in Korean history.

associated with low levels of government intervention and with export orientation in South Korean industry. A second view from the political centre and left argues that South Korea has been successful as a late industrializer as a result of strong direction from the state. This has involved the direct promotion of exports, linked with import substitution.

4.2 Japanese colonialism (1910–45)

In understanding the development of Korea (North as well as South), it is important to understand the role of Japanese colonialism. The Korean experience of Japanese colonialism was a brutal one, so that even now, over 45 years later, there is widespread resentment of the Japanese by the Koreans. But at the same time, South Korea has strong trading and technology links with Japan. In 1988, 31% of South Korea's imports came from Japan, while Japan accounted for 20% of South Korea's exports. There is also a strong desire to copy the Japanese. So South Korea could be said to have a 'hate/emulate' relationship with the Japanese.

However, as we shall see, there is a more important, structural reason for looking in some detail at Japanese colonialism. The period of Japanese rule had a considerable impact on the economic and political structure and on the industrial development of South Korea. Indeed, the South Korean case provides an excellent example of how changes in economic policies and conditions interact with changes in political processes. Neither can be understood on its own.

The overthrow of the Yi dynasty by the Japanese

Formally, Japanese colonial rule dates from 1910, but Japan had forced Korea to open its doors to foreign trade in 1876. At the time of the Japanese occupation in 1910, Korea was overwhelmingly an agricultural country. Over four-fifths of all households were dependent for most of their livelihood on agriculture or forestry. It was also a poor and stagnant society. The Yi dynasty had survived since the 14th century. But, particularly from the 19th century onwards, it was a society characterized by rural destitution, coupled with corruption and nepotism in the cities.

The concept of private land ownership was not well established. Legally, all ownership of land was vested in the royal household, which allocated it as favours to nobles and officials. Absentee landlordism was rife and at the end of the 19th century about three-quarters of the rural population were full or part tenants. Control was exercised through a monarchical and hierarchical social system. Power was maintained through land and inheritance rights, and

---

Box 4.2 Confucianism

Confucianism is a Western term which has no direct counterpart in Chinese. The term comes from Confucius, the Latinized form of *K'ung-fu-tzu* or Master Kung, a Chinese scholar who lived between 551 and 479 BC, about 2500 years ago.

Confucianism is sometimes viewed as a religion but it is more accurately understood as a philosophy, social ethic and political ideology. It exists alongside the organized religions such as Islam, Christianity, Shintoism, Taoism and Buddhism. It spread to all East Asian countries with the in fluence of Chinese culture, but nowhere was it more powerful than in the Yi dynasty in Korea. From the 15th century the Yi aristocracy (*yangban*) defined itself as the carrier of Confucian values, and the penetration of court politics by Confucianism was unprecedented.

The ancestors of Confucius (who was born in what is now Shandong Province in eastern China) were probably members of the aristocracy who had fallen on hard times. Confucius aimed to redefine and revitalize those feudal traditions and institutions that for centuries were believed to have maintained social solidarity under the Zhou (or Chou) dynasty in China which had ruled for the five centuries before Confucius's birth, but which had disintegrated by 551 BC.

Confucius's ideas were developed by his followers, the most notable of whom was Mencius (371–289 BC), who argued that a class of scholar officials not involved in agriculture, industry and commerce was essential to the wellbeing of the state, and that a ruler who does not act in a kingly (moral) way is not fit to rule. Confucian ideas are embodied in a number of scriptures, the most revered of which is the Lun-yu, a collection of Master Kung's thoughts.

But what is the essence of Confucianism? Brie fly, it is a belief in the continuity of authority and hierarchy from the household family up to the emperor, the 'son of heaven'. The family metaphor is extended from the household, to the community, to the court, to the country. Thus rulers derive their power from tradition, as head of a 'social family'. But they receive their 'mandate from heaven' only as long as they govern by moral leadership and exemplary teaching. The system is one of mutual dependence with a heavy emphasis on the scholarly tradition.

Thus Confucianism is seen by its critics as embodying authoritarianism, nepotism, conservatism, and male chauvinism. It is also criticized for its emphasis on 'empty' scholarship and for its denigration of manual labour and industry. However, there are those who praise it for its emphasis on trust, loyalty, consensus and particularly for the high social status attributed to education and the bureaucracy. Perhaps it is not surprising that it has been seen as a positive as well as negative force in South Korean development.

Figure 4.4   Haeinsu Temple, built by the Koreans during the Yi dynasty.

through priveleges of state office (*Allen & Thomas, 1992*, Ch. 6). Confucian orthodoxy was used to justify the hierarchical structure. Such a system provided a sort of stability but it was an obstacle to the mobilization of resources for defence and industrial development.

Thus Korea under the Yi dynasty was economically weak. The result of this weakness was that Korea was subjected to pressures from outside powers, in particular from Japan and the Ming dynasty in China. Japan and China competed for control of Korea, but after Japan's victory in the 1905 war with Russia, Japan emerged with undisputed supremacy in the Far East, including Korea. In December 1905, Korea became a protectorate of Japan, and five years later, Japan had completed the colonial annexation of Korea and the elimination of the Yi dynasty. With the onset of Japanese colonialism, large numbers of Koreans fled to Manchuria, Shanghai and Hawaii. The Japanese were to be the colonial masters of Korea for the next 35 years.

The impact of Japanese colonialism

What, briefly, was the impact on Korea of Japanese colonialism? 'In all cases of conquests',

Karl Marx had said; 'three things are possible. ... The conquering people subjugates the conquered under its own mode of production ... or it leaves the old mode intact and contents itself with tribute ... or a reciprocal interaction takes place whereby something new, a synthesis arises ...'. (Marx, 1973).

In the case of Korea, the impact is best described as mixed, as a synthesis. The early accounts of Japanese colonialism, written before 1920, were highly favourable. Then, in the 1930s, as Japan engulfed Korea in its war efforts, Japanese colonialism tended to be 'swathed in the blackest of colours' (Amsden 1989). More recently, since the 1960s, as the Korean economy has grown rapidly, the colonial period has been depicted (at least in English-language writings) as a 'modernizing' force. Thus the recent judgement tends to be that Japanese colonialism in Korea created some conditions conducive to development.

Impoverishing influence
On the one hand, Korea under the Japanese has been described as 'a well-regulated penal colony' (Hamilton 1986). Koreans were deprived of freedom of assembly, freedom of association and freedom of the press. The colonial authorities

excluded such subjects as the language and history of Korea in the schools. The Japanese took over much of the land, as much as half, according to Kuznets (1977), if government property is included. By 1913, about 40% of all farm households were pure tenants and about 80% were tenants or part-tenants. By the mid-twenties, it was estimated that the large majority of these tenants were living below subsistence level and, as many of these failed to pay their taxes, so their land fell into the hands of the colonial government. Huge numbers were driven off the land and many of these emigrated (Cumings, 1981 and Kuznets, 1977).

Japanese landlordism was not particularly good at creating a surplus in agriculture, but it was efficient at extracting the surplus created. Rents continued to be set at 50% of the crop but could be as high as 90% in the fertile rice fields of the south. Most of the rice collected as taxes was exported, so that, by the early 1930s, rice exports accounted for over two-fifths of the annual Korean output. In addition, the government took a substantial proportion of agricultural incomes as taxes. Thus while agricultural output in Chosen (the imperial name for Korea) rose by 74% between 1910 and 1940, there was a decline in per capita rice consumption.

Alongside the pauperization of the rural economy, there was extensive urban poverty, as real wages of urban workers fell by as much as a third between 1910 and 1940. The colonial administration restricted the development of indigenous capital, and, according to Joungwon Kim, the Japanese held a 'virtual monopoly in every area of the economy' (Kim, 1975).

Thus, in many respects, Japanese colonialism had an impoverishing, regressive aspect. Nevertheless there have been some 'modernizing aspects' to Japanese colonialism.

Modernizing influence

The monarchy was abolished, agriculture was commercialized, exchange was broadened (see *Allen & Thomas, 1992*, Ch. 1) and private ownership of land established. Although agricultural output grew only as fast as the rate of population growth, industrial output grew more rapidly.

This was particularly true in the 1930s as the Japanese war machine expanded with its invasion of Manchuria (1931) and its southward expansion into the rest of China (1937). Koreans were forced from the land to work in Japanese-owned factories, and by the end of the 1930s manufacturing accounted for 29% of total output, a figure which 'was high even for an advanced country' (Hamilton, 1986). Most of this growth of industry, particularly heavy industry, was in what is now North Korea. But grain processing, textiles and some machinery developed in the more densely-populated south.

With industrialization came urbanization. When the Japanese took colonial control, Seoul had a population of less than 200 000; by the end of Japanese colonialism, it had a population of over a million. With the industrial development in Korea being closely linked with Japan, trade expanded so that, by the end of the 1930s, the Korean economy was an extremely 'open' one, where over 50% of its output was traded.

Figure 4.5   Growth of Seoul; the city in 1910 (above) and in the 1980s (below).

Figure 4.6   The Korean army of independence taking an oath before going into battle against the Japanese.

Korean nationalism

Korean nationalism also grew over the period. Korea has a long established national identity and culture. It has had a separate identity for well over 2 000 years. It has a common language with its own alphabet. There are no large minority groups. Korea was a relatively small country among very large ones; China, Russia/Soviet Union, and even Japan. This strongly developed sense of nationalism was fed by the anti-Japan hatred of the colonial period.

Mixed legacy

Thus the legacy of Japanese colonialism was mixed. In spite of Korea being run by the Japan ese as a 'well regulated penal colony', it was under the Japanese that both industry and nationalism rapidly developed. The colonial period was one of industrialization, urbanization and expansion of foreign trade. Coming back to my question at the start of this section, Japanese colonialism was important for the development of social and economic processes (including industrialization); and political processes (as with the strengthening of national identity and national resistance to colonialism). Although the big push to industrialization came later, its foundations were laid in this earlier period.

4.3   The Korean War and its legacy (1945–60)

The period from the end of Japanese colonialism to 1960 was a period which witnessed the division of Korea into the communist North and the US-backed South. This was followed by the Korean war and the subsequent transformation and reconstruction of the Korean economy with massive US aid. It was also a period in which a radical land redistribution took place. These changes laid the material and political basis for the Korean 'miracle'; that is, for the rapid growth and development of South Korean industry through the 1960s and 1970s.

Japanese withdrawal, the division of Korea and the Korean War

The defeat of Japan in the Second World War brought the Japanese colonialism of Korea to an end. Korea was divided into administrative districts under US and Soviet occupation, but before the division in the immediate vacuum left by the Japanese withdrawal, popular organizations sprang up. In the South, People's Committees took control of their areas, disarmed the Japanese, released political prisoners, and punished collaborators. In the factories, trade union formation was rapid, the unions joining together to form the National Council of Korean Labour Unions which was to lead a General Strike in 1946. In the rural areas, plans were drawn up to redistribute land. A 'government' was formed under the title of the Korean People's Republic.

But the arrival of US forces a few weeks after the Japanese surrender brought a new government to South Korea. The United States Army Military Government in South Korea refused to recognize the People's Republic and instead established an administration staffed by Koreans who had served in the Japanese bureaucracy and police. Thousands of nationalist activists returned to Korea in the months immediately following liberation, some of them, like Syngman Rhee, fervently anti-communist. The US Army military government backed Rhee's National Society party and the small but wealthy Korean Democratic Party, described by Amsden as 'the most conservative political faction'. The US military government also backed a new trade union organization and control was wrested from the People's Committees, in the face of popular uprisings and the 1946 General Strike in which many were killed.

Figure 4.7   Inchon after expulsion of the North Korean army in 1950.

In 1948, following a period of martial law, elections were held for the Korean National Assembly, in which the Korean Democratic Party and the National Society gained two-thirds of the seats and Rhee was elected President. In the months that followed the elections, there was a purge of 'disloyal' elements in the army, police, press and educational establishments with an estimated 90 000 people being arrested in an eight-month period in 1948–49.

Meanwhile, in the north, the Soviet Union had recognized the People's Republic soon after liberation from the Japanese and radical reforms, including land reform, quickly followed. With the Soviet Union backing the faction in the North most amenable to their influence, and with the US government backing Rhee in the South, the stage was set for the Korean War, which started in 1950.

There is immense controversy about the specific causes of the Korean War. What is clear is that it was an international war, a product of the Cold War between East and West. A good starting point in reading more about the Korean War, is the book by Halliday & Cumings (1988). Here we are concentrating on the effects of the War on South Korea, and particularly on its industrial development. From this view-point, two outcomes of the Korean war period are important:

- a land redistribution which took place in South Korea before and after the war

- the massive increase in US aid to South Korea and the militarization of South Korean society.

Land redistribution

An extensive redistribution of land took place in South Korea before and after the Korean War. There was huge popular backing for land reform in South Korea after liberation from the Japanese, and this was to intensify following the example set in North Korea. A Land Reform bill was passed in 1949–50, but it was not implemented until after the end of the Korean War in 1953. By then many landlords had already diversified into industry and commerce, more land having been sold in anticipation of the reform than was redistributed through the reform. But while the land redistribution substantially reduced tenancy, it brought little change in the size of land-holdings actually operated by farm households. As a result, there was little disruption to agricultural production.

Table 4.1   US aid to South Korea, 1956–67

	Aid in US$ million	Aid as % of GNP
1956–58	270	15
1959–61	222	8
1962–64	199	6
1965–67	111	2

[Source: Hamilton, 1986]

The redistribution of land supported industrialization in two ways.

(i) The levelling of incomes and wealth in the countryside provided the possibility of 'squeezing' the agricultural sector through lower prices for agricultural output without causing famine. As we shall see in the next section, this is what happened in the 1960s.

(ii) The capital obtained by former landlords from land redistribution was re-invested in the manufacturing and commercial sectors of the economy.

US aid

US aid was also important in supporting industrialization. Bello claims that US 'Economic aid to South Korea totalled almost US$6 billion between 1945 and 1978, almost as much as the total aid provided to all African countries during the same period' (Bello, 1990). Even in the second half of the 1950s, some years after the end of the Korean War, US aid was still accounting for as much as 15% of South Korea's national income (see Table 4.1) and providing more than four-fifths of South Korea's foreign exchange receipts.

The most obvious effect of the Korean War and of US aid was the militarization of South Korean society. At the beginning of the war, the Korean military was not much more than a small constabulary. By the end of the war, it numbered 600 000; according to Amsden, the fourth largest army outside the Soviet bloc. Militarization accompanied the suppression of organized labour in industry but it also provided the basis for a

government which was able to take advantage of the post-war political vacuum.

Even though Rhee claimed that US aid did little to promote long-run growth, most commentators agree that US aid did help to 'modernize' South Korea. The need to administer the huge amount of aid channelled through government meant that the state officials, Rhee's power base, not only grew in numbers but also gained management skills and experience.

Alongside this growth in the power of the bureaucracy, there was a considerable commitment to education. In 1946, only 7% of the South Korean labour force had been through secondary education. By 1963 this proportion had risen to over a third. The expansion of education during the 1950s, building on previous cultural and scholarly traditions, was a major factor behind the industrial 'miracle' of the 1960s and 1970s.

Illicit wealth accumulation

US aid not only provided a basis for the growth of the bureaucracy, it also affected industrial development in other ways. Firstly, as Amsden and others point out, during this 'First Republic' period from 1948 to 1960, there was considerable corruption. Political connections were all-important in being able to buy Japanese property at below market prices, and in getting access to scarce foreign exchange allocations, loans at subsidized interest rates, tax concessions and preferential contracts for large-scale aid and other goverment projects. In South Korea, the 1950s is known as the period of 'illicit wealth accumulation'.

But in the 1950s, US aid also provided the foreign exchange to support rapid industrial expansion. Foreign exchange was needed to buy the capital equipment and know-how for setting up production and to buy the raw materials and energy for sustaining production. This combination of expansion and patronage gave birth to the *Chaebols*, the large diversified business groups which now dominate South Korean society. *Chaebols* were founded on production for a domestic market and on State support.

Between 1953 and 1958, both light and heavy manufacturing in South Korea grew at over 18%

Table 4.2 The growth and structure of the manufacturing sector

	Growth rate / % p.a. 1954–64	Composition of MVA / % p.a.	
		1954	1964
light industries			
food, beverages & tobacco	7	51	38
textiles & clothing	8	19	16
others	8	13	13
all light industries	8	83	67
heavy industries			
paper & paper products	19	1	3
chemical products	18	3	6
non-metallic mineral products	18	3	6
iron & steel metal products	16	2	4
machinery	12	4	5
petroleum products	32	2	8
transport equipment	12	2	2
all heavy industries	17	17	33

[Source: Milner, 1990]

a year, more rapidly than in any of 36 countries surveyed by the UN in 1960. At the beginning of the 1950s, the food, beverages & tobacco sector and the textiles & clothing sector between them accounted for well over two-thirds of total manufacturing value added (MVA). These industries continued to grow rapidly in the 1950s. But the most rapid growth occurred in a diverse range of heavy industries; including paper & paper products, iron & steel and petroleum products (see Table 4.2). As Amsden emphasizes: '… the cradling of enterprises in illicit wealth was not industry specific. These subsidized entrepreneurs were generalists, devoted to moneymaking in whatever industry the opportunity arose'. Nonetheless, investment was increasingly channelled into heavy industries, increasing the diversity, integration and technological capacity of South Korea.

The rapid growth in South Korean manufacturing during the 1950s was based on production for a limited domestic market. Although land reform broadened the distribution of income and

wealth, the domestic market was still small. Manufactured exports were also small; in 1960 less than 13% of total exports. In this period then, industrialization could be characterized as import substitution. But the economy was still a derivative one with industry and agriculture both dependent on imports for survival. At the end of the 1950s, the value of imports was still 10% of GNP, whereas total exports were less than 1% of GNP. The industrial expansion was being financed by US aid.

Clearly such a structure could survive only as long as US aid was maintained. If US aid fell, then economic growth was likely to slow. This is what happened in the late 1950s. Confidence in Rhee's government dwindled, and in 1960, Rhee was forced to resign after police had fired on and killed students protesting at election-rigging. Further elections in July 1960 brought the Korean Democratic Party (KDP) into office on a slogan of 'economic development first'. The new government readily agreed to two US demands which had been resisted by Rhee. One was closer supervision of US aid funds. The other was a large devaluation. Whereas in 1960, W63 could be exchanged for US$1, in 1961 it took W128 to buy US$1. This massive devaluation of the won increased the costs of imports and added to the unrest. Disunity in the KDP and further unrest on the streets led, in May 1961, to a military coup, led by a major-general, Park Chung-Hee. Park was to head the South Korean government for the next 18 years.

To summarize a period of fifteen years, war caused tremendous devastation. Out of the population of 20 million, over a million South Koreans died; proportionately more than twice the dead in the UK in the Second World War. Almost half the manufacturing capacity was destroyed. After the war a huge restructuring took place. This was based on massive US aid. It was also based on a land distribution that resulted in cheap food and relocation of investment from the land into industry.

The industrial base grew apace, doubling between 1953 and 1958. Existing industrial sectors were extended and new ones were established. New industrial groups, the Chaebols, established themselves with strong state support, building up industrial investments based on *import substitution*.

4.4 The economic 'miracle' (1961–79)

At the beginning of the 1960s, most South Koreans were still very poor. Roughly 80% of personal consumption expenditure went on food, clothing, shelter, heat and light. The infant mortality rate in South Korea was 64 per thousand compared with 24 in the rich countries, and housing conditions were miserable, with only 18% of households being connected to running water supplies.

But some basis for growth had been laid. Education was advanced, especially for a country with such a low level of income. By 1965, 35% of the relevant age group was attending secondary school and 6% of 18–21 year olds were in higher education. Under Japanese colonialism, industry had been developed and industrial expansion was

Figure 4.8   A new power station.

rapid through the 1950s. As we have seen, manufacturing growth in the 1950s was on the basis of production for a domestic market broadened by land redistribution with imports being financed by US aid.

Over the next 20 years, manufacturing output in South Korea was to expand by a staggering average of 20% a year. In this section we focus on the two questions posed earlier. Why was the industrialization process so rapid? How did South Korea establish industry so quickly? But before that we will look briefly at the political and economic framework.

The political changes

As we have seen, politically the period started with a military coup. Park Chung Hee's military government was intensely nationalistic, and its goal for South Korea was rapid development. Within 100 days of coming to power, the military had announced the launching of the first five-year development plan, and with the plan came the establishment of a powerful Economic Planning Board. The coup leaders, many of whom came from the same military year of intake, denounced the conspicuous consumption and the 'illicit wealth' of the rich. They threw into jail the most corrupt of the Liberal Party leaders but then discovered that they would only continue to get the backing of the US government if they released them, returned the country to civilian rule 'at the earliest possible date' and promised to 'normalize' relations with Japan.

The cost of not meeting these conditions was likely to be high, since the leverage of the US was still considerable. The leaders of the Liberal Party were released and, in 1963, the return to 'civilian rule' took place. But many of the leaders of other opposition parties remained in jail. With support from the Korean Central Intelligence Agency and with a record of fast economic growth since the coup, Park's party (the Democratic Republican Party) gained control.

The general election of 1963 was to be the last general (as opposed to Presidential) election for another two decades. Park Chung Hee was President for two terms. But in 1969 he forced through the National Assembly an amendment to the constitution allowing him to run again. In the Presidential election, he defeated his opponent, Kim Dae Jung, by a narrow margin. Two years later he declared a national emergency, suspended the existing constitution and introduced a new one, called the *Yushin* (restoration) constitution. The Yushin constitution replaced direct presidential elections, permitted indefinite re-election of the president and empowered him to nominate a third of the legislature. Effectively it left no way in which a president unwilling to go could be removed from office peacefully.

President Park was assassinated in 1979. By then, he had fulfilled the aim of rapid economic development. Much of the 'illicit wealth' had been channelled into manufacturing, and the period of Park's rule from 1961 through to the end of the 1970s was a period of spectacular growth. The government had been a modernizing and growth-oriented one. But, especially after the Yushin constitution, it was increasingly authoritarian.

Spectacular export-led growth

As Table 4.3 shows, the growth in the 1960s and 1970s was very fast and was largely export-led. It had to be. As we saw earlier (Table 4.1) aid from the US declined from an average of 15% of GNP in 1956–58 to less than 5% of GNP ten years later. If South Korea was to continue to grow, this source of foreign exchange had to be replaced by another since the finance for capital equipment and many raw materials, including fuel, had to be imported. South Korea had negligible natural resources to exploit and export, so that agricultural and/or manufactured exports had to provide the engine of growth. They did. Exports grew dramatically through the 1960s and 1970s. Thus whereas total exports as a percentage of GNP were only about 9% in the mid-1950s, the average for the 1960s was over 20%, and for the 1970s over 50%.

Table 4.3 Economic growth and growth in exports in South Korea

	GNP growth rate	Export growth rate
1960s	9% p.a.	41% p.a.
1970s	9% p.a.	37% p.a.

[Sources: Amsden, 1989; Van Liemt, 1988]

The causes of the 'miracle'?

At the beginning of the chapter we posed the question of South Korea's success in terms of two competing views about industrialization and economic growth; strong state direction versus low-level intervention. To assess the how and why of industrial development it is important to look in more detail at various aspects of industrial policy:

- trade policy

- financing of industry

- industrial diversification

- ownership
- technology
- the labour market
- physical infrastructure
- agriculture.

Trade policy

After the military coup in 1961, there were extensive reforms. In particular there was a shift towards the promotion of exports, as aid from the US was reduced. But this was a state-sponsored drive for exports, and not a switch which was left simply to free market forces. Nor were the exports promoted through the development of 'Free Trade' or 'Export Processing Zones' (Chapter 1, Box 1.3). By contrast with many other Less Developed Countries, there was little emphasis in South Korea on EPZs. By the early 1980s, manufactured exports from South Korea's EPZs at Masan and Iri accounted for less than 5% of South Korea's total exports.

Instead of promotion through free markets or through EPZs, the South Korean government actively promoted manufactured exports using trade policy. As Amsden has emphasized, in trade as in other areas of policy, the South Korean government mixed the carrot and the stick.

Businesses were both supported and disciplined. For example imports were generally allowed only if they were to be incorporated into exports. Otherwise imports were restricted. Similarly, through the 1960s and the 1970s, manufacturers selling in the home market continued to be given considerable protection (Box 4.3) from foreign competition, as they had been in the 1950s, but this time only on condition that they met export targets set by the government. High levels of protection for manufactures produced for sale in the domestic market was a common feature in LDCs in the 1960s and 1970s. But by contrast to the situation in many other LDCs over the same period, the carrot given by the South Korean government in the form of profitable protection on home sales was mixed with the stick of less profitable, or even loss-making, export targets. Compare this situation with that of Brazil in the last chapter.

A policy of setting targets for exports made particularly good sense when applied to products which are subject to economies of scale, meaning that the average costs of production decline with the volume of output (see Chapter 5, Box 5.3). Examples of products for which such increasing economies of scale are thought to be considerable are automobiles, televisions, steel and

---

Box 4.3   The rate of protection

If import duty is imposed on imported goods then it raises the price of the imported goods. The extent to which the domestic price is raised above the import price is referred to as the *nominal rate of protection* For example, assume that the price of a shirt imported from the USA is US$15. At an exchange rate of, say, W600 to US$1, the import price would be W9 000. But now assume that the South Korean government imposes an import duty of 10% on the shirt. This will raise the price of the imported shirt to W9 900. A company producing in South Korea for the domestic market can take advantage of this and either sell its own products at a similar price, increasing its profit margins, or increase sales by keeping prices lower. Either way, sales

revenue and profits are greater than they would be without the protection.

A more accurate measure would be based on the level of protection given to the local value added only; that is, excluding imported parts. Such protection, called the effective rate *of protection* was considerable in South Korea.

One economic study (Frank *et al.*, 1975) estimated that, in 1968, the effective rate of protection (on value added) in South Korea for import-competing industries was 92%. This suggests that if South Korean manufacturers could produce at the same costs as their foreign competitors, they would be able to make very high profits from their sales in the protected domestic market.

petrochemicals. For these goods, demand in South Korea was, by itself, too small to support the volume of output necessary to achieve internationally competitive cost levels. Even in 1991, the national income of South Korea was less than 4% of the USA's and less than 7% of Japan's. Thirty years earlier, South Korea's national income was (in real terms) less than one-tenth of its 1991 figure. This meant that if South Korea was going to establish industries with economies of scale, then it would have to export.

Under such conditions, if the South Korean government was to promote manufacturing expansion, it made good sense to protect production for the small South Korean market. This was done by issuing, to individual companies, licences allowing each to produce a particular range of products, but conditional on the company achieving certain export targets. This export targeting is also an effective way of reducing the risks facing a company which is new to the export market. The profits from the protected domestic market can be used to underwrite possible losses in an uncertain export market. As Amsden and other economists have stressed, most exports of manufactures from South Korea were unprofitable when considered in isolation from the profits earned on the domestic sales.

Thus, from the 1960s, the South Korean government induced South Korean companies to link production for a protected domestic market (import-substituting industrialization) with production for exports (export-oriented industrialization). In general, manufacturing profitability was high in South Korea, but only because losses on exports were more than compensated for by high profits on domestic sales.

The government's trade policy could therefore be said to be outward-oriented. Indeed, increasingly through the 1960s, the whole of government policy was directed at increasing exports. But this export expansion was not done through the free market. It was done through state planning with a very strong presidential commitment. Indeed, the progress of the export drive was monitored at monthly meetings of Cabinet members,

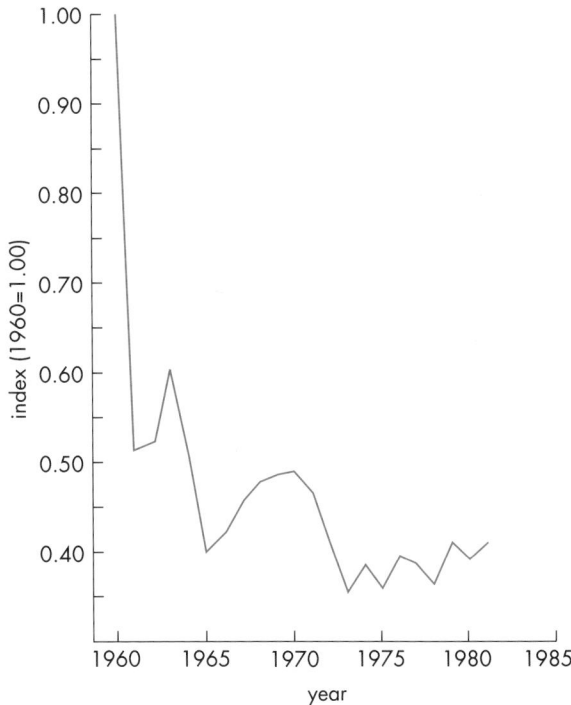

Figure 4.9   South Korea's real exchange rate.

business people and government officials chaired by President Park Chung Hee.

Government policy on the won exchange rate generally supported this export drive. As pointed out at the end of Section 4.3, following the ousting of Rhee in 1960, the won was sharply devalued. As a result, South Korean producers became more competitive in world markets.

Look at Figure 4.9. It shows the rapid real devaluation of the won from 1960 to 1965. The index is the exchange rate of the won against the currencies of South Korea's main trading partner nations, adjusted for relative inflation. A fall in the index indicates increasing South Korean competitiveness. The graph also shows that South Korea became more competitive over the period 1970–73, since the real exchange rate fell again. And note that the encouragement offered by the falling exchange rate was additional to that provided by direct and indirect subsidies already given through the tariff protection structure and export targeting arrangements. In general then, a trade policy which integrated import controls with export promotion and with exchange rate policy played a major part in South Korea's export success.

The financing of industry

As we have seen, the government's trade policy played a major role in economic growth in the 1960s and 1970s. But the state's interventionist role in the financial sector was at least as important. In the early 1960s, after the fall of Syngman Rhee, most of the commercial banking sector had been nationalized. Many economists have highlighted this nationalization of the banking sector as the most important factor explaining the South Korean miracle.

How do you think nationalization of the banking sector could help or hinder the manufacturing sector?

Some economists have argued that the nationalization of the South Korean banking sector was crucial to the success of the manufacturing sector because the state banking sector provided long-term loans to industry at preferentially low interest rates (Van Liemt, 1988). In the late 1960s, although interest rates paid to depositors were high in real terms (that is, after allowing for inflation), they were not necessarily high to approved borrowers such as companies producing for export. It is clear from Table 4.4 that, in the

second half of the 1960s, real interest rates paid to depositors were raised sharply.

It was on the basis of this South Korean experience that two American economists, McKinnon and Shaw, argued that high (real) interest rates are necessary for efficient industrial development. McKinnon and Shaw argued that the high real interest rates in South Korea had not only generated more savings and increased the quantity of investment, but had also improved the quality of investment. They argued that the quality of investment was raised because the rise in interest rates made borrowing by inefficient, unprofitable companies impossible and diverted finance to the more efficient, more profitable industries, which would otherwise be 'financially repressed'. Therefore higher (real) interest rates increased both the quantity and the quality of industrial investment.

Does this make sense? Are interest rates which are high in real terms likely to be favourable or unfavourable to efficient industrial development? These questions are important not just for South Korea but for all countries, including the UK. There have been considerable debates both about the theory and about whether the South Korean evidence supports the theory. The McKinnon–Shaw argument has been challenged, both in terms of its theory and in terms of what happened in South Korea.

Theoretically, it is difficult to see why, even if savings are raised by higher real interest rates, the quantity of investment will increase. It could just as easily be argued that investment will be discouraged by higher real interest rates. Keynesian economists have argued that high real interest rates are counter-productive to investment, and their theory runs counter to that of McKinnon and Shaw. Certainly as a description of what happened in South Korea, the McKinnon–Shaw version has been heavily criticized. For example, Laurence Harris, a British economist and former Professor of Economics at the Open University, has argued that the interest rate reform of the 1960s did contribute to growth, but that, contrary to the McKinnon–Shaw thesis, it did so because it increased the role of the state, rather than

Table 4.4 Interest rates in South Korea, 1960–79

Period	rate paid to depositers (a)	rate charged to exporters (b)
1960–64	–7% p.a.	
1965–69	27% p.a.	
1970–74	0	–16% p.a.
1975–79	–5% p.a.	–13% p.a.

Notes:

(a) Interest rate paid by the state banking sector less rise in consumer prices

(b) Interest rate charged less inflation

[Source: Dornbusch & Park, 1987]

rolling it back to liberate private market forces (Harris, 1988).

Three important points emerge from a close examination of the South Korean evidence.

(i) The rise in interest rates to depositors in the 1960s increased, rather than reduced, the power of the state banking sector as deposits were attracted out of the unofficial ('kerb') banking system into the nationalized official sector.

(ii) It is worth noting that real interest rates to depositors were only strongly positive for a short period in the late 1960s. For most of the 1960s and 1970s, they were either negative in real terms or zero.

(iii) In analysing the effects of interest rates, it is important to distinguish between the rates paid to depositors and the rates charged to borrowers. The evidence for South Korea from the 1970s shows that these rates differed considerably (Table 4.4).

The South Korean government, through its control of the banking system, paid low real rates for most of the 1960s and 1970s. In addition, by controlling the allocation of bank loans, it 'implicitly taxed depositors and channelled the proceeds to favoured sectors for investment' (Dornbusch & Park, 1987).

This interventionist role of the South Korean government was recognized by the World Bank in its 1989 *World Development Report* when it stated: 'Korea's heavily-regulated financial system was a key instrument in the government's industrial policy in the 1960s and 1970s. Interest rates were controlled and were kept low during most of this period'.

Table 4.5 External debt and debt service ratios

	External debt as % of GNP	Debt service as % of exports
1965	7	8
1975	1	14
1984	53	21

[Source: Amsden, 1989]

Low-interest loans provided to industry by the South Korean banks were crucial to the development of the manufacturing sector. But in the 1970s, South Korea also borrowed heavily from overseas to finance its heavy industrialization programme and to cover the higher costs of imported oil following the sharp price rise of 1974. As a result South Korea's external debt rose rapidly in the 1970s (Table 4.5).

Nevertheless, this rise in the value of external debt never became an excessive burden for South Korea as it did for Brazil. In the late 1970s, South Korea's ratio of payments on its external debt to its exports (its debt service ratio) was less than half of Brazil's. Why was this? Firstly, South Korea's loans were mostly long-term loans so that by the time that they were due to be repaid, South Korea's dramatic growth in export earnings was sufficient to pay them back. Secondly, South Korea took drastic action to cut its energy consumption and thus reduce its oil imports. By contrast with Brazil, the heavy borrowing from overseas did not result in an external debt crisis for South Korea.

Industrial diversification
By the early 1970s, the South Korean government's encouragement of manufacturing had already begun to reap dividends. Net manufacturing output had grown at 19% a year between 1960 and 1970 (Figure 4.1) and even as early as 1965, manufactured exports had risen to over 60% of total exports. The government had actively directed the growth in manufacturing sector through its trade policy and through other policy measures.

This industrial growth was spread across most industries. But in the early 1970s, the South Korean government took additional steps to develop heavy industries. Heavy industries are those industries which are generally more capital-intensive (that is require larger capital investments per unit of output) and which are subject to considerable economies of scale (Box 4.4). There were two reasons for this additional push into heavy industry and diversification away from light industries, which are generally more labour-intensive.

Figure 4.10   Industrial diversification: Hyundai shipyard, Ulsan.

Firstly, in spite of the falls in the exchange rate, South Korea was losing its competitive edge in some labour-intensive products, such as clothing. In the 1960s, manufacturing employment grew and, in spite of the repression of trade unions, real wages rose very rapidly. Even though this growth had been from a very low level and wage growth had been offset by increases in labour productivity, South Korea was facing sharp competition from countries in

---

Box 4.4   Different types of industry

Industry can be divided into various types (Figure 4.11).

One division is that between consumer and producer industries. *Consumer industries* are those that produce goods for direct consumption, for example, food, clothing and washing machines. Specific examples for the Third World include tea and sugar.

Producer industries are those that make goods for further industrial use. *Producer goods* are of two types: either *capital goods*, such as machinery, or *intermediate goods,* which are processed goods as inputs for further manufacture. For example, plastic pellets can be producer goods since they are often used as intermediate goods inputs for the production of plastic kitchen products (consumer goods) in another industrial

process. Many Third World countries do not have facilities for making plastics, a complex product usually made from petroleum using large-scale processing. They import it and use it in factories to make plastic kitchen products.

Another division is that between light and heavy industry.

Light industries include the food, drinks, textiles, clothing, leather, footwear, wood furniture, and paper and printing industry sectors. They are mostly *consumer* goods.

Heavy industries include the chemicals and petroleum, cement and glass, metals and metal products, mechanical, electrical and transport machinery industries. They are mostly *producer* goods.

which wage costs were even lower. Thus diversification into more capital-intensive heavy industry was undertaken.

Secondly, diversification into heavy industries was attractive to the Park government because of the needs of defence. In the early 1970s, the US government announced that it intended to reduce its defence commitments to South Korea. The South Korean military government's response was predictable; namely to promote the development of defence-related heavy industry. And so, in 1972, the drive into heavy industry was announced.

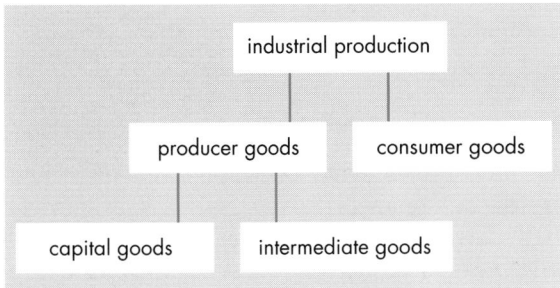

Figure 4.11

To summarize, there was a strong diversification into a new range of heavy industries. They grew rapidly in the 1970s and by 1980 the structure of South Korean industry had been transformed. Over the two decades since the military coup in the early 1960s, the manufacturing sector had grown at an average annual rate of 20%. Over the same period, the growth in national income (GNP) had averaged 9% a year. This was a growth rate unprecedented in world history for such an extended period. As Table 4.6 shows, the percentage of manufacturing net output coming from heavy industry rose from 40% in 1971 to 56% in 1980. Growth was particularly rapid in the basic metal (including steel) and transport equipment (automobile assembly, shipbuilding, etc.) industries.

Ownership

Thus it seems clear that in the 1960s and 1970s there was considerable intervention by the South Korean government in the areas of trade, finance and industrial diversification. But the state also intervened in the area of ownership. Contrary to an argument that South Korea is a huge sweatshop dominated by foreign capital, South Korea has managed to maintain considerable independence in terms of both ownership and the absorption of technology.

First consider ownership. In general, the role of direct foreign investment (DFI) in South Korea has been tightly controlled and has been small, except in electronics. Between 1962 and 1979, direct foreign investment accounted for only 1.2% of total domestic investment and in the late 1970s the share of foreign investment in South Korea's GNP was less than half of that in Argentina, Brazil and Mexico. Instead, the country's manufacturing industry is dominated by *Chaebols,* family-owned and controlled business groups. They are like the Japanese *Zaibatsu,* in the sense that their operations are diversified (they span a number of products) but at the same

Table 4.6 The growth of heavy industries, 1971–1980

| | % of net output | | % of manufactured exports | |
	1971	1980	1971	1980
light industries	60	44	86	60
heavy industries	40	56	14	40
chemical	56	49		
basic metal	15	17		
transport equipment	29	34		

[Source: Amsden, 1989]

Figure 4.12   Car assembly workers, Hyundai.

time they are highly coordinated. The four major or super-*Chaebols* are the *Hyundai* (automobiles, construction, cement, shipbuilding and steel), *Samsung* (entertainment, hotels and newspapers), *Daewoo* (construction, electronics, shipbuilding) and *Lucky Goldstar* (plastics and electronics) groups. Although the *Chaebols* are large, in the 1960s and 1970s they were tightly controlled by the state, with control being facilitated by the *Chaebols*' dependence on loans. Their ratios of debt finance to equity (or 'own funds') rose from around 1:1 in the early 1960s to almost 4:1 in the late 1970s . Compared to Brazil, South Korea's manufacturing has been dominated by medium and large firms. Table 4.7 gives a comparison for 1973.

Table 4.7 The percentage distribution of value added in manufacturing by firm size in 1973

	Numbers of workers employed		
	1–99	100–499	over 500
Brazil	27	36	37
South Korea	20	28	52
Taiwan	21	23	56
United Kingdom	16	24	60
USA	21	31	48

[Source: Amsden, 1989]

Amsden has pointed out that even the smaller firms in South Korea are tied into the large-scale sector through subcontracting. She points out the similarity between Japan and South Korea in this respect, and argues that this is a healthy structure inasmuch as it has encouraged the growth of productivity in small-scale firms.

The domestic industry which has been promoted has also been highly concentrated regionally. Highly selective intervention by the state has included the promotion of large companies producing in large factories heavily concentrated in Seoul and Pusan. As we shall see, this left a legacy of power concentration which emerged as an acute problem in the 1980s.

Technology

Is South Korea dependent on foreign technology?

Borrowing technology is not the same as technological dependence. During the last century and a half, borrowing technology was the experience of all the major industrial countries, with the exception of the UK. What matters most for technological development is not where the technology comes from (as the term technological dependency implies) but how the technologies are adapted and absorbed.

South Korea has demonstrated an impressive capability, especially in heavy industries, in choosing which technologies to import, of adapting foreign technologies to local conditions, of improving on imported technologies and of generating new technologies domestically. For example the Pohang Iron and Steel Company (POSCO) which initially borrowed technology from Japan has been in operation for less than two decades and yet became sufficiently advanced to provide technical expertise to a US steel manufacturer.

The successful absorption by South Korea of foreign technology has to a large extent been due to the interventionist role of the state in the acquisition and development of technology. Many researchers have emphasized the positive role of the South Korean government in 'de-packaging' technology. The state has promoted the overseas training of Korean managers

Table 4.8 Education in South Korea, Brazil, India and Mexico

| | Students as % of secondary age population | | | Scientists and engineers per thousand of population | |
| | secondary school | | engineering | | |
	1965	1978	1978	late 1960s	late 1970s
South Korea	29%	68%	26%	7	22
Brazil		17%	12%	6	6
India	29%	30%		2	3
Mexico	29%	30%	14%	7	7

[Source: Amsden, 1989]

and engineers, and it has encouraged the use of technical assistance from overseas, particularly in the form of independent consultants. The State has also been closely involved in the negotiations to acquire technology licenses. State coordination of technology bargaining has been extensive in South Korea.

But technology is not only about machinery. It is also, and essentially, about human capacities. Throughout the 1960s and 1970s, the State continued with its high commitment to education and by the late 1970s, even among late-industrializing countries, South Korea stood out in terms of many indices of education (see Table 4.8).

Overall, the 1970s experience of South Korea in the field of technology emphasizes the importance of the state, not so much in promoting research and development expenditure, but rather in coordinating the acquisition and application of existing technology. In the field of technology, as in the areas of trade and finance, it is the selectivity of the state's role which seems to have been significant.

The labour market

How correct is the argument that South Korea has been a huge sweatshop? Average hours of work have been high, for all people employed in manufacturing. In 1984, 73% of men and 62% of women

Figure 4.13   Photos: Schoolboys in 1985, still wearing the uniform originally introduced during the Japanese occupation.

worked at least 54 hours a week. And, although wages rose rapidly in the 1960s and 1970s (Table 4.9), they rose from a very low base . In 1969 the average monthly wage of a factory worker was between US$50 and US$70 and in the same year, the Economic Planning Board's Economic Survey admitted that South Korea's wage level did not exceed minimum living expenses to any substantial extent. In the 1960s and 1970s, wages were particularly low for female workers. In 1977, the average wage for female production-related workers in manufacturing was only 52% of that of male workers, and Amsden points out that in 1980 the male–female wage gap was greater in South Korea than in any other country for which data were available from the International Labour Office. Thus, the argument that South Korea has been a sweatshop seems correct.

Table 4.9 Growth in real wages and productivity in manufacturing, 1958–80

	Growth in real wages (% per annum)	Growth in labour productivity (% per annum)
1958–65	1.0	
1965–73	9.8	13.0
1974–80	11.1	11.4

[Source: Amsden, 1989]

However, wages grew rapidly from 1965 to 1980 in spite of the iron-fisted suppression of the labour movement. During colonialism, the Japanese employers in Korea had instituted the *sampo* system. This was an 'industrial patriotism club' in which employers and employees 'joined' together to increase production. The employees' efforts to increase production were coordinated by a company-sponsored workers' association. The *sampo* system was designed to promote productivity but also to prevent the spread of trade unionism. In the latter respect it was successful, since only a small proportion of South Korea's factory workers belonged to trade unions in the 1960s and 1970s.

In the 1960s there was some restructuring of unions along national-industrial lines and some collective bargaining was introduced. But in the 1970s, with some tightening in the labour market, the *sampo* system was reinforced and the police and the Korea Central Intelligence Agency were widely used to regulate and control labour.

Because of repression by the government, backed up by a substantial labour surplus in the economy (particularly in the 1960s), there was little militancy in the labour force through the period of the Park administration. The labour surplus is difficult to estimate precisely but unofficial estimates of unemployment put the rate at 16% in 1964, 13% in 1967, 9% in 1970 and 7.7% in 1973 (Hamilton, 1986), indicating a substantial labour surplus in the 1960s declining into the 1970s. But although the labour surplus declined in the 1970s, the pace of decline was slowed by the high rate of out-migration from the rural areas between 1967 and 1975, encouraged by the relatively low incomes in the rural sector.

Physical infrastructure
The South Korean government invested heavily in physical infrastructure. Although expenditure by the South Korean government as a percentage of GNP through the 1960s and 1970s was relatively small, a large proportion of it went on investment. In this respect, in the late 1970s, South Korea was similar to Brazil (see Table 4.10).

Table 4.10 Government expenditure: an international comparison

	Government expenditure as % of GNP 1982	Government investment as % of total investment
South Korea	20%	23% (1978–80)
Brazil	22%	23% (1980)
Chile	38%	13% (1978–80)
Thailand	20%	13% (1978–80)

[Source: Amsden, 1989]

Figure 4.14   Workers exercising outside a factory.

The South Korean public sector played an active role in building up the physical infrastructure for industry (electricity, gas, railroads, highways and irrigation). This State investment meant that the State ran a budget deficit in most years between 1963 and 1982. Deficits were financed by overseas borrowing and therefore contributed to the external debt burden, but as we saw earlier, this external debt never reached crisis proportions in South Korea.

Agriculture

In the 1960s and the 1970s, in agriculture, as in other policy areas, State intervention in South Korea was designed to promote industrialization. Earlier it was emphasized that real wages in industry were, by international standards, low in the 1960s and 1970s. Together with growing labour productivity, this meant that South Korean manufacturing production could be highly profitable but at the same time competitive in the world market. One factor which favoured the maintenance of low real wage levels in industry were the low prices (relative to international levels) of agricultural products. Higher prices for agricultural

products would have meant that urban wage rates would have had to have been higher both to entice labour away and to enable it to survive in the urban areas. Lower agricultural prices meant that labour would be ready to migrate to the manufacturing jobs and would not need to be paid as much to enable it to survive.

To develop industry, some 'squeezing' of the agriculture sector is likely. South Korea was no exception. Some researchers have claimed that, in South Korea in the 1960s and 1970s, the state did not squeeze the peasantry (see Ban *et al.*, 1980). They argue that the taxation of the agricultural sector was light and that there was little transfer from agriculture to industry. But is this sufficient evidence to establish that transfers from the agricultural sector were low?

The answer is no. The transfer can, and in South Korea did, take place indirectly through a decline in the prices paid for agricultural goods relative to those paid for manufactured goods. This price ratio is usually called the barter (or internal) terms of trade (see Box 5.2). It was through a decline in the terms of trade that a transfer out of agriculture took place at least through the 1960s. As Table 4.11 shows, the terms of trade moved sharply against agriculture between 1963 and 1967.

Table 4.11 Internal terms of trade for agricultural production in South Korea, 1963–69

	Terms of trade (1959 = 100)*
1963	163
1965	144
1967	138
1969	139

*calculated as a price index of agricultural goods divided by a price index of manufactured goods

[Source: Lee, 1979]

The fall in agricultural prices relative to those for manufactures was brought about through State intervention, and particularly through the State procurement of grain. From the 1950s, the share of compulsory government purchase of marketed grain increased steadily until in 1975 it stood at 50% for rice and 90% for barley. Through State purchasing of grain and state monopolization of fertilizer sales to the farmers, agricultural output prices which, in the early 1960s, were already low relative to production costs, were reduced relative to industrial prices through the 1960s. Indeed the government's control of marketing of agricultural outputs and inputs was so complete in South Korea that reference has been made to South Korea as 'one farm' (Wade, 1982).

Thus, in the 1960s, the State squeezed the peasantry not directly through taxation, but indirectly through the control of markets. How was this possible without destroying the peasantry? The answer is that the land reform and the associated levelling of incomes in the rural sector in the late 1940s and early 1950s made possible a squeezing of the peasantry without causing a famine. In China, at about the same time, the land reform had enabled the Chinese government to extract a large surplus from the rural sector without killing it off. But in South Korea, there was a further

favourable factor. The government was able to 'squeeze' agriculture, not only because the land reform had equalized rural incomes but also because cheap rice imports were available through the US food aid programme. The proportion of imports in total rice supply rose from zero in 1964, to 6% in 1967 to about a quarter in 1970.

In 1971, rural per capita incomes had been only about one-third of those in urban areas. Thus it is hardly surprising that the flow of labour into urban industries was easily maintained through the 1960s and 1970s, and by 1975, in spite of natural population growth, the rural population was about the same as it had been in the early 1950s.

It seems clear then that state intervention, even in agriculture, served to promote industrialization. Nevertheless it is important to point out that in the 1970s the terms of trade were shifted back in favour of agriculture as US food aid was sharply reduced. Such a switch was partly a response to an erosion of support for the Park regime in the rural areas, particularly in the South West area of the opposition candidate, Kim Dae Jung. This swing in the terms of trade in favour of agriculture brought a recovery in rural incomes in the early 1970s which meant that, by the mid-1970s, 'it would … appear that there (was) no pervasive absolute poverty in rural South Korea as measured by a nutritionally based poverty line' (Lee, 1979). And as Hamilton has argued, the level of exploitation of the peasantry in independent South Korea (that is, since the end of Japanese colonialism) has been fairly mild by historical standards.

Summary
Changes in all of the aspects of development policy that we have considered (trade, finance, diversification, ownership, technology, labour, infrastructural investment and agriculture) have played some role in the South Korean economic miracle. No one of these can be isolated. But we can make the following observations:

(i) The overall integration of policy through strong state intervention under military authoritarianism, a very 'top down' approach, was linked to often repressive measures.

(ii) There has also been a close attention to detail, as with trade policy and its monitoring at monthly meetings of Cabinet, business leaders and government officials chaired by the President. The multiple interest rate policy favoured industrial investment, a very proactive but at the same time ad hoc approach to policy. At one level the state seemed omnipotent, at another it allowed the development of a very disciplined private capitalist industrial structure that was internationally competitive and competent.

4.5 Riding the storm: economic crisis, growth and the drive to democracy in the 1980s

Economic and political crisis (1979–80)

President Park's assassination in 1979 had followed three years of economic boom. From 1976 to 1978, real GNP rose by 41%, real investment rose by more than 100% and real wages rose by an annual average of more than 15%. The won was devalued over this period but not by enough to compensate for the rise in unit labour costs. Thus the real exchange rate actually rose slightly (Figure 4.9). As a result, in 1979, the volume of exports fell. At the same time there was a sharp rise in the price of imported oil and South Korea's external terms of trade fell by 13% between 1979 and 1980.

The government was belatedly cutting back its public expenditure in response to the boom, and as both exports and public expenditure were cut back, there was a sharp recession. All of this coincided with a bad harvest; with real output in agriculture, forestry and fishing falling by more than one-fifth in 1980. In the same year, real national output fell by 5%, the first fall since the end of the Korean War. The rise in oil prices and the fall in exports meant that South Korea ran a deficit on the current account of its balance of payments (Chapter 2, Box 2.2) of more than US$4 billion in 1979 and of more than US$5 billion in 1980. As South Korea increased its borrowing from overseas to finance the external deficit, there was a rise in the percentage of its exports taken up by payments on long and medium-term external debt.

So 1980 was a year of economic crisis. It was also a year of political crisis. The assassination of Park was followed by a series of strikes and student demonstrations for a rapid return to democracy. These were followed by the imposition of martial law and then in May 1980 by another military takeover, this time by General Chun Doo Hwan. Demonstrations against martial law were brutally suppressed especially in the area in the south-west dominated by the opposition leader Kim Dae Jung, with hundreds of people being killed in May 1980 in what is known as the Kwangju massacre. Following the massacre, Kim Dae Jung was sentenced to death, but after pressure from overseas, the sentence was commuted and Kim deported to the USA.

Reconstruction and growth (1981–84)

In 1981, the South Korean economy faced severe problems. There was a sharp drop in the growth rate of the rich industrialized countries and South Korean national output had fallen by 5% in 1980. Yet, between 1981 and 1984, in the face of this depression in the world economy, South Korea achieved an average growth rate of over 7% a year. Even in 1982 when the volume of world trade in manufactures declined by 1.2%, South Korea managed an increase in national income of more than 6%. By 1984 the current account deficit had been reduced to US$1.4 billion and the inflation rate had been reduced to under 4%. And between 1981 and 1984, real wages rose by 5% a year. How was this dramatic recovery accomplished?

The over-valuation of the US dollar in the early 1980s made South Korea's exports extremely competitive in the US market. So exports grew rapidly. This was accompanied by a much slower growth in imports. As oil prices stabilized between 1981 and 1984, international prices moved in South Korea's favour, with its external terms of trade rising by more than 7%.

Government intervention
Was the solution to the crisis a liberalization of the economy, as suggested by the prevailing ideology of the 1980s? This question has been much debated in trying to understand why South

Korea recovered while many other countries floundered. The evidence is difficult to assess, as Amsden says, as hard 'as assessing godliness in a reformed heretic'. She argues that government policy between 1979 and the end of 1982 should take much of the credit for the recovery. When private investment fell, the State compensated by expanding public investment, much of it being financed by external borrowing. Internally, the State acted to lower interest rates and to bail out many of the companies which faced difficulties. In many cases the State encouraged mergers and restructuring through 'reorganization' programmes. The most conspicuous example of this was the 1986 programme which reorganized six industries (automobiles, electronic switching systems, copper smelting, heavy electrical machinery, power generating equipment and diesel engines). Groups were forced to merge, specialize or pull out of some industries. This was coupled with some nationalization.

But this is only part of the story. The government did introduce an austerity programme in 1983 that was supported by a stand-by agreement with the IMF. Government expenditure was cut and agricultural price supports which had been introduced in the 1970s were a prime target. There was a mass exodus from agriculture; over half a million people are estimated to have left agriculture between 1982 and 1985. Amsden also concedes that in the period after 1979, there was liberalization in both trade and finance as well as some moves towards encouraging greater competition in the domestic economy, through for example an Anti-Trust Law implemented in 1981 and, in 1984, through some relaxation of restrictions on foreign investment into South Korea.

In the financial sphere, interest rate subsidies on loans to finance exports were abolished in 1982, and in 1984 some of the banks were denationalized. Nevertheless, who should get what loans and at what rate of interest were issues still decided by the government. Furthermore, the *Chaebols* had bought substantial holdings in the banks, so that paradoxically the liberalization of the banking sector may have encouraged, rather than reduced, economic concentration.

Amsden's claim is that liberalization in trade and finance has been more apparent than real in the 1980s. By contrast, in studies sponsored by the World Bank, liberalization in Korea is presented more positively as a cure for the economic diseases supposedly caused by the government intervention of the 1970s. However, the World Bank's 1987 *World Development Report* concedes that 'the view that substantial liberalization is under way is not universally shared ... by all who watch the Korean experience with care'.

The anti-trust law of 1981 was associated with a growing public and political concern about the growing concentration of economic power in the economy. One estimate is that the biggest ten *Chaebols* account for almost 70% of GNP. This is almost certainly an overstatement but it is probably true that South Korea has the world's biggest share of GNP produced by the 10 biggest business groups.

Borrowing and investing overseas
Over this 1981–84 period South Korea's external debt continued to rise and by the end of 1984 was US$43 billion compared to US$32 billion in 1981. But increasingly, in the 1980s, at the same time as South Korea has been borrowing from overseas, it has also been investing overseas, including about US$6 billion between 1980 and 1984.

By the 1980s, South Korean companies were searching out sources of cheap unskilled labour overseas. They were relocating the 'sunset', labour-intensive industries such as footwear and clothing to lower labour-cost countries such as Thailand, Malaysia, Indonesia and the Philippines (Asian Development Bank, 1990). The country was by now on the brink of developed status. The heavy industries had come of age. Pohang was producing highly competitive steel, the car industry was penetrating foreign markets and the electronics industry was increasingly developing its own technology. South Korea's companies were increasingly selling under their own brand names and their competitive advantage was increasingly in cheap skilled, rather than unskilled, labour.

Political changes
While there are debates about the extent of economic liberalization in this period, there is little

disagreement about the speed of political liberalization. It was slow. The Kwangju massacre of 1980 had been followed by martial law and then by the designation of Chun as President by an electoral college. Chun took office on terms which limited him to one seven-year term. In 1983, on the third anniversary of the Kwangju massacre, an opposition leader, Kim Yong Sam, went on hunger strike for democracy. In spite of this, in the same year, Chun announced that his successor in 1987 would be 'elected' as before, indirectly through an electoral college. The announcement unleashed a widespread campaign for direct presidential elections.

The growing struggle for political liberalization (1984–90)

Figure 4.15   Distribution of trade union leaflets outside Hyundai shipyard.

Economic growth and wages
In the second half of the 1980s, the South Korean economy continued to grow very fast indeed. Between 1984 and 1988 real GDP grew at more than 10% a year, with the contribution of manufacturing being particularly spectacular. Between 1983 and 1988, net output (in real terms) in manufacturing doubled, so that by the end of the 1980s, the sector accounted for almost a third of GDP, while the share of agriculture, forestry and fishing had fallen to about 10%. By 1988, agriculture's share

of South Korea's labour force had fallen to 19%, down from 35% in 1978. In 1988 the labour force in manufacturing was 4.7 million, over a million more than the number employed in agriculture.

Between 1983 and 1988 real wages in manufacturing had risen by more than 45%, continuing the rapid rise of the 1960s and 1970s. But once again it is important to note that these rises were all from a very low base. In 1988 average monthly earnings were W393 000 equivalent to about US\$537. Since (as we saw earlier) average hours worked in South Korean manufacturing are among the highest in the world, in 1988 over 56 hours a week, the average hourly wage was still only a little over US\$2. Thus in spite of real wages rising at more than 10% a year for the past twenty-five years, the low base wage has combined with rising labour productivity to maintain the competitiveness of the South Korean manufacturing sector.

Debt
In 1980, South Korea had a deficit on its current account of more than 8% of its GDP. Its external debt was more than 45% of its GDP. By 1988 there was a current account surplus of US\$14 billion, almost 9% of GDP. And by the end of the 1980s, South Korea's net foreign debt was next to nothing, since its gross foreign debt of about US\$29 billion (less than 20% of its GNP) at the end of 1989 was almost completely offset by its investments held overseas (Asian Development Bank, 1990).

Economic and political liberalization
In this period, there were signs of further economic liberalization with a reduction in the number of goods under import restriction. But alongside this, the government continued to direct the restructuring of industry and its investment. In 1986, the Industrial Development Law was enacted and used to rationalize the textile, steel, fertilizer, automobile, diesel engine, heavy electrical equipment and heavy construction equipment industries.

While there is some doubt about whether there have been moves towards economic liberalization in South Korea, there is no doubt about the growing pressures for political liberalization. In 1987, after Chun had ordered that all discussions of direct elections be discontinued until after the 1988 Olympics in Seoul, another General (Roh Tae Woo) was nominated as Chun's successor. But in June 1987, Roh announced that he was in favour of holding the direct Presidential elections which were due that December. With the two opposition leaders Kim Yong Sam and Kim Dae Jung split, Roh was elected President. Nevertheless Roh's pro-democracy announcement of June 1987 was 'like a match set to timber waiting to be kindled' and 'decades of pent-up humiliations were let loose resulting in wave after wave of worker demonstrations and union organizing" (Ogle, 1990). The period since June 1987 has seen the rapid growth of a *minju* (democratic) labour movement confronting the official state-sponsored KFTU. Amsden has pointed out that 'Paternalism in (South) Korea since the military coup in 1961 has witnessed almost three decades of relatively peaceful labour relations'. The age of paternalism may well be over.

4.6 Conclusions

Four decades of growth in manufacturing

The growth record of South Korea has been spectacular. Over the four decades since the end of the Korean War, real Gross Domestic Product has grown at an average rate of more than 8% per year, with the growth being even faster if attention is focused on the 25 years since 1965.

The engine behind this growth has been the manufacturing sector which since the early 1960s has averaged more than 17% a year. The changes in structure and orientation of the sector over the period have been dramatic. The composition of the manufacturing sector is summarized in Table 4.12, which shows that the emphasis has shifted from food, beverages and tobacco and textiles in the early 1950s to chemicals, non-metallic mineral products and basic metals in 1970 to machinery and transport equipment in 1985. Thus, there has been a strong diversification of industry from consumer to producer industries. Such diversification has been generally associated with strengthened technological capacity and long-term industrial and economic growth.

Table 4.12 The composition of South Korean manufacturing output

	% of manufacturing output		
	1954	1970	1985
Light industries			
Food, beverages and tobacco	51	19	11
Textiles and clothing	19	20	17
Leather and footwear	2	1	2
Wood and wood products	4	4	2
Paper, printing and publishing	6	6	5
Heavy industries			
Chemicals and petroleum products	5	21	19
Non-metallic mineral products	3	7	4
Basic metals	1	5	6
Metal products	2	3	5
Machinery: non-electrical	3	2	5
Machinery: electrical	1	4	11
Transport equipment	2	6	8
Others	1	2	5

[Sources: Chong-Hyun Nam in Milner (ed), 1990 and Bureau of Statistics and Economic Planning Board, South Korea]

We have seen that there have been various phases in the development of the manufacturing sector. Four are summarized here.

(i)   In the 1950s the manufacturing sector developed on the basis of production for the domestic market (import-substituting industrialization), with capital derived from land redistribution being directed into trade and industry. There was a substantial commitment to education in this period, and US aid was crucial in financing the large balance of trade deficit.

(ii) As US aid dried up in the 1960s, the emphasis switched to manufactured exports. Almost every government policy (including trade, exchange rate, nationalized finance and infrastructure) was geared to promoting the growth of a nationally-owned industrial sector with a high export content. In spite of low food prices and the repression of organized labour, wages rose as the labour surplus was absorbed.

(iii) In the 1970s the emphasis switched to relatively capital-intensive heavy industries. At the same time the continuing commitment to the education of the labour force and the rapid absorption of technology helped to maintain the growth of labour productivity.

(iv) In the 1980s, as the heavy industries became more and more internationally competitive and the labour-intensive industries less competitive, the South Korean *Chaebols* began to relocate the labour-intensive industries to countries with lower labour costs, such as Malaysia, Thailand, Indonesia and the Philippines. Meanwhile in South Korea there was a much greater emphasis on local research and development.

Looking at why and how rapid industrialization has taken place, we can see that the industrialization process has been changing. There have been important changes of 'tack' over time.

External and internal influences on growth
In explaining this process of rapid industrial transformation, there are both external and internal factors. The external factors include massive US aid in the 1950s and easy access to the US market in the 1960s and 1970s.

One of the internal factors is the nature of state intervention in South Korea. In attempting to explain why State intervention has been so successful in South Korea when it has failed in other countries, many writers have placed stress on the interaction between politics and economics. More specifically they point to the particular class structure that evolved in South Korea. As Amsden puts it:

> "The state in (South) Korea was able to consolidate its strength with respect to both business and labour for what appear to be historical reasons. In the early 1960s there were no financiers to challenge the government's power because the state-owned banking system of the colonial period was re-

nationalized; the business community was as weak as the financial community and beholden to the state for largesse; the working classes were small in number; and the countryside, through a land reform, was devoid of large land-holders."

(Amsden, 1989)

Thus, a highly militarized state and centralized business groups have been able to pragmatically and proactively develop and implement economic and industrial policy. The story has been one of continuous industrial transformation with the government attempting to anticipate rather than react to change. Thus, the state has been central but has been selective about the ways it intervenes. For example, it has acted to discipline and repress labour, but has also helped to bring into being a highly concentrated ownership structure (the *Chaebols*) roughly on the Japanese model, that works with government in what seems to be a highly disciplined way.

Korea: another Japan?
Is South Korea heading towards advanced developed country status? Amsden's book on South Korea and late industrialization has as its main title, *Asia's Next Giant,* implying that South Korea will follow the path of Japan. Certainly, like Japan, South Korea's industrial growth has been spectacular. And, like Japan, South Korea's future growth prospects seem to be good. It has a well educated labour force. It has a well developed physical infrastructure. In recent years, it has had a high investment rate; 30% of its gross domestic product compared with between 15 and 20% for the US and UK. Korea has now reached a stage of development where a substantial impetus for growth is coming from domestic demand (Asian Development Bank, 1990). The signs look good for South Korea's economic future.

Is South Korea's future, though, linked to the future of all the East Asian countries of the Pacific Rim? It certainly seems that we are witnessing a massive change in the global 'centre of gravity' from 'West' to 'East', with Japan, South Korea, Taiwan and increasingly other countries of East and even South East Asia moving through a high growth period.

Or is South Korea an unexploded social volcano?

Wealth and income inequalities, which were reduced significantly by the land redistribution of the 1940s and 1950s, have increased in the 1970s and 1980s. The growth of the *Chaebols* has given rise to increasing concerns about the centralization of economic power. Housing and social conditions remain inadequate given the average income level.

Within South Korea the massive economic transformations have generated new social movements, including freer trade unions and democratic youth movements. There have been violent student demonstrations every year since 1987.

Although the political system has begun to be democratized, it remains highly authoritarian.

The Korean War ended in stalemate and settled nothing. North Korea now has an army estimated at 700 000 compared with the South's 540 000. A quarter of South Korea's population lives within 35 kilometres of the frontier with the North and given that some 40 000 US troops are still stationed between the capital Seoul and the demilitarized zone, it is perhaps not surprising that South Korea has been dominated by military governments. But there are signs that with 'talks about unification talks' getting under way, the conditions for political liberalization are becoming increasingly favourable.

South Korea is not a testament to the virtues of free markets; rather to capitalist development backed by an authoritarian state. But it is not at all clear that authoritarian state intervention can (or should) be replicated by other LDCs.

Summary of Chapter 4

Since the 1950s, South Korea's industrial and economic growth has been very rapid by any standards, in spite of enormous difficulties it faced as a result of the Korean War.

The economic miracle after 1960 was built on a base of previous 20th century industrialization and in the context of strong national cultural identity which goes back to the 14th century or earlier.

The Second World War, followed by the division of Korea into the Soviet-backed North and the US-backed South, set the scene for the Korean War. Two outcomes of the Korean war were important in explaining South Korea's subsequent rapid industrialization; land redistribution and massive US aid in the 1950s. South Korean landlords, with strong State support, invested in industry and commerce. As a result, South Korea's capacity to manufacture goods for its domestic market (import substitution) expanded rapidly.

In the 1960s, US aid declined. The 1960s and 1970s saw spectacular export-led growth and industrial diversification. The reasons lie in a combination of factors. One factor was strong intervention in the economy by a repressive state, whose pragmatic policies allowed the growth of an internationally competitive private capitalist industrial structure. Another contributing factor was the high standard of education among the workforce.

A brief economic crisis in 1980 was rapidly overcome. Favourable international exchange rates, combined with investment overseas, led to a greatly increased penetration of world markets. At the same time, within South Korea there were increasing demands for political liberalization.

The signs are positive for South Korea's future economic development, though the political situation is still highly authoritarian.

5

THEORETICAL PERSPECTIVES

RHYS JENKINS

5.1 Interpreting industrialization

The first four chapters in this book have laid out the international context within which the Third World has industrialized and described the industrialization of two of the leading NICs, one from Latin America and one from Asia. It is time now to take stock.

Chapter 1 showed that a group of NICs in Latin America, East and South East Asia have experienced rapid industrial growth since about the mid-1960s, and have increased their share of world industrial production and trade in manufactures. These countries succeeded in participating in the rapid growth of world trade at a time of globalization of production and reduction of tariff barriers in the developed countries. More recently, however, they have had to face new forms of protectionism in these markets.

Chapter 2 showed how foreign borrowing helped to maintain industrial growth during the 1970s, despite the slowdown in world trade and production. When new loans dried up and interest rates rose, many Third World countries faced major economic difficulties.

In Chapters 3 and 4 the experience of two NICs was described to show how both international conditions and the specific history and government policies of Brazil and South Korea combined to bring about rapid industrialization.

There are still some unanswered questions.

Q Why did these particular countries succeed in industrializing more rapidly than others?

Q Did they enjoy some peculiar advantage from their history or geography? Is the key to understanding their industrial success to be found in the policies which their governments adopted?

Q Why too was South Korea able to continue its industrial expansion during the 1980s, while Brazil suffered a decade of economic crisis?

To answer these questions we need to do more than just describe the experience of these two countries. We have to interpret that experience. Inevitably, interpretations have differed considerably. Compare for instance the following two quotations about South Korea since the early 1960s.

"This remarkable growth record was achieved by the combination of a set of appropriate governmental policies and indigenous efforts that took advantage of the high level of human resources and a favourable external environment. ...

As a set, the government's policies liberalized the foreign trade regime to make it as attractive to produce for the export market as for the home market.

Other government policies were deliberately chosen to improve the allocation of resources. Price distortions were removed and prices were brought closer to a reflection of real costs."

(Meier, 1984, p.59)

"Korea is an example of a country that grew very fast and yet violated the canons of conventional economic wisdom. ... In Korea, instead of the market mechanism allocating resources and guiding private entrepreneurship, the government made most of the pivotal investment decisions. Instead of firms operating in a competitive market structure, they each operated with an extraordinary degree of market control, protected from foreign competition ... not only has Korea not gotten relative prices right, it has deliberately gotten them 'wrong'."

(Amsden, 1989, p.139)

These quotations give such a different picture of Korea that Meier and Amsden could be talking about two different countries; North and South Korea perhaps? But they are not, they are both discussing the phenomenal growth of South Korea in the 30 years or so since 1960.

Meier views South Korea as a model of a country which has followed sound economic doctrine and has reaped the benefits from it. The role of government has been limited to providing the conditions within which private enterprise and the market can function. Trade has been liberalized and prices have been determined by market forces.

For Amsden, in contrast, the state has been the key factor in Korean development, acting not in accord with conventional economic wisdom which emphasizes the role of free markets, but in direct opposition to it. Prices have been deliberately distorted and the government has played a central role in resource allocation, while domestic production has been protected from foreign competition.

It is not only for South Korea that one can find contrasting interpretations. Compare the following two views of the Brazilian 'miracle', the period of rapid economic growth which followed the 1964 military coup.

"The reorientation of economic policies, involving varying degrees of financial and goods market liberalization constituted a cautious drawback from the autarchic economic policy of the 1950s towards a more outward-looking economic strategy. These liberalizing market-oriented policies were seen to pay handsome dividends in terms of restoring high rates of economic growth.... The market mechanism was generally strengthened during this period, and government policies functioned through that mechanism."

(Tyler, 1981, pp. 5 &13)

"The growth of the state sector was the most substantial structural change in ownership of industry during the period of the 'miracle'. In quantitative terms the state has become the most important source of investment capital. Along with its entrepreneurial contribution, the state has been fundamentally important in the construction of alliances. ... Finally, of course, pressure from the regulatory side of the state apparatus has been important in fostering joint ventures between local and foreign capital even when state enterprises are not directly involved as partners."

(Evans, 1979 p. 278)

As in the case of South Korea, there is a marked difference between writers such as Tyler, who emphasize the role of market liberalization and a more outward-oriented, less protectionist strategy, and those such as Evans who stress the central role played by the state in Brazilian development through its intervention in resource allocation and in mediating relations with the international economy.

Why then have the same experiences of industrial development in the two countries been interpreted so differently? These writers vividly illustrated that facts do not speak for themselves but are viewed through the lenses of particular theoretical perspectives. Different perspectives put different 'facts' in the foreground and relegate others to a marginal position.

In both South Korea and Brazil, the contrasting interpretations involve two key issues which are central to development strategy. The first is the *role of the state*. Did it provide a framework within which the market mechanism was allowed to function, or did the state play a much more active role, directly intervening in the allocation of resources? The second issue relates to the *links between the local economy and the world economy*. Was it openness to international market forces and competition which was the key to successful industrialization, or was it state support for domestic production and local capital which laid the basis for international competitiveness?

To understand why there are such different interpretations of Brazilian and South Korean development, we will need to look in this chapter at the way in which development theory has evolved, and in particular to contrast two main perspectives, the *structuralist* and the *neo-liberal* approaches. Each was represented in the quotations above and each provides contending interpretations of development problems.

This chapter takes a detailed look at both approaches and at the policy recommendations which each perspective generates. Before moving to this it will be useful to put the evolution of development theories into a historical context. This is done in Section 5.2.

5.2 Changes in development thinking

The dominant approach to development issues in the early 1990s, as exemplified by the pronouncements and policy advice of the world's leading international development agency, the World Bank, emphasizes the importance of market forces and the need for developing countries to take advantage of international market opportunities. Within this framework, the role of government is to provide a suitable environment within which private initiative can flourish.

This view has not always been dominant in development thinking. Indeed during the first twenty years or so after the Second World War, when Third World development became a major field of

concern and study, quite the opposite view prevailed. Economic development was not seen as something that came about naturally, but as something that could only be achieved by active government intervention. Furthermore, it was believed that international exchange between rich and poor countries tended to exacerbate international inequality.

In this section, we shall trace the evolution of thinking about development from its origins during the Second World War, through the immediate post-war period and up to the present day.

The origins of development theory

Initial concern with development issues in the developed world coincided with the independence of many Asian and African countries in the aftermath of the Second World War. Until the 1940s, there was little Western academic interest in the development problems of these areas. Their role was well defined within the colonial empires. Development was identified with the exploitation of their natural resources and the opening up of their markets for the benefit of the 'mother country'. Raising the standard of living of the mass of the colonized population was not regarded as a priority.

Classical economists such as Smith, Ricardo and Marx had studied intensively the problems of capital accumulation and growth, but their focus

Figure 5.1 The Bandung conference of the non-aligned movement was held in 1955 as an Afro-Asian solidarity conference. Virtually all the independent countries of the time attended.

had always been the development of western capitalist economies, particularly Britain, rather than that of the non-European world.

There were of course exceptions. Faced with the problem of how a relatively backward country, such as Germany, could catch up with the nineteenth century world leader, Britain, the economist List formulated arguments for the protection of 'infant industries', which were later taken up in a Third World context. Even so the focus was on capitalist development in Europe.

Several processes combined to influence the development of development theory in the immediate aftermath of the Second World War. The growing number of independent governments in Asia and Africa created a market for advice on development strategy. Even in Latin America, where independent states had existed since the early nineteenth century, the collapse of primary commodity exports during the Great Depression had led to a questioning of traditional *laissez-faire* policies based on the orthodox economic theories of the developed world. The stage was therefore set for the emergence of development theory.

1945-65: The post-war orthodoxy

The particular brand of development theory which dominated the discussion of Third World problems from the late 1940s to the early 1960s came to be known as *structuralism*. As the term itself suggests, these theories are concerned with underlying economic and social structures and see economic development as involving changes in these structures.

Economic structures refer to:

* the weight of different activities such as agriculture, mining, manufacturing and services within the economy
* the country's links with the world economy (What products does it import and export? What role does foreign investment play?)
* the levels of productivity in different activities
* the type and scale of enterprises.

Social structures involve ownership and control of resources. For example, when economists or sociologists talk of agrarian structures, they usually mean:

* who controls land and how that control is maintained
* how agricultural production is organized (who produces what, how and for whom)
* how the benefits of crop or livestock production are realized and by whom.

In many ways, structuralism was a child of its times. The Great Depression of the 1930s and the acceptance of Keynesian ideas in Britain and the United States had undermined the traditional faith in the free market system (Box 5.1). Government was being given a much more central role in managing the economy and was seen as the main agent in overcoming 'structural obstacles' to economic growth.

Not surprisingly, Third World governments were seen as central to overcoming the enormous problems of economic backwardness. It was only by the state playing an active role that industrialization and a vastly increased rate of capital accumula-

---

Box 5.1   Keynesianism

The British economist J M Keynes (1883–1946) was influential in changing economic thinking between the two world wars. Before his death, he played an important part in the discussions at Bretton Woods (see Box 2.3 in Chapter 2 and *Allen & Thomas, 1992*, Ch.11).

Keynesian economics, in general terms, puts forward the following views.

* Overall (aggregate) demand, rather than supply, plays a key role in determining the overall level of output in an economy.

* There is no natural tendency for the market alone to create full employment.

* Government interventions through fiscal policy can influence overall demand and thereby reduce levels of unemployment.

tion, regarded as essential for economic development, could be achieved. The exact role which the state should play differed from country to country. In Latin America the emphasis was on protection of domestic industry and the provision of infrastructure. In India, where the Soviet model was more influential, state ownership was more extensive and planning was seen as the key to economic growth.

However, there was agreement on a number of key points.

1 Market forces alone had failed to bring about economic development and therefore the state must actively seek to promote it.

2 Development was to be achieved by transforming predominantly agricultural economies into industrial ones.

3 Economic growth and structural transformation required an increase in the level of investment in the economy.

This last point fitted in well with the ideas of the economic historian W.W.Rostow, who suggested that an increase in the level of investment to between 10% and 12% of national income was required for economic 'take-off' (Rostow, 1960), as well as with the growth models of economists such as Harrod and Domar in which investment played a key role.

The dominant development strategy of this period in the Third World was *import substitution industrialization*. Protectionist barriers were erected against competing imports to promote domestic production of a variety of manufactured goods.

Typically this began with the production of simple non-durable consumer goods such as clothing and footwear, and moved on to more complex consumer durables such as domestic appliances and cars, and intermediate goods such as steel and chemicals. Governments also supported this strategy by granting incentives to foreign investors in manufacturing, and by investing in road-building programmes and in energy production. Often government expenditure ran ahead of revenue, but this was not regarded as a major problem because investment would create additional future income.

Figure 5.2   Import substitution industry: VW car factory in Puebla, Mexico.

It is worth bearing in mind at this point that the economic growth of the Third World far exceeded the expectations of most economists during this period. World industry grew at an unprecedented rate after the Second World War, and the Third World shared in this growth (Chapter 1, Figures 1.1 and 1.2).

1965–80: The breakdown of consensus

Despite remarkable success in terms of economic growth, in the 1960s structuralist ideas came under increasing criticism. Initially perceived as a simple recipe for structural change and freeing the national economy from the constraints of the international system, import substitution became more difficult as simple imports were replaced by domestic production and those which remained tended to require large investments and increasingly complex technology. Economic growth failed to eliminate mass poverty in the Third World. As state bureaucracies expanded, awareness increased that government did not always act in the 'national interest'.

It is possible to distinguish three main lines of criticism along which the post-war consensus fractured. The first two came from within the structuralist 'school' itself, while the third began to look again to market solutions to development.

(a) Dependency theory

Within Latin America, the main challenge to structuralist ideas came from dependency theory, which focused on import substitution's failure to create an independent national economy and the absence of a 'national bourgeoisie' to lead economic development. It was argued that import substitution had led to transnational corporations taking over most of the dynamic sectors of the economy and to local industrialists becoming 'dependent' on international capital.

There were a number of different strands within dependency theory, including Marxists such as Andre Gunder Frank and Theotonio dos Santos, and disillusioned structuralists such as Celso Furtado and Osvaldo Sunkel who had worked previously for the UN Economic Commission for Latin America. They converged in their criticism

McKale USA

Figure 5.3   One view of dependency.

of the structuralist strategies of the 1950s, and their ideas were subsequently applied to other parts of the Third World.

(b) Basic needs

Other structuralists began to question the social consequences of post-war development at about the same time. These included Hans Singer and Dudley Seers among others. These writers focused on how economic growth had failed to create sufficient employment to absorb the growing labour force of the Third World, and had created increased income inequality and poverty in many countries.

A number of reports by the International Labour Office in the early 1970s reflected these views. They focused on the employment problem in Third World countries and promoted 'basic needs' strategies which emphasized the provision of a minimum standard of living to the poorest groups. 'Basic needs' included food, shelter, clothing and access to essential services such as safe drinking water, sanitation, transport, health and education.

For these writers, economic growth and structural change alone were important but were not enough. Development required attention to the pattern of income distribution and the standard of living of the poor as well. While the early structuralists believed that the benefits of economic growth would 'trickle down' to all members of society, the basic needs approach explicitly rejected the notion.

(c) Neo-liberalism

A third line of criticism was based on a revival of traditional economic orthodoxy, which emphasized how most Third World countries had failed to take advantage of the opportunities offered by the rapid growth of international trade. These critics also pointed to the inefficiencies associated with import substitution and extensive state intervention.

A number of influential studies in the late 1960s and early 1970s by the Organization for Economic Cooperation and Development (OECD), the World Bank and the US-based National Bureau for Economic Research documented the inefficiency of import substituting industrialization and the misallocation of resources which resulted. At about the same time the examples of Hong Kong, Taiwan, South Korea and Singapore were increasingly cited to show how countries which emphasized expanding exports could achieve rapid economic growth.

The stage was thus set for the emergence of neo-liberalism as the new orthodoxy in development but there were several detours before this happened. In the early 1970s the basic needs approach and dependency theory seemed to be gaining ground. The success of the OPEC countries in sharply increasing the price of oil in 1973 led to an increased assertiveness on the part of Third World governments in international economic relations. Following the Non-aligned Summit meeting in Algiers in 1973, the United Nations General Assembly formally issued the Declaration and Programme of Action on the Establishment of a New International Economic Order in May 1974 (see Box 5.2). Later in the same year, the UN adopted the Charter of Economic Rights and Duties of States. (For a more detailed discussion of these events, see Chapter 12 of *Allen & Thomas, 1992*.)

This was the high point of Third World economic nationalism which sought to restructure international economic affairs to reflect more closely the interests of the South. It soon became clear however that passing resolutions in the UN General Assembly was one thing, but changing the way in which the world economy functioned was quite another. The ability of OPEC to operate as a cartel to raise oil prices depended on very specific conditions which were not repeated with other commodities, and the bargaining power of the Third World in international economic relations generally remained weak.

One response to the issues raised by Third World governments was *The Brandt Report* which appeared in 1980. This report of the Independent Commission on International Development Issues sought to meet some of these demands but emphasized the mutual interest of North and South whereas proponents of a New International Economic Order had a more confrontational stance. The Commission numbered amongst its members several people who had been major Western leaders: the chairman, former West German Chancellor Willy Brandt; the former British prime minister Edward Heath; the Swedish Prime Minister, Olaf Palme.

However by the time that the report was published, the wind had changed. Margaret Thatcher was already in Downing Street and Ronald Reagan had been elected to the White House. The reformist Keynesian ideas which informed the Brandt Report were already falling from fashion in the developed countries, and it would not be long before the neo-liberal revival was in full swing internationally.

1980: The new orthodoxy

It was not only the political and intellectual climate in the West which changed during the 1980s. The international context for Third World development also altered significantly. The prices of primary commodities exported by less developed countries fell sharply in the early 1980s. Even the

Box 5.2　The new international economic order

In the early 1970s, the countries of the Third World put forward a number of demands for reform in the international economic system. These covered international trade, the operations of transnational corporations, international aid and the functioning of the major international financial institutions. Amongst the most important were the following:

(a) Trade

- reductions in trade barriers on exports of manufactures from the Third World
- the establishment of an integrated programme for commodities to stabilize and support the prices of the major primary commodities exported by Third World countries
- indexation of Third World export prices to tie them to the rising prices of manufactures exported by developed countries.

(b) *Transnational corporations (TNCs)*

- regulation of TNC activities in the Third World
- establishment of mechanisms for technology transfer to the Third World, separate from direct investment by TNCs.

- elimination of restrictive business practices
- the right to nationalize foreign property in accordance with a country's own law.

(c) *Aid*

- attainment of UN development assistance targets
- development of an International Food Programme
- us of funds released by disarmament for Third World development.

(d)　　*International institutions*

- reform of the procedures and structures of the IMF and World Bank
- creation of Special Drawing Rights by the IMF linked to development assistance

In addition to these specific demands directed at the developed world, there was also a general call for greater cooperation between developing countries. By the late 1970s it was already clear that the developed countries were not going to meet these demands.

(Source: Frank, 1980)

"Do you realize I have you under my control?"

Figure 5.4　The Brandt Commission emphasized the mutual interest of North and South.

oil producers, who had managed to increase prices once more in 1979, were unable to maintain the high price level for their exports during the 1980s.

The most significant international factor affecting development during the 1980s was the debt crisis (see Chapter 2). Not only did this lead to severe recession in many indebted Third World countries, but it also meant that they were forced to turn to the International Monetary Fund and the World Bank for financial support when bank credit dried up. This weakened their international bargaining power and gave the international financial institutions leverage over their economic policies.

In these circumstances, it was not surprising that the IMF and the World Bank, which are dominated by the developed countries, advocated the policies which were currently in fashion with their governments. These included monetarist measures to bring down the rate of inflation, public expenditure cuts to eliminate budget deficits and a reduced economic role for the state. In addition, despite the growth of protectionism in Europe and North America, Third World governments were urged to reduce their protectionist barriers and give greater emphasis to exports. Third World countries, it was said, urgently needed to increase their exports in order to earn foreign exchange for servicing foreign debt.

Neo-liberal approaches have therefore dominated the discussion of development policy since the early 1980s, but not to the exclusion of all others. Structuralist theory and its more radical offshoot, dependency theory, have both evolved since the 1960s. It is no longer a widely held view that economic and political dependence is the fundamental cause of underdevelopment, and attempts to construct a general theory of underdevelopment have been largely abandoned. However, dependency theory's focus on the interaction between the Third World and the world economy continues to have an important influence. This is reflected in the work of those writers on 'dependent development' who reject the traditional opposition of dependence and development in favour of using dependency as a methodology for analyzing the specific situation of particular Third World economies (Evans, 1979).

New structuralist ideas have emerged in recent years, particularly in reaction to the debt crisis and the policies imposed by the IMF on many Third World countries (Chapter 2). New structuralists recognize that prices matter rather more than the early structuralists realized, but continue to emphasize the particular characteristics and economic processes of less developed countries, in opposition to the universal theorizing of the neo-liberals. It has also highlighted the critical importance of institutions and technology in explaining economic development.

5.3 Structuralist development theory

What exactly is structuralism?

The term structuralist was first used in development theory to refer to the ideas of a group of social scientists at the United Nations Economic Commission for Latin America (ECLA). This group was led by Raúl Prebisch, who in the late 1940s and 1950s analysed the economic problems of Latin America. They particularly stressed:

- the position in the international economy of Latin America, which was seen as peripheral to the centres of capitalism in the United States and Western Europe

- the heterogeneous structure of the Latin American economies, which were characterized by very uneven levels of development between different sectors.

Subsequently the term 'structuralist' came to be used more broadly; to refer to a much wider group of social scientists, particularly economists, concerned with issues of economic development. Indeed for some writers structuralism is virtually synonymous with 'development economics' (Hirschman, 1981; Lal, 1983).

In addition to their concern with structural change, and in common with the ECLA structuralists, these writers rejected much orthodox economic theory. Dudley Seers, who had worked at ECLA and was a leading proponent of structuralist ideas, argued that mainstream or 'orthodox' economics was the theory of the 'special case', relevant only to a small group of advanced industrialized countries during a relatively short period of their history (Seers, 1963).

Structuralist theory, therefore, developed as an alternative to orthodox theory. It started from the premise that 'certain special features of the economic structure of the underdeveloped countries make an important portion of orthodox analysis inapplicable and misleading' (Hirschman, 1981, p.375).

This is the sense in which the term structuralism is often used in current discussion of development theory. However we have cast the net even further to include other approaches which are more explicitly radical or Marxist in their orientation. Dependency theory, which developed in Latin America in the 1960s, partly out of and partly as a critique of ECLA theory and practice, is the best known of these (Chapters 6 and 11 of *Allen & Thomas, 1992*).

In terms of political positions, therefore, structuralist theories range from mild reformists who advocate a degree of state intervention or guidance of the economy, to revolutionaries who believe that development can only be brought about under socialism.

What then can such a broad group of writers have in common to justify putting them under one umbrella? There are five central features which they all share:

1 *Scepticism about the beneficial effects of the free market.* Structuralism questions the belief that the free play of market forces can bring about economic development in the Third World. This applies both to the domestic market and international market, leading to a questioning of the theory of comparative advantage in international trade.

2 *An emphasis on structural change.* Development is seen as a process of transformation of economic and social structures in which industry, particularly manufacturing industry, plays a cru-

cial role. The level of development cannot be derived simply from levels of per capita income or simplistic measures of economic growth.

3 *Concern with issues of ownership and control of resources.* Structuralists believe that highly concentrated ownership and control of resources in the Third World affect the outcome of economic policies and processes and have to be taken into account when trying to understand development.

4 *An emphasis on the dynamic aspects of technology.* Technology is seen as playing a key role in economic development. Technological dependence and technological capability are highlighted.

5 *A central role for capital accumulation.* A high rate of capital accumulation is seen as crucial for rapid economic development. This is a necessary condition for bringing about structural transformation and increased productivity levels.

This section looks at how these characteristics fit together in a theory of economic development.

Links to the world economy

A major innovation of the original Latin American structuralists was to emphasize the links between the Third World and the advanced industrialized countries. They used the notion of *centre–periphery relations* (i.e. relations between the developed capitalist centre and the underdeveloped periphery) to highlight the differences between the developed world and the Third World, and also to highlight the unequal nature of the relationship.

The developed and the less developed world are linked through movements of goods, capital and labour. Although the last of these is important for some countries, immigration controls in the industrialized countries limit the overall extent of labour migration, so we shall ignore it here.

Structuralists see these links leading to increased international inequality between the countries of the centre and the periphery. For some the periphery is actually made worse off as a result of its links with the international economy. They also see the countries of the periphery being subject to international forces over which they have little influence.

The terms of trade

A number of arguments have been put forward over the years to explain why international trade operates to the detriment of the Third World. Perhaps the best known of these is the theory of the deterioration of the terms of trade of LDCs, also known as the Prebisch–Singer theory after the two authors who first put it forward (see Box 5.3).

Prebisch and Singer noted that, contrary to the expectations of earlier economists, the prices of primary products tended to fall relative to those of manufactured goods over a long period of time. Therefore, since LDC exports were almost entirely made up of primary commodities and LDC imports were mainly of manufactured goods, they concluded that there was a long-term tendency for the terms of trade of Third World countries to

---

Box 5.3   Terms of trade

The terms of trade refer to the relative prices of a country's exports and imports. It is calculated by dividing the index of export prices by the index of import prices. Taking an initial year, in which the index of both export and import prices are taken as 100, the terms of trade are said to deteriorate if import prices increase faster than export prices, or export prices fall faster than import prices. Similarly, the internal terms of trade are used to describe the relative prices of one country's agricultural and industrial output.

To take a numerical example, with 1980 as the base year, if export prices have increased 20%

and import prices 50% by 1990, the terms of trade will have declined from 100 to 80.

	Export price	Import price	Terms of trade (= export price / import price)
1980	100	100	100
1990	120	150	80

A number of studies have estimated the long-term trends in the terms of trade both of primary commodities and of LDCs.

Figure 5.5   Unfair terms of trade? Heavy machinery for import to Nigeria (above). Cotton exports from Mozambique (right).

decline. They explained this both in terms of differences in the demand for primary products and manufactures, and in terms of the supply conditions under which they are produced in the periphery and the centre.

Demand: As an economy develops, the demand for manufactured goods tends to grow more rapidly than the demand for primary commodities, particularly agricultural products. This means that the growth in demand for LDC (mainly agricultural) exports to the developed countries is unlikely to keep up with growth in LDC demand for (mainly manufactured) imports from developed countries (see Chapter 1, Section 1.6).

Supply: In Third World countries, the existence of surplus labour tends to keep wages down. So when productivity in the export sector increases, production costs fall because fewer workers are required to produce a unit of output. With wage rates remaining the same, the total wages paid for the same output falls. This leads to falling prices for primary products. In the developed countries, on the other hand, the supply of labour is limited and workers are organized in trade unions. They are therefore able to increase wages in line with productivity. Thus the developed countries gain both from their own productivity increases

(through higher incomes) and from the periphery's productivity increases (through lower prices).

The notion that trade operates to the detriment of Third World countries was further developed in Emmanuel's theory of unequal exchange (1972). Although many would disagree with the precise formulation of the problem by Emmanuel, most structuralists would agree that international markets are in some way biased against less developed countries. In the aftermath of the OPEC price rise in 1973, one of the main demands of the new international economic order (Box 5.2) was improved prices for the products which developing countries exported.

Although the empirical evidence presented by Prebisch and Singer to support their thesis was subject to heavy criticism in the 1950s and 1960s, the deteriorating external environment for LDCs in the 1970s and 1980s led to renewed interest in their views. A number of recent studies have lent support to their view that the terms of trade tend to move against primary products (Figure 5.6).

Foreign investment and the flow of capital

Whereas orthodox economic theory suggests that capital will tend to flow from rich countries where

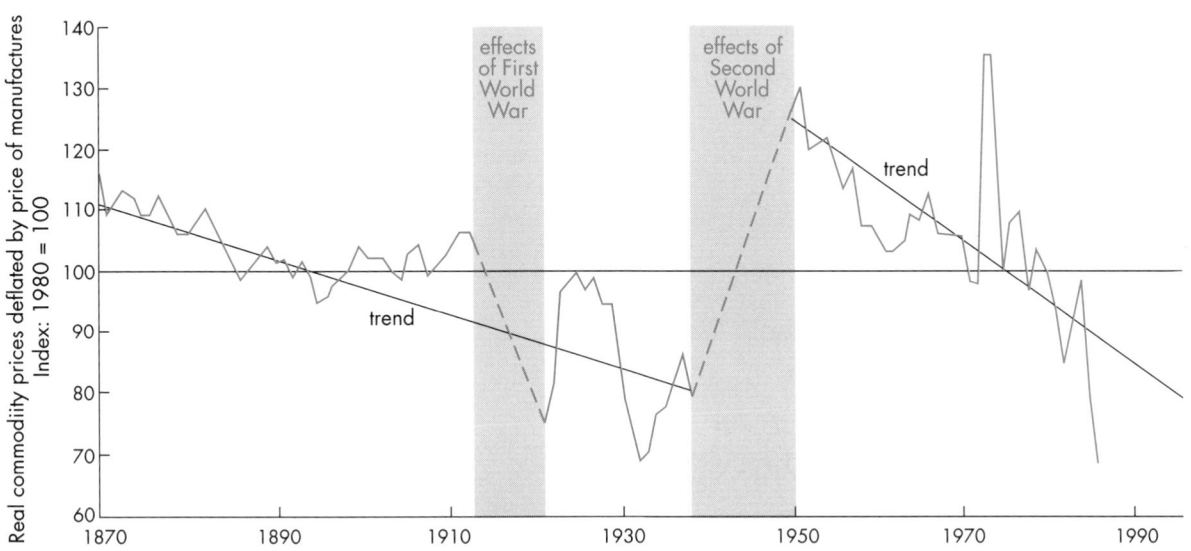

Figure 5.6   Terms of trade for primary products, 1870–1986.

it is abundant to poor countries where it is scarce, structuralist theories suggest the opposite. Structuralists say that capital is attracted to the developed countries where the necessary economic infrastructure and large markets exist and political stability is guaranteed, so that free international movement of capital leads to capital flowing from the periphery to the centre.

Direct foreign investment

This is not to deny that inflows of foreign capital do occur in the periphery from time to time and that these can contribute to economic growth by adding to the availability of foreign exchange and increasing the level of investment. However, some structuralists claim that foreign investment displaces local saving so that total investment is not increased. And in any case, this inflow of capital leads to growing outflows over time in the form of profits, dividends and interest payments. Difficulties arise when the outflow of payments exceeds the new inflows of foreign investment.

A number of comparative studies of different Third World countries support this argument (Bornschier & Chase-Dunn, 1985). These studies found that, although the inflow of direct foreign investment tends to increase with economic growth, the increased foreign capital penetration acts as a brake on further growth, because a large stock of foreign capital also increases the outflow of profits. This, and other negative consequences of foreign ownership, constitute a kind of 'negative feedback' effect on growth. The scale of negative flows of capital from developing countries is shown in Chapter 2, Table 2.4. It is also discussed in more detail for Brazil in Chapter 3.

Loans

The same argument applies to foreign loans. This is vividly illustrated by the experience of many Third World countries with foreign debt in the 1970s and 1980s (see Chapter 2). In Latin America in the 1970s for instance, the availability of foreign loans enabled governments to maintain high rates of growth in the aftermath of the 1973 oil price increases. These countries were able to continue growing until the early 1980s, by borrowing on an ever increasing scale. However, since 1982, outflows of interest and dividends have massively exceeded new loans leading to a transfer of resources out of Latin America of over US\$30 billion a year. This of course has had a devastating effect on the region's economic growth.

Capital flight

One factor which contributed to the debt crisis in a number of countries in the late 1970s and early 1980s was capital flight. In the absence of strict controls on foreign exchange, part of the loans received by Third World countries ended up in the Swiss bank accounts of their nationals or invested in property in California or Florida. This again underlines the attractions of the developed countries for internationally mobile capital.

Debt crisis

The debt crisis also illustrates the extent to which Third World economies are subject to international forces which are beyond their control. A major factor in the crisis was the sharp rise in international interest rates in the early 1980s as a result of the tight monetary policies of the United States. Since a large part of the debt contracted by Third World countries in the 1970s was at floating rates of interest, this suddenly increased the costs of debt servicing. At the same time, the banks became increasingly reluctant to increase their lending to the Third World (see Chapter 2 for a detailed explanation).

While the cost of debt servicing was increasing and the availability of new loans to repay the old ones was diminishing, many Third World countries found that their export earnings were falling. Primary exports were hit by falling commodity prices, while manufactured exports were faced with increasing protection in developed country markets. Moreover, oil-importing countries were hit by the sharp rise in oil prices in 1979 which further increased their import bills. It has been estimated that the loss of export earnings due to falling commodity prices accounted for roughly half the increase in debt between 1981 and 1983.

Structural change

For structuralists, economic development requires structural change, that is, a shift in the relative contribution of different sectors of the economy away from agriculture and towards industry (particularly manufacturing). This is hardly surprising. As we have seen, many structuralists saw the specialization of LDCs in primary production as a major factor contributing to economic backwardness. Moreover the relationship between industry and development was amply confirmed by empirical evidence.

In the 1950s when the structuralist model took root, one could look back over the history of the developed countries and see a steady increase in the importance of industry since the industrial revolution (Chapter 1, Figure 1.11). Moreover, studies which compared the economic structure of developed and less developed countries revealed that the major difference was in the size of their industrial sectors compared with their agricultural sectors.

Whereas orthodox economic theory does not generally concern itself with sectoral differences, treating all economic activity as equivalent, the structuralists believed that a number of features of industry enabled it to play a dynamic role in terms of economic development.

Economies of scale

First, industrial production is particularly subject to economies of scale. In other words, as the volume of production increases, the cost per unit of production tends to fall (Box 5.4). A car plant producing 200 000 cars a year will produce cars much more cheaply than one producing only 2 000 cars a year. This is not true to the same extent in agriculture, or indeed in many services. So in LDCs, although initially production may be high-cost because of small-scale production, these costs can be reduced rapidly as output expands.

Externalities and linkages

A second reason for supposing that industry is particularly important for economic development is that externalities are more significant than in other sectors. Externalities occur when the setting up of one activity creates benefits for others. In other words the benefit of a particular activity for society is greater than the benefit to the direct producer. An example might be where one firm creates a pool of skilled labour from which other producers can draw thus reducing their training costs.

Figure 5.7   Economies of scale: cars and lorries waiting for delivery outside São Paulo factory.

Box 5.4   Economies of scale

Economists speak of economies of scale where the unit cost of production falls as the volume of production increases. For example, look at the following index of costs for the assembly of vehicles.

Output per annum	Cost index
3 500	300
5 000	245
10 000	215
25 000	185
50 000	155
100 000	122
200 000	103
300 000	100

[Source: Jenkins, 1977]

This indicates that, at an output of 3 500 cars a year, the cost of assembling a vehicle is three times as much as with an output of 300 000 a year.

There are a number of reasons why costs are lower with a larger volume of output. There may be fixed costs which are independent of the amount produced as for example in making and setting up dies for stamping. At large levels of output both workers and equipment can be more specialized so that productivity is higher. In some industries, such as cement, there are economies from increased dimensions. The cost of a kiln increases in proportion to its surface area, whereas the output obtained increases in proportion to the volume of the kiln. These all refer to economies of scale at the plant level, but there may also be further economies to a firm which operates several plants in an industry, or in more than one industry.

Some recent technological developments have made it possible to achieve low costs at rather smaller scales than in the past (see Chapter 1). This has been noticeable in the motor industry, for example, where the Japanese have introduced more flexible manufacturing techniques, reducing set up times and have moved away from the highly specialized machinery and extreme division of labour which characterized Fordist production.

A more specific application of this is the notion of linkages. The setting up of a car factory creates both backward and forward linkages. Backward linkages arise because of the demand for inputs to supply the car factory e.g. to the steel industry, the glass industry, the rubber industry. Forward linkages occur downstream from the initial activity, for example to service stations and repair workshops. Structuralists argue that manufacturing creates more linkages than other sectors particularly agriculture and can therefore give a much greater impetus to economic development.

Productivity increases

Finally, industry is also characterized by more scope for increases in productivity than other sectors. It has been observed that the faster manufacturing output increases, the greater the rate of productivity growth. This reflects increased learning and the incorporation of new, higher productivity technology, which depends on the rate of growth of output. Moreover, since the industrial sector provides machinery and equipment for other sectors, increases in productivity in manufacturing can reduce costs elsewhere in the economy, thus contributing to the development of other sectors.

In the Third World, some of these arguments are weakened by the fact that the industrial sector may be linked to that of the developed countries. Thus, while manufacturing may create linkages, there is no guarantee that these linkages will be created locally rather than abroad. While a car factory in Mexico creates a demand for steel or glass, these inputs may be supplied from the United States or Japan rather than from Mexico. Equally, if domestic industry is confined to producing consumer goods, productivity gains will not be passed on to other sectors of the economy because capital and intermediate goods are not produced locally.

This has led some structuralists to emphasize the need for an integrated industrial sector, similar to those found in the developed countries, which produces machinery and equipment, and intermediate inputs as well as consumer goods.

There is some empirical support for the emphasis given to industrialization by structuralists. Table 5.1 is taken from a Presidential Address given by Professor A K Sen to the Development Studies Association in 1982 (Sen, 1983). He drew the audience's attention to the fact that in the low-income country grouping, the three countries with the fastest rate of growth (China, Sri Lanka and Pakistan) were also among those with the highest share of industry in GDP. Similarly in the middle-income grouping, the countries with the highest growth (Romania, South Korea and Yugoslavia) were among the five most industrialized countries. This correlation is illustrated in Figure 5.8.

Uganda has the lowest growth rate and lowest share of industry amongst the low-income coun-

tries. Ghana occupies the same position among the middle income countries, but the evidence is not so clear cut among the slowest growing countries as it is for the fast growth economies. Nonetheless, Sen believes that the importance of industrialization in economic growth cannot be denied on the basis of this evidence. The view that manufacturing is the key to economic development has traditionally been accompanied by a rather negative view of the other sectors in most structuralist thought.

Supply rigidities in agriculture

Agriculture is characterized by supply rigidities. That is, higher prices for agricultural products do not lead to significant increases in production and/or marketed output. This means that supply is unable to expand sufficiently rapidly to meet the increased demand for food from the expanding urban population. This was seen as one of the principal structural bottlenecks by the early Latin American structuralists. Moreover, agriculture is characterized by a high level of surplus labour, which produces at very low levels of productivity. This was initially seen as an opportunity for industrialization, enabling workers to be withdrawn from agriculture with minimal impact on production. But more recently it has come to be seen more as a problem, as employment creation in industry has failed to keep pace with the stream of migrants from the rural areas to the cities.

The service sector is regarded in the main as unproductive. The rapid growth of employment in services is seen primarily as a result of the displacement of labour from agriculture and the slow growth of new jobs in industry. So most rural migrants end up in low-paid or casual service jobs. Thus a further structural characteristic of Third World economies is an overblown service sector.

Ownership

As one US writer, sympathetic to the structuralist approach, has written,

> "It is possible to study a great deal of economics without ever encountering a serious question about ownership. The core of the subject is a logical system that treats capital and

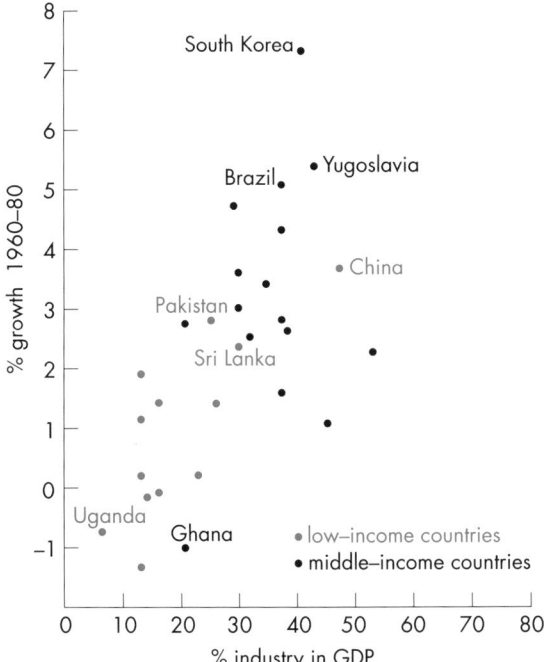

Figure 5.8   Correlation between industrialization and growth for low-income and middle-income countries (data from Table 5.1).

Table 5.1 Growth, investment and industrialization in 1980

Country	GNP per head US$	% Growth 1960–80	Gross domestic investment as % of GDP	% Industry in GDP
Low-income				
Bangladesh	130	1.3*	17	13
Ethiopia	140	1.4	10	16
Nepal	140	0.2	14	13
Burma	170	1.2	24	13
Afghanistan	—	0.9*	14	—
Zaire	220	0.2	11	23
Mozambique	230	−0.1	10	16
India	240	1.4	23	26
Sri Lanka	270	2.4	36	30
Tanzania	280	1.9	22	13
China	290	3.7*	31	47
Pakistan	300	2.8	18	25
Uganda	300	−0.7	3	6
Sudan	410	−0.2	12	14
Middle-income				
Ghana	420	−1.0	5	21
Kenya	420	2.7	22	21
Egypt	580	3.4	31	35
Thailand	670	4.7	27	29
Philippines	690	2.8	30	37
Morocco	900	2.5	21	32
Peru	930	1.1	16	45
Colombia	1 180	3.0	25	30
Turkey	1 470	3.6	27	30
S Korea	1 520	7.3	31	41
Malaysia	1 620	4.3	29	37
Brazil	2 050	5.1	22	37
Mexico	2 090	2.6	28	38
Chile	2 150	1.6	18	37
South Africa	2 300	2.3	29	53
Romania	2 340	8.6	34	64
Argentina	2 390	2.2	—	—
Yugoslavia	2 620	5.4*	35	43

[Source: World Bank, 1982]

The table includes all countries within the 'low-income' and 'middle-income' categories, except those with less than 10 million population, members of OPEC, and those without figures for GNP or GDP growth.

* Growth rates based on GDP growth figures per head.

land as factors of production to be analyzed by universally applicable techniques without regard to who owns them."

(Sheahan, 1987, p.130)

This is not true however of structuralist analysis. In societies characterized by highly unequal ownership, these issues cannot be disregarded by economic analysis the structuralists claim.

The analysis of agriculture regards ownership as central. The problems of agricultural supply discussed above, derive in large measure from prevailing patterns of land tenure and control over resources such as water rights, as well as access to complementary inputs and credit. In Latin America the traditional pattern of large estates and small peasant plots, gave rise to a situation in which the best land was farmed extensively by large landowners with low yields, while marginal land was farmed intensively by the peasant family. This tended to limit agricultural output and productivity increases. The peasantry did not have the resources to respond to agricultural policies while large landowners lacked the incentive. The result was agricultural stagnation.

In industry too, ownership affects economic performance. Here the particular concern is with foreign ownership. Although most structuralists

Figure 5.9 'Here, Señor Carter is the statue of Simón Bolívar, who liberated Latin America from foreign domination.'

recognize the contribution which foreign ownership can make by introducing advanced technology and providing access to foreign markets, they are also concerned about the negative effects of unrestricted foreign ownership.

Transnational corporations (TNCs) exercise considerable market power which enables them to earn monopoly profits. These do not always appear in the tax returns of the foreign subsidiaries because of various accounting procedures used by the TNCs, particularly transfer pricing (see Box 5.5). This enables TNCs to repatriate a large part of their earnings to the parent company, further intensifying the 'drain of surplus' from the periph-

---

Box 5.5   Transfer pricing

Transfer prices refer to the internal prices charged on transactions between different parts of the same corporate organization. They are contrasted with the 'arm's length' prices which are set in external markets for transactions between independent parties.

There has been considerable concern in recent years that TNCs are able to manipulate these transfer prices in order to reduce their tax liabilities in particular countries or to avoid government controls on profit remittances by their subsidiaries.

Numerous examples have come to light where TNCs have used transfer pricing to under-declare their profits in LDCs. One of the earliest was in Colombia where it was found that in the late 1960s TNCs over priced the inputs which they sold to their subsidiaries, compared to free market prices, by 155% in the pharmaceuticals industry, 54% in the electrical industry, 44% in rubber and 25% for chemicals. For individual products levels of over pricing of as much as 3000% were recorded in certain cases (Vaitsos, 1974).

The manipulation of transfer prices by TNCs is difficult to control because governments often lack the necessary information and organization required in order to monitor such practices.

ery and worsening the balance of payments problems from which most developing countries suffer.

Since TNCs are primarily concerned with maximizing profits globally, they often act individually and collectively to restrict competition in various ways. These include imposing restrictive clauses on subsidiaries and licensees who depend on them for technology, tying inputs of raw materials, machinery etc., to the technology supplier or restricting exports in order to divide world markets. TNCs also engage collectively in cartels and informal collusion through market sharing arrangements or the allocation of spheres of influence, which may restrict economic growth.

For structuralists, ownership is relevant, not only because of its impact on economic growth, but also because of its impact on income distribution and poverty. Neo-liberal theorists tend to emphasise population growth and insufficient opportunities for alternative employment in explaining rural poverty. But for structuralists, access to land (or lack of it) is crucial. Income distribution also feeds back into economic growth because of its impact on the pattern of consumer demand and on capital accumulation.

Another area of concern relates to the cultural impact of foreign ownership. TNCs use their market power to create demand for their products through advertising and sales promotion. This leads to 'taste transfer' and the expansion of the market for products which may be inappropriate for local conditions. The classic example of this is powdered baby milk.

Figure 5.10   Taste transfer: cans in an Angolan market.

Finally the more radical structuralists emphasize the link between property ownership, economic power and political power. Ownership and control of resources not only influence the outcome of development policies but also, through the state, can influence the formulation and implementation of those policies. In many Third World countries, despite industrialization, large landowners continue to enjoy considerable political influence, through their control of export crops.

Technology

One of the key features of Third World economies is the co-existence of very different technological levels both between sectors and between different enterprises in the same sector.

Technology does not drop like manna from heaven but is rather the outcome of research and development by firms or research institutions and of on-the-job learning. As such it is conditioned by the historical and economic conditions in which it developed. Importing foreign technology does not therefore necessarily offer a short-cut to development.

Structuralists have been concerned with the problems of technological dependence which may arise as a result of excessive reliance on imported technology. This is seen as creating a number of problems.

Expensive and outdated technology

First, on the international market, technology is not free. In many cases, firms in developed countries provide technology which is no longer state of the art to firms in the Third World, charging them excessively high prices. Third World buyers are in a weak bargaining position because of their lack of expertise, inadequate information and lack of alternative source of supply. Because of the competitive advantages which they can derive from using the technology in the local market, they are prepared to pay over the odds.

Inappropriate technology

A second problem relates to the nature of the technology imported. Because it has been developed in the developed countries it may often be inappropriate for conditions in the Third World. It may be too capital-intensive so that very few jobs are created, or too large scale for the small markets of many developing countries so that there is a great deal of unused capacity.

Lack of local technological capabilities

These problems are both linked to a third, which is the lack of local technological capabilities within Third World countries. This both weakens the bargaining power of firms in negotiating to acquire imported technology, and limits their ability to adapt the imported technology to local conditions. What is more, dependence on imported technology tends to perpetuate the problem. Particularly where countries import a technology package through a TNC where all the principal elements are provided from abroad, there are no opportunities for local learning. Thus when, for example, another plant needs to be built in the same line of business, no local capabilities have developed which can substitute for the foreign inputs.

Modern structuralists therefore tend to emphasize the importance of developing local technological capability. Achieving this has many ramifications and is taken up in more detail in Chapter 7 of this book.

Accumulation and financing

Capital accumulation is an *increase* in the stock of productive assets in an economy (investment in machinery, buildings and so on). In its simplest form there is a direct relationship between a country's capital stock and its total output. The higher the rate of capital accumulation, the faster the rate of increase of the capital stock and hence the greater the rate of growth of output.

This of course is an oversimplification. It is possible that the relationship between the capital stock and output changes so that increases in accumulation do not give rise to a faster rate of growth. Indeed if resources are wasted on prestige projects of little economic benefit (white elephants) then this is precisely what will happen. While a high rate of accumulation is a necessary condition for economic growth it is not a sufficient condition.

The structuralists are aware of this, emphasizing the need for the surplus to be channelled into productive investment and not into consumption. This links back to questions of ownership and income distribution discussed earlier. For example if a large part of the surplus is in the hands of owners of traditional estates, it may be spent mainly on luxury consumer goods or on acquiring more land for the estate, rather than invested in raising agricultural productivity.

It also leads to concern over the mechanisms through which the surplus is directed to productive use. For instance, how can urban elites be persuaded to invest in industrial enterprises rather than using their wealth to speculate in real estate or transferring their money to foreign bank accounts?

This also links to the emphasis on the key role to be played by industry for the structuralists. Rapid industrialization requires a transfer of resources from agriculture into industry. We have already mentioned the role which surplus labour plays in this context, but particularly when the industrial sector is initially small and therefore only able to generate a small surplus itself, growth also depends on a transfer of other resources to industry.

Glance back now at Table 5.1 and look at the share of investment in GDP for the fastest growing and the slowest growing countries in the two groups. Do the data support the view that fast growing countries tend to have high levels of investment, while low growth countries have low investment rates? Sen certainly thinks so. He comments,

> "So both in terms of cases of success and those of failure, the traditional wisdom of development economics is scarcely contradicted by these international comparisons. Quite the contrary."
>
> (Sen, 1983, p.750)

5.4 Structuralist policies

The inexorable conclusion of the structuralist paradigm is that development is too important to be left to the market. The state must take an active role in promoting economic development.

This was almost universally accepted by writers on development in the 1950s and early 1960s, apart from a few lone voices swimming against the tide. Since the mid-1960s that tide has turned. Those who advocate an active role for the state in developing countries are on the defensive. Nevertheless the structuralist analysis provides strong arguments for state intervention in Third World countries. There are a number of key areas in which structuralists see an important role for the state. These are discussed below.

The international economy

At the international level, structuralists believe that the free play of market forces tends to lead to further polarization. The state must therefore intervene to mediate the relations between the national and the world economy.

As far as primary commodities are concerned, there is little that individual Third World governments can do, except where they enjoy a degree of monopoly in the world market (e.g. Brazil with coffee) and can impose export taxes in order to improve the terms of trade. Collectively, however, there is more that can be done. Together they can create international commodity agreements which will help to stabilize the prices of primary commodities. Or they can form producer cartels like OPEC, in order to raise prices. However in practice such initiatives have not prospered because of the leverage of developed countries and because of conflicting interests among developing countries.

Third World governments have more control over their domestic markets and structuralists argue for protectionist policies particularly in order to promote infant industries. In the past protectionist policies have been applied indiscriminately in many Third World countries giving rise to gross inefficiencies with extremely high levels of protection. Despite this, structuralists continue to argue that there is a sound theoretical case for selective protection over a limited period of time. Indeed when account is taken of learning and the acquisition of technological capability, protection may be justified for periods of as long as a decade.

Another area of international economic relations in which the state needs to play an active role is in controlling capital flows. Total freedom of movement of capital is undesirable because it may lead to flows of 'hot money' in and out of the country which will have a destabilizing effect on the economy. It is particularly important for poor countries, which can ill afford to lose capital, to have some mechanism such as exchange controls in order to prevent capital flight.

Industrialization

Industrial policy in the Third World is closely linked to trade policy. Competition from the advanced industrialized countries constrains the development of local industry. So protecting infant industry is a crucial part of any structuralist industrial policy.

The extreme 'export pessimism' of the early structuralists (see Section 5.3) has been at least partly dispelled as regards the possibilities of exporting manufactured goods. Most structuralists now recognize that government policies should not be an obstacle to exporting. Therefore where the domestic market is protected, firms should also be offered export incentives to enable them to compete on international markets.

In most advanced capitalist countries, the state's role in manufacturing industry is relatively limited. It provides infrastructure in the form of roads, railways and public utilities such as gas and electricity. But it does not generally engage directly in manufacturing production.

In the Third World however there may be few if any agents other than the state able to set up certain key industries. Often, the risks are too great, or the capital investment too large, for local entrepreneurs and foreign capital is not interested either. So in order to establish industries such as steel or petrochemicals, which are essential to the creation of an integrated industrial sector, the state may have little choice but to set up production facilities itself.

Figure 5.11   State investment in heavy industry: pouring metal into moulds at an Indian steel plant.

The structuralists also believe that the state should play a role in determining the structure of the industrial sector. In an economy in which manufacturing is mainly in the private sector, credit allocation can have a key role in promoting investment and can be used to ensure that priority sectors are developed. The government should also intervene to determine the balance between large-scale and small-scale industry. Specific policies may be required to strengthen small industry in order to generate employment.

Ownership and control

Structuralists do not regard property rights as sacrosanct, and certain changes in ownership are seen as an essential part of development strategy. Where traditional patterns of land tenure are an obstacle to agricultural development, radical land reform involving land redistribution and changes in tenure relations are necessary, even though this may encounter strong political opposition.

Similarly where a primary export sector is controlled by a foreign TNC, nationalization may be necessary in order to appropriate the full benefits in terms of foreign exchange earnings and government revenue. Measures short of full nationalization which give the government a measure of control and an increased share of revenues should also be considered.

In the 1950s most Latin American structuralists welcomed foreign investment, provided that it was not of the traditional 'enclave' variety in mines or plantations. Direct foreign investment (DFI) in manufacturing was seen as an important way to bring about import substitution in complex manufacturing industries. Industries which would be necessary to change the region's positions in the international division of labour.

However structuralists soon came to recognize that such optimism concerning foreign investment was misplaced. By the 1970s most structuralists recognized the potential conflict between the global interests of the TNCs and national economic development. It was no longer axiomatic that what was good for General Motors was also good for the Third World.

One area of particular concern is transfer pricing and a number of countries have been able to save foreign exchange through setting up agencies to monitor and control the pricing practices of TNCs. Other negative consequences of TNC behaviour such as tie-in clauses and export restrictions in technology contracts are also subject to monitoring by host governments.

Direct bargaining with TNCs has also enabled host LDCs to obtain much more favourable terms than would have been the case with the free market. In many oil and mineral industries governments have increased their share of revenue through taxation, royalties and share ownership. Similarly government intervention in technology transfer deals between TNCs and local firms have strengthened the latter's bargaining power and reduced the level of royalty payments and hence the outflow of foreign exchange.

Thus while recognizing the benefits which TNCs offer in terms of technology transfer and access to foreign markets, most structuralists argue that state controls on the behaviour of TNCs are necessary if the costs of foreign investment are to be minimized. The more radical structuralists go further. They argue that foreign TNCs should be excluded, because the ability and willingness of Third World states to control TNC activities is in doubt.

Technology

As already mentioned, government intervention in technology transfer can reduce the cost of imported technology. It can also be used to require the 'unpackaging' of technology so that only those elements which are not locally available are imported. Unpackaging, by increasing the opportunities for local firms and consultants, can help promote local technological development.

Local technological capacity can also be encouraged more directly by government both through direct support for applied research and through fiscal incentives for such expenditure by the private sector. There may also be a particular case for promoting capital goods industries such as machine tools because of their role in diffusing technological change throughout the economy. Again, see Chapter 7 for more detailed discussion.

Accumulation

In contrast to liberal theorists who, as we shall see, emphasize the need for high interest rates in order to encourage savings, most structuralists are more concerned with keeping interest rates low in order to encourage investment. In addition, as pointed out above, subsidized credit can be used to promote particular industries.

The state can play a crucial role here, if necessary borrowing in order to lend at low rates of interest. The government itself can also be an important source of saving, as can state corporations, although in practice they frequently have deficits.

Structuralists are concerned with long run economic development and are reluctant to see long term prospects compromised by short term austerity measures which lead to large cut backs in investment. They are therefore opposed to the types of policies advocated by the IMF in the face of their debt problems. Austerity is seen as a temporary stopgap which does nothing to resolve the long-term problems and indeed can only serve to intensify them. Structuralists therefore believe that Third World countries should opt for growth, and either negotiate for substantial debt reductions or default. Not surprisingly we have returned here to the external constraints facing Third World countries.

5.5 Neo-liberal theory

What is Neo-liberalism?

As we saw in Section 5.2, structuralist approaches to economic development came under increasing attack from about the mid-1960s. By the 1980s, structuralism had been replaced by neo-liberalism as the dominant development orthodoxy. In this section we shall look in more detail at this approach and the policies which have been advocated by the World Bank and the International Monetary Fund from this perspective.

Neo-liberals reject the structuralist view that the conditions prevalent in the Third World make it necessary to develop a special economic theory. Instead they believe in the universal validity of certain economic principles. Neo-liberalism is based on neo-classical (or 'orthodox') economic theory which, it is argued, is as relevant to Africa, Asia and Latin America as it is to Europe or North America.

One of the leading advocates of the relevance of neo-classical economics for development has defined the approach in the following terms:

> "A neo-classical vision of the world is one of flexibility. In their own or their families interests, people adapt readily to changing opportunities and prices … In short, the price mechanism can be expected to work rather well."
>
> (Little, 1982, p. 25)

This quotation encapsulates three key features of the neo-classical perspective.

(i) Individualism

The basic building blocks are individuals rather than economic or social structures. As Mrs Thatcher once said 'There is no such thing as society, only individual men and women and their families'.

(ii) Exchange relationships

The focus of analysis is on market relations. Social interactions are reduced to market exchange and 'neoclassical economics can thus be described as a paradigm that tells one to investigate markets and prices' (Little, 1982). The expectation is that markets will work well in the sense of leading to an efficient allocation of resources (see Box 5.6). Issues of ownership and control of resources tend to be neglected and considerations of equity ignored.

(iii) Flexibility

Whereas the structuralists emphasized the prevalence of structural rigidities in Third World economies, neo-classical theory assumes flexibility. Thus both producers and consumers respond readily to price incentives. If producer prices for farmers are

*Figure 5.12   In tandem: Margaret Thatcher and Ronald Reagan —
leading 1980s advocates of neo-liberalism.*

Box 5.6   Markets and resource allocation

In any economic system, mechanisms must exist to determine what is produced, how and by whom. This is the problem of the allocation of resources. In a centrally planned economy this is determined by planners. In a market economy it is solved through the 'invisible hand' of the market.

An economy is considered production-efficient if the allocation of resources is such that it is impossible to increase the production of some goods (or services) without reducing the supply of some other goods (or services). When, in addition, these goods and services are distributed in such a way that no one individual can be made better-off without making someone else worse-off, the economy is efficient, and not just production-efficient.

Neo-classical economists have shown that under certain restrictive assumptions, the free market leads to an efficient allocation of resources .

---

increased, agricultural output will expand. If wages are kept low, firms will have an incentive to use more labour-intensive production techniques and employment will grow. If the currency is devalued consumers will buy locally produced goods instead of the now relatively more expensive imports.

Price distortions producing inefficiency

Central to recent neo-liberal thinking is the notion of price distortions. It can be shown, under certain assumptions, that theoretically a competitive market system will result in an efficient economy.

This theory underlies the belief that market prices provide the best indicators, or 'signals', for decisions about resource allocation. If prices diverge from their free market level (i.e. if they are distorted) because, for example, of government price controls or subsidies, then the economy will not attain efficiency. For a small Third World economy, the relevant free market prices, it is argued, are those set on the world market.

In the real world, prices are often distorted. While this can be the result of monopolistic tendencies in the private sector, neo-liberals hold that

> "In most instances, however, price distortions are introduced by government directly or indirectly in pursuit of some social or economic objective."
>
> (World Bank, 1983, p.57)

There is a case therefore for removing distortions and moving prices closer to 'efficiency prices'. Market forces should be allowed to operate both as far as a country's international economic relations are concerned and in its domestic economic transactions.

The World Bank and others have therefore sought to back these theoretical arguments with studies which show that a low level of price distortion tends to be associated with high levels of economic growth and does not lead to high levels of inequality. The results of one such study are reported in the 1983 *World Development Report*.

The scatter diagram in Figure 5.13 plots the level of price distortion against annual GDP growth rates for 31 LDCs which account for 75% of the population of developing countries excluding

China. In calculating the level of distortion, The World Bank identified seven key prices and classified them as having a low, medium or high distortion (given a score of 1, 2 and 3 respectively). To calculate a country's distortion index, the distortion scores for each key price are added up and the result is divided by seven.

The prices selected fell into three main groups:

(i) *Prices affecting foreign trade*
   protection of agriculture
   protection of industry
   exchange rate

(ii) *Prices affecting the factors of production (capital and labour)*
   interest rates
   wages

(iii) *Prices affecting domestic prices*
   power tariffs (taken as a proxy for pricing of infrastructure)
   inflation

We will return to Figure 5.13, but first let us see how these prices affect the economic performance of a country. The first set of prices, foreign trade, is obviously closely connected to an outward-oriented strategy. They are examined in detail in the next section, under gains from trade.

The second set of prices concerns interest rates and wages. In many LDCs, governments interfere in the money markets in order to keep down the rate of interest. Where inflation is high, this has often led to negative real interest rates (i.e. rates of interest which are below the rate of inflation). This has a number of unfavourable effects. First, it is argued that interest rates need to be positive in real terms in order to encourage saving. Second, a higher rate of interest will increase the efficiency of investment. Where interest rates are artificially low, credit has to be rationed and the large (farmers and industrialists) are favoured at the expense of the small. Removing interest ceilings will play a major role in ensuring that funds go to those who can use them most efficiently rather than those who have contacts or ample security.

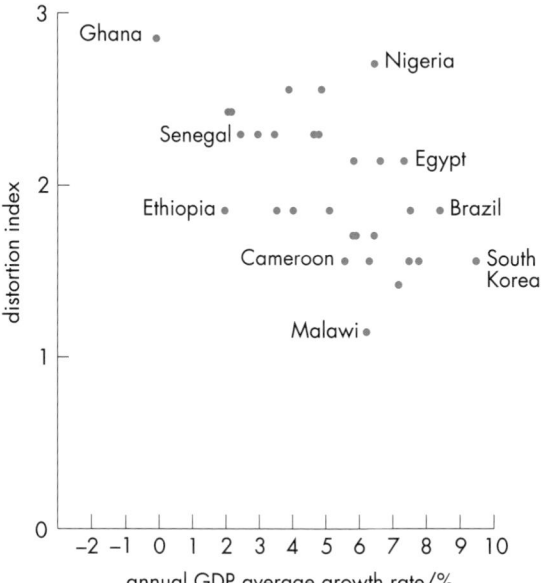

Figure 5.13   Price distortions and growth in the 1970s.

In the neo-liberal view interest rates and wage rates are also the key factors determining the type of technology used in production. If interest rates are too low, and wage costs are inflated through government labour legislation, this will encourage firms to replace workers by machines, which will have a negative effect on the growth of employment opportunities. It is also argued that the rate of wage increase needs to be restrained in order to maintain international competitiveness.

In the third set of prices, underpriced infrastructure can create problems because it leads to inadequate investment which gives rise to bottlenecks with adverse effects on economic growth. For example, a government may decide to keep the price of electricity low in order to encourage industrial production. Price controls will reduce the profitability of the electricity companies if they are in the private sector and they will be unwilling to invest in new generating capacity or perhaps even maintain existing capacity adequately. If the electricity industry is in public ownership, it will also lack internally generated funds for its investment programme and may be starved of cash by a hard pressed central government. The result of this lack of investment will be inadequate power supplies, leading to frequent power cuts so that industrial firms may even be forced to install their own electricity generators in order to guarantee supplies. This will involve additional costs compared to adequate investment in the electricity industry, and thus cause an inefficient allocation of resources.

Finally high and/or rapidly accelerating inflation is seen as a major distortion which affects the efficiency of resource allocation because it creates uncertainty and encourages unproductive activities. It is not uncommon for the well-off to invest in financial markets or real estate as a hedge against inflation, rather than investing in industrial production.

Distortion index

These seven distortions were added together to give a composite distortion index for each country, which was then compared with the economic growth rate during the 1970s (Figure 5.13). This showed that the low-distortion countries performed best on average, growing at 6.8% per annum compared with 5.7% for the medium distortion group and 3.1% for the high-distortion countries (World Bank, 1983). In other words, countries with little price distortion tended to grow fast while those in which prices were highly distorted tended to perform badly.

On the surface, this appears to be a neat correlation which takes into account a range of price variables. But does this reflect the fact that high-distortion countries have given greater emphasis to social objectives rather than rapid economic growth and have therefore done better in terms of income distribution? The World Bank argues not. There is no notable difference between the three groups of countries in terms of income inequality. If anything, the low-distortion countries have done better.

This evidence lends support to the view that 'getting prices right' is a crucial factor in economic development.

Gains from free trade; critique of import substitution

Alongside the importance of freeing up prices, neo-liberal theory strongly emphasizes the virtues of trade. It shows that countries can gain from trade by specializing in those goods in which they have a comparative advantage (Box 5.7) and importing other goods. Such specialization will come about if countries adopt free trade, or at least keep trade restrictions to a minimum.

As one of the principle tools of neo-liberal thinking and as a critique of past import substitution policies in developing countries, it is worth spelling out the theory of comparative advantage in more detail.

Comparative advantage theory says that a country, in fact all countries, will benefit from freedom to import and export without restriction. The idea is that each country will concentrate on producing the things in which it has a relative (comparative) advantage instead of trying to produce items

Box 5.7 Comparative advantage

The theory of comparative advantage was developed by Ricardo in the early nineteenth century and has been the cornerstone of international trade theory ever since. Ricardo demonstrated that two countries could benefit from trade even when one of them had an absolute productivity advantage in all lines of production. The country with the higher productivity would gain from importing those goods in which its advantage was smallest, while the low productivity country would gain from importing those goods in which its productivity disadvantage was greatest.

Thus, what matters in international trade is relative productivity levels or comparative advantage. It is impossible for a country not to have a comparative advantage in anything, unless by chance its relative productivity level is the same in all lines of production, in which case it could not gain at all from trade.

Under free trade, in other words where there are no trade restrictions or subsidies, competitive market forces will lead countries to specialize according to their comparative advantage. Providing that there is no coercion, for example through colonial rule, both countries will gain from trade and the resulting specialization.

---

which it is particularly ill-equipped to produce and which could be imported cheaply from countries producing them at much lower cost.

The problem with import substitution is that it deliberately interferes with trade in order to encourage the local production of goods which are produced more cheaply abroad. From a neo-liberal point of view, this has a number of negative effects.

Inefficiency

First it is argued that protectionism has led to inefficiency. Inefficiency means a number of different things in this context. Firms which are protected from international competition do not need to cut costs and increase output in the same way as those in open markets. They can afford waste and poor quality without having their survival threatened. This is reflected in the high cost and low quality which often characterize import substituting industries in Third World countries.

Inefficiency can also arise in terms of resource allocation (see Box 5.6). For example, a country pursuing an import substitution policy may impose quotas on textile imports to protect its own textile industry which produces for the domestic market. It may well find that, even with relatively low-paid labour, its textile factories produce cloth at a cost of US$1 per metre while importers could bring in cloth produced in the ultra-modern factories of Japan for US$0.80 per metre. If the domestic industry produced 1 million metres of cloth, this would save US$800 000 of foreign exchange which would otherwise have been spent on imports. However the local cost of producing this cloth would have been US$1 million. The theory of comparative advantage tells us that the country would have been better off devoting this US$1 million to some other activity in which it is more competitive internationally, and importing cheaper foreign cloth. This would make it possible for the country to enjoy the same level of consumption of cloth, at the same time as releasing some resources for additional production of other goods.

Discrimination against agriculture

One of the major ways in which protectionism has distorted the allocation of resources in LDCs involves discrimination against agriculture. Because import substitution strategies have concentrated on promoting manufacturing, industrial protection has generally been much higher than that given to agriculture. As Table 5.2 shows, the ratio of protection in agriculture is less than one in all the countries listed apart from South Korea, indicating that manufacturing receives a higher level of protection. Discrimination against agriculture

Table 5.2 Relative protection rates for agriculture and manufacturing

Country	Year	Relative protection ratio[1]
Philippines	1974	0.76
Colombia	1978	0.49
Brazil[2]	1980	0.65
Mexico	1980	0.88
Nigeria	1980	0.35
Egypt	1981	0.57
Peru[2]	1981	0.68
Turkey	1981	0.77
S Korea[2]	1982	1.36
Ecuador	1983	0.65

[1] A ratio higher than 1.00 means that agriculture is more protected than industry. A ratio lower than 1.00 means that agriculture is less protected than industry.

[2] Refers to primary sector

[Source: World Bank, 1986]

is particularly marked in Nigeria and Colombia where the ratio is less than 0.5.

This means that agricultural producers face unfavourable internal terms of trade (see Box 5.3), because the manufactured inputs and consumer goods which they buy are sold at prices well above those prevailing on the world market, but they are not paid correspondingly higher prices for their products. This has a depressing effect on agricultural production and investment, contributing to agricultural stagnation.

Bias against exports

Another bias created by import substitution is against exports. Paradoxically, according to the neo-liberals, the export pessimism of the structuralists became a self-fulfilling prophecy because the policies which they advocated discriminated against exports.

Consider the example given earlier of the textile industry. If high-cost textile mills are set up behind protective barriers, this will increase the cost of cloth to the garment industry. Production of clothing, which might have been able to compete internationally if it had access to cloth at the same price as its international competitors, will no longer be able to do so and exports will contract (or not even get off the ground).

The end result is that traditional exports will tend to stagnate and new export lines will fail to emerge, so that shortages of foreign currency will be exacerbated rather than relieved by import substitution.

Empirical evidence

These theoretical arguments have been backed up by a number of empirical studies which claim to show that countries which have adopted 'outward

Table 5.3 Characterization of trade regimes

Outward-oriented	Inward-oriented
low levels of protection	high levels of protection
few quotas and import licences	extensive use of controls
export incentives	few incentives to new exports
realistic exchange rate	overvalued exchange rate

'oriented' trade policies have done better economically than those which have been 'inward oriented'.

One of the most influential of these studies, covering 41 countries was carried out by the World Bank and reported in the *World Development Report* for 1987. Countries were classified according to their degree of outward/inward orientation in two periods, 1963–73 and 1973–85 (see Table 5.4).

A number of aspects of the economic performance of the different groups of countries was compared for both time periods. The results can be seen in Figure 5.14.

Table 5.4 Classification of 41 countries by trade orientation

Period	Strongly outward-oriented countries	Moderately outward-oriented countries	Moderately inward-oriented countries	Strongly inward-oriented countries
1963–73	Hong Kong SouthKorea Republic of Singapore	Brazil Cameroon Colombia Costa Rica Côte d'Ivoire Guatemala Indonesia Israel Malaysia Thailand	Bolivia El Salvador Honduras Kenya Madagascar Mexico Nicaragua Nigeria Phillipines Senegal Tunisia Yugoslavia	Argentina Bangladesh Burundi Chile Dominican Republic Ethiopia Ghana India Pakistan Peru Sri Lanka Sudan Tanzania Turkey Uruguay Zambia
1973–85	Hong Kong SouthKorea Republic of Singapore	Brazil Chile Israel Malaysia Thailand Tunisia Turkey Uruguay	Cameroon Colombia Costa Rica Côte d'Ivoire El Salvador Guatemala Honduras Indonesia Kenya Mexico Nicaragua Pakistan Philippines Senegal Sri Lanka Yugoslavia	Argentina Bangladesh Bolivia Burundi Dominican Republic Ethiopia Ghana India Madagascar Nigeria Peru Sudan Tanzania Zambia

[Source: World Bank, 1987]

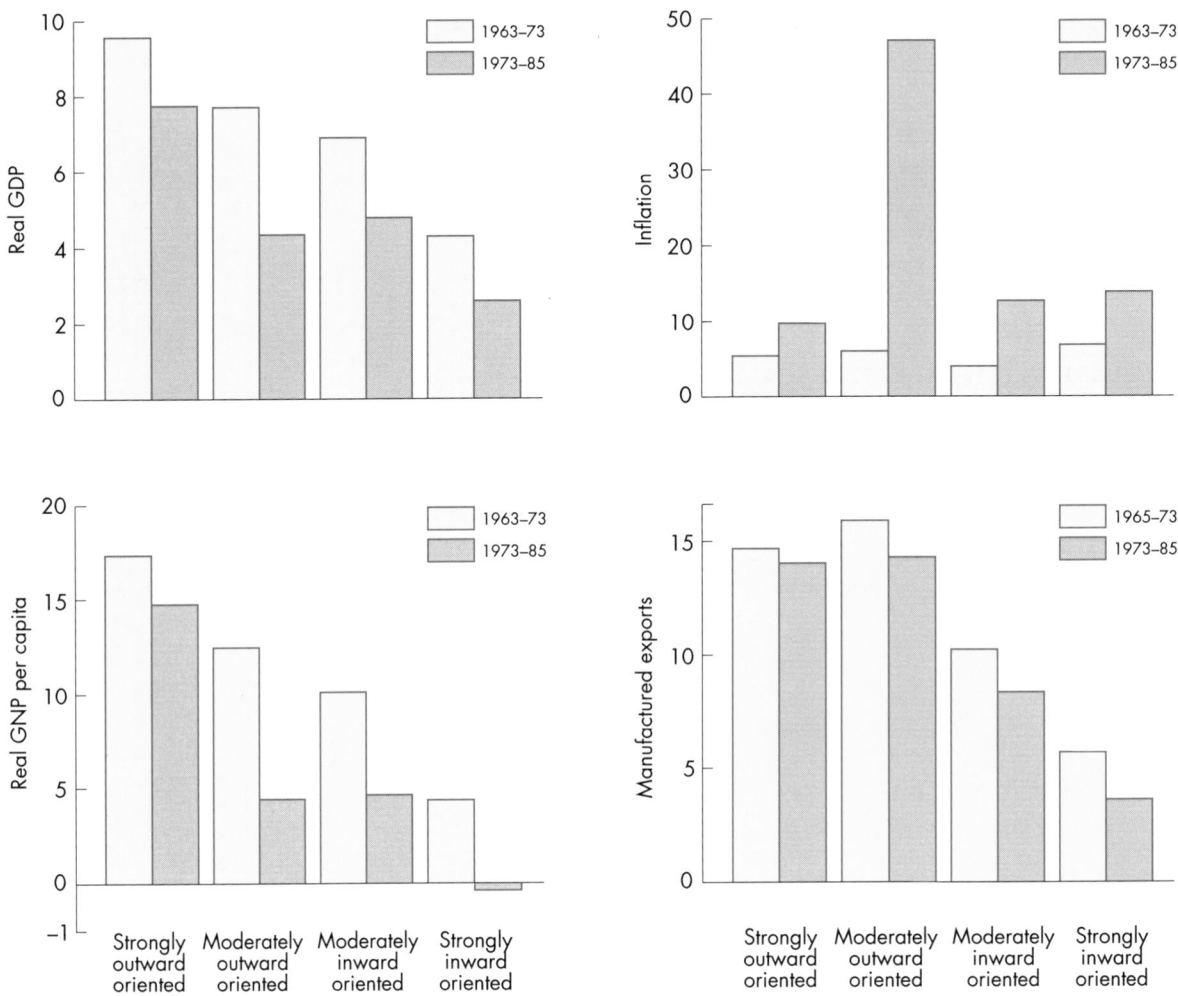

Figure 5.14   Economic performance of 41 countries by trade orientation.

The first two diagrams show that the strongly outward oriented countries did best in terms of economic growth in both periods, whether measured in absolute or *per capita* terms.

Look closely again at the first two diagrams. Can one also say that the more outward oriented a country, the better its growth performance? Is this the case both in the period 1963–73 when international conditions were relatively favourable, and in 1973-85 when external conditions deteriorated? (See Chapter 1.) Redrawing the first diagram of Figure 5.14 separately for 1963–73 and 1973–85 will show that the relationship between trade and growth is not clear-cut.

The bottom two diagrams show inflation and the rate of growth of manufactured exports. Not surprisingly, manufactured exports have grown faster from the outward-oriented than from the inward-oriented economies. In terms of inflation however, the moderately outward oriented economies are the worst performers.

Although not indicated in Figure 5.14, the World Bank also argues that:

"... a good case can be made for suggesting that outward orientation leads to a more equitable distribution of income. First the expansion of labour-intensive exports means higher employment. Second, reinforcing this, outward orientation removes the bias in favour of capital-intensive industries which is often implicit under inward-oriented policies. Third, the direct controls of an inward-oriented strategy generate rents that channel income to those with access to import licenses or subsidized credits."

(World Bank, 1987, p.85)

Thus a liberal trade policy is considered superior to protectionism for Third World countries on both theoretical and empirical grounds.

The critique of state intervention

While neo-liberals see protectionism as the main problem affecting the international economic relations of Third World countries, other forms of state intervention are prevalent in the domestic economy. These too have been subject to criticism by neo-liberal theorists.

Development Planning

In the 1950s and early 1960s, development planning was in fashion. In many countries these were largely paper exercises drawn up to convince donors of the need for foreign aid. Some countries, most notably India, took planning seriously however and used Five Year Plans to guide their economic policies. Nevertheless, in the late 1960s comprehensive planning was increasingly criticized as planned targets were not met and many plans were not even implemented.

The neo-liberal critique of planning is largely based on the limited capabilities of government planners. First, they lack adequate information on which to base the plans. Not only does planning require detailed information about current production techniques and consumer demand, but it also requires foresight concerning how these will evolve. In the real world, say neo-liberals, individual entrepreneurs are in a much better position to exercise judgement than government planners. So the price mechanism is a much better means of influencing investment decisions than a comprehensive plan. As one critic of planning has put it:

"The strongest argument against planning of the Soviet or Maoist variety, therefore, is that, whilst *omniscient* planners might forecast the future more accurately than myopic private agents, there is no reason to believe that flesh-and-blood bureaucrats can do any better — and some reason to believe that they may do much worse."

(Lal, 1983, p.75)

Second, planners often lacked the levers or instruments necessary to see that their plans were implemented. Unlike the Soviet Union where the state directly controlled the entire economy, in Third World countries, major sectors remained in private hands so that plan targets were often little more than exhortations.

A third criticism is that planning occurred at the wrong level. Thus while national plans were drawn up, insufficient attention was devoted to the individual projects which would have to be implemented in order to make these plans a reality. Often, well thought out and socially profitable projects simply did not exist. It was this realization that led to the development of techniques of social cost–benefit analysis in the late 1960s.

Rent Seeking

The neo-liberal critique of state intervention is not confined just to development planning. The suspicions directed at government bureaucrats is all pervasive. Although development planning is no longer in vogue, most Third World economies are characterized by numerous government controls over economic activity, including production licences, price controls, exchange controls and import quotas.

Neo-liberals maintain that if governments intervene in markets and impose controls, people will devote much of their time to attempting to gain some leverage, some privileged position that enables them to make profits out of the controls. They will increasingly switch from productive activity to unproductive activity and this represents a waste of resources. This is known as 'rent seeking' because the profits that can be made by cornering a special position are known as 'monopoly rents' in economists' jargon (even though these profits have nothing to do with the rent of housing or land).

Figure 5.15.

Rent seeking can best be illustrated by an economy with import controls and foreign exchange controls. A trader who obtains a licence is entitled to buy foreign exchange and purchase imports of particular goods. For example a trader who obtains a licence to import television sets can buy these cheaply on the international market, but because the government puts a limit on the number which can be brought into the country, the local price is much higher, reflecting their scarcity. The lucky trader can then pocket the difference.

If traders can make high profits from obtaining licences, it is worth their while devoting resources to obtaining them. So some traders put a lot of effort into lobbying government officials, into buying and selling licence rights and, once they have a licence, into seeking out 'black market' deals on imports or foreign exchange. These activities are often a relatively easy route to enrichment. They may also lead to corruption as traders attempt to bribe key bureaucrats. But even in the absence of corruption, resources will be diverted away from production and national welfare. Similar arguments apply with other types of direct control. Price controls for instance can lead to companies artificially inflating their costs to obtain price increases.

State expenditure and inflation

Neo-liberals regard the level of state expenditure as excessive both in developed and less developed countries. The 1980s saw a major attempt to cut back on the size of the state sector in Britain. Neo-liberals support similar measures in Third World countries.

In its *World Development Report* for 1988, the World Bank comments,

> "The public sector has grown rapidly in almost all countries during the past few decades. This Report has shown how the poor conduct of fiscal policy has contributed to serious economic problems in parts of the developing world. Unsustainable budget deficits have led many countries into heavy foreign borrowing, high inflation, and stagnant private investment. Public revenues have failed to match spending. ... Too many public funds have been spent on unwise investment, costly subsidies, and excessive public employment; too few have been spent on investment to support development."
>
> (World Bank, 1988, p.182)

The growth of government spending is seen as having two major negative consequences. First, it is argued that it tends to 'crowd out' private investment and initiative. In other words, as the public sector grows there is less and less room for the private sector.

Second, there is a tendency for government expenditure to grow at a faster rate than government revenue. The result is a growing public sector deficit which is often financed by printing money. This leads to inflationary pressures in the economy which tends to disrupt economic growth.

State enterprises

An important factor contributing to the public sector deficit is the burden imposed by subsidies to loss-making state firms.

Commenting on these firms, the World Bank notes that:

> "... their record has frequently been poor, particularly in developing countries. They have failed to play the strategic role in industrialization that governments had hoped for. Financial rates of return have generally been lower for SOEs (state-owned enterprises) than for the private sector. ... They have often put large burdens on public budgets. ... One study has found that countries in which SOEs accounted for higher shares

of gross domestic investment generally had lower rates of economic growth.

> (World Bank, 1987, pp. 66–67)

5.6 Neo-liberal policies

The neo-liberal view has been put into practice in many Third World countries as a result of the implementation of policies drawn up by the World Bank and the International Monetary Fund. These policies are often referred to collectively as *structural adjustment* (see Chapter 11, Box 11.4 in *Allen & Thomas, 1992*).

In this section we will look at three aspects of these policies which link back to the discussion of neo-liberal theory in the last section:

* market liberalization, often referred to as 'getting prices right'

* trade liberalization to move the economy towards greater outward orientation

* reducing the role of the state in the economy through privatization and cuts in government spending

Taken together these are said to result in a more market-oriented economy both domestically and in relation to the international economy.

Getting prices right

Removing price controls

In many Third World countries governments attempt to control the prices of key commodities for social, political or other reasons. They may provide subsidies as well in certain areas. Reform is required in order to remove these distortions. Prices should be allowed to reflect the true scarcity of goods rather than being artificially restrained. A common recommendation therefore is for removing price controls and subsidies (Box 5.8).

Direct control of investment and output also impedes the functioning of the market mechanism in Third World countries. A number of countries including Brazil, Egypt, India, Indonesia, Mexico

Box 5.8 Removing price controls in Ghana

The World Bank noted the success of Ghana in removing price controls in the mid-1980s. Price controls had existed in Ghana since 1962. By 1970 nearly 6000 prices were controlled, but with inflation reaching 100% a year the frequent requests for price adjustments far exceeded the administrative capacity of the Prices and Incomes Board. Numerous distortions resulted, with smuggling becoming rife and many goods in scarce supply.

In 1984 a major reform was introduced whereby for most goods producers simply had to notify the Prices and Incomes Board of price changes. The list of prices requiring prior approval by the Board was reduced gradually to eight. In 1985 inflation fell to 10% compared to 122% in 1983 and 40% in 1984.

"On the supply side, the incentive effects of price liberalization helped in four ways: hoarded consumer goods were released, scarcity rents were shifted from distributors to producers, agricultural producers responded to favourable rainfalls by greatly increasing food availability, and industrial producers sought additional foreign exchange through a newly opened auction window for foreign exchange …

These policies generally improved the market situation. Increased local supplies of some commodities such as milk, bread, soap and beet brought market prices down, sometimes below the previous official prices, while increased imports eliminated scarcity rents for other goods (for example tires and vegetable oil)".

(World Bank, 1987)

Figure 5.16   Accra market.

and Pakistan use industrial licensing to regulate new investment. This leads to bureaucratic delays and may discourage investment, while at the same time favouring large firms and reducing competition. Under these circumstances deregulation is advocated as a means of increasing competition and improving efficiency. In India for instance, relaxation of licensing in the scooter industry has led to rapid growth of the industry and greater competition has stimulated the production of technically superior products at international standards of price and quality (World Bank, 1987).

Financial liberalization

Financial liberalization is also a key part of the package. Interest rates are often kept artificially low and, where inflation rates are high, the real interest rate (taking into account inflation) may be negative. Removal of government controls over the capital market, leading to higher interest rates which are at least positive in real terms, can increase the efficiency of investment and may also encourage a higher level of saving. Several countries such as Argentina, Chile and Uruguay have carried out such reforms, although not without a number of problems, as Box 5.9 illustrates (World Bank, 1987).

Less intervention in labour market

Reduced government intervention in the labour market is also desirable. Repeal of minimum wage legislation, more realistic (i.e. lower) wages in the public sector, and reform of labour legislation which gives job security or requires substantial redundancy pay are all seen as measures which should be introduced in order to increase the efficiency of the labour market.

Trade liberalization

A second major area of policy reform relates to trade and is designed to bring about a shift to more outward-oriented development strategies.

Removing import quotas

First, import quotas should be removed. These are seen as doubly undesirable. Not only do they protect domestic producers from international competition, permitting them to operate inefficiently and increase prices, but they also give rise to rent seeking (see Section 5.5). Removing quotas, even if they are temporarily replaced by import duties, is therefore seen as being particularly desirable.

Reducing tariffs

Having removed quotas, a second step is to reduce the level of tariffs. At the same time the variability of tariff rates between different products should also be reduced since this is a major source of price distortions. Tariffs need not be totally eliminated but they should be kept low.

Box 5.9 Trade liberalization in Chile

One of the best known and most dramatic cases of trade liberalization is that carried out in Chile during the 1970s under the Pinochet regime. In 1973 Chile was one of the most protected economies in the world, with tariffs averaging 105%, some tariffs as high as 700% and a large number of other restrictions on imports. There was also a highly distorted multiple exchange rate system.

The new military government initially reduced the maximum tariff to 220% later in 1973. By 1976 it had removed all quantitative restrictions on imports and unified the exchange rate and by 1979 the tariff rate had been reduced to a uniform level of 10%. In this way one of Latin America's most protected economies became the most open.

Exports grew rapidly during the 1970s and Chile began to enter international markets for new products such as fruit, vegetables and forestry products. There was a major restructuring of domestic industry, with dramatic falls in production in previously highly protected industries such as textiles and footwear and rapid growth of industries which processed local natural resources such as fish processing, furniture and timber. In aggregate, the share of manufacturing in GDP fell from 29% in 1974 to 19% in 1982. At the same time unemployment rose from 5% in 1973 to 15% in 1981.

(Gwynne, 1990)

Where tariffs continue to exist, export incentives should be provided in order to offset the bias against exports implied by the tariff. The objective is neutrality, in the sense that the incentives which firms face should be roughly the same, whether they are producing for the domestic market or for export. They should also be the same whether they produce shoes or cars. This is based on the neo-liberal assumption that free market prices are the most efficient for resource allocation (see Box 5.6). When prices are distorted by, say, protective tariffs then it is argued that the distortion must apply equally to all prices.

Realistic exchange rate

Finally, outward orientation requires a realistic exchange rate. Since inward-oriented policies are often associated with an over-valued exchange rate, a devaluation is usually an essential part of the package. This is argued on the grounds that outward orientation requires an economy to be internationally competitive. An over-valued exchange rate which makes imports cheaper also makes exports more expensive relative to world market prices. Devaluation to make exports more competitive is, therefore, deemed to be essential.

Reducing the role of the state

The third major strand of structural adjustment is to reduce the role of the state in the economy.

Privatization

An important element of this is the privatization of state-owned enterprises. This has been pro-

ceeding rapidly in a number of countries in recent years. Governments staggering under the burden of servicing their foreign debts and subject to pressure from the IMF have sold off public companies in order to raise additional funds or to reduce the drain on public finances from loss making firms. In Mexico for instance, the number of state enterprises was reduced from 1 100 in 1982 to 350 by 1990. Some, such as the loss making airline Aero Mexico, have been turned into profitable private companies. A similar process of privatization was started in Brazil in 1991 by the government of Fernando Collor (see Chapter 3).

Cutting government expenditure

The second aspect of reducing the role of the state has been cutting government expenditure. This is often achieved through reducing public sector employment and restraining the wages of civil servants. These cuts are intended to reduce the government's budget deficit and bring down inflation. It complements the policies to reduce government intervention in the market and cuts in subsidies in order to 'get prices right'.

In the neo-liberal view, the government should confine itself to those areas in which it is particularly well equipped to function and leave the rest to the market. It must be responsible for establishing clear, even-handed rules of the game within which markets can operate. It should also ensure the provision of certain essential infrastructure such as transport, communications, power and education, although it need not always provide these directly itself.

Summary of Chapter 5

This chapter has presented two contending theoretical perspectives on development, the structuralist and the neo-liberal approach. At different times, each approach has exercised a dominant influence over development thinking, and the debate is by no means over.

Central to the conflict between the two approaches is the role which the state should play in economic development. For structuralists, an active state is essential for overcoming the problems of economic backwardness. Neo-liberals place their faith in the market.

The different elements of structuralists and neo-liberal theories can be summarized as follows.

1 Structuralists are concerned with the workings of the social and economic structures of society. They therefore analyse development in terms of changes in the sectoral composition of economies (agriculture, industry and services), of social classes and ownership, and of the unequal relationship of developing countries to developed in the international economy.

2 A common feature of structuralist thought is that the nature of individual developing country economies or regions is sufficiently different from developed countries to merit a separate analysis.

3 Another common feature of structuralism is that the state in developing countries should pursue active or strategic interventions in order to promote development. In recent years, this view has fallen into disrepute. However, a new generation of structuralist thought is again emphasizing that the state should play a key role in promoting development.

4 The main elements of structuralist theory and policy are:

- links to the world economy and the terms of trade
- structural change linked to industrialization
- ownership and control of agricultural land and industrial production
- technology
- capital accumulation
- the role of the state in development.

5 Neo-liberalism, in direct contrast to structuralism, is concerned with universal laws of economic development. This theory posits that, in principle, the same rules of economic development can be applied across the board from the most developed country to the least developed.

6 The emphasis of neo-liberal theory is on the individual and on the free play of market forces. While structuralists tend to view development in the long term, neo-liberals emphasize the short term in the belief that the long term will take care of itself.

7 Relying on the market as the best arbiter of prices and efficiency, neo-liberals recommend that the state should take a hands-off approach to development. Economic decisions should be left to private individuals and the state should only provide those goods and services (such as infrastructure) which would not otherwise be provided by the private sector.

8 The main elements of neo-liberal theory are:

- price distortions produce inefficiencies

- trade liberalization (e.g. reducing protective tariffs) produces a more efficient economy.

- the direct role of the state in the economy should be reduced.

Before going on to the next chapter, look at the quotations about South Korea and Brazil in Section 5.1 again. How closely do the views of Meier and Tyler reflect the neo-liberal approach, and how far can those of Amsden and Evans be characterized as structuralist?

6

(RE-)INTERPRETING BRAZIL AND SOUTH KOREA

RHYS JENKINS

The accounts of Brazilian and South Korean industrialization in Chapters 3 and 4 have highlighted a number of key aspects of the development process. In some ways the two experiences are rather similar. Both countries belong to a small group of countries, the newly industrializing countries (NICs), which have experienced rapid rates of industrial growth. In other ways they are often seen as contrasting models. Brazil is often cited as an example of import substitution industrialization while South Korea is seen as having adopted export-oriented industrialization.

Certainly both Brazil and South Korea have experienced rapid economic growth and major structural transformation during the past quarter century. Up to 1980, their record has been impressive compared to the average performance of developing countries. But after 1980, Brazil's growth rates have not compared so well. Refer to Table 6.1 for growth rates of GDP and other economic indicators.

Manufacturing industry has played a dynamic role in both countries. Production and exports of manufactures have grown rapidly, particularly in South Korea. In the 1960s and the 1970s, Brazilian manufacturing also grew faster than for the Third World as a whole but has not kept pace with the phenomenal growth of South Korea. Moreover in the 1980s, with the debt crisis,

Table 6.1   Average annual growth of economic indicators

		GDP	GDP per capita	Manufacturing	Export of manufactures	Inflation
Brazil	1965–80	8.8%	6.4%	9.8%	31.1%	31.5%
	1980–88	2.9%	0.7%	2.2%	12.3%	188.7%
S Korea	1965–80	9.6%	7.6%	18.7%	39.7%	18.7%
	1980–88	9.9%	8.7%	13.5%	15.3%	5.0%
LDCs	1965–80	5.8%	3.5%	8.2%	—	16.5%
	1980–88	4.3%	2.3%	5.9%	—	46.8%

[Data source: World Bank]

Table 6.2 Comparison of economic indicators

		GNP per capita	Manufacturing as % of GDP	% employed in industry	Manufacturing exports/ million US$	Debt service as % of GDP
S Korea	1960s	—	18	15	104	20.4 (1970)
	1980s	US$3 600	32	27	31 931 (1986)	11.5
Brazil	1960s	—	26	20	134	21.8 (1970)
	1980s	US$2 160	29	27 (1980)	9 068 (1986)	42.0
LDCs	1960s	—	20	12	—	—
	1980s	US$750	—	16 (1980)	—	—

Unless indicated otherwise, 1960s data is for 1965 and 1980s data is for 1988.

[Data source: World Bank]

Brazilian industry fell further behind, failing even to keep pace with growth in the rest of the Third World (see the growth rates for manufacturing in Table 6.1).

Brazil has suffered much more severely from the debt crisis than South Korea. Although in 1965, both countries had rather similar debt service ratios, by 1988 South Korea's had been cut almost by half, while that of Brazil had almost doubled (see Table 6.2). Brazil has also suffered from far more serious inflationary problems than South Korea, particularly in the 1980s.

As well as outperforming Brazil in terms of some economic indicators, South Korea has also done much better in terms of the major social indicators of development. In the 1960s life expectancy was similar in the two countries. By the 1980s, South Korean life expectancy had improved far more than Brazil's, which was regressing towards the average for developing countries. Infant mortality rates were initially lower and showed a proportionately greater improvement in South Korea than in Brazil, which has remained near the Third World average. Literacy

Table 6.3 Comparison of social indicators

		Life expectancy	Infant mortality per 1000	Literacy	Income distribution (Gini coefficient)
Brazil	1960s	54 years (1960)	104	61% (1960)	0.50 (1960)
	1980s	65 years	61	77%	0.58 (1980)
S Korea	1960s	54 years	62	71% (1960)	0.34
	1980s	70 years	24	93% (1980)	0.39 (1980)
LDCs	1960s	49 years	117	—	—
	1980s	62 years	67	55%	—

Unless indicated otherwise, 1960s data is for 1965 and 1980s data is for 1988.

[Data source: World Bank]

levels too are much higher in South Korea than in Brazil (Table 6.3).

Gini coefficient: A measure of relative size of household incomes. If the Gini coefficient is 0, income is evenly distributed (10% of the population receive 10% of the income, 20% receive 20%, and so on). If the Gini coefficient is close to 1, a tiny proportion of the population are receiving most of the income.

There is undoubtedly a link between these social indicators and the degree of income inequality. Income is much more evenly distributed in South Korea than in Brazil, although rapid economic growth during the 1960s and 1970s was accompanied by increased inequality in both countries.

These differences in income distribution and in social indicators are not related to differences in the nature of the political regime. Both countries were ruled by authoritarian governments for most of the past three decades following military

Figure 6.1   Authoritarian regimes in Brazil and South Korea.
(Top) A military rally in Brazil after the military takeover in 1964.
(Bottom) A South Korean student being arrested in Soeul, 1990.

coups in the early 1960s. These regimes were similar in terms of restricting democracy and freedom of speech, and in exercising tight control over labour.

In summary, we can say that the economic performance of both countries, compared with other developing countries, was impressive, at least until the debt crisis of the 1980s. Two notable differences are clear between Brazil and South Korea. First, whereas South Korea continued to do well in the 1980s, Brazil ran into serious problems. Second, throughout this period, the social consequences of economic growth have been much more favourable in South Korea than in Brazil. The political conditions under which this was achieved, were rather similar in the two countries.

These then are some of the 'facts' concerning development in Brazil and South Korea during the past quarter century. While Chapters 3 and 4 provide a more detailed account of developments in the two countries, the purpose of this chapter is to show how the two theoretical approaches presented in Chapter 5 differ radically in their interpretation of these development experiences. They do this in two ways: by emphasizing different aspects of development, and by interpreting the same aspects very differently.

6.1 A neo-liberal view

As we saw at the beginning of Chapter 5, neo-liberals such as Meier explain the economic success of South Korea largely in terms of the policies pursued by the government. They believe that in South Korea, as in the other East Asian NICs:

> "Rapid economic growth ... during the past two or three decades was achieved not by economic tricks, but by sensible policies based on sound neo-classical principles."
>
> (Tsiang &Wu, 1985, p.329)

Similarly in Brazil they associate the 'economic miracle' with a change towards more market-oriented policies following the military coup in 1964.

The neo-liberal story can be illustrated in two ways. The first is to compare the policies and performance of Brazil and South Korea over the past three decades, both with each other and with those of other Third World countries. This should show whether good economic performance tends to be associated with neo-liberal policies. The second is to look at how policies evolved over this period in Brazil and South Korea, to see how policy changes in the two countries have contributed to economic performance.

Comparing Brazil and South Korea

As was seen in the previous chapter, neo-liberals believe that rapid economic growth is associated with a low level of price distortion, an outward-oriented trade strategy and a low level of state intervention and ownership.

According to the World Bank's index of distortion for 31 developing countries in the 1970s (see Figure 5.13 in Chapter 5), South Korea has the fourth lowest index of distortion amongst the countries listed. Brazil, although not as low as South Korea, also has a lower than average distortion index.

Table 6.4 lists the various factors. We can see from this table that for both countries the World Bank considers that there is little distortion in terms of the exchange rate, wages and infrastructure pricing. South Korea performs better than Brazil on two counts, the distortion in interest rates and the protection of manufacturing.

It is argued that South Korean real interest rates have been more realistic than those of Brazil. While both were negative (see Chapter 5), South Korean rates averaged –5% in the 1970s whereas they were –8% in Brazil. The lower negative interest rates would lead to a higher level of savings in South Korea and more rapid employment growth, it is argued, because there would be less of an incentive to replace workers by machines. For the neo-liberals this is a major element explaining the greater income equality in South Korea.

Table 6.4 Distortion indicators in Brazil and South Korea

Distortion indicator	Brazil	S Korea
Exchange rate	low	low
Protection for manufacturing	medium	low
Pricing in agriculture	high	high
Interest rate	high	medium
Wages	low	low
Overall price level	medium	medium
Infrastructure pricing	low	low
Average distortion index	1.9	1.6

[Source: Agarwala, 1983]

The lower level of protection for manufacturing in South Korea is also an important element in the greater outward orientation compared to Brazil and other less developed countries. A strong outward orientation involves low levels of protection, incentives for exports to compensate for any import barriers, absence of direct controls and licensing, and a competitive exchange rate.

Most Third World countries continue to follow inward-oriented policies. Of the 41 countries analysed by the World Bank, as many as 30 had either moderately or strongly inward-oriented policies between 1973 and 1985 (see Table 5.4 in Chapter 5). These countries pursue policies which emphasize import substitution and discriminate against exports. They do not follow their comparative advantages, but instead set up high-cost, inefficient industries for the domestic market. As a result their economic performance suffers.

The World Bank classifies South Korea as one of only three countries, along with Hong Kong and Singapore (Taiwan was not among the countries considered), to have strongly outward-oriented policies between 1963 and 1985.

Brazil is classified as having moderately outward-oriented policies, one of only three countries (the others are Israel and Malaysia) to be classified in this way both in 1963–73 and 1973–85.

Thus a major factor in the superior economic performance of South Korea and Brazil compared to the average for Third World countries is their outward orientation. Moreover South Korea has outperformed Brazil because it adopted an outward-orientation policy both sooner and more vigorously than Brazil.

The final component of the neo-liberal view focuses on the role of the state. Neo-liberals are fond of quoting Adam Smith who wrote in *Wealth of Nations*:

> "Little else is requisite to carry a state to the highest degree of opulence from the lowest barbarism, but peace, easy taxes, and tolerable administration of justice; all the rest being brought about by the natural course of things."

> (Smith, 1776; quoted in Riedel, 1988, p.1)

In South Korea the government has allowed market forces to operate, and has avoided an excessive growth of the state sector. By contrast, the bureaucracy in most other Third World countries stifles private enterprise, and large, inefficiently run public enterprises are a drain on the economy. The public sector deficit has played a major part in fuelling inflation and the growth of the foreign debt in many Third World countries, whereas South Korean industry is almost entirely in the hands of the private sector, and the government has kept public expenditure and the growth of foreign debt under control.

Figure 6.2   Both Brazil and South Korea have increased their outward orientation over time. (Top) VW cars being exported from Brazil. (Bottom) Assembling cars at Hyundai, Ulsan, South Korea.

Brazil is seen as much nearer to the norm for the Third World. It has a large budget deficit, and a number of the country's major firms in areas such as steel and petrochemicals are state owned. Table 6.5 shows that, compared to South Korea, Brazil has a much larger share of government expenditure in GNP, and whereas the South Korean government ran a small budget surplus in 1988, the Brazilian government has a massive deficit. State enterprises are also much more important in Brazil in terms of their participation in production and investment.

Brazil

The neo-liberals' interpretation of Brazilian development reinforces the general points made in the last section. Their view is the following. In the 1950s, Brazil followed inward-oriented, import substitution policies. Tariffs were high, imports of many goods required licences, while others were banned under the 'law of similars' (see Box 3.4 in Chapter 3). The state also intervened extensively in the domestic economy, controlling key economic sectors. There was a high level of price distortion which gave rise to

Table 6.5 Public sector indicators, 1988

Indicator	Brazil	South Korea
Government expenditure/GNP	25.1%	15.7%
Government surplus/GNP	-12.2%	1.6%
Share of state enterprises		
in GDP (1982)	11.0%	4.0%
in GDI* (1978–80)	39.0%	23.0%
in manufacturing (1980)	23.0%	11.6%

* Gross domestic investment

[Sources: World Bank, 1990; Balassa *et al.*, 1986; ILO, 1988]

bottlenecks in infrastructure; for example in power and transport where investment was low. Distortions in the labour market and the capital market gave rise to an extremely capital-intensive industrialization, so that manufacturing employment did not grow fast enough to absorb the growing labour force. Moreover, the inward-looking policies created a bias against exports, so that Brazilian foreign exchange earnings stagnated. Neo-liberals such as Krueger (1978) attribute Brazil's rapid economic growth despite these policies during the 1950s to inflows of foreign private investment which reduced the impact of stagnant export earnings.

The decline in the growth rate in the early 1960s is seen as a result of the cumulative effects of the distortions of the 1950s. Import substitution became increasingly difficult, bottlenecks more severe and new inflows of foreign capital declined.

The military coup in 1964 brought about a major shift in economic policy which lay the basis for the 'Brazilian economic miracle'. According to the neo-liberal interpretation, the crucial element in this change in policy was a shift from an inward- to an outward-oriented trade strategy.

"For Brazil there seems little doubt that the outward looking strategy of the late 1960s was responsible for the heightened pace of economic growth."

(Krueger, 1978, p.278).

The first steps, taken in 1964 and 1965 involved tax exemption to help reduce the bias against exports. Exporters of manufactured goods were exempted from paying tariff duties on their imports and from paying value added tax. In 1967, a reform of the tariff system reduced the level of import duties. As a result, both exports and imports grew rapidly in the late 1960s and early 1970s. Furthermore, in 1968 the government adopted a policy of frequent mini-devaluations of

Figure 6.3   São Paulo's stock exchange.

the cruzeiro against the US dollar to maintain the international competitiveness of Brazilian exports.

Although the shift towards outward orientation was the critical element of economic policy under the military, other markets were also liberalized and distortions reduced. The rate of inflation was reduced from 87% in 1964 to a moderate 20% in 1973. Employment legislation which made it difficult to dismiss workers was removed, enabling the labour market to function more efficiently. There was also a mild financial reform, although not as far-reaching as that carried out in South Korea after the military coup.

Brazil became increasingly integrated with the world economy and economic growth accelerated. Moreover, greater outward orientation and the reforms in the labour and capital markets contributed to much faster employment growth in the manufacturing sector than before 1964.

The oil price increases of 1973 marked the end of the 'Brazilian economic miracle'. But for the neo-liberals, it was not the changing external circumstances which were primarily responsible for the deterioration in Brazil's economic performance. It was the way the Brazilian government responded to these changes.

Faced with the increasing cost of oil imports, the Brazilian government reversed its trade liberalization. Administrative controls over imports were tightened and the real exchange rate became overvalued. (See Figure 6.4. The index of

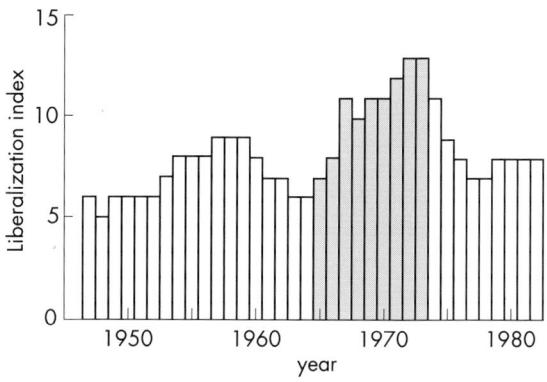

Figure 6.4   Index of trade liberalization in Brazil, 1947–82. Note the rise during the 'economic miracle' years (shaded).

trade liberalization is a subjective numerical estimate, with a value of 0 for totally restricted trade and a value of 20 for completely free trade.) In order to cover the current account deficit, the government borrowed heavily overseas (see Table 3.1). Rather than adjust to the external shock via devaluation, the Brazilian government postponed adjustment and further distorted its domestic economy through administrative controls. These problems came to a head in the 1980s with the second oil price increase and the reversal of capital inflows with the debt crisis.

Despite the more outward-oriented policies adopted by the military government in the 1960s, the state continued to play a major role in the economy throughout the period of military rule, investing in basic and intermediate industries, controlling the prices of many goods and intervening extensively in economic life. As

---

Box 6.1   Battling the bureaucracy in Brazil

"Wherever modern government structures are built on an already highly developed legal and administrative system, bureaucracies are bound to multiply. Brazil is no exception. What is exceptional is the degree to which Brazilians have managed to circumvent the more rigid and obstructive bureaucratic rules. In addition, the government has recently had some success in attacking the rules themselves.

Brazilians have described their federal administrative system as excessively centralized, for-

mal, and distrustful of the public. This view dates back at least to the temporary transfer to Brazil of the Portuguese kingdom and its centralized administration in 1808, and perhaps even further, to 1549, when the first governor-general arrived with a framework of laws and regulations even before there were people to conform to them. The formalism embodied the prejudice that documents are more important that facts. The distrust showed in the controls that required endless lists of certificates, attestations, licenses, and other documents. Not many years ago the case was reported of an export license that required 1 470 separate legal actions and involved thirteen government ministries and fifty agencies.

The *jeito* was employed to overcome such difficulties. This Portuguese term, corresponding roughly to 'knack', 'way', or 'fix' in English, refers to the varied ways that Brazilians, like people in other countries, get around the maze of regulations and legal requirements. The *jeito* principle has been remarkably effective. It relies significantly on the *despachante* [roughly, an expeditor]. The *despachante* has counterparts in many countries but has been especially active in Brazil, where the lubrication of sticky administrative processes has been essential for social mobility and rapid economic development.

The *despachante* is an intermediary who, in return for a commission or fee, purchases and fills out the multiplicity of legal forms, delivers them to the proper persons, and extracts the needed permission or document. The system developed when simple transactions, such as obtaining a marriage license or identity card, could take only a few hours or could take months; depending on whether *despachantes* were used and how much they were paid. The *despachantes* are thriving, specialized professionals and have their own union and competitive examinations. Some specialize in police work, naturalizations, auto licenses, marriages, or 'legalization of real estate'. The *despachantes* who arrange imports and exports have long enjoyed a legal monopoly. Each typically has several employees, and almost all sizable businesses maintain their own *despachantes*.

Brazil's rapid economic growth and social evolution demonstrate that a complex bureaucracy need not be a barrier to development. The costs are nevertheless substantial. Moreover, such resourceful adaptations of the *jeito* may have been too effective and may have undermined attempts to reform public administration.

The most recent efforts to reform the system,

rather than live with it, began in 1979. A National Debureaucratization Program was designed to simplify administrative procedures and, more broadly, to reverse what was seen as the relentless trend toward growth in government, excessive centralization, and abundant regulation.

The results in 1979–84 were impressive. On the basis of a citizens' project (which surveyed all the points of contact of individuals, throughout their lives, with bureaucratic requirements) it was possible to eliminate, or simplify, a long list of documents and procedures ranging from notarization requirements and driver's licenses to passport extensions, university enrolment processes, and income tax returns. Evidence of residence, economic dependence, and so on, could be established simply with a written statement by the interested party, rather than legal certificates and third-party attestation. A 'presumption of truth' displaced the 'rule of distrust'. Other legal procedures were simplified. In all, more than 600 million documents a year were removed from circulation. The savings have been estimated at close to US$3 billion a year, equivalent to about 1.5% of Brazil's GDP.

In the economic field the main achievements were to simplify rural credit procedures, to change commercial registration procedures so that forming a company could take three days rather than three to six months, and to bring relief from bureaucracy to 1.5 million small enterprises. For the time being, however, the program has left many areas of regulation untouched, including some that are important to industrialization and trade.

It is significant that, although a Minister of Debureaucratization was appointed, no new government department was formed. The programme was implemented by an executive secretary and just twelve assistants At the very least, and on a limited front, some progress has been made in simplifying the rules and changing the relationship between citizens and civil servants."

[Source: World Bank, 1987]

Box 6.1 illustrates, the massive Brazilian bureaucracy, despite having been reduced in the 1980s, continues to impose substantial costs on the private sector.

In summary, the neo-liberals say that the 'Brazilian miracle' was the result of the application of neo-liberal policies by the military government in the mid-1960s, particularly a shift from an inward-looking to an outward-looking strategy. The deteriorating economic performance of the late 1970s and the economic crisis of the 1980s resulted from incomplete liberalization in the 1960s and the subsequent reversal of neo-liberal policies in the 1970s.

South Korea

How do neo-liberals interpret South Korean development? As in Brazil, the 1950s in South Korea were characterized by inward-oriented policies. Economic growth was under 5% a year between 1954 and 1959, and this was only made possible by massive inflows of US aid. The period was characterized by the worst features of a controlled, inward-oriented economy. Rent seeking was widespread and political connections were the key to economic advancement (Section 5.5 of Chapter 5).

The major turnaround in South Korea's economic fortunes came with the adoption of outward-oriented policies and other economic reforms following the 1961 coup. The major measures are summarized in Figure 6.5. The new regime devalued the exchange rate and introduced export incentives in the early 1960s. In 1965 quantitative restrictions on imports were gradually relaxed and in 1967 the government switched from an import control system based on a list of goods that could be imported to the more liberal device of a list of goods that could not be.

The second half of the 1960s also saw reductions in price controls, and liberalization of foreign capital transactions and domestic financial markets. The last of these reforms led to a sharp increase in interest rates (see Table 4.4), which encouraged domestic savings and made investment more efficient.

However, neo-liberals see South Korea's attempt in the 1970s to develop the heavy and chemical industries as a policy mistake, because it involved increased levels of protection and generous supplies of credit at subsidized rates of interest. The greater emphasis on import substitution and increased price distortions slowed down economic growth in the late 1970s

However a further phase of import liberalization began in 1978 and despite being temporarily interrupted by the economic and political crisis of 1980, continued in the 1980s. Controls on imports were relaxed further and tariff rates reduced (Figure 6.6).

Neo-liberals regard South Korea's success in maintaining high rates of economic growth in the 1980s as further support for their analysis and policy recommendations. The economy grew despite the deteriorating external situation and in sharp contrast to the experience of Brazil. Far from being vulnerable to changes in international conditions over which it has no control, South Korea's strongly outward-oriented economy was in a better position to adjust to changing circumstances, because of its low price distortions and greater flexibility.

Comments and questions

This chronology of economic policies in Brazil and South Korea indicates that the timing of policy measures can help explain differences in economic performance. Whereas South Korea began to move towards a more export-oriented

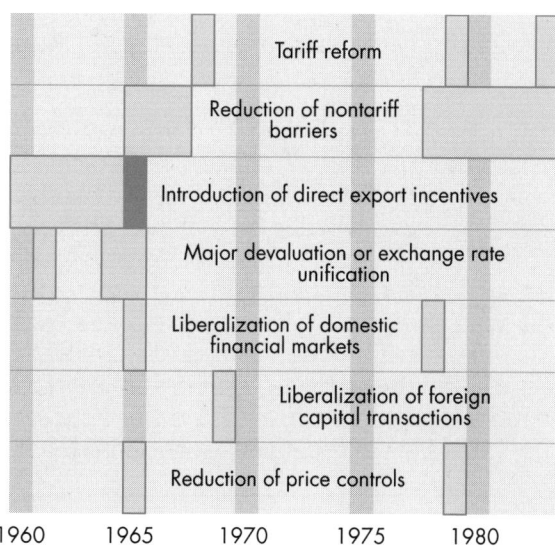

Tariff reform

Reduction of nontariff barriers

Introduction of direct export incentives

Major devaluation or exchange rate unification

Liberalization of domestic financial markets

Liberalization of foreign capital transactions

Reduction of price controls

1960   1965   1970   1975   1980

■ Policy reversal

Figure 6.5   Major economic liberalization policies in South Korea, 1959–83.

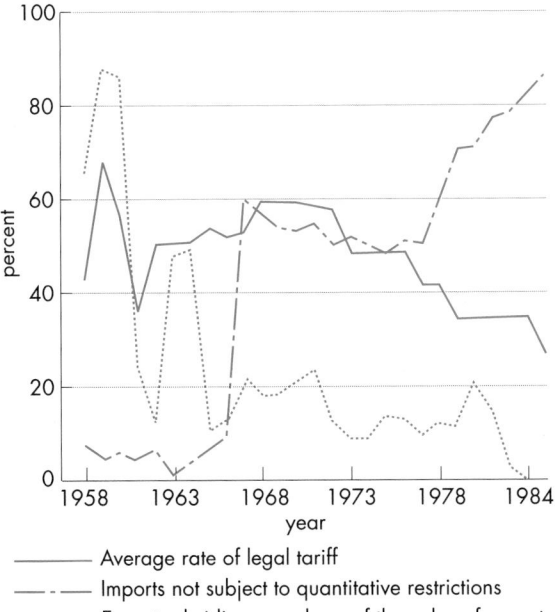

percent / year

— Average rate of legal tariff
— · — Imports not subject to quantitative restrictions
·········· Export subsidies as a share of the value of exports

Figure 6.6   Evolution of trade incentives in South Korea, 1958–84.

strategy in the early 1960s, Brazil did so in the late 1960s. More significantly, South Korea began to promote exports after a fairly short period of import substitution in non-durable consumer goods, in the 1950s. Brazil had a much longer history of import substitution and by the late 1960s import substitution in consumer durable and intermediate goods was well advanced. In other words when Brazil began to change its trade orientation, it already had a legacy of high-cost import substitution industries, which held back its progress.

Before going on to the next section stop to think about the following questions:

Q How well does the neo-liberal interpretation fit what you learnt about Brazil and South Korea in Chapters 3 and 4? In particular, do you think that any important aspects of South Korean and/or Brazilian development have been left out of this analysis?

Q Does the experience of Brazil and South Korea vindicate the neo-liberal position discussed in Chapter 5?

6.2   A structuralist view

In contrast to the neo-liberal view, with its emphasis on a universally valid economic theory, structuralists are much more concerned with the specific historical and institutional context within which development occurs. Economic policies are a part of the story but they have to be placed in a wider context.

Let us start by comparing development in Brazil and South Korea with that in other less developed countries, but now emphasizing those aspects of development which play a major role in structuralist theories of development. This will illustrate in slightly more detail how structuralist theory interprets the historical experience of both Brazil and South Korea.

Comparing Brazil and South Korea

As we saw in Chapter 5, structuralist theories put considerable emphasis on how centre–periphery relationships affect development in the Third World. Although the 'export pessimism' of the early structuralists proved to be exaggerated in the 1950s and 1960s, this did not contradict their more fundamental insight that development strategy had to take account of the particular international circumstances facing Third World countries.

The economic performance of South Korea and Brazil bears this out. Initially South Korea depended on massive economic aid provided by the United States, reflecting its particular geopolitical position in the Cold War. Subsequently both South Korea and Brazil launched their export drives during the 1960s at a time when world markets were expanding, and in the 1970s they were able to borrow heavily on the international capital market as a result of the vastly increased liquidity of the international banks following the 1973 oil price rises.

However, in both Brazil and South Korea, the state has always mediated the relationship between the country's economy and the world economy. While both Brazil and South Korea put considerable emphasis on promoting exports of manufactures, they did not do so by adopting free trade policies. Indeed both countries continued to grant substantial protection to production for the domestic market while exports were promoted.

Similarly, although there were large capital inflows to Brazil and South Korea, particularly in the 1970s, these were not totally uncontrolled. In South Korea especially, preference was given to foreign loans channeled to domestic firms via the nationalized banking system and not to direct foreign investment. As a result South Korea had one of the lowest levels of dependence on direct foreign investment anywhere in the Third World.

Capital flight

Outflows of capital were subject to very strict controls in Brazil and South Korea. In contrast, countries such as Mexico had traditionally not used foreign exchange controls. Others like Argentina and Chile had liberalized their financial markets in the 1970s. As a result, capital flight was much less extensive in the late 1970s and early 1980s from Brazil and South Korea than from other countries.

Debt

Despite controls on capital flight, both Brazil and South Korea accumulated large foreign debts. In the case of Brazil this has been a major cause of economic problems in the 1980s. Structuralists would stress two points.

(i)   The debt crisis was brought about by events over which Brazil and South Korea had no control, particularly the deterioration of their terms of trade and the sharp rise in US interest rates in the late 1970s and early 1980s. Sachs (1985) estimated that the combined effect represented a loss of around 5% of GDP in Brazil and almost 4% in South Korea.

(ii) The impact of debt on development depends on what the loans are used for. In South Korea loans were used more productively than in Brazil, particularly in generating and saving foreign exchange. This helps to explain why South Korea was better able to weather the debt crisis in the 1980s.

Structural change

Both the South Korean and the Brazilian cases amply support the structuralist emphasis on the role of manufacturing industry in bringing about structural transformation. South Korea's impressive economic performance has been associated with a phenomenal rate of growth of manufacturing; averaging more than 15% per annum sustained for a quarter of a century. In Brazil too, industry was the fastest growing sector in the late 1960s and 1970s. And the poor performance of Brazil in the 1980s has been associated with industrial stagnation.

In both countries, the manufacturing share of GDP increased sharply. As shown in Table 6.6, South Korea ranked second (after Singapore) and Brazil fourth out of 35 countries, in terms of the increased share of manufacturing between 1960 and 1980.

Not only did the share of manufacturing in total output increase but the structure of industry also became increasingly complex, with extensive linkages (see Chapter 5, Section 5.3). The United Nations Industrial Development Organization (UNIDO) has developed an index to measure structural change within manufacturing. If each branch of industry had continued to contribute exactly the same share of the total manufacturing output over a period, then this index would be zero. But if, say, the food processing industry had declined while the computer industry expanded, then this will be reflected in a higher value of the index. On the basis of this index, between 1965 and 1980 South Korea and Brazil ranked second and third in terms of the extent of structural change (Table 6.6).

Ownership and income distribution

We also find striking differences between Brazil and South Korea in land ownership and in foreign ownership of capital. South Korea has one of the most equitable land distributions in the Third World, while Brazil has one of the most unequal. This difference results from the history of land reform in South Korea (see Chapter 4). In Brazil, where large estates persist, there has been no serious land reform.

Table 6.6 Structural change in selected economies

Country	% Change in share of manufacturing in GDP (1960–80)	Index of structural change in manufacturing (1965–80)
Singapore	16.7	48
S. Korea	14.2	31
Malaysia	13.8	16
Brazil	13.0	30
Turkey	8.9	23
Egypt	8.3	22
Portugal	7.3	22
Thailand	7.0	18
Tunisia	6.1	17
Costa Rica	5.4	6
Philippines	5.3	11
Mexico	4.9	15
Colombia	4.8	11
Kenya	3.9	28
India	3.7	21
Ivory Coast	3.6	17
Uruguay	3.6	10
Greece	3.1	14
Israel	2.9	16
Peru	2.9	14
Algeria	2.9	19
South Africa	2.0	19
Morocco	1.5	12
Argentina	1.1	16
Iran	1.0	19
Spain	1.0	25
Syria	0.5	18
Venezuela	0.2	8
Hong Kong	0.0	10
Dominican Republic	−2.3	4
Iraq	−4.0	9
Ireland	−6.7	19
Yugoslavia	−6.9	12
Ecuador	−7.2	19
Chile	−7.2	13

[Source: UNIDO,1985; Chenery *et al.*, 1986].

Figure 6.7   Shipbuilding was one of the heavy industries developed under protection in both Brazil and south Korea. (Top) Ishibras shipyard, Rio de Janeiro. (Bottom) Welding panels, Hyundai Shipyard, Ulsan, South Korea.

Figure 6.8   (Left) Large estate in Brazil. (Right) Smallholding in South Korea.

Brazil's less equitable land distribution is reflected in a less equitable income distribution (Table 6.3).

Similarly, Brazil and South Korea occupy sharply divergent positions in terms of foreign ownership. An index of foreign capital inflow calculated by Bonschier & Chase-Dunn (1985) ranks Brazil 29th in the degree of inflow, out of 103 countries covered. South Korea in contrast comes near the bottom of the list in 95th place. In the key manufacturing sector, foreign owned firms account for 40% of output in Brazil compared to less than 20% in South Korea where much tighter control was exercised.

As a result, local capital is much stronger in South Korea than in Brazil. The bulk of manufactured exports are accounted for by the large Korean groups *(chaebols)* which have also themselves become foreign investors, expanding both into other parts of Asia and into markets in developed countries.

Technological development

Technological development has played a key role in the economic success of both South Korea and Brazil. The acquisition of technological capability is difficult to measure (see Chapter 7), but on some indicators, both countries perform well, particularly South Korea (see Table 6.7).

South Korea spends 1.1% of its GNP on research and development (R&D), a higher proportion than in any other Third World country, while Brazil is in third place after India. Similarly the number of scientists and engineers engaged in research and development (relative to the size of population) is higher in South Korea than in any other developing country apart from Singapore and although Brazil lags behind, it still performs

Table 6.7 Indicators of technological capability in selected countries, 1986

	R&D/GDP	Scientists and engineers in R&D per million population	% of patents to nationals
S. Korea	1.1%	781	69.0
India	0.9%	37	20.0
Brazil	0.6%	240	9.1
Mexico	0.6%	212	8.7
Singapore	0.5%	923	8.4
Argentina	0.4%	344	30.8
Chile	0.4%	132	10.5
Venezuela	0.4%	264	11.9
Indonesia	0.3%	153	—
Pakistan	0.3%	97	—
Thailand	0.3%	—	—
Egypt	0.2%	411	3.1
Philippines	0.2%	88	9.8
Sri Lanka	0.2%	—	12.2
Turkey	0.2%	154	7.4
Colombia	0.1%	38	4.3
Kenya	0.1%	—	—

[Source: Evenson & Ranis,1990; Fishlow, 1985]

better than most other countries in the list. In South Korea, too, the majority of patents issued for innovations are granted to nationals, whereas in other Third World countries, the overwhelming majority go to foreigners.

Another indicator of successful acquisition of local technological capabilities is the growth of technology exports in recent years. South Korea and Brazil have been the leaders amongst the newly industrializing countries in this field, along with India.

Technological development is closely linked to the capital goods industry which provides the source of many technical improvements (see Chapter 4, Box 4.4). In most Third World countries, the capital goods industry is small or non-existent. However industrialization in Brazil and South Korea has extended to include a significant capital goods industry. During the 1970s, local production of capital goods increased almost sevenfold in Brazil and fifteenfold in South Korea.

One reflection of the acquisition of technological capabilities is a rapid rate of productivity growth. Comparative studies show that productivity grew at high rates in Brazil during the 1950s and in South Korea during the 1960s and early 1970s. Manufacturing productivity in South Korea grew particularly rapidly in the 1960s and 1970s, faster even than in Japan.

Growth of investment

Rapid growth in both South Korea and Brazil has involved high levels of capital accumulation. Between 1965 and 1980, investment grew in both countries at rates well above the average for developing countries (see Table 6.8). Although South Korea began the 1960s with low levels of

Table 6.8 Indicators of investment

	Brazil	South Korea	Developing countries
Investment as % of GDP			
1965	20%	15%	20%
1988	23%	30%	26%
Investment growth			
1965-80	11.3%	15.9%	8.6%
1980-88	0.0%	10.5%	2.7%
Price of producer goods (1975)*	0.93	0.92	1.19†

* A value of less than 1 indicates that prices of producer goods are lower than the average of all goods. (See Figure 4.11 for definition of producer goods.)

† Average for 8 Developing countries other than Brazil and South Korea.

[Sources: World Bank, 1990; Bradford, 1987]

investment this was doubled between 1965 and 1988. In Brazil, there were increased levels of investment in the 1960s and 1970s. But these were reversed with the crisis of the 1980s when economic growth slowed and the rate of investment stopped.

The rapid growth of investment in Brazil and South Korea during the 1970s was associated with a relatively low price for investment goods, particularly compared to a sample of other developing countries. Moreover, as we saw in Section 6.1, interest rates in both countries during this period were negative, giving further encouragement to investment.

Brazil

The structuralist view of Brazilian economic development emphasizes the major role played by the state throughout the post-war period. Indeed far from the 'economic miracle' being associated with liberalization, it was accompanied by an increase in direct state involvement in the economy (see Chapter 3, Section 3.4).

Import substitution

The import-substituting policies of the 1950s played a major part in building up the diversified industrial base which later enabled Brazil to break into international markets with its manufactured goods. The motor industry is a good example of this. Established on a manufacturing (as opposed to assembly) basis under Kubitschek in the 1950s, it became an important export industry from the 1970s (see Box 3.7).

The difficulties which import substitution ran into in the early 1960s were an outcome of the failure to change underlying economic and social structures of the country during the 1950s; rather than a result of inward-oriented policies *per se*. For example, the failure to carry out land reform meant that a large part of the population lived in rural poverty and did not constitute a market for industrial goods. So import substitution was forced to take place in ever more sophisticated goods for a restricted market. Moreover, the continuing inequalities in land ownership meant that agricultural output did not increase significantly in response to increased demand for food from the growing urban population. This and other bottlenecks, such as in infrastructure, contributed to accelerating inflation in the early 1960s.

Another problem with the import substitution of the 1950s was emphasized by some structuralists. This was the increasing role of foreign firms in the industrial sector. Industrialization was based on providing generous incentives to foreign capital, as well as protection for the domestic market. While these policies encouraged inflows of foreign capital and technology in the 1950s, by the early 1960s remittances of profits and dividends were running ahead of new investment.

Paradoxically, the problem of markets for industrial goods was solved after the 1964 military coup by increasing concentration of income and income inequality. The increasing wealth of the middle classes and better-off fuelled the demand for consumer durables such as cars, television sets and refrigerators, which were the fastest growing industries during the 'miracle' years .

Continued government intervention

In fact many structuralists regard the 'Brazilian miracle' as something of a mirage; arguing that it can 'best be described as a vigorous economic recovery rather than as an 'economic miracle' …' (Bacha, 1976, p.7). The period of extremely rapid economic growth in Brazil was fairly short-lived. The first three years of military rule were characterized by a major recession, which came on top of the slowdown in growth in the early 1960s. Thus the fast growth in the late 1960s and early 1970s merely brought the country back to where it would have been had growth continued through the 1960s at the same rate as in the 1950s.

From this point of view it makes sense to consider the three decades up to 1980 as one period. The change in policy after 1964 is much less marked than the neo-liberals claim. The shift from import substitution to outward-oriented policies after 1964 were at most partial. Protection for the domestic market continued throughout the period. Although exports were indeed promoted, this often involved increased government intervention rather than liberalization, with firms being set export targets in return for reductions in import duty (see Box 3.4).

The state also played a major role in the Brazilian economy throughout the post-war period.

Far from the military reducing government involvement in economic activity, it expanded it and consolidated the triple alliance between state, private and foreign firms (see Box 3.5). Between 1968 and 1974, public enterprises accounted for more than half of total investment and more than 70% of loans for development purposes came from the state and regional development banks (ILO, 1988). State firms were also an important factor in Brazil's export drive.

The government also intervened in technology transfer to reduce the costs of imported technology and to increase local technological capabilities. Brazil has relied to a greater extent than South Korea on importing packaged technology through multinational corporations. A notable exception to this has been the 'market reserve' policy in the computer industry (see Box 3.10) which structuralists regard as a positive example of what can be achieved through state intervention.

Foreign investment and capital accumulation

There was also considerable continuity in the role played by foreign investment in Brazilian development throughout the post-war period. From the mid-1950s incentives were offered to attract foreign capital and multinational corporations arrived in large numbers. The slowdown in direct foreign investment in the early 1960s was quickly reversed after the military takeover, with transnational companies being offered advantageous conditions. Although in the 1970s, the Brazilian government began to bargain with, and even exclude, foreign capital from certain sectors to obtain more favourable results, particularly in terms of the balance of payments, policies remained more liberal than those of South Korea.

As we saw in Table 6.8, the 1960s and 1970s in Brazil were characterized by a high rate of growth of investment. The military coup in Brazil in 1964 led to a reduction in real wages for unskilled workers, and a shift of income from labour to capital. This contributed to increased income inequality during the 'miracle', but it also helped to create favourable conditions for capital accumulation during the late 1960s and 1970s.

Figure 6.9   The Brazilian 'economic miracle' period was characterized by large investments in infrastructure.
The Furnas hydroelectric project on the Rio Grande in Minas Gerais.

External and internal causes of crisis

The economic crisis which hit Brazil in the 1980s is seen by structuralists as primarily resulting from deteriorating external conditions. In the early 1980s, Brazil's international terms of trade (see Box 5.3) fell by almost 30% at the same time as real interest rates payable on the country's foreign debt rose from –2.7% to +8.5% (Sachs, 1985). This external shock gave rise to accelerating inflation and falling output. Investment which had grown rapidly in the 1960s and 1970s stagnated. At the same time the return to civilian rule in Brazil created increased pressures to satisfy the social needs which had been neglected during the years of military rule.

Figure 6.10 'The eternal debt of Latin America … What can we do?' One Latin American view of debt.

Despite three decades of rapid industrial growth, many of the underlying economic and social structures in Brazil, particularly in the rural areas, remained largely unchanged. Landlords, for instance, continue to exercise considerable political influence, placing constraints on government policies which would harm their interests, and ensuring their access to subsidized credit and inputs provided by the government.

These structures combined with the external constraints, particularly the massive net transfer of resources from Brazil to service the foreign debt, and the continuing reliance on foreign finance and technology, to hinder further rapid economic growth.

South Korea

Whereas the neo-liberals emphasize policy changes which began in the 1960s to explain rapid economic growth in South Korea over the past three decades, structuralists stress the importance of developments before 1960 in laying the basis for later economic success. Chapter 4 showed how the economic and social structure of South Korea emerged from a particular historical experience; particularly the impact, both positive and negative, of Japanese colonialism. After the defeat of the Japanese, the land reform and the massive inflow of US aid in the 1950s contributed crucially to the structural transformation of the South Korean economy and society.

Land reform

For structuralists, the land reform carried out in South Korea in the early 1950s provided a crucial basis for subsequent economic development. This effectively abolished the landlord class and gave tenants their own land, providing the basis for the relatively egalitarian income distribution found in South Korea. Land reform also eliminated the political power of large landowners. As a result it was possible for the government to adopt policies which transferred resources out of agriculture into industry, laying the foundations for rapid industrial growth. One central policy was the compulsory purchase of grain at prices which were below market prices and which, in the 1950s, were below production costs (Lee, 1979). The relatively equal income distribution in South Korea also provided a mass market for simple consumer goods such as textiles which formed the basis for industrialization in the 1950s.

Geo-political position

Structuralists also point to South Korea's unique geo-political position. The Cold War led to the United States providing massive economic aid to the South Korean government until the mid-1960s. More than two-thirds of gross investment and imports in South Korea were financed through aid. Some structuralists would argue that aid and the special relationship between Korea and the United States during the Vietnam war were crucial to its economic success.

State intervention

Structuralists disagree fundamentally with the neo-liberals on the role of the state in the South Korean 'miracle'. As one author has commented,

> "No state outside the Socialist bloc, ever came anywhere near this measure of control over the economy's investible resources."
>
> (Datta-Chaudhuri, 1981, p.56)

State intervention in itself does not necessarily promote economic development. The neo-liberals are quite right to point out that it can often give rise to rent-seeking and corruption, and the extent to which this occurred in South Korea during the 1950s is well documented. However the South Korean experience since 1961 suggests that a state with a high degree of autonomy from vested interests, an efficient bureaucracy and a strong commitment to economic growth can indeed achieve impressive results.

In 1961 President Park created the Economic Planning Board which has played a major part in determining industrial priorities through a series of five year development plans. Thus although private enterprise accounts for the bulk of industrial production in South Korea, the general direction of development has been determined by the government. This is clearly illustrated by the big push into heavy and chemical industries which was initiated by the state in the early 1970s (Chapter 4, Section 4.4).

The nationalization of banks in the early 1960s gave the South Korean government a crucial instrument to influence the direction of economic development. Favoured sectors received loans at very low rates of interest, in return for implementing government policies and meeting certain targets.

Faced with a decline in US aid in the early 1960s, a priority for the government was to increase export earnings. This was done not by adopting free trade policies, but by an aggressive policy of export targeting combined with continued protection of the domestic market. Throughout most of the 1960s and 1970s, over 40% of import items were subject to quantitative restrictions and the average legal tariff was between 40% and 60% (Figure 6.6). Thus firms which met government targets benefited from high profits on sales in the domestic market and from cheap credit and inputs.

Restricted foreign investment

The government also ensured that the main beneficiaries of these policies were Korean-owned firms. In the 1960s and 1970s foreign capital in South Korea was subject to tight investment screening and extensive government interferences and reporting requirements and control. Preferential consideration was given to joint-ventures and foreign capital was excluded from all areas unless otherwise specified. As one commentator has remarked,

> "... the government was able to exert comprehensive influences on the patterns of foreign investment in Korea ... competition with domestic firms was seldom allowed, both in domestic and export markets, and Korea became one of the few countries with very restrictive foreign investment regulations."
>
> (Koo, quoted in Luedde-Neurath, 1984, p.23)

The greater willingness of South Korea to restrict foreign capital, and to direct it where it offered specific advantages in terms of access to foreign technology or export markets, is reflected in the limited role played by TNCs in the Korean economy.

Technology transfer and investment

The development of local technological capabilities has been crucial to South Korea's industrial success. As with foreign investment, Korea exercised strict control over technology transfer in order to maximize learning effects. Unpackaging of imported technology has been encouraged, minimizing dependence on direct foreign investment. Like Japan, South Korea also resorted to copying foreign products through 'reverse engineering' or 'depackaging technology' (Chapter 4, Section 4.4). As a result South Korea has now become one of the Third World's leading exporters of technology.

The state also played a crucial role in bringing about high levels of investment in South Korea. A significant share of capital investment was undertaken within the state sector and government policies also encouraged investment. Contrary to the neo-liberal view, the state promoted accumulation through a policy of deliberately introducing distortions into the economy. As one study of capital accumulation in South Korea has concluded,

> "…our results support the view that investment in Korea has been influenced by government policy and targeting, and to a lesser extent by the standard neo-classical variables."
>
> (Yusuf & Peters, 1985, p.45)

A further factor contributing to high levels of investment in South Korea was the control of labour. In the early 1960s, wages were already low and fell in real terms after the military coup by President Park (ILO, 1988). Although wages grew rapidly from the mid-1960s onwards, labour productivity grew even faster (Table 4.9). As in Brazil, this created favourable conditions for investment.

Restructuring and growth

Rapid economic growth requires not only a high level of saving but also the productive use of investment. In the case of South Korea, many of the usual channels for non-productive investment were closed off. Land reform limited the opportunities for large-scale investment in land, while public ownership of the banking system meant that financial investment was less attractive. Opportunities for making large profits simply through trade and access to foreign

exchange were also eliminated under the Park government.

Like Brazil, South Korea faced an economic crisis in the early 1980s. However, it has been much more successful than Brazil in weathering the storm and achieving renewed economic growth. Structuralists deny that this is a result of more liberal economic policies in South Korea. They claim that liberalization in the 1980s has been more apparent than real.

In fact the South Korean government intervened strongly in the face of economic difficulties, increasing public investment and embarking on a major industrial restructuring in the early 1980s. This brought about a rapid resumption in export growth and a reduction in the balance of payments deficit. Thus the speed and effectiveness of state intervention was a major factor in successful adjustment in the 1980s, just as it had played a crucial role in rapid economic growth in the 1960s and 1970s.

Questions

Now repeat the exercise which you carried out at the end of Section 6.1.

Q How well does the structuralist view fit what you know about Brazil and South Korea?

Q Can you see areas in which the neo-liberal and structuralist views directly conflict? If so, looking back at Chapters 3 and 4, which seems most consistent with the accounts given there?

Q Are there still important gaps which neither approach has dealt with adequately?

6.3 Lessons from the NICs

What do the experiences of Brazil and South Korea demonstrate? We have seen that different theoretical perspectives can lead to very different interpretations of the same development experiences. This is not just a matter of academic interest. The way we interpret the past influences the lessons we draw for the future. In this section we examine some of the lessons which neo-liberal and structuralist theorists draw from their analysis of the NICs.

Neo-liberal lessons

For the neo-liberals the lessons are clear. One neo-liberal writer sums up the four East Asian NICs (Hong Kong, Singapore, Taiwan and South Korea) in the following terms:

> "... success is almost entirely due to good policies and the ability of the people — scarcely at all to favourable circumstances or a good start."
>
> (Little, 1981, p.25)

He goes on to argue that, although entrepreneurial ability and the responsiveness of producers will vary from country to country, this will only affect the time it takes for these policies to be successful. Thus any country which adopted sound neo-liberal policies could expect to reap the benefits which have been enjoyed by the East Asian NICs. Indeed they believe that a second tier of NICs (such as Malaysia, Thailand and Colombia) is already emerging, following in the wake of the East Asian pioneers.

So, for neo-liberals, there are some fundamental policies to achieve economic growth:

- Price distortions have to be reduced through the removal of price controls and subsidies, deregulation, particularly of financial markets, and reform of labour legislation which increases the cost of employing and laying off workers.

- Trade and exchange rate reforms need to be carried out in order to remove the bias against exports resulting from import substitution strategies, and to reduce price distortions for traded goods. These reforms usually involve devaluation to make the exchange rates competitive.

- The role of the state in the economy should be reduced by cuts in government expenditure and privatization of the majority of state owned enterprises. The state should concentrate on providing an enabling framework for private enterprise.

Structuralist lessons

Structuralists are far more cautious concerning the transferability of the experience of countries such as Brazil and South Korea to other Third World countries. They emphasize the specific historical, institutional and geographic conditions of these two countries which are not necessarily replicated elsewhere.

Specific circumstances

South Korea for instance benefited from large inflows of US aid during the 1950s and early 1960s because of its geopolitical position. It began to expand its manufactured exports in the 1960s when international trade was growing rapidly and developed countries were reducing trade barriers. The history of South Korea and particularly the legacy of Japanese colonialism and the impact of the Korean War gave rise to a high degree of state autonomy from local vested interests which might otherwise block government policies.

Even though Brazil faced problems of limited demand for basic manufactures, so that import substitution only really took off with increased concentration of wealth and the production of luxury goods, there are few Third World countries with a domestic market of comparable size, apart from China and India. Given Brazil's large population, even a relatively small percentage of the total constituted a numerically large pool of middle class consumers of manufactured goods.

Brazil's physical size also gives it a diversified natural resource base for agricultural production and mineral extraction. Even before the rapid industrial growth of the 1960s and 1970s, Brazil had a long history of industrialization and a well established industrial base (see Box 6.2).

Limited international markets

A second point stressed by structuralists is that even if other countries were able to replicate the success of the NICs, they would soon run into market problems. The advocacy of export promotion as a strategy for Third World countries is subject to what is known as the *fallacy of composition*. This is the fallacy of believing that what one country can produce and profitably sell can be replicated in a large number of countries or in all countries, regardless of the size of the international market for that product.

To take a simple example, training shoes are currently imported into Britain from a small number of East Asian countries including South

---

Box 6.2   The preconditions of the Brazilian model of industrialization

Brazil's pre-existing industrial base: Although Brazil went through periods of rapid industrialization in the 1950s and during the economic miracle, there was clearly a significant and sophisticated industrial base before either of these phases. This started at the beginning of the 20th century and, in contrast to many other Third World countries, Brazil already had a steel industry and a chemicals industry in the 1950s. It also had large and long-established textile, food and clothing industries.

Brazil's size: In the Third World, Brazil is also rather exceptional in terms of its size (geographical and population) and the extent of its natural resources. It is half of the continent of South America, with a population of over 120 million. This provides certain advantages for industrialization; particularly economies of scale resulting from the size of the internal market. In addition, in spite of the sparseness of oil resources, Brazil is well-endowed with other energy, mineral and agricultural resources; such as water for hydro-electric power, uranium for nuclear power, iron ore, bauxite and gold.

Favourable international conditions: In the 1950s and 1960s the two factors most favourable to industrialization at the international level were stable cheap finance and cheap oil. The Kubitschek government strategy was introduced at a time when US multinationals were turning their attention to the Third World generally. Following the Korean War boom and the period of US aid to Europe after the Second World War, North American capital was prepared and able to invest in the Third World where conditions were right. Until 1973 there were investible funds in the Western economies, which countries such as Brazil were able to tap into, attracting both foreign investment and loans. In addition to this, when the developed countries were expanding they were able to absorb exports from the Third World. This gave a chance for countries such as Brazil to export manufactured goods abroad and also to export raw materials as a means of paying for imports of machinery. Generally speaking, then, the economic miracle occurred at a favourable conjuncture in the international economy.

State control of the working class: The Brazilian miracle occurred in political conditions that are not general in the Third World. The 1964 coup gave an air of political 'stability' to the country that proved very attractive to foreign firms. The government's control over unions and workers was an incentive to investment, since it created the conditions at the point of production that would guarantee low wage costs and high productivity. At the same time, the overall control of the government over the working class and opposition political parties and groups gave all firms a sense of security. They did not live in fear of a sudden change in the regulations governing production and investment.

Creating the conditions for rapid expansion: The government not only controlled the working class, it also provided incentives in the form of institutional and infrastructural back-up to companies to ensure growth. It provided loans, tax relief and investment support to companies, assured supplies of energy, improved transport and reorganized the financial system in the years following the military coup.

The State sector: In spite of the Brazilian government's acceptance of foreign companies and its stress on the market economy, the government was not at all adverse to the expansion of the State sector. Although the government's own bureaucracy was cut down and the terms and conditions of service of many public servants were worsened by reforms after 1964, the so-called 'productive' State sector providing goods and services to industry and consumers expanded rapidly during the period of the economic miracle.

[Source: Adapted from Humphrey & Wield, 1983]

Korea, Taiwan, Indonesia and Thailand. These supply the bulk of the UK market and provide valuable foreign exchange for these countries. Should we therefore recommend that India, China, Pakistan, and every country in Sub-Saharan Africa and Latin America undertake a major export drive to sell trainers in Britain? Clearly not. The effect would be to drive down the price of training shoes to such a low level that exporting would be unprofitable. Thus, while it may make sense for a single country taken in isolation to begin exporting training shoes, it cannot be a solution for the Third World as a whole.

This suggests that the success of countries which adopted export-oriented industrialization strategies in the 1960s was at least partly because most other Third World countries at that time were following import-substituting policies, so that the few had a fairly clear run at the market.

In the 1980s a new twist was given to the fallacy of composition argument by the growth of the 'new protectionism' in developed countries (see Box 1.2 in Chapter 1). One author estimated that manufactured exports from developing countries would increase sevenfold in the 1980s if other Third World countries were to export as much

Figure 6.11   One early internationally competitive industry in South Korea was textiles. A textile worker on a spindle in Seoul.

(adjusted for country size and level of development) as the East Asian NICs did in the mid-1970s (Cline, 1982). Such an expansion of exports would be certain to lead to a protectionist backlash from the developed countries. These conclusions have been disputed by neo-liberals, but they remain a concern for structuralists.

Active state intervention

Does this mean structuralists believe that other countries cannot draw any lessons from the Brazilian or South Korean experience? Not at all. While structuralists reject the neo-liberal view that policies can simply be transferred elsewhere, they maintain that both the Brazilian and South Korean cases vindicate the long-held structuralist belief in the need for active state intervention to promote development. More specifically, they argue that the two countries bear out the need for the state to intervene to regulate links with the world economy and to give priority to industry.

From this point of view the adoption of structural adjustment programmes in many Third World countries under IMF/World Bank conditionality is likely to have an adverse effect on industrialization. Writing in the mid-1980s on the prospects for industrialization in the coming decade, Kaplinsky commented that

> "Structural adjustment programmes, by undermining the pervasive role of the state and focusing on short-run static efficiency is placing significant obstacles in the face of long-run industrial strategies."
>
> (Kaplinsky, 1984)

In other words, from a structuralist perspective, neo-liberal policies which reduce the role of the state in the economy and dismantle the instruments of trade policy will be counter-productive in terms of industrial development.

The experience of South Korea, and to some extent Brazil, indicates that state intervention is not necessarily always doomed to be plagued by 'government failure' as a result of the incompetence and corruption of bureaucrats and the rent-seeking activities of businessmen, as the neo-liberals imply. Effective state intervention,

however, requires the creation of institutions which can formulate and implement appropriate policies. This in turn depends on broader political conditions which determine the degree of state autonomy from vested interest groups and the commitment of those in power to economic development.

For structuralists, the cases of South Korea and Brazil show that three factors are vital for successful economic development: fundamental structural change, high levels of capital accumulation and development of local technological capabilities. Structural change, particularly land reform, has been a crucial element in South Korea's development. Brazil's development has been limited by the lack of structural and social change.

Apart from these general lessons concerning the need for state intervention and structural change to bring about economic development, contemporary structuralists are reluctant to generalize about policy. They emphasize the need for policy to be tailor-made for particular countries and one of the criticisms that they often make of the IMF is that it imposes a standard policy package in all Third World countries irrespective of local conditions.

6.4 An evaluation of theoretical perspectives

So far in this chapter we have seen that both neo-liberal and structuralist theories can provide coherent interpretations of industrialization in Brazil and South Korea. How then can we choose between them, especially as they suggest very different policy prescriptions for other Third World countries?

Before trying to answer that question, we might ask why we need theory at all? In social science, theories generally help us interpret the past, intervene in the present and make predictions about the future. In development studies which is by definition concerned with economic and social change, intervention in the present is crucial. As Karl Marx wrote

"The philosophers have only *interpreted* the world in various ways; the point is to *change* it."

(Marx, 1888, p.123 of 1974 edition)

Some theory is in any case inevitable. The social and economic reality of the Third World is extremely complex and any account will be selective. Theory identifies the key features of any specific case because it is impossible to reproduce reality in full. To do so would be similar to the king who asked his cartographers to produce a map of his kingdom which was exact down to the last detail, only to find that when they had finished, the map was so large that it covered the whole kingdom.

The accounts of Brazil and South Korea given in Chapters 3 and 4 are highly selective. As such they assume that some things are more important than others and therefore have an implicit theoretical foundation. The account of South Korea, for example, highlights many of the factors stressed in structuralist theory, while tending to contradict many of the claims made by neo-liberals.

We can therefore say that theory is both inevitable and necessary for action. How then can the rival merits of the two theories discussed in this chapter be assessed? Clearly in social science it is impossible to test conflicting theories under laboratory conditions and hence there may be more than one theory to explain the same reality. Choosing between different theories thus becomes much more of a matter of judgement. This involves evaluating how consistent the theory is, both internally in terms of its own logic, and externally in terms of the extent to which it mirrors reality. It also involves considering the relevance of the theory in terms of what issues it addresses. In so far as different theories can be seen as serving different interests, a political element will also enter the choice between theories. As in other areas of life, it is always worth asking who benefits.

Theories are not static. As we saw in Chapter 5, they evolve in reaction to social and economic developments which pose new problems and solutions. They also feed off each other through debate and convergence. In the light of all this, it is essential to approach all theories critically, with an eye to strengths and weaknesses, and not to accept them always at face value.

A critique of neo-liberal theory

Neo-liberalism is based on orthodox neo-classical economic theory. The neo-classical arguments in favour of the free market are subject to a number of limitations. First, they apply to a competitive economy whereas in the real world, particularly in the Third World, production may be in the hands of a small number of monopolistic firms, or trade controlled by a few large merchants and access to land and resources by large landowners. In other words, many markets are far from competitive.

Second, this theory is primarily concerned with issues of resource allocation at a point in time. It has very little to say about problems of economic growth or development. As such there is a crucial theoretical gap between the view that countries should 'get prices right' according to neo-classical theory and the claim that this will bring about a faster rate of economic growth or increased development.

Finally, neo-liberal theory says nothing about income distribution. An efficient economy in terms of resource allocation (see Box 5.6) could be one in which income inequalities are unacceptably high.

Given the theoretical tenuousness of the neo-liberal case, it is not surprising that considerable effort has been devoted to empirical linking of economic growth with low price distortions and outward orientation. The claims made by the World Bank in this area have in fact been hotly debated.

Price distortions only explain about a third of the differences in growth rates between different countries, indicating that other factors too are significant. South Korea and Brazil are identified as two countries which grew at a significantly higher rate than would be expected on the basis of the degree of price distortions. Neo-liberals suggest that this exceptional growth is a result of political and institutional factors. On the other hand Ethiopia, Jamaica and Ghana are three countries where growth was lower than expected in relation to the degree of price distortion. Again, neo-liberals attribute this to political factors.

There is also a highly subjective element involved in calculating the distortion index. For example, Chile, which underwent a major liberalization of the economy under the military regime in the 1970s, but grew slowly over that decade, is classified as having a high level of price distortion. Finally, any relation between price distortions and growth may be the result of some third factor. Structuralists could argue that the structural problems which slow down economic growth can also give rise to large price distortions. This would require structural changes to bring about less distortions and faster growth.

There are similar problems with World Bank evidence of links between outward orientation and growth (see Table 5.4 in Chapter 5). The strongly outward-oriented group of countries which performs so well consists only of South Korea and the two city states, Hong Kong and Singapore, and can hardly provide a model for other Third World countries with large agricultural sectors and rural populations. There are moderately outward-oriented countries such as Chile and Uruguay where GNP *per capita* and manufacturing output have stagnated between 1973 and 1985, and inward-oriented economies such as Cameroon, Nigeria and Indonesia where manufacturing has grown at more than 10% a year over the same period.

It has also been noted that many of the strongly inward-oriented economies are amongst the least developed economies in the Third World, and that in recent years the least developed countries have grown more slowly than the middle income countries. Thus the apparent relationship between growth and trade orientation may simply reflect the greater obstacles to growth faced by the poorest countries.

Thus, somewhat surprisingly, in the light of the neo-liberal emphasis on both low price distor-

tions and outward orientation as factors explaining growth, there seems to be no consistent relationship between the two variables. Cameroon and the Philippines both have low price distortions but are classified as inward-oriented, while Chile and Turkey both have high indices of distortion, but are regarded as outward-oriented (compare Table 5.4 and Figure 5.13).

The neo-liberals can point to numerous examples of the negative effects of state intervention in Third World countries. They deny the need for state intervention beyond the minimal requirements for the functioning of the market and the provision of certain public goods, and they ignore examples of positive results from state intervention. However they can produce no clear evidence that countries in which government spending is a relatively small proportion of GDP grow faster than those with high levels of state expenditure.

The detailed evidence which has been amassed by structuralists to demonstrate the extent of state intervention in South Korea is dismissed on the grounds that intervention is not …

> " … on balance *responsible* for Korea's success. Indeed, it could be argued that success has been achieved *despite* intervention."
>
> (Lal, 1983, p.46)

Indeed neo-liberals often imply that, had the South Korean government not intervened so extensively in the economy, growth would have been even more rapid.

Given the fact that the sustained rapid rate of growth of South Korea is unprecedented, and matched only in recent years by that of Taiwan and Singapore, the view that even faster growth could have been achieved if the state had not intervened is rather difficult to swallow. It is little wonder that one critic of the neo-liberal perspective has commented with reference to the four East Asian NICs that,

> "Before the four existed, it had been necessary to invent them in order to justify the theory; and after they expanded, not a little invention went into rendering the facts of

their performance consistent with the postulates of the free market."

(Harris, 1986, p.30)

A further criticism of neo-liberal theory is its neglect of certain issues which are central to understanding development. The individualist basis of the theory prevents it from addressing issues of income distribution between individuals and social groups in a meaningful way. Emphasizing market relations leads to all economic activities being regarded as equivalent so that the complex and unevenly developed nature of Third World economies is obscured and structural transformations ignored. Finally, the neglect of issues of ownership and control of resources prevent the conflicts of interests from being analysed. All these are crucial factors in any effort to eliminate poverty and hunger in the Third World.

While one should be careful not to reduce different theories to mere expressions of particular group interests, it is important to consider whose interests are best served by particular theories and policies. Classical liberalism and the doctrine of free trade in the nineteenth century clearly served the interest of British industrialists who wanted cheap inputs of raw materials and markets for their manufactured products, and agro-exporting elites in areas such as those in Latin America who enjoyed growing markets for their exports and a free flow of imported luxury goods.

Who then are the main beneficiaries of contemporary neo-liberalism?

- Internationally mobile capital, both industrial and financial are amongst the most obvious beneficiaries of increased integration of Third World countries into the international economy.

- Traditional exporters, as in the nineteenth century, are also likely to benefit from the removal of the anti-export bias associated with restrictive trade policies.

- Local industrialists in less developed countries also stand to gain, if they are internationally competitive. But if they are uncompetitive, they face the threat of in-

Figure 6.12   Mobile capital: transporting multinational company's workers in Malaysia.

creased competition from imports and higher interest rates.

- Domestic financial capital in developing countries, often organized into large conglomerates is able to benefit from liberalization of domestic financial markets and increased access to foreign capital markets.

A critique of structuralist theory

A central weakness of much structuralist theory is the view of the state as an autonomous entity, above society, making decisions in the national interest. The rationality of state intervention has been overestimated: state intervention can occur for private gain as well as, or as opposed to, the good of the national economy.

So although the structuralist case for state intervention to overcome economic backwardness was sound, the economic and social structures which made state intervention necessary also meant that the state was often unable to carry out effectively the policies which structuralists proposed. Vested interests could also pervert those policies to serve their own ends. For example, infant industry protection, which should have been granted only for a limited period while local producers became internationally competitive, has often been granted indefinitely because of the influence of the protected industrialists.

Empirically, the rigidities which structuralists believed were pervasive in less developed countries proved to be less extreme than they assumed in many cases.

"Countless empirical studies have shown that ... changes in relative prices always have effects on supply and demand, including food supplies and foreign exchange. This means that structuralist prescriptions that ignore the incentive effects of relative prices, often cause serious trouble, sometimes creating shortages that could readily have been prevented."

(Sheahan, 1987, p.13)

There is also a question of how relevant structuralist theory is in today's context. The traditional emphasis on import substitution was based on the belief that developing countries faced deteriorating terms of trade for their primary products and obstacles to developing non-primary exports. However, many middle-income countries now obtain a significant and growing part of their foreign exchange earnings from manufactured exports.

The growing internationalization of production and finance described in Chapters 1 and 2 also raises the question of whether the national economy, which is the central object of structuralist analysis, still exists as a meaningful entity. Within an increasingly integrated world economy, national development strategies may decline in relevance.

Finally who benefits from structuralist strategies? This depends on the precise nature of the strategy pursued.

- In South Korea, there is little doubt that the prime beneficiaries have been a relatively small number of local *chaebols* which account for a large share of the economy's output (see Chapter 4).

- In Brazil, the Triple Alliance (see Box 3.5), within which foreign capital played a key role, has been the principal beneficiary.

- In both cases, industrial capital has benefited from a protected domestic market, low rates of interest and government subsidies.

- State bureaucrats have also benefited from the expanded role of the state in the economy. This helps explain the consider-

able resistance which often confronts attempts to liberalize the economy.

6.5 Limitations of the theories

So far we have considered specific criticisms of both neo-liberal and structuralist theories. To some extent, each theory is an implicit (and often even explicit) critique of the other. Structuralists emphasize 'market failure' in their critique of neo-liberalism while neo-liberals stress 'bureaucratic failure' in criticizing structuralism.

Despite this, there are a number of ways in which the two theories share common ground. This last section will highlight these similarities and the limitations of both the theoretical approaches which we have discussed.

First, both theories emphasize economic variables and put social, political and cultural variables firmly in the background. For instance neither the neo-liberals nor the structuralist interpretations of South Korea give any importance to Confucianism (see Chapter 4, Box 4.2) in explaining Korea's economic success. Where social variables such as land tenure are considered, they are regarded as important because of their impact on economic variables such as agricultural output and the structure of demand.

I'VE QUICKLY UNDERSTOOD THAT, IN A BUREAUCRACY, THE ESSENTIAL THING IS ALWAYS TO KEEP YOURSELF COVERED

Figure 6.13   Bureacracy.

Figure 6.14   Authoritarianism and neo-liberalism: three of Chile's leaders listening to prayers on the first anniversary of military rule, 1974.

Second, both theories are primarily addressed to government. Their main objective is to provide a basis on which government policymakers can act in order to promote economic growth. Put in this way, we can see that although the advice is different, the audience is the same for both theories. Theory however does not necessarily have to be for government consumption and theories designed to inform government will not necessarily answer the questions posed by other groups. Neither theory addresses the concerns of peasants, rural and industrial workers, or women.

These two limitations are reflected in the inadequate theory of the state within both approaches, which I commented on in the case of the structuralists. Structuralists' concern is primarily with identifying the correct policies which the state should implement, and not with the political conditions required for implementing the policies. Occasionally the need for a 'strong state' in order to implement the policy package is mentioned, but both theories are somewhat coy about the links between their theories and authoritarianism.

It should be remembered that both the South Korean and the Brazilian 'miracles' followed military coups in the 1960s, and continued under authoritarian regimes. Elsewhere, probably the best example of a real neo-liberal strategy was that of Chile under Pinochet after the bloody military coup which overthrew socialist President Salvador Allende in 1973. Despite this affinity with authoritarianism in both cases of liberal and interventionist development strategies, neo-liberal and structuralist theories do not directly address these issues of political economy. If development is defined broadly to include political participation and human rights, neglect of the political dimension is a severe limitation.

A third limitation of both theories is that they are concerned with the 'big picture'. They are macro-economic theories. They focus on what is going on at the level of the national economy as a whole and tend to neglect micro issues, such as what happens within and between firms and households.

Part 2 of this book tries to fill some of the gaps left by both the neo-liberal and the structuralist approach. It does so by focusing on a selected number of issues which are important features of the industrialization process, and which can add to, or throw a new light on, the case studies of Brazil and South Korea and the analysis of industrialization in Part 1.

Summary of Chapter 6

The first section of this chapter compares a number of economic and social indicators for South Korea and Brazil with the average for less developed countries as a whole between 1965 and 1988. This shows that South Korea's performance has been quite exceptional throughout the period, while Brazil did relatively well until 1980 but has fallen back since then.

Some other writers draw a contrast between the East Asian NICs, which are described as having followed a neo-liberal development strategy, and the Latin American countries, which are said to have adopted structuralist policies. The approach here has been different, in showing that South Korea and Brazil can be interpreted from both a neo-liberal and a structuralist perspective.

In explaining South Korea's rapid economic growth, the neo-liberal interpretation emphasizes export-oriented policies; 'getting prices right' and the low levels of government expenditure and public ownership. Where state intervention has occurred, this has been more of a hindrance than a help. The structuralists on the other hand, believe that there is a direct connection between state intervention and economic growth in South Korea. The government deliberately 'got prices wrong', as well as bringing about major structural changes such as land reform in order to promote economic development.

In the case of Brazil, the endorsement of the neo-liberals is less whole-hearted since many distortions remain; considerable protection of import-substituting industries, high government expenditure and extensive public ownership. However the 'economic miracle' of the late 1960s and early 1970s is clearly attributed to the shift in policy towards greater market orientation after the 1964 military coup. Structuralists on the other hand stress the importance of state intervention and import substitution as the backbone of Brazilian industrial growth from the early 1950s to the 1980s.

Neo-liberal and structuralist interpretations have very different implications as far as the lessons to be drawn for other Third World countries are concerned. This gives particular importance to the ideological struggle between the two camps.

Two questions are then raised. First, why do we need theories of economic development? Second, given that there are competing explanations, how can we choose between them? Both neo-liberal and structuralist theories were then subject to a critical evaluation.

Both neo-liberal and structuralist theories suffer from certain shared limitations. As a result neither can deal adequately with some important aspects of the industrialization process. Some of these issues will be considered in more detail in Part 2 of this book.

PART 2

Favela Vila Prudente, São Paulo, Brazil.

7

TECHNOLOGY AND INDUSTRIALIZATION

TOM HEWITT AND DAVE WIELD

This chapter is the first of four dealing with subjects that cut across the macro-economic theories in Part 1 of this book. Technology is an integral part of industrialization and development. But it is not often the prime focus of attention. In the first part of this book, the subject of technology, and its importance to industrialization, has cropped up regularly but seldom centrally. The following points have been raised.

- Internationalization of production means that manufacturers are faced with many choices about what to produce, how and where to produce it, and therefore what technologies to use. (Chapter 1)

- Technological changes, including the introduction of microelectronic systems and associated information technologies, have increased flexibility of production. One factory can now produce a wider range of products and services. (Chapter 1)

- Technological levels and capabilities vary between different Third World countries, between enterprises in the same country and even within enterprises. (Chapter 6)

- Technological capabilities have been critical in countries, such as Brazil and South Korea, where industrialization has been rapid. (Chapters 3 and 4)

- Low technological capabilities weaken the bargaining position of most developing countries in acquiring technology from elsewhere. (Chapter 6)

- The choice of technologies available to developing countries is limited. So inappropriate technologies are often developed locally or imported. (Chapter 6)

So debates about technology and how (even whether) it should be developed are central to studies of development. Some people even doubt whether developing countries can succeed in developing their own technological capability.

One important argument about technology and development runs as follows. Developed countries have a comparative advantage in industrial technologies (see Box 5.7 in Chapter 5). This is the result of long experience, ample financial resources and human capacities (skills). Developing countries do not have any of these on the same scale. Therefore they would be better off using the limited resources available to them in areas where they do have a comparative advantage. In short, developing countries should not re-invent the wheel but should import existing technologies as and when they are needed. An extension to this argument is that it is at best irrelevant, and at worst dangerous, to introduce technologies that bias development away from basic needs.

These points will be reviewed in the light of experience in developing technological capability in developing countries. This chapter asks two questions:

Q Why is technological capability important for development?

Q What influences the acquisition of technological capability?

This chapter argues that there is more than one way of acquiring the technological capability needed for economic and social development, but that there are some basic ground rules.

Although we will focus partly on Brazil and South Korea, the discussion is relevant to other late industrializers. These countries confront similar technological challenges to those of developed countries. Yet their social, political and economic conditions are quite different. In short, there is no one route to technological modernization.

The debate is not about whether or not to develop technological capability. In practice that choice does not exist. A more pertinent question is how to approach technological development. So this chapter concentrates on the *constraints* on developing countries in the choice and use of technologies and the *opportunities* open to them for technological development. The role of technological capability in the process of industrialization raises some important questions about the different positions of developing countries in the 1990s.

One argument is gaining ground. The argument is that developing countries would do better to focus on the accumulation of technological capability by learning to use and change technologies little by little (or incrementally) rather than expecting to gain technological capability in quantum leaps by setting up advanced factories and hoping technological capability will 'trickle down'.

The chapter is structured as follows. Section 7.1 sets out the terms of debate about technological capability and sets up a framework for thinking about technology. Section 7.2 focuses on national approaches to the acquisition of technology capability. While Section 7.3 explores how foreign technology has been acquired in developing coun-

tries. Section 7.4 puts people centre stage and argues that skills and training are the key to technological capabilities, and Section 7.5 concludes by discussing the learning process in its entirety.

7.1 Approaches to technological capability

Technology as a black box

The role of technology in social and economic development has long been neglected, by economists as well as by others. For many economists, as long as investments led to outputs, it did not really matter what particular combination of machinery, organization and know-how, or in other words what technology, brought about the transformation. The relationship between steady technical change and economic growth was not often explored, nor was the issue of technical choice. Models of economic activity could deal better with analyses of demand and supply, capital and labour. Technology was treated as something of a 'black box'. There was no need to look into it because all that mattered was what went in and what came out.

Technology, neo-liberalism and structuralism

Nevertheless some economists, among them structuralists and neo-liberals, have thought seriously about technology and how to acquire technological capability. At opposite extremes, two approaches to acquiring technological capability have been identified:

- by integration into the world economy, relying on foreign technology, through direct foreign investment and/or licensing

- by building a local capacity in technology through a process of 'technological learning'.

In general, neo-liberal or market-oriented theorists would prescribe the first strategy, while structuralists would opt for the second.

In the first case the argument is that, for each project requiring investment in new equipment and production systems, there is probably existing technology that can be used 'off the shelf'. This, it is said, is cheaper than developing it from scratch. The decision-making process therefore consists of choosing the cheapest option from among the competitors and buying it in. The technology thus bought can be used immediately, and gradually know-how will be acquired by a trickle-down or demonstration effect.

In the second case, know-how is acquired by 'doing' in a gradual process. Structuralists would argue that technological capability is best developed locally, to avoid technologies that are inappropriately transferred from other countries. Inappropriate technologies will slow down or even block longer-term technological development.

In practice, most approaches to building technological capability have been in between these two extremes. For example, South Korean and Brazilian policies have sometimes been based on an *ad hoc* combination of the two approaches. But in neither of these countries have technological capabilities come automatically. In both cases, considerable financial and human resources have been necessary.

Table 7.1 sets out a simplified form of the neo-liberal and structural views.

Neo-liberals are against state intervention and prefer to rely on the market to choose the technology most appropriate for a given industry in a given country. This applies both to the production and to the use of technology. Because neo-liberals generally view technology as a 'black box', they treat it merely as a production cost. This means that, although they may see technology as an important variable in the cost calculations, they will usually recommend that developing countries should use tried and tested technologies.

Many structuralists, by contrast, would argue that there are opportunities for developing countries to build their own technological capability at an early stage of development. To do this there is a need for strategic state intervention which plays a coordinating role among different subsectors of industry and between users and producers of technology. Know-how is built up over time and requires considerable effort to acquire.

An alternative approach: taking technological capability seriously

There is a third and more interesting approach: that technological capability should be taken seriously in its own right. If we put technological capability centre stage, how does this affect our analysis? There are some key concepts associated

Table 7.1   Neo-liberal versus structuralist approaches towards technology in developing countries

	Structuralist	Neo-liberal
Focus of analysis	interactive learning	short-run cost
Role of the state	strategic state intervention	reliance on market forces
Point of entry	early stage entry	mature stage entry
Concept of technology	technology as acquired capability not easily transferred	technology as a tradeable recipe or blueprint
Innovation process	links between producer and user	separateness of production and diffusion of technology
Concept of labour	labour as a resource	labour as cost

[Source: adapted from Schmitz & Cassiolato, 1991]

with technological capability and innovation, which have relevance for building technological capability in developing countries.

Box 7.1 lists six key elements of technological capability, based on a definition of technological capability as the ability to make effective use of technology. Fransman makes the following points about the list:

Although the last two capabilities, institutionalized R&D facilities and basic research, will usually represent more complex (and costly) activities, the first four capabilities are not necessarily presented in ascending order of complexity. The capabilities required, for example, in the search for alternative ways of generating large quantities of electricity might far exceed those required for the modification of agricultural implements in order to adapt them to local conditions. The copying of a complex machine might be a more difficult (and costly) task than the design of a simple new machine. Nevertheless, it is important to note that there is a fundamental distinction to be drawn between the capabilities involved in 'know-how' ((i)–(iv)) and those involved in 'know-why' ((v) and (vi)).

Although the ability to develop completely new technologies, through basic research and innovation, is a crucial element of technological capability, it is by no means the only aspect. One can develop technological capability without doing R&D for new technologies. Most textbooks make the assumption that technology comes from applying science and that to produce new technology one must first have new science to apply. The implication for developing countries of such an assumption is important: that more indigenous technological capability depends on having local R&D laboratories.

Histories of innovation usually describe the heroic nature of science and the success that applying science brings. But that is only part of the story. In the heroic histories less is said about the difficulties of applying science, the failures, the problems, the length of time it takes, and so on. Very little is mentioned of how technological capability can be acquired without huge R&D investment. South Korea, for example, could be said to have acquired sufficient technological capability by appropriating imported technology rather than investing in R&D; to the extent that it is now a leading exporter of sophisticated technical products.

Box 7.1   What is technological capability?

Technology is defined broadly in this book. As well as machinery, it encompasses organization of production; knowledge, whether embodied in hardware or software; people; institutionalized practices (see also Chapter 16 of *Allen & Thomas,* 1992).

It follows that technological capability is the ability to make effective use of technology. This includes the capability to choose technology, operate processes and produce goods or services. It also includes the capability to manage change in products and processes, and in the associated procedures and organizations.

Thus, technological capability involves the following:

(i)   the ability to search for available alternatives and to select appropriate technologies

(ii)   the ability to make selective use of technology in producing goods and/or services

(iii)   adaptation of technology to suit specific production conditions

(iv)   the further development of the technology as a result of minor innovations

(v)   the development of institutionally organized research and development (R&D) facilities

(vi)   conducting basic research.

[Source: adapted from Fransman & King, 1984]

Constraints

What are the 'facts' about the complex process of technological innovation? We begin with three 'facts' that make it difficult for developing countries to acquire technological capability.

- Technological innovation is uncertain. The results of investigation cannot be known with precision; scientifically or technologically, economically or socially. There is an element of gamble in any search for ways of designing and making new products and services.

- Contemporary technological innovation is indeed increasingly reliant on scientific knowledge and thus investment in high level skills and facilities.

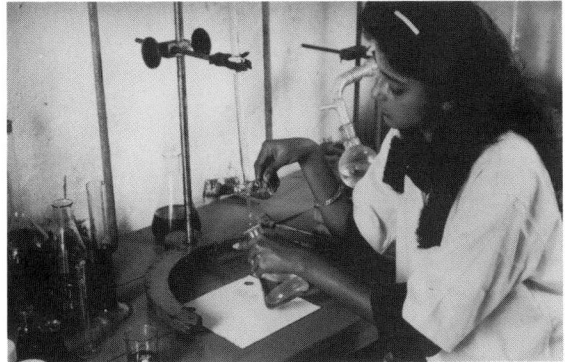

Figure 7.1   R&D: an analytical test laboratory in India.

- Research and development is increasingly based on laboratories rather than individual inventors.

Opportunities

A fourth 'fact' offers opportunities for developing countries rather than constraints.

- Significant numbers of innovations are originated by people through learning by doing and learning by using.

> "People and organizations, primarily firms, can learn how to use/improve/produce things by the very process of doing them, through their 'informal' activities of solving production problems, meeting specific customers' requirements, overcoming various sorts of 'bottlenecks'."
>
> (Dosi, 1988, p. 223).

Linked to the increasing awareness of the importance of learning by doing is awareness of the importance of 'tacit' over 'codified' knowledge:

> "There is a vast range of technological knowledge embodied not so much in published literature as in the minds and muscles of many varieties of working technologists."
>
> (Kline, 1989, p.10).

Figure 7.2   Innovation through adaptation: manufacturing wooden bus frames for export in Penang, Malaysia, as an alternative to metal construction.

User innovation

Recently, the importance of learning by using has become apparent. In some sectors, new uses of existing technology are more significant than the original uses. Scientific instruments, for example, are often developed as one-off designs for a particular task. Then they are adapted by instrument equipment manufacturers who find new applications. Many important medical innovations have been developed in this way. But even sectors that are more basic to industrial development have significant user innovation. In information technology, for example, user companies have been very important in developing new uses, customizing products to individual use, and developing software so that later computer companies add new attributes to their new models.

To summarize, the idea that innovation and technological capability depends on user innovation, and not just on science and basic research, gives a variety of possibilities to developing countries. In particular, as we suggested earlier, it points to the possibility of gradually building technological capability whilst keeping some local control over the process of technological acquisition, rather than hoping for dramatic transformations by importing new technologies.

7.2 Building national technological capability

This section looks at the acquisition of national technological capability based on local processes. How can national technological capability be established? The lesson from the previous section is that research and development (R&D) is just a small part of the process of acquiring technological capability in developing countries. We saw earlier that an exclusive focus on R&D misses the more significant *learning* which takes place through *incremental* changes in technology, particularly in the production process. As one leading technology analyst, O'Connor, points out:

> "... the strength of R&D capabilities in a given country is not a function simply of the existence of formal research institutes and

laboratories. Perhaps equally important is the accumulated informal and frequently undocumented knowledge acquired by the indigenous work force through a protracted process of learning by doing and transmitted through formal or informal on-the-job training."

> (O'Connor 1985, p.324)

This was a welcome change of emphasis since it gave a broader scope to understanding technology and how it can be acquired in developing countries. However, in some industries such as electronics (and, more recently, biotechnology and new materials) the human research component takes on a renewed importance. For example, O'Connor goes on to say:

> "The computer industry is essentially a knowledge-intensive industry wherein skilled, highly trained scientific, engineering and technical labour power is probably the single most important asset. Without such labour, even access to adequate financial resources and material inputs would not be a decisive advantage in a country's effort to develop an indigenous industry."

> (O'Connor 1985, p.325)

How can a developing country acquire technological capability in such unpromising circumstances? Let us apply O'Connor's ideas to a case study of the Brazilian computer industry.

The Brazilian computer industry

The key to the start of the industry was the creation of a 'reserved market' for Brazilian firms in the mid-1970s. That is, only firms that were 100% Brazilian owned were allowed to produce in certain areas of the computer market; the small and medium sized computer segments (see Box 3.10 in Chapter 3 for a description of the growth of the Brazilian computer industry). This sealing off allowed a significant growth in the ability to produce computers, develop the relevant skills, and provide locally made inputs to the industry, in the space of just a decade.

There are no precise measures of research and development in the context of Brazilian electronics. Part of the reason for this lies in a confusion over what constitutes R&D itself. It is usually defined as work undertaken to acquire new scientific and technical knowledge or to produce new materials, products or processes, and it is usually seen as an activity that starts with basic research. Measuring it usually involves counting the expenditure on R&D and the number of scientists and engineers engaged in it. By conventional definitions, research and development in all segments of Brazilian industry is limited. In fact, by international standards, R&D in Brazil as a whole is limited.

To put the situation in perspective, Brazil invested US$1702 million in all R&D in 1982, whereas US$2053 million was invested globally by just one US firm, IBM, in the same year. Nevertheless, there has been a consistent commitment on the part of Brazil's policymakers to promote science and technology. The share of the national government budget devoted to this increased from 0.84% in 1970 to 3.64% in 1982. Similarly, R&D expenditure as a proportion of GNP grew from 0.24% in 1971 to 0.65% in 1979 and the number of scientists and engineers engaged in R&D per million population rose from 75 in 1974 to 208 in 1978.

Such aggregate measures obscure important pockets of R&D. To give some idea of the kind of R&D investment in Brazilian electronics, we contrast three subsectors: mainframe computer producers, consumer electronics producers, and producers of small–medium computers and peripherals (e.g. printers and disk drives). Below we look at their different approaches to R&D in the 1980s.

Mainframe computers

Foreign computer firms producing mainframe computers relied on research carried out in parent companies (such as IBM and Unisys) and had very restricted local R&D activities. In Brazil, these local R&D activities have been limited to:

- some applications software
- software linkages to nationally produced peripherals
- increasing the number of locally produced parts and components.

The technological complexity of the products makes these activities no simple task. The engineers and technicians involved (often trained in the parent company) are highly qualified in their particular fields. However, because these foreign firms have no research facilities in Brazil, the local engineers have only controlled a small part of the R&D process. The bulk of research has been carried out in the parent company.

Consumer electronics

In consumer electronics, foreign firms based in the Manaus Free Zone (MFZ) have controlled a large segment of the market, particularly televisions. Product technology has come from overseas, mainly Japan. Research and development, when it existed at all in MFZ, has been strictly limited to increasing local production of inputs and quality control activities. The major R&D activities there were 'features' (or cosmetic) modifications and the adaptation of nationally produced inputs. In other words, not basic research or product development, but very minor product modifications. This is reflected in the almost complete lack of engineers in this subsector.

Smaller computers and peripherals

By contrast to the foreign-owned firms in mainframes and consumer electronics, it is the firms with wholly national ownership of capital who have employed by far the most human and financial resources in R&D. Most of these have been producing smaller computers and peripherals. In 1986 more than 5000 professionals were employed in R&D by national firms and their R&D expenditure reached US$154.1 million, which amounted to approximately 10.1% of total sales. Relative to the size of the national industry, this is a significant sum. However, in absolute terms it is still little, even when allowing for wage differentials of R&D personnel in Brazil and the United States. Similarly, the absolute number of people in R&D is small by international standards, although in the industry they represent approximately 10% of the total labour force. To give an idea of the magnitude of investment of these resources, take the case of IBM and its global R&D activities. It has been estimated that in 1985 IBM invested US$2.7 billion (6% of total sales) in R&D.

This quantity was spread between three basic research institutions of 2500 employees (amongst which count 1000 PhDs) and numerous other research centres employing more than 50000 people (700 PhDs).

Stages of technological capability

There are those, including some neo-liberals, who have dismissed R&D by national computer firms in Brazil as simply 'reinventing the wheel'. This, they say, is a waste of valuable resources which could be employed more productively in areas appropriate to Brazil's existing endowments. In other words, these firms may just as well give up.

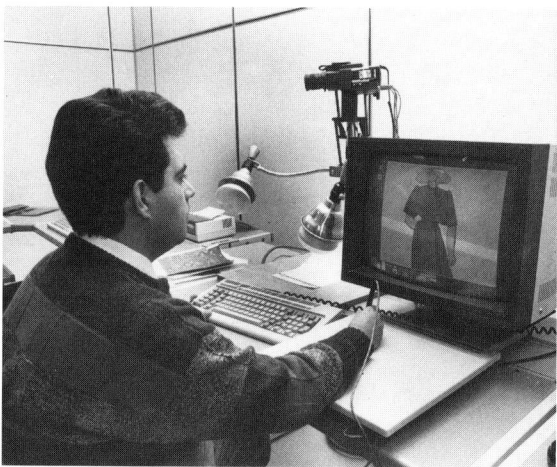

Figure 7.3   Brazilian computer being used for computer-aided design of clothes.

A competing, and perhaps more interesting, view is that learning about existing technologies through R&D is a cumulative process which passes through various stages of capability. In this view, technology is something that is learnt about over an extended period rather than a blueprint which is merely bought (see Table 7.1). These stages can be divided into activities resulting in: *imitation, modification, redesign and major innovation*. The labour requirements for these activities differ. For example, imitation requires mainly manufacturing (or even just assembly) and organizational skills. With the progression towards innovation the skill requirements increase accordingly, with more and more emphasis on design capability. (See Boxes 7.1 and 7.2.)

> ### Box 7.2   Stages of building technological capability
>
> **Imitation:** Making a product identical to an original developed elsewhere. Such a process can vary in complexity. It can be very easy for a simple tool, much more complex for a modern machine tool. When complex production systems and design is needed just to copy a production process, it is a very important achievement; as for example when a country builds the ability to produce clone cars.
>
> **Modification:** Specifying minor improvements and modifications, for example to fit a product to local conditions.
>
> **Redesign:** Deciding on changes needed for new markets, or to update models, and then carrying through the manufacturing changes needed to produce the new design.
>
> **Major innovation:** Developing something entirely new, usually requiring some formal R&D.

Imitation and modification

The distinction between imitation and modification, or what has been termed 'creative imitation', is stated clearly by Tigre:

> "It is important to distinguish between simple copying, often with clandestine import of components, and creative imitation. The latter consists of more than merely making a carbon copy of the original product. Rather, it is an improvement, correcting eventual faults and adapting the product to local needs. In many cases, the requirement to incorporate national components necessitates redesign of the equipment since local parts do not always abide by the specifications of the original manufacturer overseas. Thus, the activity offers opportunities for learning which could eventually be used to develop own designs [i.e. to innovate]."
>
> (Tigre 1986, p.154)

Carbon copy imitation has become a standard practice in microcomputer production. This is a

Figure 7.4 Learning in production: making adjustments in textile factory in Kenya.

world-wide phenomenon facilitated by the use of standard off-the-shelf components (particularly microprocessors) by the major manufacturers. Amongst the 150 manufacturers of microcomputers in the US in the 1980s, there were an estimated 20 or more so-called 'compatibility houses' producing copies of the IBM-AT alone. There are many more spread around the world, particularly in East and South East Asia. In Brazil, in 1985 there were no less than 37 firms producing models of the IBM microcomputer family (PC, PC-XT and PC-AT).

Copying and understanding, having know-how and know-why, is not a task that can be underestimated in its complexity. Neither can the returns in terms of learning for those engineers and technicians involved in the process. But there are also limits to this kind of learning:

> "... the maximum that can be achieved in the case of [microcomputer] compatibles is to make modifications and minor improvements, always within the limits of compatibility."
>
> (*Data News*, 4.2.86, p.23).

Even this may become difficult if there is a greater move towards the use of proprietary components in the newer generations of microcomputers. Proprietary components, as the name suggests, are not available to anyone except the patent holder.

Redesign

The redesign of already existing products may be viewed as a form of 'minor innovation'. It appears that those firms which have, in the past, invested considerably in technological learning through creative imitation are in a position to redesign products to enter niche markets. This, for example, is the case for firms which have developed specialized applications for microcomputer hardware and software.

Innovation

Major innovation represents the highest level of R&D activity and, according to some observers, is not yet a viable proposition for Brazilian firms:

> "The Brazilian market does not seem to be sufficiently large to support firms which, in isolation, would have the financial means to conduct R&D in the scale and depth neces-

sary to introduce major innovations; neither would most firms be able to undertake the efforts to go inside the 'black box' and unlock the proprietary technologies characteristic of newer systems."

(Frischtak 1986, p.22)

Copying or imitation appear to be easier ways to enter the microcomputer market and also an effective means of beginning the process of learning. But, innovation in the general purpose computer market is a tall order for all but the few leading firms in the world.

Computers for finance

Significant innovation has, nevertheless, been characteristic of market niches in Brazil's computer industry, particularly in the area of banking and commercial automation systems. Banking automation equipment in 1985 accounted for 30% of computer sales. Amongst the ten largest nationally owned computer firms, five are directly or indirectly controlled by financial institutions. The banking automation systems developed by these firms are unique as they are specific to the needs of Brazil's financial system. In a highly inflationary economy such as Brazil's, it becomes desirable to invest in and develop technology which increases the speed of circulation of money, such as on-line terminals and electronic fund transfer systems. Inflation has been so high in recent years that specialized computer systems were necessary to cope with daily changes in financial reckoning (and so many zeros!). Learning by using in the banking sector has been amply demonstrated by Cassiolato (1991) who argues that the close interaction between producers and users has compounded the learning process.

Comparing Brazil and South Korea

How does the experience of Brazil compare with that of South Korea, the most advanced Third World computer producer? In 1986, Brazil had, overall, a larger computer industry than South Korea. More significantly, Brazil has progressed further in designing and producing what are called 'non-commodity' computers. These are inputs to other industries and can be exported to specialized markets rather than having a huge direct consumer market. Nevertheless, South Korea is more competitive in producing 'commodity computers' (personal computers made to the 'PC' standard). In other words, it appears that while Brazilian firms have been learning how to innovate using R&D, South Korean firms have been learning how to build strong technological capabilities in imitation and modification, involving close attention to production.

This brings us back to the argument at the beginning of this section. R&D is very important in certain industries, but *learning in production is equally so*. While the computer industry in Brazil was relatively successful in building up design capability, there were problems with its production capability. One of the reasons that the Brazilian computer industry in the example above has only been a qualified success is that it has not learnt to be competitive in production.

Sugar production in India

Approaches to building local technological capability include areas other than 'high technology'. One interesting case is that of crystal sugar production in India. In the last few decades a traditional sugar production technology has been significantly upgraded to become nationally competitive with modern technologies. This technological capability has been developed through R&D, redesign and significant modification of existing technology. The sugar production process involves crushing the cane (or beet) and then concentrating the cane juice by boiling it. Technological changes over more than a century have increased the yield (weight of sugar crystals per unit weight of sugar cane) from 5% to 12%. In principle, by far the most productive means is by vacuum pan (VP) techniques, building the sugar-based liquid under vacuum.

Kaplinsky (1984a) has described the development of an alternative technology to vacuum pans. The first VP sugar-cane factories were set up in India in the 1920s. Indian VP factories, all built locally, operate at only 20–40% of the full scale economies obtained in industrialized countries where production processes are highly automated. While Indian VP plant manufacturers compete in supplying equipment to other developing countries,

Figure 7.5   Large scale (vacuum pan) sugar mill, Mumias Sugar Company, Kenya.

there are no cases of them supplying to advanced country markets, mostly because the Indian manufacturers cannot meet the demand for automated processing systems in sugar refineries.

Around 1955, Indians set out on a different technological trajectory. They began to upgrade traditional technology. They substituted mechanical rollers for bullock crushing of cane and began improving the process by which cane juice was boiled not in vacuum but in open pans. The process was called open pan sulphitation (OPS). By the late 1960s the attainable sugar recovery had increased from 5% to around 7%.

But the disparity in yield between 7% and the 12% obtainable by VP techniques, meant that OPS could not compete. OPS only thrived and grew because of government protection, and in some cases the 'natural' protection of locations that were very isolated and could not easily transport their cane to the big VP mills.

But Indian engineers recognized that, precisely because OPS was sub-optimal (whereas VP was

close to its achievable maximum yields) the return on low levels of investment in OPS research and development might be high. A traditional technology from Quebec was imported and modified, significant improvements made in the crushing technology, and the furnaces used in boiling were redesigned and made more efficient.

> " The consequences are that OPS technology can now stand on its feet, without any government subsidy or protection, in relation to the sorts of VP plants currently used in India. It is a striking example of indigenous technical capability."
>
> (Kaplinsky, 1984a, p.152).

What the sugar cane case study suggests, Kaplinsky argues, is that, even in the age of the microelectronics, a lower-level technology can be improved significantly and can compete with more sophisticated technologies. In this case the acquisition of local technological capability was for improvement of a particularly appropriate technology for developing countries. It was appropriate

Figure 7.6 Open pan techniques for sugar production. (Above) Straining raw sugar. (Below) boiling pans.

in the sense that it maximizes use of home-produced materials and labour and is at a level of technological sophistication within the scope of available resources for production, operation and maintenance. It is not simple technology but has relevant scale for its context of agricultural inputs, industrial production and use.

Figure 7.7 'It's all right sir, It's only suffering from a hangover!' In Brazil, a huge industry has grown to produce sugar for alcohol used as car fuel.

The acquisition of technological capability came about through:

- careful thought about which parts of the production process could be improved to most effect

- searching for and gathering of information from other countries, (i.e. the imitation of Quebec technology)

- local R&D to adapt, modify and redesign

In short, this was a gradual process involving much effort in R&D and production.

Some conclusions

The experiences of the computer industries in Brazil and South Korea, and the sugar industry in India illustrate four ways in which national technological capabilities have been acquired. They show that:

1 Technological capability goes beyond R&D, but that different levels of R&D have been relevant in all cases.

2 A range of technological capabilities have been developed in different ways in a relatively integrated fashion.

3 Building technological capability takes investment of effort, time and financial resources.

4 Developing countries are not completely dependent on technologies from developed countries. On the contrary they show that imported technology is only useful if there is a developing capability to use it.

7.3 Foreign technology and technological capability

Building local technological capability is one approach. But importing and using of foreign technology is more common. Local effort, by itself, may just take too long and by the time a country has caught up in a particular technology, or 'closed the technological gap', the international technological goalposts will probably have moved. On the surface, importing technology may be an appealing short cut. However, this route is fraught with dangers and successful use of foreign technology really depends on the manner and terms of its acquisition.

The 3-way relationship involving governments, foreign corporations and local capital is complex and has been the focus of much of the debate about development policies. In the so-called 'modern' industries (such as cars, electronics, machinery and chemicals), large corporations from the US and Japan, and to a lesser extent Western Europe, dominate both the technology and the markets for goods and services.

For developing countries, interaction with foreign corporations is necessary and inevitable. However, for the governments of developing countries, well as for the investing companies, to be able to attain what they want from direct foreign investment, the governments have to be in a position to bargain over the way the companies operate. Otherwise the foreign corporations simply achieve their own corporate goals regardless of the country's needs. But this is not necessarily a zero sum game where developing countries always lose out, as is argued, for example, in the literature on the new international division of labour (see Chapter 1). So how can foreign technology best be assimilated to build up technological capability?

In some of the earlier chapters of this book, the dangers associated with 'buying in' technologies have been broached. For example, many countries in Africa, with very weak technological capability, did resort in the 1960s and 1970s to buying in whole factories. The rationale was that they needed to deal with only one set of negotiations and thus could simplify the process of acquiring technology. Such arrangements are often called *turnkey agreements*. Instead of buying all the parts of a factory and the skills needed separately and putting them all together, one company would put the lot together and sell them as a package, set it up and often run it for a while. Then, it would be handed over, needing just a simple 'key' to turn it on and keep it working. Such initiatives were usually either established by Third World governments or begun as joint ventures between governments and a foreign turnkey partner. While the aim to gain control over a technology with little or no experience of it, it turned out to be more difficult in practice.

Technology consists of more than hardware. It also includes social organization (sets of procedures and human relations), and a body of understanding. To control technology there must be enough 'know-how' in the organization. There must be procedures and knowledge of why it works, the 'know-why'. Otherwise the technology cannot be kept working, maintained, or modified

Turnkey agreement: the sale, as a single package, of a complete factory along with the expertise to build and operate it.

to suit local conditions. In short, the build up of technological capability from turnkey projects has often been weak.

Algeria

Other approaches to the import of foreign technology have been developed. One approach is to import sophisticated technology, make the big investments needed, and aim to assimilate it by building capabilities as quickly as possible. The Algerians took this decision in the 1960s and 1970s. They were attempting to use high oil revenues to diversify their economy, which included introducing electronic and advanced manufacturing technologies. Initially, Algeria used turnkey deals linked to plans to build technological capability through local production with an emphasis on on-the-job training. Huge complex 'multi-factories' with various plants were bought in. But the resulting build-up of technological capability was quite slow and the ability to adapt and modify did not grow significantly.

Over time, Algeria changed its strategy. The government made a decision to break down its new investments into smaller parts that were more easily controlled. It began to set up much more decentralized tender systems and to develop bargaining skills to acquire foreign technologies. The ability to adapt and modify increased. New production lines emerged in some plants, closer links developed with customers that led to changes in product range. But overall, the hope that importing very sophisticated production technologies would lead to an advanced innovative capacity has not been achieved. In particular, the different elements of technological capability described in Box 7.1 have not been completely integrated.

Tanzania

Another alternative to developing some technological capability from scratch is to choose a less than 'state of the art' version of technology to import. The Tanzanian government made this decision for one of its textile factories in the 1960s. On one hand, the factory (which was built with Chinese aid) used just 40% of the capital of a second Tanzanian plant built around the same time. On the other hand, while the Chinese-built factory used two and a half times as much labour, it still managed to produce at lower cost. However, there has been little evidence of more sophisticated capability building than that involved in keeping a factory running.

South Korea

South Korea provides an example of how a country with more production technology capability can systematically use links with foreign buyers of exported products to adapt and modify local technologies. Foreign buyers were almost as important as foreign suppliers of equipment and materials in initiating innovations. They made regular visits to inspect facilities and were involved in programmes to control and improve quality:

> "... through such things as suggesting changes in individual elements of the production process and improvements in the organization of production within the plant and in management techniques generally, buyers helped many exporters achieve greater efficiency and lower costs. It thus appears that the transfer of know-how from export buyers has been a major contributor to minor process innovations of the sort that sequentially lead to gradual improvements, the cumulative effect of which can be extremely significant."

> (Westphal *et al.*, 1984, p.286).

Foreign capital investment

We have not yet mentioned the simplest method of importing foreign technology: encouraging foreign capital investment. This would be a major means of transferring technology and building national capability if, for example, direct foreign investment were encouraged in ventures that subsequently diffused technology to nationally owned companies.

Of course, foreign firms will only be interested in setting up production where they see gains for themselves. In the 1960s and 1970s, it was argued that foreign firms tended to locate where there were sources of cheap labour. This applied to assembly-intensive industries such as clothing and electronics, sometimes called 'screwdriver'

industries. They became recognized as the fly-by-night factories employing 'nimble-fingered' young women (particularly in Mexico and South East Asia). But there were other reasons for direct foreign investment.

From the point of view of multinationals, potentially large markets were equally, if not more attractive, than cheap labour (as was the case in Brazil during the economic miracle). In addition a series of tax incentives offered by developing country governments added to the attraction of investing in certain countries. Such incentives persist, for example, in Malaysia's free trade zones and in the border industries of Mexico.

From the point of view of developing country governments, employment creation is often cited as a reason for offering incentives to direct foreign investment. Foreign exchange generation is also an important reason, since most of such industries use developing countries as 'export platforms'. A final reason is that direct foreign investment has been seen as a way of transferring technology.

Licensing of foreign technology in Brazil

But simply inviting (or luring) foreign firms to set up production is not sufficient to persuade them to part with the technological capability they brought with them. To gain access to and, thereby, have the chance to assimilate foreign technology depends crucially on one's bargaining power over technology transfer. This point can be demonstrated in the case of licensing of foreign technology in the Brazilian computer industry.

As we said earlier, the Brazilian government excluded foreign firms from certain parts of the computer industry which were 'reserved' for nationally owned firms. So how did they gain access to computer technology?

The argument is straightforward. In the early days of state intervention, foreign firms were uninterested in sharing technology with Brazilian firms, that is, foreign firms wanted to hang on to their technological advantage or nothing. By the end of the 1980s foreign firms were more amenable to negotiate with Brazilian firms and the government over collaboration.

How did these changes come about? Initially, the large computer firms were unwilling to license technology to Brazilian firms. Nevertheless, they were interested in operating within the Brazilian market, as evidenced by the applications to the government by foreign firms to manufacture mini-computers in Brazil. National firms, in their turn, were forced to turn to smaller foreign computer firms as a source of technology. Even then, some of these licensors imposed marketing restrictions on the licensee. Direct foreign investment was not permitted at this time since, it was argued, national firms would not be able to compete on the internal market even with licensed technology from other sources. More importantly, the explicit objective of policy intervention in the computer industry was to build up the competitiveness of national firms by fostering the technological capability of these firms. At the time of putting up protective barriers, the issue at stake was not about the exclusion of foreign capital itself but about access to technology and know-how on terms favourable to the development of capabilities locally. If the big firms had negotiated at all, a reserved market may not have been necessary.

In the intervening years, there appears to have been some pay-off to the policy of exclusion. Brazilian firms have built up a considerable technological capability not only in manufacturing but also in R&D (see Section 7.2). They have also increased their bargaining strength with foreign capital. The licensing of super-minicomputers from the market leaders, DEC, Hewlett Packard and Data General to local firms, and the entry of IBM into a joint venture with a local firm, is a clear indication of this.

Negotiating technology transfer

Would it have been possible to build up this capability to negotiate over technology transfer without restricting the entry of foreign capital? The experience of other developing countries can throw light on the question. In electronics, three developing countries which have followed restrictive policies towards foreign capital are Brazil, South Korea and India.

South Korea

In South Korea there has been a close collaboration between political and industrial interests in electronics, which has allowed a strong basis for restriction of foreign capital. The Koreans, however have done this from a national position of technical and political strength, with the result that they have been able to 'negotiate much su perior technology transfer deals' (Mody, 1987). This is not a situation peculiar to the electronics industry in South Korea. As Chapter 4 suggests, the extensive (formal and informal) controls over direct foreign investment in the economy as a whole included: tight investment screening; extensive government interference in corporate decisions; and extensive reporting requirements.

India

India, by contras,t has not been so successful in building up the negotiating power of South Korea and as it moves into a period of liberalization towards foreign capital, local firms are becoming increasingly marginalized. A study by Grieco (1984) which examined the Indian computer industry up to the late 1970s concluded that the policy of excluding foreign capital had opened up opportunities for local development of the industry . A more recent study, however, documents a change of situation. Since 1984, there was a growing liberalization: entry of private capital, some removal of duties and import restrictions, and growing investment by foreign capital. The impacts of these changes ...

> "... do not appear to have been particularly beneficial in terms of building indigenous technological capability. The majority of firms have so far shown an inability to move beyond the stage of 'kit assembly' and to conduct R&D and therefore to innovate. Linked to both of these problems has been an increase in the level of foreign collaborations, with which liberalization has been associated. Only those firms with skills that pre-date the major liberalizations of the decade have such skills in the late 1980s ..."
>
> (Heeks, 1991)

Benefits from restrictions

It seems that the beginning of technological capability in India built during a period of strong control over foreign investment has not been consolidated. Liberalization has, so far at least, acted as a brake on technology capability. Thus, the two countries besides Brazil which have had the most restrictive practices towards foreign capital push us towards the conclusion that negotiating power needs to be built up not only at the political level but also at the economic and technological level.

Within Brazil also, those subsectors giving free access to foreign subsidiaries appear to generate little or no local R&D capability. The unrestricted entry of foreign corporations prevented the process of technological learning from taking place. Brazil has managed to increase negotiating power with foreign capital by restricting entry at the early stage of the computer industry. Thus, for those nations attempting to build technological capability:

> "The dilemma facing all importers of technology is that if restrictive clauses are rejected outright, access to the desired technology may be refused. If on the other hand such clauses are too readily accepted, the value of the technology may be seriously undermined."
>
> (Luedde-Neurath 1988, p. 92)

We can conclude that access to foreign technology on favourable terms is dependent on bargaining power. This is not to argue for a blind dismissal of foreign capital and the belief that developing countries can go it alone. On the contrary, foreign firms remain a most important source of technology. However, that technology is only useful in developmental terms if local firms, supported by the state, are able to find effective means of transferring it, and the know-how that goes with it, into local hands. From the above analysis, it appears that at least two prerequisites can improve bargaining power. The first is to build up a local capacity that knows what to do with the technology once it is obtained, and the second concerns the timing of restrictions on foreign capital in order to build up the capacity.

This section has considered how technology imports can lead to the development of technological capability. It has argued that developing countries can use foreign technology but that considerable and continuing technical, political and economic efforts are needed to effectively turn the large initial investments into increasingly innovative industries. Much effort is needed but there are a variety of means and much experience to draw on.

7.4 Education and training

Whether it is through importing foreign technology, using, adapting, modifying or redesigning it, and/or through R&D, it is abundantly clear that there are a variety of approaches to building up technological capability. What have they in common? The tremendous effort required depends on people and their skills; individually, in groups and institutionally. Building technological capability, of whatever form, depends fundamentally on education and training.

As we saw above, the traditional view of the electronics industries of developing countries has been of one based on direct foreign investment in free trade export zones. Foreign corporations, in this view, have exploited cheap female labour to carry out repetitive assembly tasks. This view has been subsequently criticised for being too simple in its emphasis on corporations' need for cheap labour and for ignoring a more complex set of global investment decisions by corporations which were driven just as much by accessing growing developing country markets (see Chapter 8).

There has also been a decisive transition to a new pattern of demand for labour in many developing countries. It is one which uses a much wider range of skills and, in particular, a high proportion of skilled engineering and technical labour. The origin of this increased demand for skills is the attempt by some developing countries to stimulate a local technological capability.

The employment and skill implications of such attempts reinforce the argument that labour needs

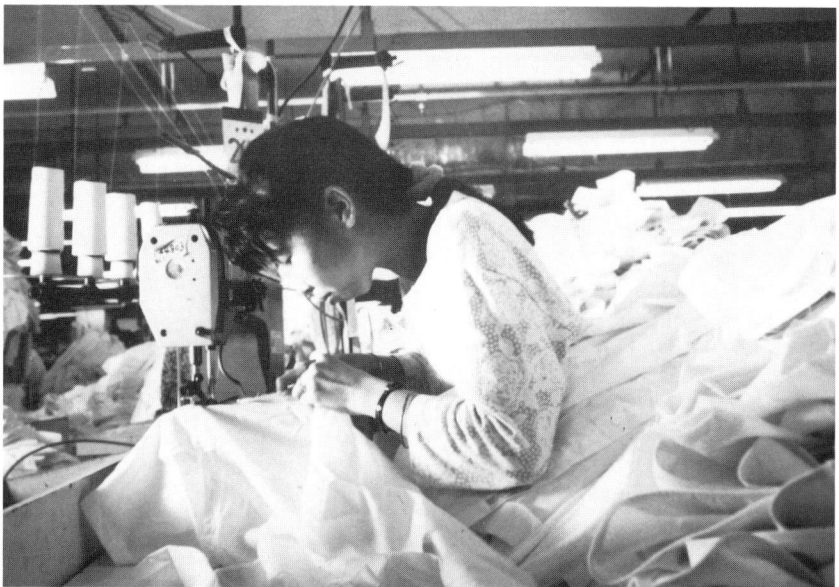

Figure 7.8   Textile worker in Malaysia.

Figure 7.9   Computer training in Zambia.

to be viewed as a resource, not as a cost (see Table 7.1). In Brazil in the last decade there was a substantial increase in the skill base of the electronics industry within the protected segments of computer production. This increase is due not only to the expansion of the industry in Brazil, but also to the way that the industry has developed; generating in-house capabilities to design and produce computers for a range of different market segments.

Figure 7.10   Gilbert Workey runs an engineering business in Kumasi, Kenya. Here he is with a second-hand machine imported from Britain.

The build-up of skilled labour has been more impressive in other NICs however. In some cases the statistics compare well with Japan (Table 7.2).

State involvement in training is accepted in other developing countries where the supply of skilled labour has not been a strong point to date. State intervention is seen as an important stimulus to building up a skilled labour supply. In Singapore, South Korea and Taiwan (not to mention Japan) the state has considered scientific and technical

education to be a priority, and there is certainly a role for government in the formation of 'human capital' through education policies. This has taken several forms. For example, in Singapore education policies have attempted to supply the labour market with highly skilled local labour to be involved in integrated circuit design and software development. In South Korea and Taiwan, public policy has put emphasis on graduate and technical training in electronics. The argument is that, through upgrading the educational levels of the labour force, the growing demand from industry can be met and the industry itself can be upgraded from simple assembly tasks to more knowledge intensive activities. As Kaplinsky says:

> "The past experience of Japan and the Asian NICs has shown that an educated labour force has been as much a source of industrial success as its cheapness."
>
> (Kaplinsky 1988, p. 47)

The result has been that as the demand for certain types of labour increases so too do the demands on governments to participate more in training schemes. However, in practice, such policies are difficult in most developing countries because of the shortage of adequate financial resources and a general retreat of the state's direct involvement in the economy.

Table 7.2   Educational indicators for selected countries, 1985

Country	% of age group in secondary education	% of age group in tertiary education	Engineering students as % of population	Science, maths & engineering students as % of population
Japan	96	30	0.34	0.40
S. Korea	94	32	0.54	0.76
Taiwan	91	13	0.68	0.78
Singapore	71	12	0.61	0.73
Hong Kong	69	13	0.41	0.51
Brazil	35	11	0.13	0.24

[Source: Freeman, 1990]

7.5 Conclusions

We have come a long way from the view that technology is an uninteresting and uninvestigated black box. Opening the box has given us some clues to answering the questions posed at the start of the chapter:

- Why is technological capability important for development?

- What influences the acquisition of technological capability?

The capacity to transform the economy is crucial if developing countries are not to stagnate. The transformation may take many forms, but at its centre lies technological capability. It is often assumed that 'late industrializers' can relatively easily learn to use and change technologies that are in routine use elsewhere. On the contrary. This is not something that is acquired overnight or without effort. It requires more than a strong base of skilled people and investment resources. If there is one important notion to emerge from this chapter then it is about learning.

Learning

In common use, learning means the various processes by which skill and knowledge are acquired by individuals and groups. In this chapter we have turned to two kinds of learning:

- the acquisition of technological skills and knowledge by individual and, through them, by organizations

- the acquisition of increased technological capability (or technological learning).

We considered the idea that the accumulation of technological capability (that is, technological learning) can take place little by little by 'learning by doing', 'learning by using', and 'learning from changing' technologies, rather than by huge investments in basic research and innovative development. These activities do not come that easily or freely. They happen best with planned and organized effort. Nevertheless, they are a window of opportunity for national technological learning that does not depend on large R&D facilities that many, or most, developing countries cannot afford and do not have.

We listed four stages of technological capability: imitation, modification, redesign and major innovation. Learning by doing and learning by using correspond most strongly to imitation, the first stage. Learning from changing corresponds to modification, the second stage. It is a development from learning by doing and learning by using:

> "Opening the black box of a particular production technology and manipulating its contents is much more likely to generate additional knowledge and understanding than is continued operation of a given production system. One probably learns little from facing problems (and even less from ignoring them), but a great deal from solving them. One may learn little from using improved methods, but a great deal from defining and implementing them."

> (Bell, 1982, p.192).

Learning by searching

Redesign, the development and manufacture of changed designs, requires the organizational ability to learn from changing. But it involves more besides that. For example, it may require the searching out of knowledge from other places. Thus, another type of learning is 'learning by searching'. This can be searching for knowledge about the practical lessons of similar types of production elsewhere. It can also be the start of formal R&D; as happened in the Brazilian computer industry in which R&D began through the automation of banking systems.

Learning through training

Finally, there are several studies that illustrate the importance of 'learning through training'. These studies suggest that formal education and training produces the best results when associated with the other elements of learning. For example, the development of capability, from 'learning by doing and using' to 'learning from changing', is strongly associated with increased training and education at all levels. It requires a population with a broad base of training and not just a small group of extremely well educated people. Note that in Table 7.2, Japan does not have the highest proportion of science and technology students, but does have the highest proportion in secondary education.

Technology is important but has often been marginalized in studies of development. In particular, the narrow idea of technology as the shiny new equipment that will develop people is erroneous. Making effective use of technology to improve the living standards of people involves developing the broad capabilities of people in technology. Examples of industrial technologies support these arguments. But the arguments hold for other technologies: agricultural, construction and medical.

We have not delved into the values associated with technology and choice of technology. (This is covered in more detail in Chapter 16 of *Allen & Thomas*, 1992). For example, we have not dealt with ethical decisions involved in technological choice. Our examples cover clothing, computers in banking, agromachinery and sugar; but not military systems, nuclear power stations, or medical technologies.

Nor have we investigated the advantages and disadvantages of adopting different technologies to different social groups. Our argument has been that technological capability is important for development and that building a broad understanding of technology is a key component of empowering people to be involved in technological decisions that affect and can change their lives. The impact of technological change on women's employment and on the environment are addressed in Chapters 8 and 10.

Summary of Chapter 7

1   Developing countries are not totally dependent on foreign technologies. There is some technological capability in all developing countries, though there are tremendous differences. It is important that technological change builds on existing capability.

2   The relevant use of technology depends on learning how to acquire technological capability. This involves much effort. It certainly does not happen automatically or passively. It requires organized and broad systems of acquisition to build technological capability.

3   There are different and interdependent levels of technological capability: imitation, modification, redesign and major innovation.

4   There are different ways of acquiring technological capability and many different experiences and lessons for late industrializers in developing countries. Technological capability does not happen by just letting in foreign capital. However, importing foreign technology can be the beginning of a new learning process if linked to other elements of learning — access to foreign technology on favourable terms depends on bargaining power.

5   Technological capability depends on developing human resources and skills, which places increasing demands on the state for training.

6   Technological capability is about command over knowledge — individual and technological learning. Both involve learning by doing and using, learning from changing, learning by searching, and learning by training.

8

GENDER ISSUES IN INDUSTRIALIZATION

RUTH PEARSON

As the previous chapters have demonstrated, industrialization and industrialization strategies in the Third World are concerned with the transformation of economic structures. The economies of some (but by no means all) Third World countries have moved from the production of raw materials and agricultural products for internal consumption and First World markets to the production of manufactured goods. Discussion of this transformation has concerned economic policies, investment strategies, technological change, and international trade and finance. Is there anything in these analyses which can possibly relate to a discussion of *gender*, or can be illuminated or explored by applying a gender perspective?

There is one central issue which has not been dealt with specifically in the previous chapters: the industrial labour force. Once we bring people into the analysis of industrial development, we need to know who they are, what they do and, in particular, whether they are men or women. Or, put another way:

Q What kind of jobs does the development of industrial production in Third World countries provide? And who are these jobs for?

If one of the objectives of development is to improve the standard of living and provide employment opportunities for people, it is important to ask which people have had access to industrial employment, and how they have benefited.

This chapter examines the implications for women of the employment opportunities and income generation resulting from industrialization in the Third World. Gender divisions are one of the basic social divisions in all societies (*Allen & Thomas, 1992*, Chapter 15). It would be as valid to look at the effects of industrialization according to other social divisions, such as class, race, ethnicity, religion, urban/rural differences, but that is beyond the scope of this chapter. However, it is important to remember that any social division is affected by other social relations. So if, for example, we refer to the impact of industrialization on women and men as groups or categories, we need to remember that their social positions as a whole (e.g. their class and ethnic backgrounds) will affect the extent to which a gender-based analysis provides a representative or complete account.

8.1 Industrialization and women

The impact of industrialization on women is one which is much discussed and disputed. When this question was first examined in the 1970s the consensus was that *industrialization marginalizes women*. This consensus was consistent with a linear view that saw industrialization as moving through time between two poles. One pole is the non-industrial economy in which manufacture is carried out by handicraft or artisan producers working in households or workshops using traditional methods of production to make simple handicraft goods such as garments, basic tools, household goods, etc. The other pole is the modern, technologically sophisticated and dynamic industrial sector in which production is organized on a large scale, using modern technology which tends to substitute for labour.

This kind of modern industry — the basis of much of the industrial strategy of Third World countries up to the 1960s and 1970s — was associated with the creation of a new industrial workforce. Workers in modern industry were required to have the skills and education necessary for modern methods of production, and the commitment to the requirements and pace of modern industrial work, and to be amenable to the industrial discipline and organization necessary for efficiency and high productivity. For many years it was assumed that these characteristics were associated almost exclusively with male workers. However the notion of 'skill' is a gender-based concept. Many case studies and analyses have indicated that jobs and tasks performed by women workers are considered 'unskilled', whereas male jobs are associated with skilled work.

As Anne Phillips and Barbara Taylor put it:

> "… skill has become saturated with sex … the equations — men/skilled, women/unskilled — are so powerful that the identification of a particular job with women ensured that the skill content of the work would be downgraded. It is the sex of those who do the work, rather than its content, which leads to its identification as skilled or unskilled."
>
> (Phillips & Taylor, 1980)

The bulk (but not the total) of the workforce employed in import-substituting industries in Latin America and South-east Asia in the period since the Second World War — particularly in capital-intensive sectors such as steel, shipbuilding and heavy industry — was in fact male. The empirical evidence did indeed appear to support the view that industrialization marginalizes women.

Figure 8.1   Skilled or unskilled work? Women pack soap and men control the machines: a soap factory outside Lusaka, Zambia.

Figure 8.2   Manufacturing diesel engines in Poona, India (1959).

A second consensus on this question was that *Third World industrialization is based on the exploitation of women workers.*

Since the 1970s the increased emphasis on export-oriented industrialization (EOI) and production of manufactures for the markets of rich industrial countries has substantially modified the structure and composition of the industrial labour force in many Third World countries. EOI was often based on a limited number of industrial sectors which were relatively labour-intensive (Box 8.1). Some of this production involved assembly type production, often of materials and components imported from the industrialized countries. But as the statistical and sectoral indicators of industrialization grew in many Third World countries (see Chapter 1) women's share of employment also grew. A new consensus was therefore established. No longer was it argued that industrialization marginalized women; on the contrary, the increase of

---

BOX 8.1   Capital and labour intensity

"… producers (firms and farms) are assumed to face a given set of relative factor prices (e.g. of capital and labor) and to utilize that combination of capital and labor which minimizes the cost of producing a desired level of output. They are further assumed to be capable of producing that output with a variety of technological production processes, ranging from highly labor-intensive to highly capital-intensive methods.

Thus, if the price of capital is very expensive relative to the price of labor, a relatively labor-intensive process will be chosen. On the other hand, if labor is relatively expensive, our economizing firm or farm will utilize a more capital-intensive method of production — that is, it will economize on the use of the expensive factor, which in this case is labor."

(Todaro, 1981)

women's share of employment seemed to go hand in hand with the successful industrialization of many Third World economies from 1970 onwards. As more and more countries were successful in locating export-processing within their economies, women were being drawn into the labour force in greater numbers. It was argued that a major feature of Third World industrialization was the employment opportunities offered to women, though there was much dispute as to why women were the new industrial labour force, and what such employment offered to women in terms of wages, training, promotion, working conditions, etc.

In the early 1990s this second consensus is also under attack. In some countries the rising share of women in industrial employment has slowed down and in some cases reversed; in other cases, women's share continues to rise. Some observers argue that *the increase in women's employment signifies only a stage in the industrialization process,* which will be surpassed once more mature and technologically advanced industries are established in the Third World. Or, as has happened in mature industrialized economies, technological change is displacing large sections of the industrial workforce, particularly in so-called 'unskilled' work where women tend to be concentrated. The new workers for the era of flexible specialization (see Chapter 1) are required to be multiskilled with technical qualifications, which tends to work against the interests of Third World women workers who, like their counterparts in industrialized countries, have more restricted access and fewer opportunities to gain technical qualifications or on-the-job training.

Other observers argue that the macro-economic policies, which international agencies such as the World Bank and IMF and many national governments have imposed on Third World economies in the wake of the debt crisis, have significantly undermined any protection of wages, working conditions and rights of organization. It is suggested that these policies are leading to a *feminization of the workforce.* This has two distinct aspects: firstly, women workers make a more attractive workforce because they

have been historically less militant and cheaper to employ than the traditional male working class; secondly, all working conditions are being reduced to those previously endured only by women workers, making the preference for women to carry out low-paid 'unskilled' work less imperative.

Still others argue that the figures are misleading. Although the growth of women's employment in the formal sector (i.e. registered factories of the type associated with modern industry) has slowed down or halted, this does not mean that women's industrial employment has not continued to grow. However, *much of the extra employment is located outside the large factories,* in small workshops, sweatshops, or homeworking, where women provide an even cheaper, more flexible and less protected workforce than any to be found in the modern industrial sector. Moreover it has become apparent that, while rapid growth of export-oriented industrialization did increase women's share of industrial employment in many Third World countries, this did not happen in every case. In countries where there has been little growth of industry, such as those of Sub-Saharan Africa, employment opportunities for women in the industrial sector remain very limited.

It is likely that all these factors are present as we move towards the end of the twentieth century and that gender divisions of labour in industrial employment in the Third World are highly uneven, responding in different countries and sectors to different processes. In the following sections I set out the evidence and arguments for the first two consensuses: that women are marginalized by the process of industrialization, and that industrialization in the Third World has been based on the expansion of women's share in the industrial labour force. I then examine the contradictory evidence of recent years and the issues that arise in understanding how industrialization has affected men and women differently, particularly in employment and skills creation. This will lead us to a better understanding of the dynamics of industrialization itself.

8.2 The first consensus: 'industrialization marginalizes women'

The view that women are left behind as economies are transformed and modern industry takes root came from two distinct, but influential, sources. The primary influence on development academics and practitioners was the publication in 1970 of the path-breaking study by Esther Boserup, entitled *Women's Role in Economic Development*. The second was the experience of industrialization in Latin American countries since the 1930s, which gave historical credence to Boserup's thesis that women were marginalized by the process of economic development, particularly by the establishment of modern industry.

Boserup's thesis: women are excluded from development

Boserup's book dealt with the impact of economic development on the productive roles of men and women. She wrote, in the Preface to a new edition of the book:

> "The main theme of this book is the difference in work conditions between the sexes in countries which are in a process of economic development. ... The characteristic features of economic development are increasing specialization of labour, increasing quantity and quality of equipment and infrastructure, and better and better education and training of the labour force. Gradually as economic development proceeds, more and more processes and services cease to be performed within the family household and become supplied by specialized enterprises or public institutions. As a result, a larger and larger share of the population is transferred from production within the household for family needs to wage labour or management jobs in private enterprises and public institutions. ... The process of increasing specialization of labour is accompanied by an increasing hierarchization of the labour

force and a gradual adaptation of the sex distribution of work, both in the family and in the labour force to the new conditions. Since men are decision makers both in the family and in the labour market, are better educated and trained than women and are less burdened with family obligations, they are much more likely to draw benefit from these changes than women who end up at the bottom of the labour market hierarchy."

(Boserup, 1987, p.iii)

Boserup argued that in the process of economic modernization production was transferred from domestic or home industry to units which required specialization of labour and capital, resulting in higher efficiency and productivity. Because such employment required educated and skilled workers, male labour was recruited. This contrasted with earlier forms of industrial production in home industries where there was a very high female participation.

> "However, when in a given country, a manufacturing industry is gradually being built up in competition with existing home industries manned by family labour, much of this labour is likely to change over to wage employment in the larger industries, be it successful enterprises in the home industries which expand and move to special premises, or a foreign or domestic large-scale industry which is recruiting labour. The important problem in the context of the present study is how this process of change will affect the large female labour force in the family industries. In other words, will the expanding employment of wage labour in industry proper absorb not only the male labour force released from home industries but also the female labour force formerly occupied in such industries?"

(Boserup, 1987, pp.10–11)

By examining labour force data from the 1960s for a number of developing countries, Boserup established that women accounted for a much lower percentage of wage labour in industry than they did when industrial production was carried out by small enterprises using own-account or family labour:

> "In nearly all developing countries women in industrial occupations account for less than one fifth of the employees while they often account for one third to one half of own-account workers and family aids"
>
> (Boserup, 1987, pp.111–112)

The explanations for the decline in women's employment as industrial production is transferred from 'traditional' home industries to 'modern' factory production are similar to those advanced for the growth of the industrial labour force in Britain and other countries which went through an industrial revolution (Pinchbeck, 1981; Berg, 1985). On the *demand* side Boserup cited the specific regulations governing employment of women workers, including maternity benefits, childcare obligations, exemption from night work and equal-pay legislation which in large industrial enterprises add to the employers' costs of hiring women, and concluded that "the result may indeed be to make it more profitable to employ men than women workers" (Boserup, 1987, p.113). She pointed out that high fertility rates amongst African women were cited by the International Labour Organization (ILO) as a possible explanation as to why employers were hesitant about recruiting women workers. She also discussed the differences in educational levels of men and women amongst potential industrial workers, and the lack of relevant training opportunities for women to train as skilled industrial workers in developing countries (Boserup, 1987, p.141).

Boserup also provided explanations from the *supply* side of women's labour as industrial workers. She argued that terms of employment in large-scale industry are too inflexible for women, particularly those with domestic and childcare responsibilities. In addition she pointed out that factory work is not thought to be appropriate or respectable for women in many cultures, and in some cases women are not permitted to carry out productive work in places where there are men who are not family members.

This argument is consistent with some aspects of neo-liberal theory, which argues that individuals respond to market conditions, while stressing that the flexibility of women to respond to changes in the labour market is hampered by domestic responsibilities, social conventions of what is appropriate work for men and women, and lack of access to appropriate education and training.

In Boserup's view it was the development of industry itself which caused a change in the nature of the labour markets in Third World economies, and to which potential women workers have difficulty in adapting. A structuralist view, on the other hand, would say that the conditions imposed on the labour markets of Third World economies by the world economic system tend to exclude equal participation of women.

Boserup's study, first published in 1970, was especially influential because it was the first comprehensive study of the effect of economic development — both agricultural and industrial — on women. Much more research has been carried out since then, and much more information is now available. However, Boserup's study remains of central importance because, as well as focusing international attention on the question of development, industrialization and women's employment, it provides a market-oriented theoretical model to explain the differences. Boserup, as others who espouse this theoretical view, suggested measures to prevent the market discriminating in job generation for women and men. These included:

- improving women's education and training,

- reducing women's fertility, and

- mechanizing domestic work to reduce the time spent on domestic chores.

Dependent industrialization and the marginalization of women in Latin America

In contrast to Boserup's position, the analysis of women's marginalization from industrialization in Latin America came from a totally different perspective — the perspective of dependency theory (see Chapter 5).

> **BOX 8.2   Women in the economically active population**
>
> The **economically active population** (EAP) includes that sector of the total population of working age that is either in employment or actively seeking work.
>
> In situations where jobs are not readily available to women, or where women tend to be concentrated in activities in which the nature of their work is disguised or invisible (such as agricultural work on family farms, or irregular jobs in the service sector) women tend to be viewed by census enumerators, family members, and even themselves, as being 'housewives' or 'helpers' rather than as workers in active employment.

Certainly the experience of many countries during most of the twentieth century appeared to support the marginalization thesis. In the case of Brazil, Helieth Saffioti (1978) argued that as the industrial sectors grew from the latter part of the nineteenth century up to the 1960s, women were systematically excluded from the economically active population (see Box 8.2).

Data from the 1872 census of Brazil showed that 45.5% of the workforce were women. Of these, 35% worked in agriculture, 33% in domestic service, 20% in dressmaking, 5.3% in textiles and 6.7% in other jobs (Saffioti, 1978, p.184). Saffioti pointed out that, largely because of the importance of the textile industry, women constituted the majority of the industrial labour force. Similar figures were established for 1900. By 1920, however, women's share of the economically active population had fallen to 15%, and during the acceleration of import-substituting industrialization after 1930 the percentage of women in industrial employment declined:

> "contrary to general belief, industrial development did not bring about a substantial increase in the employment of female labour. Although there was an increase in the absolute number of women employed in the three major sectors, the increase in the number of men employed was substantially greater, so that the proportion of working men to working women was almost the same in 1940 as it had been two decades earlier."
>
> (Saffioti, 1978)

In the 1950s and 1960s, which included the beginning of the planned industrialization strategy known as the 'Brazilian miracle' (see Chapter 3), whilst women's industrial employment increased overall, their share relative to men in the industrial labour force declined. By 1960 women's share of the total employed labour force had risen (since 1950) by 3.2% to 17.9%, and by 1970 to 21%. However, women constituted only 12.2% of industrial workers in 1970.

This does not mean that women were not employed at all in factories in the early stages of industrialization in the the Third World. In some industries, particularly in textiles and food processing, the technology of production initially differed little from the kind of techniques previously utilized in home-based industries; in the early stages, technological change was slow, productivity and wages were low and working conditions were poor. In fact, Brazilian women continued to occupy a major share of employment in the slow growing, technologically static industries: 60% of workers in textiles and one-third of those in the chemical-related sectors were women in 1950, compared to much lower shares in the more dynamic and technologically advanced metal working industries (Humphrey, 1987, p.23). The very fact that women had the lowest share of employment in the fastest-growing industrial sectors accounted for the systematic fall in women's share of industrial employment in Brazil up to the 1960s.

Saffioti and other Latin American writers of this era recognized the difficulties that women have had in adapting to the changing demands of the labour market in the context of industrialization and restructuring of the economy. But they explain the low level of demand for women's labour on two grounds. The first is that the nature of industrial growth in peripheral economies reduces the overall demand for labour. Because women had little education, few skills, and were concentrated in those sectors of industry such as textiles which are not 'dynamic' (in the sense of fast-growing and technologically advancing), they were excluded from the bulk of the new jobs created by this kind of capital-intensive industrial expansion. Second, the fact that industrialization was taking place in a 'dependent' economy — relying on investment and capital goods imported from the mature industrialized economies — was seen to be the reason why Brazil's industrial expansion up to 1970 did not provide work opportunities for women as well as for men. Saffioti argued that women's work and economic contribution were an essential part of pre-capitalist production which was not based on labour, but 'In Brazil, the establishment of a full-fledged capitalist system of production accelerated the expulsion of women from directly economic roles' (Saffioti, 1978, p.188). Whereas women were prominent in pre-capitalist economic organization, structurally 'dependent' economic development in the Third World has led to an industrialization process based on imported, capital-intensive technology to which men have been recruited rather than women. In other words, the type of industrialization experienced in the Third World has led to the systematic exclusion of women from the industrial labour force.

Let me summarize the two strands of the first consensus. Both Boserup and Saffioti, together with many later writers, identified industrialization as a process which excludes women from employment. As modernization takes place (as Boserup would argue) or capitalist accumulation and capitalist relations of production become established (as Saffioti would argue), there is a decline in the importance of artisanal production and an increase in factory production.

As household and workshop commodity production was transferred into factories, using wage labour, jobs tended to go to men. In this process the urban 'home' became the site of social and biological reproduction with which women became strongly identified, rather than being employed in the new factories which were the basis of modern industrial expansion. In the earlier periods of industrialization in the Third World, import-substituting industrialization tended to focus on consumer goods and intermediate goods, relying on imported technology which had a tendency to displace labour; this further contributed to the view that industrialization marginalizes women.

> **Reproduction**: The various elements or 'inputs' of any production process first have to be produced, and then replaced: that is, they require *reproduction* for production to continue in the future. The most vital element of the whole process – namely the producer – also needs reproducing. *Social reproduction* replaces the inert elements of the process. The 'production of the producer' involves *biological reproduction* (childbearing), *generational reproduction* (childrearing) and *daily reproduction or maintenance* (provision of human needs like food, shelter, etc.).

8.3 The new consensus: 'industrialization is based on the employment of women'

From the 1970s onwards, the pattern of industrialization in the Third World shifted from industrial production for supplying domestic markets to exports for the markets of industrialized countries. This export-oriented industrialization (EOI) was largely based on the availability of cheap labour, which allowed Third World economies to compete in Western consumer-goods markets (see Chapter 1). The expansion of export-oriented, labour-intensive manufacturing industry has been located primarily in Mexico, Brazil, the East and South-east Asian countries of Hong Kong, Singapore, Taiwan and South Korea, and subsequently in Malaysia, Indonesia and other parts of the Third World such as the Caribbean and Mauritius. It was based on two processes:

- the relocation by multinational companies of production previously carried out in Western economies; and

- new investment and international sub-contracting in developing countries which offered low wage costs, comparable productivity and a range of incentives to encourage the growth of manufacturing production for export.

Although industrialization aimed at export markets was carried out in a wide range of countries, and covered a number of industrial sectors, attention has focused on a narrow range of products and production processes which employ relatively large amounts of labour, in particular the apparel and textile industries, the assembly of semiconductors, and other parts of the electronics industry. A major reason for the relocation of production in these sectors was the nature of technological developments which allowed the fragmentation and standardization of production processes. This meant that parts of the production process, particularly assembly-type operations such as sewing pre-cut pieces of clothing together or soldering microchips into standardized circuit boards, could be relocated to Third World countries where low-cost labour with little or no industrial training or experience could be utilized.

Many countries established special industrial estates where production for export could be carried out exempt from import and export tariffs, and where there were other incentives such as exemption from local taxation, waiving of labour legislation concerning minimum wages and rights to organize, as well as the provision of utilities, local roads and telecommunication facilities. By the late 1980s around 80 of these export processing zones (EPZs) or free trade zones (FTZs) (see Chapter 1, Section 1.3) had been established in Third World countries, with at least 40 more planned or under construction.

Figure 8.3   Assembling electronic circuit boards in the free trade zone of Kaohsiung, Taiwan.

Output and employment trends: the growth of women's employment

Export of manufactures from LDCs had tended to be concentrated in a limited range of industrial sectors, which have employed a predominantly female labour force:

"... manufacturing for exports began only in the 1950s, first in local and then in multinational firms. It has been concentrated in labor-intensive industries, which tend to be female-intensive in all countries, since these industries are sensitive to wage costs and female labor is typically cheaper than equivalent male labor. The job characteristics of these industries also fit well with the needs and characteristics of female labor constrained by the sexual division of labor. Readily learned skills requiring manual dexterity and patience with tedious tasks make women appropriate workers, conditioned as they are by culture and extensive experience with sewing, food processing and other household tasks."

(Lim, 1990)

The growth of industrial output and employment in Third World countries since the 1970s has been based to a considerable extent on the increase in exports of consumer goods — mainly textiles, garments, footwear, electrical and electronic goods and components. The production processes and products were labour-intensive and the implications for employment in manufacturing industry substantial. However, the expansion of employment in manufacturing was not uniform throughout the available labour force. Unlike the earlier period of industrial expansion discussed in Section 8.2 a significant proportion of workers were women. This is shown in Table 8.1, which records the trends in women's share of manufacturing employment since 1975.

The figures in this table are constructed on an aggregate level and include a wide variety of occupations within the industrial sector. Although it is quite difficult to establish the accuracy or comparative value of aggregate data such as these because of problems of definition and criteria for inclusion and exclusion, many small-scale studies corroborate that the overwhelming majority of the workforce engaged in manufacturing was, and in many places continues to be, women. While women's share in the industrial labour force, although rising rapidly, is rarely more than 30–40% in most countries, the percentage of women workers in export processing factories producing textiles, electronics components and garments is much higher than this, with figures as high as 90% in some cases.

Why women?

As the production of garments, textiles and electronic goods was relocated to Third World countries, the gender composition of the labour force reflected the pattern found in these industries in the industrialized countries (Glucksman, 1990). Much of the explanation of why women workers were employed rests on their universally lower costs compared with those of male workers. Given that a high percentage of total costs in labour-intensive production processes is related to the cost of the labour, wage levels are a significant determining factor in employment strate-

gies. But compared to industrialized countries, wage levels in less developed countries are very low. For example, the differentials for average industrial wages between the USA and Mexico are 5:1, and 25:1 between the USA and Bangladesh. East Asian industrializing countries fall somewhere between these figures.

Given these differentials, why was it not sufficient to recruit male workers for Third World industries to retain a competitive advantage in international markets? The reason why women were targeted for the labour force is because they almost always command lower wages than men working in similar occupations. Table 8.2 shows the relative male and female industrial wage rates in selected countries. It is important to note that male wage rates and earnings are higher than women's in both industrialized and developing countries. However, for those developing countries where production and employment in manufactured exports grew fastest over the last two decades, the differential is particularly high. In South Korea in 1985, women's earnings were only 47% of equivalent male earnings; in Singapore, the figure was 63%.

Unpacking the 'cheap labour' arguments

Is the reason that new export industries targeted women workers solely attributable to their lower wages compared with men? Is it just that women were 'cheap labour'? Wage rates are not in fact the only relevant factor. The final cost of labour is measured in terms of the *unit cost* of production which, as well as wages, includes how much a given quantity of labour will produce in a given period of time (i.e. labour productivity). Throughout history, women have been employed for tasks requiring meticulous and repetitive work. Although such work is generally classified as 'unskilled', it usually requires considerable degrees of manual dexterity — which it is assumed that women have acquired outside the workplace. Managers were clearly convinced that women workers constituted their ideal labour force:

> "The manual dexterity of the oriental female is famous the world over. Her hands

Table 8.1 Women's share of manufacturing employment: selected countries

Bangladesh	1961[a]	2.7%		Puerto Rico	1978[b]	48.9%
	1974[b]	1.0%			1982[b]	49.1%
	1981[b]	5.1%			1987[b]	47.5%
Germany (F.R.)	1961[a]	32.2%		Singapore	1970[a]	34.3%
	1970[a]	31.3%			1980[b]	47.6%
	1987[a]	30.3%			1987[b]	47.5%
Ghana	1966[a]	12.5%		South Korea	1960[a]	26.4%
	1984[a]	21.3%			1970[a]	35.1%
					1980[b]	37.9%
Hong Kong	1961[a]	34.8%			1985[b]	39.7%
	1971[a]	43.5%			1987[b]	40.5%
	1981[b]	49.8%				
	1987[b]	49.6%		Sri Lanka	1963[a]	17.9%
					1971[a]	29.7%
India	1951[a]	9.1%			1986[b]	45.3%
	1961[a]	5.8%				
	1981[b]	9.8%		Thailand	1960[a]	27.1%
	1987[b]	9.1%			1970[a]	37.9%
					1980[a]	43.3%
Indonesia	1971[a]	34.7%			1986[b]	45.2%
	1980[a]	35.4%				
	1985/6[a]	34.6%		Turkey	1970[a]	13.6%
					1975[a]	15.9%
Jamaica	1982[a]	23.0%			1980[a]	14.4%
	1986[b]	30.4%			1985[a]	15.1%
Japan	1960[a]	26.4%		UK	1966[a]	31.1%
	1970[a]	35.1%			1971[a]	30.0%
	1980[b]	37.9%			1981[a]	30.7%
	1985[b]	39.7%			1987[a]	29.9%
	1987[b]	40.5%				
				USA	1960[a]	25.4%
Mauritius	1962[a]	6.6%			1970[a]	28.7%
	1972[a]	6.6%			1980[b]	30.4%
	1978[b]	55.0%			1987[b]	32.3%
	1983[b]	59.1%				
	1982[b]	57.4%				
Philippines	1960[a]	34.9%				
	1970[a]	36.9%				
	1980[b]	47.2%				
	1985[b]	50.4%				
	1987[b]	47.8%				

Note that two data sources are used, each using different categories. Source (a) reports employees in receipt of wages and salaries. Source (b) reports all paid employment, which may include outwork, piecework and other forms of non-regular employment.

[Data sources:(a) ILO, 1990 (b) ILO,1988a]

Table 8.2 Relative wage rates and earnings of males and females in selected Asian and European countries, 1980 and 1985

Asia

Hong Kong
rate/day   1980 77.7%   1985 79.2%

Japan
earnings/month   1980 43.6%   1985 42.1%

South Korea
earnings/month   1980 45.1%   1985 46.9%

Singapore
earnings/week   1980 61.5%   1985 63.4%

Sri Lanka
earnings/day   1980 75.4%   1987 70.3%

Europe

France
earnings/week   1980 77.0%   1985 79.1%

West Germany
earnings/week   1980 77.0%   1985 79.1%

UK
earnings/week   1980 68.8%   1985 69.3%

[Data source: ILO, 1988a]

suitable for export processing employment. Women were also considered to be 'naturally' more docile and willing to accept tough work discipline, 'naturally' less inclined than men to join trade unions, and to take 'naturally' to tedious, repetitive and monotonous work. In addition to the grounds that women's work was unskilled, low wages were rationalized on the basis that women did not have the primary responsibility of earning a family wage: high levels of productivity could be attained at minimum costs, with little investment in training or compensation for formal qualifications. As one economist writing in the 1970s explained: "It takes six weeks to teach industrial garment making to girls *who already know how to sew*" (Sharpston, 1976, p.105, emphasis added).

If it can be argued that such knowledge is acquired in the course of women's socialization, it can be projected as part of women's natural attributes, rather than as a skill or training which should be rewarded with higher wages:

> "... manual dexterity of a high order may be required in typical sub-contracted operations, but nevertheless the operation is usually one that can be learned quickly on the basis of traditional skills. Thus in Morocco, in six weeks, girls (who may not be literate) are taught the assembly under magnification of memory planes for computers — this is virtually darning with copper wire and sewing is a traditional Moroccan skill. In the electrical field the equivalent of sewing is putting together wiring harnesses; and in metal-working, one finds parallels in some forms of soldering and welding."

(Sharpston, 1976, p.334)

are small and she works fast with extreme care. Who, therefore, could be better qualified by nature and inheritance to contribute to the efficiency of bench-assembly production line than the oriental girl."

(quoted in *Far Eastern Economic Review*, 18 May 1979, p.76)

Given assumptions made in earlier periods of industrialization that women were unsuited to or unavailable for industrial work because of domestic duties or social norms constraining their activities outside the domestic sphere, it is ironic that women's suitability for this type of employment was projected as an extension of their 'natural' attributes. Women's nimble fingers were not the only quality that made them

The preferential recruitment of women therefore assumed that lower unit costs would be achieved because of lower wages and higher productivity. Unlike the kinds of employment generated by capital-intensive, import-substituting industrialization, assembly and manufacture of consumer goods and components for exports did not rely for their productivity and quality control on the technology embodied in the machinery, nor

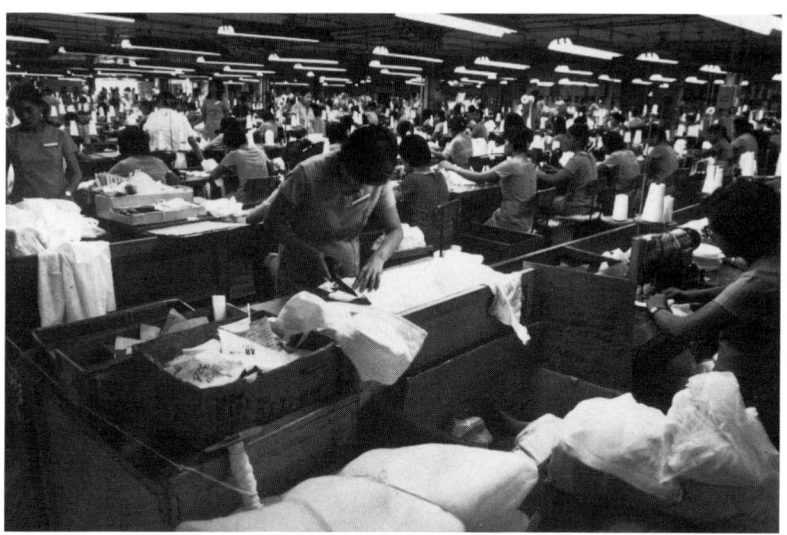

Figure 8.4 "It takes six weeks to teach industrial garment making to girls who already know how to sew": women machinists in the Philippines.

on the physical strength or technical qualifications of the workforce. Instead they relied on the ability of the workers to carry out repeatedly the kind of detailed work necessary to sew sleeves into garments, solder wires or etch electronic circuits under microscopes. And, for these kinds of jobs, women proved to be the most productive workers.

There are few actual examples where the productivity of men has been tested in the same production conditions as women on assembly lines, as jobs tend to be sex-typed when they are created. However there are some reported case studies in which substitution of female by male labour was abandoned because male workers were unable to reach the level of productivity achieved by the women. Only with changing technology and changes in the real wages offered by factory work in comparison with other employment has the proportion of male labour in some sectors of export production increased (Pearson, 1991).

Other factors contributing to the high levels of productivity achieved by women workers included much longer working days and weeks than those customary in industrialized countries. There was limited alternative wage employment and state controls effectively prevented the growth of labour organizations to improve working conditions and pay. In larger companies, 'scientific' management procedures, as well as complex systems of piecework rates and bonuses, all contributed to levels of productivity that were often far higher than those in similar factories in industrialized countries. Whilst these factors applied to all workers in Third World countries, women workers, particularly new entrants to the labour force, were particularly vulnerable to exploitation and manipulation.

Women workers in Third World industrialization: stereotypes and beyond

Although earlier accounts of export-led industrialization appeared to ignore or to be indifferent to the gender of the industrial workforce, later writers emphasized the central role of women workers:

> "Exports of manufactures from developing countries have been made up in the main of the kinds of goods normally produced by female labour: industrialization in the post-war period has been as much *female* led as *export* led."

> (Joekes, 1987, p.81).

The rapid growth of export processing and the concomitant rise in the employment of women in this sector contributed two further aspects to the 'new consensus'. The first concerns the composition of the female workforce. A widely held stereotypical picture emerged of the average or ideal Third World woman factory worker. It comprised four essential components:

- that she is *young*: recruited from an age cohort ranging from 15–25, concentrated in the 18–21 age group;

- that she is *single* and *childless*;

- that she is *'unskilled'* in the sense of having no recognized qualifications or training;

- that she is a *recent migrant* from the rural areas and has no previous experience of formal wage employment in the industrial sector.

These stereotyped notions of Third World women workers have increasingly been revealed for what they are. There is some empirical basis to this stereotype in that the first generation of export processing factories were able to select quite carefully which women they wished to employ. Where there was a large potential female labour force, it was deemed rational to employ women before they were encumbered with the domestic responsibilities associated with marriage and motherhood, and many case studies show that the age profile of the workforce, particularly in the electronics and garments sectors, is concentrated in the 15–21 age group (Pearson, 1991; Wolf, 1991). In countries which have relatively recently initiated or expanded the export of light manufactures based on labour-intensive assembly production processes, such as Bangladesh and Indonesia, the profile of the female employees indicates that, at least initially, young single rural migrants form a major part of the initial recruitment. However, recent studies have revealed the differences or variations in employment conditions and labour force composition of women workers in different developing countries. While many women do leave the industrial labour force when their work schedule is incompatible with childcare and other domestic responsibilities, there are also a substantial number who have remained in employment into their 30s and 40s, as in industrialized countries.

The second aspect of the new consensus is that women's industrial work became almost exclusively identified with the employment of women workers in export factories. While the vast majority of workers in exports were women, such employment only accounted for a fraction of women's productive work within the industrial sectors of Third World economies in the 1970s and 1980s. According to one analysis of international labour statistics, 'only three million or so are totally engaged in export led production … the remainder of the 166 million women workers are employed in production activities that are largely geared to domestic markets' (Mitter, 1989, p.27).

Focusing so much attention on the role of a very small section of the industrial labour force (such as export factory workers) tends to obscure the importance of the female workforce in factories producing for the domestic market, the growing number of women working in small sweatshops or in their own homes under subcontracting arrangements (for export and domestic markets), and the range of industrial activities carried out in the informal sector, Box 8.3 (Benería and Roldán, 1987). It also tends to obscure the fact that in most countries where rates of industrial output, employment and exports were highest in the 1970s and 1980s men continued to comprise the major part of the *total* industrial labour force.

Why the new consensus?

Many writers continue to identify Third World industrialization with export processing and thus almost exclusively with the employment of women workers. It is not just economists and analysts of international economic relations who hold that view. The very visibility of clothing, footwear and consumer electronics goods imported from various parts of the Third World has increased general public awareness in the developed countries of the sources of these goods. Indeed, few readers will be unaware that many consumer goods they purchased from chain

---

BOX 8.3 The informal sector

The **informal sector** is a term which is applied to the range of activities undertaken by the working poor in Third World cities (and elsewhere). It is variously defined according to the nature of the enterprise, activity or worker involved, and its characteristics are contrasted with those of the formal sector.

Some analysts assume that the informal sector is quite separate from formal sector activities, while others emphasize the many links between the two sectors. In general terms, it refers to all the work people do outside factories or offices, often with no recognized employment contract or fixed wages. The following table contrasts the characteristics of the two sectors.

Formal sector	*Informal sector*
Barriers to entry	Ease of entry
Often uses foreign capital	Relies on indigenous resources
Capitalist enterprise	Family ownership
Large scale	Small scale
Uses imported technology	Labour-intensive and adapted technology
Formal training and apprenticeship	Skills acquired outside formal education and training
Regulated and non-competitive markets	Unregulated and competitive markets
Within government control/policy	Outside government control

---

stores in the 1980s were either imported directly from Third World countries, or contained components fabricated there. Even now an investigation of each summer's T-shirts in high street shops, or the soles of training shoes, would reveal the current geography of the export of clothing and footwear from developing countries. While Third World industrialization is primarily associated with low-budget consumer goods, and contributes to the tendency to identify women as the principal industrial workers in those countries, it is also important to remember that women work outside these factories in a variety of other workplaces, and that Third World industry also produces steel, ships, chemicals and pharmaceuticals — sectors which employ a predominantly male labour force. Export processing, and its female workforce, is only one aspect of industrialization in the Third World.

8.4 The end of consensus: diversity and difference

At the beginning of the 1990s it is clear that no general or simple typology can be used to describe or explain the gendered effect of industrialization. The earlier consensus — that women were excluded from employment opportunities offered by industrialization — and the later consensus — that Third World industrialization was based on activities that required a predominantly female labour force — have been shown to be partial and inadequate.

Both these earlier versions concentrated only on waged employment in factories large enough to be recorded and included in official industrial censuses. This excludes all the myriad other activities that take place in small businesses and workshops, in sweatshops and in people's homes. The development literature refers to the latter as the *informal sector*, as opposed to the *formal sector* where regular waged employment in factories takes place. However, much informal sector activity is an integral part of the industrialization process in Third World countries, and has to be taken into account if the gendered nature of the industrialization process is to be properly examined (see Section 8.5 below).

A second major shortcoming of the earlier approaches is that they concentrate on the employment experience of women during the limited time in which they are employed in the formal sector. There has been little consideration of what happens to women after that. Do they cease to be affected by industrialization once they lose their factory jobs? Do they carry out any other productive activities in the industrial sector or elsewhere when they are not employed in factories? The idea that once women take on reproductive roles as wives and mothers they no longer need to be considered as productive workers underlies the failure to look beyond the factory gate.

The global feminization of labour: a third consensus?

There have of course been attempts to produce a new consensus for the 1990s. After decades of rapid technological change, and radical restructuring of industrial production in both industrialized and Third World economies, the buzzword of the 1990s is *flexibility*. Instead of industrial efficiency being related specifically to economies of scale, smaller units of production equipped with programmable and flexible technology are found to be more cost-effective under certain conditions. Flexible production systems require flexible labour that can be deployed over a variety of production tasks, whereas the major feature of large-scale production is labour specialization. Instead of firms continually expanding as a result of the increasing scale of production, it can be more efficient to have a series of small firms linked together, or to divide enterprises into smaller autonomous units. It has also been suggested that this new technological flexibility may be organized around firms having a permanent, core labour force, with a periphery of casual workers (Mitter, 1986).

Whatever the plot, a flexible labour system does not only require multiple skills. The demand for such labour is also immediate and temporary. It is employed only when directly needed in production — an extension of the Japanese 'just in time' principle: rather than hoarding stock (which has the labour element built in), the parts, components and final goods are produced only when they are needed. This kind of labour force usually has no permanent status, no statutory protection against dismissal, is subject to short-time working or retrenchment, and cannot demand a wage above what is competitive in the market. This concept of the flexible workforce, in which the norms of previously 'inflexible' or male jobs are replaced with conditions historically associated with women's work (i.e. irregular forms of employment) has been described by Standing (1989) as *global feminization*. By this he refers not only to the increase in women's share of industrial employment, but to the terms and conditions of work and employment, and the substitution of women in activities previously carried out by male workers under 'inflexible' conditions.

In some ways the global feminization of labour can be seen as an extension of the 'new consensus' outlined in Section 8.3 above. Instead of suggesting that industrialization relies primarily on the employment of women, it is postulated that industrialization depends on the conversion of all industrial employment to the conditions of female employment.

This is another generalization which should be closely examined before it gains currency as the latest consensus on women and industrialization. First, statistical evidence of an inverse relationship between women's and men's participation in industrial labour markets is far from convincing (Elson, 1991). Second, it again seeks to explain a series of complex and often countervailing trends within a single dynamic.

Diverse trends

There is not, nor has there ever been, a single uni-directional trend in the relationship between industrialization and women's employment. In the late twentieth century, how industrialization affects the gender composition of the labour force within and outside factories depends on the specific context. There are various considerations: the kind of industrialization strategy; the sectoral composition ·of newly established and expanding industrial production; above all, the *supply* of men's and women's labour for industrial employment.

The supply of labour is always affected by the conditions and rewards offered by industrial em-

Figure 8.5(a) Global feminization? Assembly worker at Hyundai, Ulsan, South Korea.

Figure 8.5(b) Global feminization? Shipbuilding at the China Shipyards, Kaohsiung, Taiwan.

ployment. In the case of the male labour force, skills and qualifications, and the availability of alternative and commensurate employment, will affect its composition. There is extensive evidence from both industrialized and developing countries that even within particular production lines jobs are sex-typed, and that men are reluctant to apply for or work in jobs which are socially constructed as 'women's work'.

This can of course change over time, but even in cases where men have been recruited to jobs traditionally created as women's jobs, such employment is associated with a reorganization of production because of technical change (Sklair, 1989). Conversely, where management has recruited women into occupations previously the exclusive preserve of male workers, the jobs have been redesignated as women's jobs to facilitate such substitution (Humphrey, 1987). The supply of women's labour is affected by similar considerations; in addition a crucial factor which affects the supply of women's labour for industrial employment — and indirectly their ability to move beyond the bottom of the occupational hierarchy — is the ease or difficulty of combining paid work (especially industrial shift work) with the domestic responsibilities of marriage and motherhood.

Two roads to the factory: the experience of the female workforce in Singapore and South Korea compared

It is instructive to compare the experience of women in Singapore and South Korea since both countries followed a similar export-oriented industrialization strategy since the 1960s, involving the rapid incorporation of women into the industrial workforce. The following extracts are from a case study by Phongpaichit.

Singapore

Singapore began its labour-intensive industrialization strategy only in 1960 for which it relied heavily on foreign capital from multinational companies [MNCs]. At that time it had a large pool of unemployed and underemployed workers, and participation rates among women workers were still rather low. The industrial strategy required female labour and the government did several things to facilitate their recruitment such as locating industrial zones near communities with underemployed women

workers. In the 1960s young women workers were mobilized into industrial employment in large numbers. They were subject to long hours of work and relatively low pay, compared to the men. The two main industries at the time were garments and electronics. These industries experienced rapid technological change and retrenchment was common; workers could be laid off very easily and women workers were the first to suffer. They were also susceptible to industrial diseases. Liberals and feminists wrote several articles against these conditions and the maltreatment of women workers. The government limited trade union activities and prohibited strikes, thus colluding with the MNCs to exploit labour.

The late 1970s, however, presented a rather different picture. Successful industrialization had created a tight labour market for both men and women, and women's wages began to increase, making for a narrowing gap between male and female wages. The Government began to assist married workers in continuing to work by subsidizing the cost of childcare in some cases. Attempts were also made to upgrade the skills of both men and women workers. It is not difficult to see that the government's assistance was motivated by the fact that the Singapore economy needed its female labour to keep industrialization going, as Singapore has rather a small population. But even then the government's move came rather late; from the beginning it was the household which played a very important role in women's continued employment in industry.

According to one study, the factory women who entered the job market during the first phase of labour intensive industrialization and managed to remain in the industrial work-force into the second phase, were often upgraded into positions of higher pay and greater permanence. These were women who had family support for childcare and other household chores, or who, at the start of their careers had been educated up to the primary level or above. Family support enabled the women to continue working long enough, even after marriage, in order to acquire the tenure and skill necessary for further upgrading, as industries moved from labour intensive to more capital intensive operations; a high educational level enabled them to acquire more skills and move up the wage scale in the industrial hierarchy. Higher wages in turn allowed the women to pay for the cost of childcare, and remain in the work-force even after marriage. The women who had neither family support or educational qualifications tended to suffer most as they had to quit work upon marriage.

The '60s and '70s still had the prevalence of the extended family system among the Chinese and this assisted the women a great deal. Many factory workers were able to rely on family support because their families were close at hand. Singaporean women workers were mainly recruited from within the relatively small state of Singapore and government contrived to locate factories close to kampongs (village homes) with surplus women workers to ensure a good supply of labour with minimal disruption. This situation differs from that of many other Asian industrializers, where new industries rely heavily on migrant labour drawn from a wider hinterland. Such migrant labour cannot depend on a family support system near at hand.

Towards the end of the early '70s the extended family system went into a decline as the result of the mushrooming of public housing through the Housing Development Board which aimed at resettling families from kampongs that often housed large extended families, into modern flats designed for nuclear families. In this situation only women who could afford child care remained in the workforce. Here too, the household played an important role: kin members were prepared to look after the children of working mothers in return for some compensation, which was usually cheaper than private childcare services.

In the second phase of industrialization, tight labour markets and higher wages compelled the government to shift its industrialization strategy from labour-intensive to capital- and skill-intensive enterprises. In order to achieve this the development of human resources was of utmost importance, and since Singapore had a small population, it could not afford to discriminate against women. Thus public policies to upgrade the educational levels and skills of all those who had not had the opportunity to do so in the previous phase, were open to both men and women. In this second phase more women entered professional occupations, and in industry, more were upgraded into supervisory positions. The need for female labour compelled the government to provide assistance in childcare, and even encourage men to play a more active role in household work.

Thus by the early '80s in Singapore, women became a permanent part of the industrial labour force, in every sphere of work from unskilled to skilled and professional. ...

South Korea

In terms of the long-term consequences of industrialization on women and the household, the case of South Korea is markedly different from Singapore. South Korea has also undergone two main phases of industrialization — the labour-intensive phase in the '60s and early '70s, and a more capital- and skill-intensive phase from the mid '70s onwards. As far as women workers are concerned, they still constitute what may be termed a 'floating' or 'peripheral' labour force.

Women's industrial working lives are still rather short, extending from their late teens up to the time they get married or have children. The reasons for this can be found both in the economic and the social sphere. In the economic context South Korea has a much larger population than Singapore (40 million as against 2.5 million), and thus in terms of the labour market it has a much larger supply of both male and female labour; the competition between males and females for industrial jobs is thus much keener overall. Further the source of supply of workers, females included, for factories in the early phases of industrialization was the large rural hinterland. Migrant women workers had to travel a long way from home and were thus deprived of their family support systems.

Despite the fast growth of industrialization in South Korea, the rate of labour absorption was still not rapid enough to create a tight labour situation as in Singapore. It is also possible that the social bias against women was stronger in South Korea and militated against change, even for example in education. ... As industries progress from labour-intensive to capital-intensive technologies, men move up the ladder through re-training programmes and incentives and encouragement to study while women remain behind, so that those with poor social backgrounds move from outdated labour-intensive industries into jobs discarded by men.

In South Korea, a woman's place is still seen to be very much in the home. A married woman is supposed to look after the household affairs of not only her immediate family but her husband's as well. Despite the emergence of the nuclear family, this custom is so prevalent that, even where a woman is living with her parents-in-law, she is not in a position to ask them to help with childcare or other household chores, to enable her to continue working. This is in marked contrast to Singapore, where, as we have seen, the extended family is very supportive to the working woman.

Without family support, factory women are at a great disadvantage in the labour markets, as they find it difficult to remain in the labour force long enough to acquire tenure and skills. In most cases, therefore, they cannot return to industrial jobs until after their child-rearing responsibilities are over. In the urban slum of Seoul there is now a large number of poor married women in their late 30s and 40s who were factory workers in the labour-intensive industries of the '60s. Most of them came from rural areas as migrants, and married and settled in the outskirts of Seoul.

The unwillingness of the family and society to accept the woman's role in social production disadvantages Korean women in other ways as well. Their household work is not valued in economic terms. This coupled with the unwillingness of the family and society to accept women's role in the public sphere, acts to lower the economic value of women's work in industry. Thus we find that women's wages in Korean industries (for unskilled and semi-skilled jobs) are about two thirds of men's wages or less (after adjusting for differences in age and length of service), and there is very little sign of a narrowing in the gap between male and female wages. This means effectively that women cannot afford surrogate childcare.

Another striking difference between Singapore and South Korea is society's or government's view of women with regard to policies on human resource development. Whereas in Singapore women are not discriminated against in education and professional jobs because of the shortage of labour, in South Korea they do not seem to enter the government's development goals as part of the human resource factor in economic development at all. They are pushed into the labour market when required, as during the labour-intensive phase of industrialization, but must leave their jobs and return home when their families demand. While government policy in Singapore attempts to upgrade the educational level of both men and women who could not benefit from compulsory education in the early phase of industrialization there is no such policy in South Korea; all vocational school education and attempts to upgrade skills in the private sector have been concentrated on men.

Rapid industrialization and the shift towards capital-intensive industry in South Korea have created rather a tight labour market situation for industrial workers in skilled and technical jobs. We would expect that the women would now be in a position to get better jobs and better pay; recent developments however have shown that they inherit only those work opportunities which are discarded by men. Welding is a case in point: traditionally a male occupation, Korean women have recently been encouraged to take it up in shipyards and factories. The Korean Employers' Federation has even suggested that more women be trained in welding techniques. This suggestion, ostensibly a radical move aiming at diversifying women's role in the industrial sphere, reveals itself, on closer inspection, as the old imperative at work again. Welding is characterized by a high turnover rate and, in advanced countries like Japan, for instance, robots are increasingly replacing manpower. The reasons for this are two: the high efficiency of robots and the difficulty in getting men to weld when they can choose other occupations instead. South Korea cannot afford robots but it can offer women the unpleasant jobs that men no longer want. Doubtless, once robots are introduced, women welders will be discarded and ushered back to their kitchens again.

Thus, in South Korea, women, despite having contributed to successful industrialization, have not been able to escape the hold of the household as defined by social custom. The relatively slack labour market as compared to Singapore, and a different industrialization strategy may be said to be the main reasons responsible for this state of affairs. In the period we are studying there was no real imperative to change

women's status as was the case in Singapore where there was a clear dependence on women's labour in the second phase of industrialization. It should also be pointed out that the subordinate position of women in South Korea is not confined to factory women; even the educated are oppressed. Although more Korean women now have access to education, very few can get satisfactory jobs. In government service for instance, there are hardly any women in executive or professional grades.

The Korean government is only just beginning to talk about ways to encourage married women to continue working in those occupations where male labour is tight. Yet, neither government or employer is prepared to subsidize the cost of childcare. The general feeling is that this is the responsibility of NGOs [non-governmental organizations] or social welfare organizations, and family norms, as we have seen, provide little support for women.

(Phongpaichit, 1988)

This account of the different experiences of women workers in Singapore and South Korea should alert us to the dangers of making simple generalizations about Third World women workers, even in countries whose industrialization strategies have been relatively similar. It also demonstrates how little can be deduced from aggregate statistics about women's share of the industrial labour force. Table 8.1 indicated that women's share of industrial employment in Singapore continued to rise through the 1970s and 1980s: from just over a third in 1970, to nearly a half in the 1980s. A simplistic analysis of these figures without reference to the labour market situation, or the nature of industrialization in the 1980s, might conclude that women are still confined to low-skilled labour-intensive production processes. From the aggregate figures, how could we distinguish the experience of Singapore from that of South Korea, where women's share of the industrial workforce also rose: from 35.1% in 1970, to 37.9% in 1980, and to 40.5% in 1987? Both could be seen as evidence supporting the 'global feminization of labour' thesis. But both countries represent very different trends which can only be understood by going beyond the statistical data and examining the employment strategy linked with each industrialization process.

8.5 Industrialization beyond the factory: women's work in the informal sector

There is a further dimension to the experience of industrialization which even Phongpaichit's useful comparison does not take into account. A great deal of industrial production, as well as the distribution and marketing of industrial products, takes place within the informal sector, outside formally organized factories and markets.

An increasingly important aspect of informal-sector employment for women consists of various forms of industrial subcontracting. Phongpaichit's account assumes that women factory workers are excluded entirely from industrial work when they marry and have children. In recent years it has become apparent that large numbers of married women and young mothers, many of whom are ex-factory employees, are involved in a network of industrial subcontracting within their own homes.

A survey undertaken in a low-income area of Seoul, South Korea, found that at least 10% of the economically active female population was engaged in some form of industrial homeworking, involving production activities using materials delivered from large factories. The range of activities carried out included the sewing of sweaters, sheets and suits, embroidery (by hand and machine), and the stitching of hats, socks scarves, leather luggage, jackets, boots, gloves and jogging shoes. A substantial percentage of women carrying out home-based activities were involved in some kind of 'finishing' task, chiefly removing threads from factory-sewn garments or textiles. Women were also employed in food processing (chiefly garlic peeling and packing), in sub-assembly of electronics and electrical goods, and in a variety of miscellaneous packaging and other activities (Kim, 1991).

The reasons for using homeworkers, who operate through a web of subcontractors, are various. Outworking allows the main supplier responsible for the export contract to minimize overheads, to adjust the size of the workforce to changes in demand, and to save on labour costs. The study estimated that main contractors saved between 20 and 40% on wage costs, with additional savings through avoiding non-wage payments such as taxation, social insurance and welfare payments, not to mention factory space, storage space, utilities and materials.

The women interviewed complained of low earnings (only 57.3% of the equivalent factory wage), overdue payments from subcontractors, living space being overrun by uncollected sweaters and other goods, and instability in the supply of materials or work (and therefore of earnings). But the reasons why they undertook the work is very clear: at least half of the women had children under the age of six and/or elderly or sick relatives for whom they were responsible. The majority of the husbands in the households worked in manual occupations such as construction work, as mechanics or taxi or truck drivers, and earned only half of the average urban wage. Without the continued earnings of the women, the household would find it impossible to survive. But, as the researcher comments: "Women in these low income families are in need of gainful employment, but ... face difficulties in entering the formal workforce. ... When questioned why they do home-based work the majority (3/4) cite the need for childcare and housework as main reasons. Two thirds express their willingness to remain as homeworkers even if jobs with better work conditions are available. This result represents either the poor alternatives, [an inadequate] care system, or how deeply women themselves are internalized with the socially defined responsibilities of running the family" (Kim, 1991, pp.12–14).

Subcontracting and various forms of outwork including homework have long been a feature of other Third World industrial sectors, especially those which produce for exports, although there is little systematic research available with which to estimate its extent. Case study material from

Figure 8.6   Sewing at home, at Kibarague, Nairobi, Kenya.

Figure 8.7   Bidi rollers working at home. These women have actually joined the Self Employed Women's Association in Ahmedabad, India, and obtain higher rates for their work than unorganized homeworkers.

Mexico (Benería & Roldán, 1987) Brazil (Schmitz, 1982) and the Philippines (Pineda Ofreneo, 1984) supports the findings of the South Korean example:

* Married women do not leave the industrial labour force even when they leave the factories

* There is an increasing trend towards subcontracting of manufactures for export to reduce costs and to cushion firms against fluctuations in an increasingly competitive market.

* A very high proportion of urban households rely on income from non-factory industrial work for their survival.

This aspect of Third World industrialization, by definition hidden from researchers and governments alike, is further evidence of the inadequacy of previous notions of industrialization experiences and the role of women workers. Far from being a remnant of previous, pre-industrial forms of production, homework and other kinds of production based on payment by volume rather than time (i.e. piece rates rather than wages) are a feature of the *current* phase of industrialization in the Third World.

Whether industrial outworking and home-working have increased over the last 10–20 years, or whether they have become slightly more visible and therefore recognized, is not clear. Whichever is the case, the high participation of women, especially those with domestic responsibilities, points to two conclusions:

1 The economic activity rate of women in industrial production is very much higher than that indicated by statistics primarily based on formal-sector recorded employment.

2 There are clear sexual divisions of labour within informal sector activities, which are just as persistent and rigid as those prevailing in the formal sector.

Some writers claim that women's participation in the informal sector in industrial and related

activities has increased over the last 10 to 15 years as the result of the generally poor levels of economic output and negative rates of growth particularly in Latin America and Africa (Moser, 1989; Gerhart, 1989). Certainly it is clear that the number of women in the urban labour force has grown dramatically. While the male labour force in Latin America doubled between 1950 and 1980, the female labour force grew by more than three times, and it is projected that another 22 million women will enter the labour force by the year 2000 (Berger, 1989). This is only partly the result of falling urban incomes linked to the *failure* of industrialization in the region, and increasing urbanization accompanying industrialization in the post-war period. Indeed, the growth of the female wage labour force in South-east Asia, and women's increasing participation in the informal as well as the formal sectors, can be seen as a result of the *success* of industrialization strategies. Either way, it is clear that the formal industrial labour market is unable to absorb the growth in the wage labour force which has accompanied industrialization in the latter part of this century.

There has also been a significant growth in the number of urban households where women are the primary income earners. Female-headed households account for an estimated third of all urban households in Latin America (Berger, 1989, p.5), and similar or greater proportions are estimated for urban Sub-Saharan Africa and parts of Asia (although, again, it is difficult to make comparisons because of differences in definitions). Since few women in this situation in the Third World have any access or entitlement to state benefits to meet the requirements of their own and their children's subsistence, women in female-headed households have a higher rate of economic activity than women in male-headed households. And because they often have the same kinds of domestic and childcare responsibilities as married women, they form a large share of the growing number of home-based industrial workers in cities all over the world.

8.6 Gender and industrialization: some conclusions

Challenging the polarized consensus about the place of women workers in the industrial workforce, and revealing the diversity of female workforces, have done more than challenge some dearly held stereotypes. They have also laid the basis for understanding the interaction of two different but connected sets of social relations: (capitalist) relations of production, and gender relations. In its search for cheap labour, or for labour which will minimize the unit labour cost of production, capital is not necessarily free to target women as the most exploitable and least resistant sector of the population. In order to provide cheap labour women have to be available for production; in some cases this means employing them when they are least constrained by domestic responsibilities, in other cases it means finding a form of employment that is compatible with their domestic responsibilities. In every case it is necessary to understand that women are constructed in terms of gender roles and relations as well as being a source of potential productive labour power, and that this construction will affect the precise nature and mode of women's employment in industry.

By focusing on the implications of industrialization for women's employment we have also learned something about the process of industrialization which is not necessarily apparent in the gender-blind analyses we often read. Given the widespread evidence that thousands of women are involved in industrial production outside the factory, we have to appreciate that analysis of industrialization cannot be confined to what happens in organized industry. Although the existence of the informal sector has been long recognized, its direct connection with the informal industrial sector has not always been so apparent. The fact that women are working in the same sectors, for the same markets, and often on the same products as those that are processed within the factories, and that very often those outside the factory have been factory workers at other points of their lives, is sufficient to prevent us from taking a narrow or inadequate definition of industry and industrialization.

There are further insights which derive from this analysis. Exploring the gendered nature of the workforce also reveals the variety of forms of industrial organization; moreover many of these forms are not alternatives to factory production, or remnants of pre-factory production, but are new and contemporary adaptations to prevailing conditions. The prevalence and variety of non-factory industrial work should warn us against linear models of industrialization in which 'superior', higher-productivity organization or production technology supersedes 'pre-industrial' forms. Non-factory production is a facet of the industrialization process rather than a feature of pre-industrial economic organization.

To understand fully the implications of industrialization for women we would also need to examine the impact of women's earnings on intra-household income distribution and decision-making. In other words, we would need to analyse whether earning a wage empowers women within households, and increases their autonomy and ability to resist coercion or oppression. We would also need to examine whether employment in factories is 'women's choice', or whether such employment carries costs such as reduced access to education, restrictions in timing and choice of marriage partner, or alternatively, whether employment actually increases women's choices in these spheres. Once we begin to investigate the gender issues implicit in industrialization we begin to ask questions and see dimensions which may not have been obvious, and ultimately we throw light on the whole process.

Summary of Chapter 8

1   This chapter has examined the employment and income-earning opportunities brought by industrialization, and their implications for women. It has done this by reviewing the debates on how industrialization has affected women and by examining data on the changing composition of the industrial labour force in the Third World.

2   The first consensus was that women were marginalized from industrial development. This consensus arose from focusing on early experiences of import substitution (especially in Latin America) which were associated with capital-intensive production and male employment generation.

3   The second consensus suggested that industrialization was based on the increasing employment of women. This view focused on the export-oriented industrialization since the 1970s which has used labour-intensive techniques, particularly in textiles, garments and electronics production, and where women have formed the majority of the labour force.

4   No single consensus has an adequate explanation of the relationship between industrialization and women's employment. Women appear to be excluded at certain points and targeted at others. Understanding which characteristics are demanded of women workers and comparing case studies reveals the diversity and differences. Industrialization is a dynamic process, as is the nature of the labour force which changes with different skill requirements, production technologies, specialization, and social and political contexts.

5   A gender-based analysis of industrialization enables us to see dimensions and issues and raise questions that other gender-blind approaches do not. Industrialization is not linear; the informal sector is as much a part of industrialization as organized factories; women's participation in industrialization may take many forms from homeworking to permanent waged employment. Industrialization — its process and impact — therefore concerns a wide spectrum of social relations from households to companies.

9

CULTURE AND INDUSTRIALIZATION IN BRAZIL

VIVIAN VON SCHELLING

The relationship between culture and industrialization is a subject which can be approached from various angles. It is possible to focus on broad socio-cultural changes over a whole period and the way in which the momentous transformation in the whole fabric of society brought about by industrialization is connected to given cultural configurations and patterns. This offers us a deeper insight into the relationship between different dimensions of society in the process of social change. Alternatively, we can narrow the focus and concentrate on a particular social group or agent and its experience of industrialization as manifested in its language, customs, world vision and artefacts. The benefit of this approach is that, although it cannot give us the same sweeping overview, it highlights the 'subjective' side of an objective social process. This enables us to explain not only the underlying causes of industrialization, such as the emergence of new classes and the development of technology, but to understand a human experience and thus to interpret the significance and impact of industrialization.

This chapter will adopt a two-pronged approach, taking into account both broad changes in the structure of society and the experience of social groups. It will address the following questions.

Q In what way has the development process in Brazil been linked with ideological and cultural change?

Q How have different social groups responded to industrialization in Brazil?

Specifically, the chapter will focus first on some important relationships between culture and industrialization as a whole since the 1920s (Sections 9.2 and 9.3). It will then concentrate on the culture of the peasants and rural labourers who have migrated to the city of São Paulo, and look at the carnival associations or 'Samba Schools' of Rio de Janeiro (Section 9.4). However, before we turn to Brazil, there are a few general observations on the relevance of culture for development studies, and most importantly, some definitions of culture used in this chapter.

9.1 The relevance of culture

Culture has come to be seen as an essential element of development studies, rather than as a 'residual factor' to be tacked on after the more important work of economic and social analysis (Chapter 17 of *Allen & Thomas, 1992*). This does not mean replacing 'economic reductionism' with 'cultural reductionism', but acknowledging the importance of culture in understanding industrialization.

In much of the literature about industrialization, particularly that associated with modernization theory, an assumption is made that the transition from an agrarian to an industrialized society occurs according to a set pattern, a fixed 'logic of industrialism'. Changes in the methods of production involving the use of science, machine technology and the factory system are automatically linked to a series of associated changes in social institutions, beliefs and social relations. These in turn are regarded as a precondition for the successful unfolding of the industrialization process. According to this view, the increasing specialization of labour and the growth of a national market for labour and goods lead to social mobility and the emergence of an open society. Education is linked to industry, while respect for science, achievement and rationality become the pillars of a new and secular value system. Simultaneously, with the development of industry and the concentration of workers in factories and in the bureaucracies which administer the production process, the city emerges as the centre of the economic, political and cultural life of the society. Finally, as the personal relations characteristic of the rural community disintegrate, the impersonal and contractual relations which govern large industrial organizations provide the individual with new roles and identities adapted to the new social order.

This set of interrelated social changes, elaborated by sociologists into a model of the industrialization process, presents us with several problems. The idea that there is a universally valid model of industrialization ignores the fact that, in each case, industrialization takes place in a particular society and is shaped by the history and culture of that society. With respect to the Third World, a similar mistake is made in assuming that the countries are homogeneous. This approach also fails to recognize that industrialization takes place 'under the shadow and direction' of the First World, which interferes with the unfolding of a fixed pattern of industrialization (Kumar, 1978, p.123).

A further problem with this approach is that it is based on a form of evolutionary thinking inherited from the Enlightenment and much of nineteenth-century sociology, which sees history as the progression of humanity from a simple, 'primitive' state to a state of 'civilization' through stages involving the development of technology and an increasing specialization of tasks within societies. According to this view, industrialized society is the final and most advanced stage of the evolutionary process.

The danger, then, of assuming the existence of a universal 'logic of industrialism' is that the varied historical and cultural contexts within which industrialization occurs are considered only in so far as they fit the prescribed model. As Henry Bernstein points out: 'the methodological approaches of Western social and political scientists ... often assume that developing countries are infant or deviant examples of the Western experience and can be studied in terms of a shortfall from the norm' (Bernstein, 1971, p.147).

How can we avoid substituting a model for reality? It is essential that we understand the interaction between the general social processes involved in industrialization — the changes in the methods of production — and the particular historical and cultural circumstances through which industrialization acquires a specific identity and significance. Moreover, social development is not a 'natural' evolutionary process. It is brought about by individuals and social groups pursuing particular goals and interests guided by their respective visions of the world. Their culture, how they perceive social events, their aspirations and beliefs are therefore equally important. They are as much a part of reality as the rate of capital investment or the role of multinationals in the process of industrialization.

As discussed by Tim Allen, the term 'culture' contains a number of meanings and assumptions (Chapter 17 of Allen and Thomas, 1992). The next section looks specifically at three of these meanings. They overlap to some extent with the meanings set out by Tim Allen: namely, culture as 'expressive', 'pluralistic' and 'hegemonic'. However, in order to clarify the the use of the term here, we will focus briefly on the history of the development of culture as a concept.

The concept of culture

Culture was originally used to describe the act of cultivating crops and rearing animals. Subsequently, towards the end of the eighteenth century, it came to define the analogous process of the growth and development of the human mind. In the nineteenth and twentieth centuries, culture came to encompass not only the products of artistic and intellectual activity, but also the customs, traditions, language and artefacts of a particular group. This was partly due to the influence of the German philosopher Herder, who developed the idea that the 'symbolic forms' of society — music, poetry, rituals — expressed the psyche or, in his words, the 'spirit' of a people (Williams, 1981). These forms not only included the recognized artistic and intellectual products of the learned, but also the customs, language, legends and songs of the 'common people'. Taken together, they formed a pattern, a culture, through which the identity of the people was expressed.

This idea was later elaborated by anthropologists in two ways. On the one hand, culture is seen as the shared set of meanings, values and behaviour patterns, the 'whole way of life' of a society or social group. Transmitted from generation to generation, it helps the individual to adapt to his or her environment and maintains the continuity of the society or group. Individuals are born into a culture which constructs and shapes the way they perceive the world. On the other hand, culture is not only that which ensures the continuity of the social order, but is also a transforming force because it embodies the specifically human capacity to create, to invent new ways of life. In other words, human beings do not survive merely by adapting to their environment, but also by transforming it through the use of tools and new forms of knowledge; in other words, by creating novel forms of culture.

Thus there are a number of interconnected meanings contained in the concept of culture:

1 Culture as 'the whole way of life' of a society or a group.

2 Culture as the artistic and intellectual products of a society or group.

3 Culture as a pattern of meanings contained in ideas and symbols through which the social order is both reproduced and transformed.

In looking at the relationship between industrialization and culture at a structural level, we shall make use of the third meaning, as this meaning helps us to clarify how culture is connected to the establishment of an urban-industrial society. It can also help us to see how different and often conflicting groups try to change the new order and direct it towards different goals. The first and second meanings are more relevant to our examinations of the group of rural migrants in São Paulo and the Samba Schools of Rio de Janeiro. Here we concentrate on the response of particular agents to the process of industrialization, as revealed in their culture both as a 'way of life' and in the specific symbolic forms through which this way of life is expressed.

So, we have unravelled the origins of some of the meanings of culture, but there is still something missing. Is culture only about the frictionless sharing of meanings, about the smooth reproduction of society as a set of ideas and patterns of social behaviour passed from one generation to another? A cursory glance at the history of the Industrial Revolution in Europe indicates that this was not the case: the process of industrialization was accompanied by a protracted and often fierce battle of ideas. These ideas expressed the conflict between the pre-industrial way of life and a new social order organized around the factory system and described the relationship between the new class of employers and the workers, between capital and labour. The victory over the old agrarian society was achieved not only through the pursuit of economic and political transformations, but also, centrally, through the destruction of pre-industrial ways of life. Broad processes of social change are accompanied by struggles for cultural power between various social groups which have a fundamental role in determining the structure of society and, consequently, an interest in changing or maintaining that structure.

The Italian Marxist Antonio Gramsci defined this conflict as the 'struggle for hegemony' (Gramsci, 1971). In his reflections on the subject, he pointed out that the economic and political dominance of a social class is achieved, not simply through the use of force, but through gaining the consent of subordinate classes to the social arrangements and ideas favoured by the dominant class. This process could be said to be successful when the ideology of a dominant group provides the vehicle through which the governed group experience, and relate to, their social situation. It ranges from definitions about the 'proper' way to organize the economy and distribute wealth to ideas about the role of the family and the legitimacy of particular ways of seeing and acting. The result becomes established within society as a whole as a form of 'common sense' and as part and parcel of the prevailing forms of popular culture. And, once a particular way of seeing the world has become common sense, part of the culture of the people, it seems as if there is no alternative to that way of seeing society and organizing social life. While this condition of hegemony mitigates social conflict, it does not do away with it altogether. Some forms of resistance are capable of being contained within the limits set by the dominant culture. Others, particularly in periods of economic instability and crisis, constitute a more fundamental challenge to the way social relationships are ordered. Hegemony is therefore never established once and for all, it has to be continuously worked at; periods of conformity and consensus alternate with periods of resistance and opposition (Hall, 1981).

The concept of hegemony is useful in several ways:

- It highlights the fact that, since society is divided into dominant and subordinate groups (social classes, genders, ethnic and religious divides) with unequal economic and political power, the sphere of culture, in particular popular culture, is marked by a struggle to define the framework, the preferred meanings, through which we interpret the world and our place in it (Hall, 1981). Moreover, since the control and ownership of the means of cultural production (of the media, educational institutions, religious organizations and so on) is similarly unequal, it is likely that the prevailing interpretation of reality will be that of the dominant groups.

- It also, however, emphasizes that consent to the established social order is not gained without struggle and cannot occur without taking account of, and engaging with, the culture of the subordinate groups. The notion of hegemony, therefore, avoids the pitfalls of seeing popular culture merely as a passive reflection of what is imposed by the dominant culture, or, alternatively, of seeing it as an uncontaminated culture of resistance against pressures to submit and conform.

This approach has proved to be useful in the field of cultural studies as it focuses on popular culture as a product of the interaction between dominant and subordinate cultural forms. This results in complex combinations of dominant and oppositional forms, which include domination, subversion, conformity, partial acceptance and negotiation.

Let us now turn our attention to the process of industrialization in Brazil. As we come into contact with historical reality, the relevance of these concepts as tools to help us understand the dynamics of social change will, hopefully, become apparent.

9.2 The industrialization of Brazil and the emergence of 'the people'

In the following pages, we will look briefly and rather schematically at how Brazilian industrialization from 1930 to 1964 and the model of development based on import substitution were linked to broad changes at the level of culture. This will illustrate the importance of the struggle for hegemony that took place between the coalition of classes in Brazil seeking to establish a new urban-industrial civilization.

As described in Chapter 3, the break with the old agrarian order based on the export of primary products and the power of a landowning class ushered in a new period. During the 1930s under the presidency of Getulio Vargas, for the first time in 500 years of Brazilian history, the middle and working-classes, as well as rural labourers and the peasantry, participated in the economic and political decisions which affected the development of society. It was a significant epoch, often referred to as the 'Brazilian Revolution' in which, to use the phrase of the Brazilian sociologist Octavio Ianni, 'the people appear on the stage of history' (Ianni, 1971).

The fundamental change underlying this 'Revolution' was the emergence of an urban-industrial society. This change went hand in hand with major structural alterations entailing the rise of new classes, the urbanization of the south, in particular São Paulo, and the growth of a nationalist ideology.

When Getulio Vargas assumed power in 1930, the political system in Brazil brought about a new realignment of social forces. The industrialists and the middle classes were strengthened by a series of economic measures that stimulated national industrial development, the growth of an internal market and the national integration of Brazil. Simultaneously, a new working class emerged whose purchasing power and skills were necessary for industrial expansion. The allegiance of the working class in the struggle against the old agrarian order was therefore seen as a prerequisite for the success of Brazil's industrialization programme. Policies designed to secure working-class support included the introduction of labour legislation and the regulation of wages and employment through state investments. Although radical, these transformations, did not lead to a complete reorganization of society. The support of the landowning classes and their capacity to export were still necessary as foreign currency was required to finance the import of industrial machinery. The new political configuration that emerged during this period was characterized by a shifting compromise and an unstable struggle for hegemony between the national bourgeoisie, the working class and the landowning classes. This configuration, known as Populism (see Box 3.3 in Chapter 3), was reflected in a mode of thinking about Brazilian society and the aims of development that was inspired by two interconnected ideas: the Nation and the People.

The idea of the 'Nation' marked a break with the past. Brazil had been dependent on the external demand for raw materials. It now replaced the goods originally imported from abroad and gained

a progressive autonomy and control of its own resources. The terms 'national development', 'national identity', 'self-determination', and the emergence of the Nation as the 'subject' of its own history, became key elements in the struggle for hegemony in the new social order.

Inspired by this new vision of Brazil, an influential group of intellectuals and artists launched the Modernist Movement in the early 1920s. Rejecting the sense of inferiority fostered by Brazil's colonial legacy, the Modernists highlighted the value of the non-European aspects of Brazilian culture and, in particular, celebrated the black and Indian elements in popular culture. The painting, literature, history, music and anthropology produced by the Modernists and their followers in the 1930s and 40s reflect the spirit of cultural renewal, aesthetic innovation and national self-discovery characteristic of the period (see Amado, 1945, 1984, 1988; de Andrade, 1979; de Andrade, 1984; Freyre, 1933; Ramos, 1961; Rego, 1966). A powerful, although somewhat later, symbol of this desire for national affirmation was the construction of Brasília, the new capital, in 1961. Built in the geographical heart of Brazil, it represents the nationalist ideal of independence and internal development.

A second idea, closely linked to that of the Nation, is the concept of 'The People'. It became a central category in the culture of Brazil after the 1930s, and its importance as a physical presence becomes apparent if we consider it in conjunction with the process of urbanization and, in particular, with the extraordinary transformation of São Paulo during this period.

With the massive influx of Europeans, former slaves and rural workers described in Chapter 3, São Paulo became the centre for vast agglomerations of nationalities, ethnic groups and classes. It became the frontier of 'modernity', generating an intense awareness of social change and a propitious climate for the political mobilization of 'the people'. In 1917 the first general strike led by the Anarchist Movement took place and in 1922 the Communist Party was founded in São Paulo.

The role of 'the people' in the process of industrialization in Brazil was ambiguous. While their participation in the electoral process, political parties, trade unions and interest groups was seen as necessary to the advance of industrialization, it was a force which also needed to be contained within the framework of capitalist development. This ambiguity was, in turn, reflected in considerable ideological controversy during this period about who actually constituted 'the people'. For the left, the term referred primarily to the working class and the peasantry; for groups in the centre of the political spectrum, the term also included the middle classes and the national bourgeoisie. In practice, however, there was a consensus that 'the people' consisted of all groups and classes engaged in the gigantic task of overcoming underdevelopment through industrialization and the reform of social and political institutions.

From 1945 to 1964, sometimes called the period of 'Populist Democracy', the social reforms of the populist alliance and the 'national developmentalism' of the state formed the backdrop to major cultural changes. The Higher Institute of Brazilian Studies (*Instituto Superior de Estudos Brasileiros*, ISEB), created by the Ministry of Education in the mid-1950s, became a major centre of ideological debate and cultural production on the subjects of nationalism, economic development and the role of 'the people' in Brazilian history. In a manner reminiscent of the earlier Modernists, the 'Isebians' looked towards popular culture and 'the people' as the bearers of an authentic national identity. In contrast to the dominant élites who identified with and imitated European and North American culture, popular culture, in their view, expressed the genuine history and experience of the country through customs and traditions. What popular culture lacked was a 'critical consciousness' of the need to transform Brazil into an autonomous industrialized nation, although this consciousness could be obtained through educational reform and the widespread dissemination of an 'ideology of development'. The participation of 'the people' in the educational and political reforms which were a prerequisite to industrialization was an integral part of this process.

In the 1960s the concern with popular culture led to a search for new forms through which to reach 'the people', a large proportion of whom were illiterate (48% of the adult population in 1960). Theatre and cinema focused on the lives of workers, peasants, blacks, Indians and rural migrants, using their experience of suffering and oppression, their symbols, cultural practices and world vision to develop novel forms of theatre and a new cinematic language (for example, the Theatre of the Oppressed as developed by Augusto Boal and The New Cinema Movement led by Glauber Rocha).

In the predominantly rural and poverty stricken North East of Brazil a powerful and broadly-based Popular Culture Movement emerged with the purpose of mobilizing 'the people' to question their subordination to the landowning class through grass-roots education, adult literacy programmes and the promotion of popular culture. In Popular Culture Centres throughout Brazil 'the people' were urged, through 'consciousness raising', to value their culture and to see themselves as creators of a culture capable of acting on and transforming their social situation. In 1963, under the government of João Goulart, the Brazilian pedagogue Paulo Freire was invited to organize a nationwide adult literacy campaign based on his revolutionary adult literacy method. His method, known as the 'pedagogy of the oppressed', combined learning to read and write with a critical reflection on the causes of underdevelopment, inequality and domination, of which illiteracy was just one aspect. It was designed to assist 'the people' through a critical analysis of the causes of their own experience of oppression, help them acquire a voice in society and allow them to break out of their 'culture of silence' (Freire, 1972). (See Figure 9.1.)

In 1964 the populist alliance collapsed. It was replaced by a right-wing military dictatorship under which the state extended its powers as an agent of industrialization. The national-popular discourse characteristic of the period of Populist Democracy was suppressed through a combination of censorship, the abolition of former left-wing and populist parties, and the persecution

Figure 9.1   These two pictures are the first in a series of six slides used in the adult literacy campaigns of the Popular Culture Movement in the North East of Brazil in the early 1960s. They are designed to show students that the house, the well and the book are parts of human culture, which transforms nature. Hence, as the creators of culture, they, 'the people', can also read and write their own texts and transform society.

and torture of activists and intellectuals involved in the cultural politics of the 'Brazilian Revolution'.

It is beyond the scope of this chapter to analyse the complex economic and political causes of the collapse of the populist alliance. One very important factor, however, was the fact that the consensus over the direction and the beneficiaries of development and industrialization broke down. With the formation of trade unions in the countryside, the growing demands for reform of the unequal land tenure system and the spread of adult literacy linked to political radicalization, the mobilization of 'the people' to participate in the development process threatened to undermine the hegemony of national developmentalism. This threat was expressed, as well as furthered, by the struggle between the groups involved in the populist alliance over the purpose of development and their definitions of the twin concepts of 'the Nation' and 'the people'. This struggle manifested itself in ideological differences between political parties in the populist period. It was particularly evident in

the sphere of popular culture where the state's interest in generating a skilled work force that could vote through adult literacy projects (literacy was a precondition for voting) coincided and conflicted with the Popular Culture Movements' goal of fostering the capacity of 'the people' to think critically about the social order.

The period of Populist Democracy is a useful example of how social change is both reflected in, and brought about by, the struggle for cultural power, for hegemony. This is illustrated in Figure 9.2. In the figure, the circular arrows relate to the interaction between the economy, politics and culture. For example, the period 1930–64, based on an import substitution model of development, gave rise to various social groups and classes which struggled for political power, struck up alliances or entered into conflict with each other. This struggle is manifested at the level of culture, which in turn affects how the economy is organized, maintaining or changing it, giving rise to new social groups (or not) and to new forms of political power and culture.

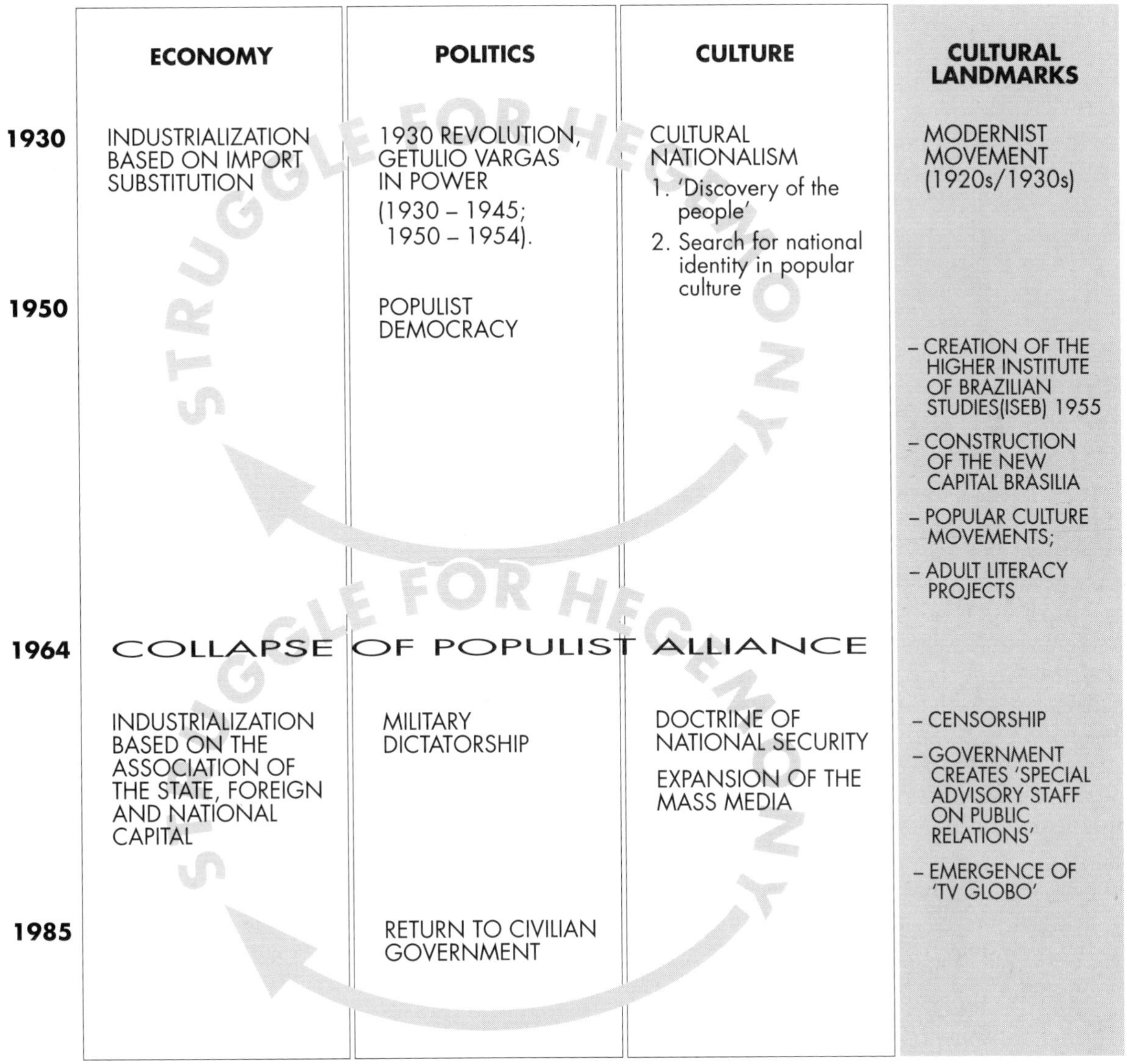

	ECONOMY	POLITICS	CULTURE	CULTURAL LANDMARKS
1930	INDUSTRIALIZATION BASED ON IMPORT SUBSTITUTION	1930 REVOLUTION, GETULIO VARGAS IN POWER (1930 – 1945; 1950 – 1954).	CULTURAL NATIONALISM 1. 'Discovery of the people' 2. Search for national identity in popular culture	MODERNIST MOVEMENT (1920s/1930s)
1950		POPULIST DEMOCRACY		– CREATION OF THE HIGHER INSTITUTE OF BRAZILIAN STUDIES(ISEB) 1955 – CONSTRUCTION OF THE NEW CAPITAL BRASILIA – POPULAR CULTURE MOVEMENTS; – ADULT LITERACY PROJECTS
1964	COLLAPSE OF POPULIST ALLIANCE			
	INDUSTRIALIZATION BASED ON THE ASSOCIATION OF THE STATE, FOREIGN AND NATIONAL CAPITAL	MILITARY DICTATORSHIP	DOCTRINE OF NATIONAL SECURITY EXPANSION OF THE MASS MEDIA	– CENSORSHIP – GOVERNMENT CREATES 'SPECIAL ADVISORY STAFF ON PUBLIC RELATIONS' – EMERGENCE OF 'TV GLOBO'
1985		RETURN TO CIVILIAN GOVERNMENT		

Figure 9.2   The struggle for hegemony in Brazil before and after 1964.

9.3   The military dictatorship and the industrialization of culture

During the military dictatorship (1964–1985) a series of measures (called 'institutional acts') gave the Brazilian State extraordinary powers over its citizens. The government could suspend the political rights and electoral mandates of any individual with politically suspect views. According to

official ideology, encapsulated in the 'Doctrine of National Security', the military acquired direct responsibility to defend the Nation against internal as well as external enemies. This doctrine, based on the Cold War assumption that 'Christian West' and 'Eastern Communism' were locked in permanent conflict, stated that to protect the West against the 'cancer' of communism it was necessary to develop a system of continental security encompassing both North and South America under the leadership of the USA. Any criticism of the government and the armed forces was defined as a threat to national security and censored. The media were placed under the control of military courts. Strikes were seen as evidence of the subversive presence of an 'internal enemy', which the state could legitimately penalize through the use of force in the name of 'security and development'. In the view of the military government and its supporters, the period of Populist Democracy had incontrovertibly shown that the Brazilian people were incapable of governing themselves and, hence, required the firm tutelage of the state.

As described in Section 3.4 of Chapter 3, which discusses Brazilian politics under the military regime, the new model of development and pattern of industrialization were based on an alliance between the state, private local capital and foreign capital. One important aspect of this collaboration, which again highlights the relevance of culture to an understanding of development issues, was the extraordinary expansion of the mass media that took place during this period, especially television. The state promoted the development of various cultural institutions, among them 'Embratel', a state-owned telecommunications company connected to the international satellite system. Gradually, with the assistance of the newly-formed Ministry of Communications, the whole territory of Brazil was integrated within a single national communications network. This was an important development for two reasons: it facilitated the control and political mobilization of the population as conceived by the 'National Security Law', and promoted the growth of a national consumer market for Brazil's expanding industry. These transformations, in a country with a large proportion of the population still illiterate, made television the main vehicle for state-controlled publicity and commercial advertising. In the late 1960s, government-granted instalment credit led to the percentage of urban homes in possession of a TV set rising from 9.5% in 1960 to 40% in 1970 (Skidmore, 1988). Jointly, these developments contributed to the emergence of Brazil's television empire, TV Globo, whose soap operas, news programmes and imported films, continuously

interspersed with commercials extolling an urban affluent life style, reached 95% of the 17 million households with a television (Guimarães & Amaral, 1988).

Let us now return to the concept of hegemony and look at some of the links between cultural change and industrialization during this period. During the first decade of the military regime the new nation-wide television network was clearly being used by the government as an ideological tool to establish its hegemony, in other words, to gain consent to the new social arrangements and model of development it sought to institute. The fact that it was continuously obliged to use force to suppress opposition to the new social order revealed a lack of consent in various sectors of society: the labour movement, the intelligentsia, members of the armed forces, and members of the middle class opposed to the coup.

In the late 1960s the government created a 'Special Advisory Staff on Public Relations'. This body, made up of journalists and social scientists, was charged with disseminating TV films advertising Brazil as a country whose rapid and triumphant economic growth would soon enable it to join the ranks of the developed nations. Using popular language, these programmes linked images of a modern and powerful Brazil with the values of hard work and the heroic role of the armed forces. Given that the 'economic miracle' was financed partly by a reduction in workers' wages, these programmes could be seen as attempts to obtain the workers' consent to the social order by inviting them to regard the reduction as a patriotic sacrifice. In 1970, when the Brazilian football team won the World Cup for the third time, the players were personally received by President Medici with carnival celebrations. The government Public Relations body wrote a song for the team *Pra Frente Brasil* (Forward Brazil), which became the theme song of the regime and was played throughout the country on radio and television. Posters were produced with images of the Brazilian 'King of Football', Pelé, scoring a goal accompanied by the government slogan: 'Nobody can stop this country now.' (Skidmore, 1988, p.112) In this way, Brazil's progress under the leadership of the armed forces was successfully linked to popular symbols of cultural identity. More indirectly, the prevalent model of development was legitimized through TV Globo's extensive coverage of the accomplishments of the regime, including opening up the Amazon region through the construction of the Trans-Amazonic highway.

As the economic and political fortunes of the military regime began to change in the mid-1970s, with the impact of the oil crisis and the emergence of considerable opposition, the allegiance of TV Globo began to shift. In the early 1980s, during the campaign for direct presidential elections, TV Globo's continuous coverage of the mass rallies and demonstrations held in most major Brazilian cities and its support for journalists who disobeyed government censorship played a crucial role in undermining the legitimacy of the military government. Similarly, in 1985 TV Globo's extraordinary capacity to mobilize public opinion in favour of its candidate Tancredo Neves was manifested in its ability to link alleged national qualities, such as a spirit of conciliation and cordiality, with Neves' manifest destiny as the restorer of democracy (Guimaraës & Amaral, 1988, p.130). And in 1989, during the first direct presidential elections since 1961, TV Globo played a crucial role in the defeat of the leader of the Workers' Party (PT), Luis Ignacio da Silva ('Lula'). On the eve of the presidential election it presented its viewers with an edited version of a televised debate between the two presidential candidates, Collor de Mello and 'Lula', which highlighted the 'Lula's' shortcomings. His popularity dropped significantly following the transmission of the programme.

Many readers may doubt that television has enough power to shape a country's fortunes. Surely, they argue, to assume that it does is to see viewers as excessively passive receptacles of media messages, with no alternative and independent views through which to interpret the world. The power of the media to shape social consciousness is a controversial issue, and one which cannot be settled here. Nevertheless, its power in the case of Brazil is not to be underestimated; not only because of its influence on the course of Brazilian politics, but also because of its effects on the

processes of social change brought about by industrialization.

In order to shed some light on television's effects on the processes of social change, we will look briefly at some of the consequences of Brazil's model of industrial development. A model which had, as one of its characteristics, integration into the world economy through massive foreign investment. In his book *Dependent Development*, Peter Evans points out that one of the characteristics of what he calls dependent development during military rule was the 'disarticulation between technology and social structure' (Evans, 1979, p.29). In other words, production technologies imported from the First World cannot absorb underemployed labour because they are capital intensive. In addition, they are designed to produce goods which most people in Brazil cannot afford. This reinforcement of an industrial structure based on 'luxury' goods leads, in turn, to a greater concentration of income in the affluent sections of society. Thus, because the pattern of capital accumulation is based on a heavy reliance on direct foreign investment, expensive consumer goods and an unequal distribution of income, the majority of the population is marginalized both as producers and as consumers. And, as allowing political participation in this context can be potentially destabilizing, state repression becomes a central aspect of this model of development.

Now, what does this have to do with television? As we have seen, television played an important role in the struggle for hegemony during the initial years of the military government in Brazil and, subsequently, was influential in the demise of that government. Should you ever have an opportunity to watch Brazilian television over an extended period, you will be struck by the fact that the programmes predominantly represent the urban, cosmopolitan life of Rio de Janeiro and São Paulo. Soap operas, in particular, concentrate on the trials and tribulations of the middle and upper classes. By rarely representing the cultures of other less 'developed' regions or non-dominant social classes, or doing so only as 'backward' or exotic manifestations, television effectively reproduces the marginalization of the majority of the population at the level of culture. In this way, it creates the comfortable illusion that poverty and underdevelopment, this 'other' Brazil, no longer exist. This illusion is reinforced by Brazil's integration into the world economy. TV Globo, for example, exports its programmes to 112 countries. But in order to compete in the world market, its programmes need to be adapted to the tastes of North American and European audiences. Moreover, for the majority of the population, a large proportion of which has migrated to the cities and become separated from its original, local culture, television becomes a means through which to make sense of the new urban-industrial environment and to participate, however marginally, in the fruits of modernity. The power of television as a symbol of modernity is heightened by the lack of an adequate educational system and the absence of civic institutions representing the needs of the marginalized majority.

9.4 Culture and industrialization: looking at 'agents'

Migration and identity

Now that we have looked at how specific models of development and cultural forms interact, and at how the struggle for hegemony is a crucial aspect of this interaction, let us turn our attention to the experience of industrialization as lived by a group of rural migrants in the city of São Paulo. In doing so, various uses of the concept of culture will come into play.

The transformation of an individual's life through industrialization entails the adaptation to, and creation of, a new 'way of life'. In this process the migrant's identity undergoes a process of change as he or she is confronted with the implications of assuming a new and different position in society.

This new identity could be seen as a synthesis of the migrant's former culture and his or her new culture in the urban industrial context. It is made up of representations, images, beliefs and concepts made available by culture, through which the migrants experience and define themselves. In other words, the migrant is not only confronted

with a new material existence as an industrial worker not a rural labourer or peasant, but is also faced with what this means, how it is defined in the context of a given culture. However, as we saw, culture itself is connected to the structure and relations of power in society. The migrant's response to industrialization and the development of a new identity inevitably entails a conscious and unconscious engagement with the varied and conflictive modes of thinking present in society at large, each struggling to make its interpretation of reality prevail over the others. Thus, for example, the dominant culture of the urban industrial context may devalue the migrant identity of peasant origin. The extent to which this influences the migrant's own sense of self and world view will depend on the extent to which alternative representations are available. And this, in turn, depends not only on the individual, but on the extent to which 'cultures of resistance' questioning the dominant view of the migrant identity have developed and become part of 'common sense', part of the broad 'popular culture'.

This enables us to see in what way, and to what extent, human beings adapt to and transform new social circumstances.

Migration and uneven development

The transformation of agrarian society brought about by industrialization has generally entailed the migration of large parts of the rural population to the city. In Brazil, however, as in some other developing countries, it has a very distinct character due to the fact that industrialization exacerbated the uneven development of different regions and created marked disparities between countryside and city. There are a number of interrelated factors involved.

Essentially, industrialization took place in the south of Brazil, while the system of land tenure in the countryside remained largely unchanged. Large tracts of land, or *latifundios*, belong to a single family or clan of families and this monopoly of the land enables them to wield great power over the peasantry and rural labourers. (To some extent, the southern region is an exception to this pattern, in that European immigration in the early twentieth century introduced small land-holdings and more advanced techniques for tilling the land.)

This inequality has in many ways been aggravated by industrialization. The need to grow cash crops for export to obtain foreign currency to import machinery has led landowners to encroach on the subsistence plots on which they allowed the peasantry living on their land to grow their own food. In the process, a large percentage of the peasantry has become proletarianized, that is, transformed into wage-labourers no longer relying primarily on subsistence agriculture for their survival but selling their labour for a wage. At the same time, the expansion of agribusiness in the hands of multinationals and the mechanization of agriculture have led to an excess supply of labour in the countryside and thus to high rural unemployment. Although relations between peasant and landlord before industrialization were highly inequitable, this was to some extent mitigated by a relationship of patronage and dependence whereby, in exchange for services and payment in kind, the peasant received the landowner's assistance and protection. With the expansion of a money economy and wage-labour this highly personalized relationship was replaced by an impersonal cash nexus undermining the traditional bonds of loyalty and dependence between landowner and peasant. In this context, migration to the city, where the services are better and the wages higher, appeared to be the only way of escaping growing impoverishment, economic insecurity and the disintegration of traditional rural values and relationships.

Arrival in the city did not, however, guarantee an improvement in the migrant's condition. Industrialization in Brazil has not been able to absorb the mass of rural migrants because:

- Industrialization is capital rather than labour intensive.

- Industrialization is based on the expansion of consumer goods for the urban and predominantly middle-class market, which are beyond the purchasing power of the majority of the Brazilian population.

- Perhaps most significantly, rural to urban migration has been on such a massive scale — some 75% of Brazil's 150 million population is now urban — that industry has been unable to absorb more than a portion of the urban labour force.

This leads to a coexistence in the cities of a relatively wealthy minority with a North American or European life style and a mass of migrants living in the shanty towns on the outskirts of the sprawling industrial cities. The North East in particular, which is the place of origin of a large proportion of rural migrants, has been an area of marked underdevelopment. Because the Brazilian economy since the colonial period has been largely based on export crops, it has been perennially vulnerable to the demand fluctuations of the world market. At the same time, the predominance of large, partially unproductive estates employing peasants as sharecroppers, tenant-farmers and seasonal labourers is the underlying cause of the widespread poverty of the area. Given the precarious conditions under which the rural population lives, the climatic conditions of the North East, characterized by periodic droughts and floods, have a devastating effect on the local economy.

In the late nineteenth century and in the mid-1930s before the 'Brazilian Revolution', a number of peasant movements emerged in response to oppression and deprivation. These movements took a variety of forms, ranging from messianic groups congregating around a charismatic religious leader to organized bandits called *cangaceiros*. Both the religious 'prophets' and the bandits Antonio Silvino ('Lampião') and his companion 'Maria Bonita' have become firmly established in the popular mythology of the region.

In order to understand the cultural background of the rural population of the North East, and before discussing the cultural impact of migration, it is necessary to point out the importance of religious belief, experience and ritual in giving meaning to existence. The North East is a large and culturally varied area, including coastal regions with a strong legacy of Afro-Brazilian culture and a rural hinterland with Iberian traditions inherited from sixteenth-century Portugal. There is a vibrant oral tradition consisting of poetry, myths, legends, teachings, religious-magical practices and medicinal knowledge. These traditions are largely embedded in, and expressed through, a form of 'Popular Catholicism' based on a cult of the Saints and the Virgin Mary. This belief system is intertwined with supernatural figures including the Devil and the souls of the dead.

The predicament of rural migrants from the North East is that their dislocation from this geographical area and cultural universe to an urban centre like São Paulo also entails, in a sense, a journey from one epoch to another. Thus, although rural culture is itself becoming increasingly urbanized, migrants nevertheless experience the clash of rural and urban cultures with great intensity. The migrant embodies in his/her career the transformation in values and social relations which take place with industrialization in a society characterized by uneven development as a whole.

Migration: the confrontation with a new 'way of life'

Migration entails a process of resocialization. The confrontation with a new 'way of life', characterized by different ways of organizing work, different behaviour and values, is accompanied by a process of re-education and the acquisition of a new identity. The aim of this process is to facilitate the migrant's integration into the urban industrial context and hopefully guarantee not only economic survival but upward social mobility, which forms the migrant's 'horizon of hope'. However, integration in the urban environment entails a devaluation of rural cultural values and, frequently, a form of de-skilling. While the labour process in a rural context enabled the labourer to understand the cycle of production in which he or she was involved, he/she becomes an appendage of assembly line production in the urban context. Moreover, infrastructural amenities such as electricity, sewage, water, public transport and educational facilities are deficient in the districts on the outskirts of towns, the places migrants tend to settle. The migrant is thus deprived of the citizenship rights which are an integral part of urban life. The rural migrant's attitude both to the city and the countryside is, therefore, ambiguous; both are alternately idealized and devalued.

The experience of migration confronts the individual with a number of oppositions and contradictions. These are expressed in representations of time, work and consumption, of everyday life and the qualities of city and country life. In the rural context, time is cyclical and measured according to the alternating rhythms of nature — day and night, harvesting and sowing — punctuated by the calendar of religious festivities. In the city, time is linear and work in the factory, often involving night shifts, breaks the link between the productive process and the cycles of nature. The migrant's aspirations of social mobility are expressed in a wish to be employed in a factory or domestic service. In the case of male migrants, the preference is often for some commercial activity which enables them to escape the discipline of factory work and maintain the relative independence which they enjoyed in a rural context. For women, however, factory work enables them to escape the control of their family, even though it entails taking on a double burden of working both within and outside the home.

Box 9.1   Some data on migration in Brazil

According to the National Census for the years 1970–1976, 14.4 million people migrated to the south-east in 1970, 18 million in 1976.

In 1970, São Paulo alone received 3 million migrants from the North East, the States of Minas Gerais and Espirito Santo, and 4.3 million in 1976.

In 1970, of 29.5 million internal migrants, 20 million had their census taken in the city. This means that the majority of migrants are either inter-city or rural–urban.

In 1960, only 45% of the population lived in the cities; in 1980, 67% lived in the cities. In 1990, 75% of Brazil's population was urban.

In the city, labour and goods are exchanged for money and the migrant's sense of identity is strongly affected by the discrepancy between purchasing power and the urban status symbol of consumer affluence. The levelling and impersonal qualities of urban social relations based on commodity exchange are compared negatively to the relations of the subsistence farm based on co-operation and reciprocity.

Thus, although the city is idealized as the centre of 'civilization', with its speed, luminosity, services, information and labour legislation, it is also seen as the world of 'illusion', of false appearances.

In Box 9.2 and Box 9.3, two migrants from the North East, Juca and Fatima, tell their stories. The representations they use illustrate some of

---

Box 9.2 Juca's story

"I came here [São Paulo] with the objective of progressing in life, to have something, which I was unable to get there [Pernambuco]. Until today I have not achieved any objective — but I do not reject my roots. São Paulo is a place of beauty, of development, of sophistication, of commercialization.

So here I am now in São Paulo struggling every-day to survive. Today I find myself unemployed and tomorrow who knows where I will find work, but returning to Pernambuco has never left my mind. What calls me there is the desire to live, to feel nature close, to enjoy life with greater freedom, to have time for my friends, to sit by a river or lie down by its bank and make a hole in the ground and, who knows, draw my sustenance from the waters. There it is easier to get things. Here things are very expensive. There you spend six months cutting sugar cane and then you are unemployed. Here it is easier to find work and eat a little bit better. I want to be the employer and employee of my own person. That is why I dream of going back to Pernambuco because there, in spite of difficulties and without work, one still lives better than here. I don't have such high-flying dreams. I dream of going back to my roots, of living without depending on a bus, on a certain time to get up and on a boss. I'd like to open up a business, a little bar, whatever, in order to live independently ... I saw a family that worked eight days in order to feed seven. That is unjust and cowardly of our government, which borrows I don't know how much money to give this country greater worth. There are good people who struggle and sacrifice themselves twelve hours a day or more like me when I was working. For Matarazzo I worked up to sixteen hours a

day. And today, where am I? Unemployed. And that is hard, it is unjust, to know that one has given one's blood and sweat but one is worth nothing ... Politics? I am not involved in politics because it only serves those who know how to debate and who have a lot of strength, for I have never seen a politician who is weak and has got anywhere. But there is a party which can do something for the North-Easterners and that's the Workers' Party. And Lula (the leader of the Workers' Party), he wants to advance workers; especially North-Easterners who are simple, peaceful but strong, and who have built São Paulo, working for the development of a state which is the spring-board of Brazil ...

... Life here is different in part for the following reasons. Pernambuco is a land with more folk-lore than São Paulo ... there people still exist who have the strength, the courage, the joy in themselves to join the June festivities which don't exist in São Paulo, even though they know they have to work for twelve hours at the end of a hoe inside a sugar cane field, risking their life for another's benefit. But here there are no certain times. Not there, there everything has a determined time. This is what I call tradition. São Paulo has no tradition. We created the Trio Pernambuco in order to remember the past ... it is an opportunity for me to be what I am and not to negate it. We may some day think of being professionals, but that depends on many opportunities and on knowledge of people who could help us because, on your own, you don't get anywhere. What is development? That depends on the person but, for example, if today I had achieved a purpose I would have developed, developed knowledge."

the themes already discussed. In reading their stories, notice how their experience of the changes brought about by industrialization in the Brazilian context define who they are.

Juca migrated to São Paulo from an area growing sugar cane on the coast of the North-Eastern state of Pernambuco when he was 15. He is now 35 and unemployed. For a few years he worked as a factory worker for Matarazzo, a firm he sued for not paying him overtime. He is also one of the founding members of a trio playing North-Eastern music in the homes of friends and relatives, in bars, at wedding parties and on other festive occasions celebrated by the population living on the outskirts of São Paulo.

Fatima came to São Paulo when she was nine years old. She has been working in a shoe factory for fourteen years, and is a co-ordinator of the Movement for Land (*Movimento sem Terra*), a grass-roots organization, active in rural and urban areas, struggling to obtain land, housing, sewage, light and water for the large mass of landless peasants and shanty town dwellers. Part of her work involves 'consciousness raising' and the political education of the members of several grass-roots organizations. Her life history is characterized by a political radicalization which developed quite suddenly when she took some courses on the nature of society organized by the Catholic Church. This led to a radical personal transformation of her identity as a woman.

Box 9.3   Fatima's story

"I have a very religious aunt who believes that everything is a sin. I was not supposed to go out or wear a low-cut dress. One night when I was waiting in a queue to pick up four tins of powdered milk, I rebelled and joined the Movement for Health and then the Movement for Land. I participated in the courses 'What is society' and 'How does society work' organized by the Catholic Basic Community. I began to wear sporty clothes, I put my rosary away and I lost weight. That is when the fights with my husband started. He did not approve of the change in me. One of the most important moments was my first land occupation with three thousand families. My job was to measure the land and partition it, there were people there who were engineers, architects, everything. Then the police came and pulled down the three thousand shacks. ... Today I see God in people — in the humble. I am particularly fond of the Gospel according to Saint Luke and the Book of Exodus. ... My work involves organizing other co-ordinators and various districts as well as the grass-roots work that leads to social transformation. People wake up in the morning at four, they go to work, they earn a pittance and are alienated ... my work of transformation with migrants is to make them see the causes of their poverty. I start, for example, with a drawing of an ox. They all know the ox.

The bankers, landowners and businessmen are in the filet, the people are where the head is, in the hooves and tail. And then they say, 'Oh, so we are in the tail?'... In another exercise I ask everybody to remember their childhood with sheets of newspaper. They make little boats and houses — their childhood illusions. Then suddenly, without any explanation, I take and destroy everything and explain, 'this is what the system does with your illusions'. These exercises are followed by discussion. They come to see that they don't just have obligations but rights. ... My illusions when I came here were to have my own house, to earn enough. The good thing about the North East was the joy of being together. We used to make our dolls with corn cobs, as there was nothing ready made. The bad thing was the strict upbringing. Here, North-Eastern culture disintegrates, they watch TV and listen to the radio, they only see the dream of getting rich. I married in order to get away from my father. I changed owners, and my husband married in order not to go to the army. My husband and I separated and he left me with all the debts. So, when the creditors came, the children put up a poster saying 'we have cancelled our debt'. And when my children were asked to write about what is good and what is bad for God, my daughter put under the heading of 'good' — land occupation."

Rural to urban migration in poetry

Now that we have explored how the process of migration is expressed in a 'way of life' and a new identity, we will consider how this experience of change is manifested at a different level of culture, or according to a different meaning of culture, expressed as 'artistic and intellectual products'. But first, a cautionary note. When trying to establish links between artistic products (poems, novels, musical forms or paintings) and social reality, it is important not to reduce these products to the status of mere reflections of social reality. The creative process and the aesthetic requirements of a particular form change artistic products into something which goes beyond a social document. Through its reshaping of language and perception, a poem or a novel creates an imaginative world of its own, enabling the reader to see reality in new and unusual ways. The skill with which this is done is part of the pleasure. Artistic products, nevertheless, can also be vehicles for communicating ways of seeing the world which move us to accept the world as it is or to change it. In this way, they connect us back to social reality. Artistic products are thus both part of, and independent of, social reality. As an example, in three poems written by peasants and rural labourers, we can detect the changes brought about by industrialization.

These poems are part of a peasant poetic tradition called string literature (*literatura de cordel*), so called because the booklets containing the poems have traditionally been sold on rural outdoor markets hung up on a string. Of medieval European origin, but also influenced by African and Amerindian elements, they were originally transmitted by travelling singers. In the late nineteenth century, the development of trade and industry in the North East gave rise to a small peasant artisan printing press which sold booklets of poems to a growing mass of transient rural workers. They contain epic medieval narratives, stories of love, tales of miracles and fantastic occurrences, religious teachings, critical commentaries on everyday life, accounts of historical events, and descriptions of the deeds and exploits of heroic figures including the bandit 'Lampião' (Figure 9.3) and the messianic proph-

Figure 9.3   A booklet containing an epic poem on the bandit 'Lampião, The Governor General of Hell'.

ets of the North East who promised to liberate their followers from poverty and oppression.

As you can imagine, given the power landowners wielded over the peasantry and rural labourers, the relationship between landowner and peasant is a core theme in string literature; it forms part of the genre categorized as 'booklets of heroic deeds'. Read the poem on page 264 and try to determine the way in which this relationship is represented. As you can see from the cover (Figure 9.4), it is about the heroic deeds of a peasant named João Canguçú on the Gameleira sugar mill (*engenho*).

One day the fearless and robust João Canguçú from the rough hinterland of the North East appears at the sugar-mill to seek employment. When he hears of the landowner's inhumanity,

Autor: Proprietário:
APOLONIO ALVES DOS SANTOS

O Heroismo de João Canguçu
no Engenho Gameleira

Figure 9.4

THE HEROISM OF JOÃO CANGUÇU IN THE GAMELEIRA SUGAR MILL

No Engenho Gameleira	The sugar mill of Gameleira
estado do Maranhão	in the state of Maranhão
foi antro da malvadeza	was a cavern of wickedness
covil da ingratidão	a den of ingratitude
abrigo da falsidade	the shelter of perfidy
abismo da traição	a pit of treachery
E era dono desse engenho	The owner of this mill
o coronel Edmundo	was the coronel* Edmundo
tipo muito agigantado	a man of gigantic build
magro, careca e corcundo	thin, bald and hunchbacked
foi o ente mais perverso	the most evil man
que já se viu neste mundo ...	the world has ever seen ...
Assim ele praticava	And there he acted
ali o que pretendia	in whatever way he inclined
matava gente e queimava	He killed and burnt people
e punição não havia	no punishment was there
daquela negra traição	for such dark treachery
ninguém não se defendia ...	nor any defence ...
Ali os trabalhadores	There the workers
não viam nunca um tostão	never caught sight of a penny
tudo quanto precisavam	everything they needed
compravam no barracão	they bought in the sugar-mill shop
desde do calçado a roupa	from their shoes to the clothes
a toda alimentação ...	as well as all their the food ...
Vestido em roupa de mescla	Dressed in colourful clothes
calçado de botinão	wearing tall sturdy boots
chapéu quebrado na frente	a hat tipped to one side
fumando n'um cachimbão	and smoking a pipe
quem o visse só dizia	anybody who saw him would think
ser Cabra de Lampião ...	'this is the brigand Lampião' ...

* Coronel is the term given to large landowners or political bosses in the North East.

the appalling working conditions and the threat of death under which the labourers are forced to work, João Canguçú takes up their cause and, in an armed battle with the perfidious landowner, sees that justice is done. Having personally vanquished the landowner he informs the authorities of the atrocities which took place on the mill. He is rewarded with a medal and money, and a new and benevolent landowner takes over the sugar-mill of Gameleira.

With vivid images this poem, which is representative of many of the poems of string literature, describes a situation characteristic of peasant life from the point of view of the peasant. One essential aspect of this poem is the way in which the conflict between peasant and landowner is perceived and resolved. The unhappiness at the sugar-mill arises out of an inequality in power and resources and is resolved at an individual level through the triumph of João Canguçú. While the landowner is the personification of evil, the latter is the personification of virile courage and justice. Harmony is restored not through a change in the structure of economic relations but by the replacement of the wicked landowner, who failed to reward his worker's labour with money or patronage.

Going back to our initial discussion of popular culture and hegemony, the social function of this poem and many others like it seems ambiguous. On the one hand they reveal an acute awareness of, and attempt to address, the oppression experienced by a subordinate class and its calls for justice. It does not, however, fundamentally challenge the traditional economic structure and patron-dependency which underlie this situation. There are exceptions to this pattern.

In the 1960s during the Popular Culture Movements and as a result of the emergence of rural trade unions, social change as a way of improving the living conditions of the peasantry appears frequently in string literature. A significant change also took place in the 1970s. The rising cost of paper and the spread of radio and television forced many of the artisan printing presses to close. A larger publishing house in São Paulo took over a considerable share of the market for this poetry. Using industrialized methods of produc-

tion and distribution, it has replaced the original wood-cut covers with coloured prints in the comic book format.

With rural migration to the city and the confrontation with a 'new way of life', new themes emerged which revealed a variety of responses to modernity and industrialization. Consider the poem on pages 267–268, called 'The Life of a North-Easterner in São Paulo'. What themes and images strike you? The poem is about Norbertino who journeys from the hinterland of the State of Bahia to São Paulo, leaving behind not only work on the land but a way of life in which 'you grow up listening to stories/of love and courage/... where 'you speak of werewolves/and other enchantments'. The poem contrasts life on the subsistence plot which belonged to his father, with life in São Paulo.

Although promising jobs, entertainment and money, São Paulo appears as a world of illusion and alienation governed by the merciless rhythm of the clock. After great efforts, Norbertino finds work in a factory. Gradually though, he makes friends and, in a confrontation with management, discovers the power of collective action.

What is striking about this poem is the presence of some of the themes that occur in both Juca's and Fatima's accounts of their lives: an idealization of the social relations of the rural context accompanied by criticism, absent in the previous poem on João Canguçú, of the structure of social relations. The poet sees these social relations as the cause of Norbertino's fate and as something that can be changed through trade union involvement.

A critical stance towards the social order is present in a number of the poems of urbanized 'string literature': focusing on the external debt, the rising cost of living and the use of nuclear energy. In some cases, the themes are linked explicitly to trade union organization. The poem 'Accidents at work and in the construction industry' exhorts construction workers, the majority of whom are rural migrants, to join the union and to take measures to avoid accidents. At general assemblies of the Construction Workers' Union, the booklet has been used with a film in which the

THE LIFE OF A NORTH-EASTERNER IN SÃO PAULO

Mesmo os tempos ingratos
trazendo dificuldades
todo mundo era unido
e naquela sociedade
uma mão outra lavando
e a dureza levando
até com naturalidade

Even in unforgiving times
bringing many a difficulty
everyone was united,
for in that society
each gave another a hand
bearing the hardship
in a natural way...

E aqueles bois bonitos
dos tempos de plantação
onde o povo alegre
plantando milho e feijão
tomava muita cachaça
comia e fazia graça
sambava com devoção

And the beautiful oxen
during sowing time,
when the people joyfully
plant corn and black beans
drink plenty of sugar-cane brandy,
eat, make merry
and dance with abandon

...

...

São Paulo, então, não era
o lugar só de requeza
aonde todos viviam
sufocado na grandeza
como ele viera pensando
pois assim que foi chegando
deu com a cara na pobreza

São Paulo then was not
a place only of riches,
where everyone lived
suffocated in wealth
as he had thought
for no sooner had he arrived
poverty stared him straight in the face

...

...

No meio do maquinário
as pessoas se moviam
tantos dentro da fábrica
mas um ao outro não via:
todos eram indiferentes
pareciam estar ausentes
da vida e da alegria

Among the machines
people moved around
so many in the same factory
yet no- one saw the face of the other:
all seemed indifferent
life and joy there
seemed to be absent

Naquele ritimo louco	In that crazy rhythm
de tantas horas por dia	of so many hours a day
e o barulho das máquinas	and the noise of the machines
que os ouvidos aturdia...	which left your ears stunned
as pessoas não se olhando	no-one looked at each other
e o encarregado passando	and the foreman passed
medindo o que fazia	measuring what was done...
Via em cada situacão,	In each and every situation
o medo e a precisão	he saw fear and need
a falta de confiança	lack of trust
e também de informacão ...	and also of information...
Olhava a realidade	He looked at reality
e dizia: -Na verdade	and said: In truth
nunca houve abolição	the abolition of slavery never took place...
Foi então entendendo	He then understood
as relações sociais	the social relations
do sistema que exige	of a system which demands
cada vez se correr mais	that you run ever faster
sem fazer muito segredo	and without further ado
vai nos empurrando o medo	we are driven
de ser passado prá trás	by the fear of being pushed under
...	*...*
Deste acontecimento	From this event
ele tirou uma lição...	he learnt one lesson...
aprendeu que na verdade	he learnt that in truth
só a solidariedad	only solidarity
suplanta a escravidão	can overcome slavery

poem itself is recited to discuss dangers on the construction site. Here we see a traditional form, originating in an oral culture, being used with the modern medium of film to raise the political awareness of the workers. This procedure validates their previous rural identity, yet also offers them tools to gain a greater control over their lives in the urban context (see Figure 9.5).

Figure 9.5 Poem on 'Accidents at work in the construction industry', published by the Construction Workers' Trade Union of São Paulo.

Not all poems in the urban context take this stance. In many the modern, secular, industrial world is seen from the point of view of an idealized, traditional past in which filial respect, marital fidelity and religious faith have not yet been undermined by greed, ambition and sexual promiscuity. Satan, a central figure in Popular Catholicism, whose demonic qualities are depicted in luring and loving detail in many of the poems of string literature, also appears in an urbanized form. Sometimes, in booklets such as 'Satan blowing the furnaces of the nuclear energy plant' (see Figure 9.6) he appears as the destructive force of modern technology, and at other times, as for example in 'Baby devil appeared in São Paulo' (see Figure 9.7) as the 'administrator of the modern world' in which children disobey their parents and women transgress their prescribed gender roles of chaste wife and devoted mother.

So, the experience of rural to urban migrants, faced with new patterns of life in the city and the demands of industrialization, is a complex one.

Figure 9.7 *'Baby devil appeared in São Paulo'.*

Figure 9.6 *'Satan blowing the furnaces of the nuclear power plant'.*

This experience is by no means an automatic response to urban-industrial life. Taking cultural change into account helps us to understand the impact and significance of diverse experiences: others, as we shall see below, have experienced industrialization under urban life in quite a different way.

Samba Schools and industrialization

This final section looks at a quite different group or 'agent' and the way in which its way of life and cultural manifestations are related to the process of industrialization in Brazil. The Samba Schools, the carnival associations of Rio de Janeiro, emerged in the early twentieth century. In order to understand their form and significance it is necessary, however, to first consider the relationship between two key institutions: slavery and Afro-Brazilian religion.

Since the early sixteenth century, not long after the Portuguese had landed in Brazil, slave labour became a cornerstone of the colonial economy (Figure 9.8). Africans, mainly from the western coast of Africa, were transported to Brazil to work in the sugar-cane plantations and mines as well as in the cities as domestic slaves and later, in the nineteenth century, in the expanding coffee plantations of the south (Figure 9.9). Although attempts were made by groups of fugitive slaves, called *quilombos*, to free themselves from slavery, they were unable to unite in defence of their interests. Resistance to their oppression was expressed mainly through culture, in particular, through religion and in ways which led to the interpenetration of African and European elements.

Figure 9.8   A lithograph of a Rio de Janeiro slave market, from a book published in 1835.

Figure 9.9   'Coffee' — an oil painting by Candido Portinari, 1935.

There are today in Brazil different varieties of Afro-Brazilian religions, some of them incorporating elements from Catholicism as well as Amerindian mythology and the French 'Spiritism' of Alain Kardec. All of them, however, stem from a common Afro-Brazilian religion known as *Candomblé*.

According to the Brazilian scholar Edison Carneiro, the first temples of *Candomblé* were set up by black women in the city of Salvador in the State of Bahia where the greater freedom blacks enjoyed in comparison to their counterparts in rural areas enabled Afro-Brazilian religion to flourish.

The core of the *Candomblé* cult is centred on the personal relationship between its followers and the gods which make up the pantheon of male and female African divinities known as *orishás*. One of the most important ways in which a believer enters into communication with his or her god is through rituals of possession in which the personality of the god is embodied. This occurs through dance and to the accompaniment of music. The extent to which the god has become incarnated in his or her follower is manifested in the degree to which the god's personality is expressed through dance and mimicry. Resistance to the destruction of the self and the ethnic group brought about by slave labour was thus expressed, not only in specific religious representations and rituals, but in the gestural language of the body. As will become clearer presently, this function of the body as a repository of ethnic identity was to have important consequences for the way in which blacks negotiated their social position in Brazil as it began to industrialize.

In the early twentieth century, as blacks fled from the plantations to the cities following the abolition of slavery in 1888, the *Candomblé* cults became centres in which not only African traditions and social relations were maintained, but in which blacks found refuge from the experience of racial discrimination and unemployment.

It is in this context, and as a result of the confluence of various factors connected to the industrialization of Brazil, that the cultural practices related to *Candomblé* go beyond the confines of the religious temple and create, in the process, profane forms of dance and music. In an unfavourable position on the labour market of the expanding urban centres, blacks congregated in the outskirts and hills of Rio de Janeiro, giving rise to a black urban subculture composed of workers, public servants, artisans, small businessmen and a host of semi-employed or unemployed individuals living on the 'margins' of society, geographically and culturally.

Marked by the memory of slave labour and the experience of exploitation and discrimination in the new social order, this culture was characterized by a fusion of rhythmic structures and musical forms tied to the religious context of *Candomblé*, and an ethos based on a contempt for work, money and authority. Thus, in sharing a similar predicament, forms of social organization and social interaction emerged in which a distinctive black identity was expressed. At the same time, the greater density and mobility of urban life led to a more intense and frequent interaction between European and African culture, producing new musical forms such as the *choro* and the, now forgotten, *maxixe*. One of the most important musical forms, however, was the samba; characterized by a collective or 'paired' form of composition, a syncopated rhythm and a melancholic-irreverent eulogy of life on the margins of society. Gradually, the repercussions of this process were amplified by the emergence of a record industry and radio stations which, in the 1930s, began to transmit the first sambas.

One specific cultural practice through which this new urban dynamic was revealed was the annual carnival festivities. With urbanization and capitalist development, two different forms of carnivalesque entertainment emerged. In the private hotels, the theatres and cafés, the middle classes, imitating the masked balls of Paris and Venice, danced to the sound of waltzes and polkas; in the streets, citizens were confronted with the image of groups of costumed blacks parading to the syncopated rhythms of samba, invading the urban landscape and transgressing class and geographical boundaries. The parades took the form of the religious processions held in the north of Brazil and known as *ranchos*. These were originally festive occasions celebrating the Nativity through a procession of allegorical floats. The procession was preceded by a master of ceremonies and a standard bearer holding the group's insignia.

The nature of the procession and the themes are intimately connected with the significance of carnival in Brazilian society. A characteristic of carnival is that, for a brief and intense period, the shared norms which uphold the social order, the social divisions of class, ethnic group, gender, and status group are temporarily relaxed. This momentary freedom from social control allows for the emergence of an idealized image of a world without inequality, a world of communion in which existing hierarchies have been transgressed or inverted. Symbolically, this 'relativization' or questioning of reality is expressed through satire, fantasy and parody, through the use of mask and disguise. Men are dressed as women, the poor as nobles. Humans take on animal form, and all the figures normally banished to the world of illusion and the uncanny territory of the unconscious take centre stage: princes and kings, ghosts, skeletons, devils, gods of ancient Greece and Rome, 'savages', criminals, clowns and prostitutes. The 'lower' sphere of the body, with its forbidden impulses and desires, displaces the 'higher' sphere of moral decorum, while samba and the sambistas transform the impersonal space of the street into a world in which pleasure replaces the worry and toil of everyday life.

This utopian or 'carnivalized' ideal of a world upside-down coexists uneasily, however, with the organization of the carnival festivities which are structured in accordance with definite differences in wealth, status and power. The Samba Schools and the carnival have, to a greater or lesser extent, been transformed from organizations which express the reality and identity of the black population to institutionalized festivities tied to economic and political interests in Brazilian society at large.

In the mid-1930s, during the populist regime of Getulio Vargas, these groups, initially seen as a threat to Brazil's self image as essentially white and European, acquired the name of Samba Schools. Their procession was officially organized by the state authorities in the form of a competition for a cash prize. One of Brazil's major tourist attractions, they now each consist of up to 4000 members and their parade can only be seen from relatively expensive stalls. Clearly, since the 1920s a significant change has taken place.

Let us now look at the nature and social function of Samba Schools in greater detail.

The Schools are active not only during the three climactic days of carnival but throughout the year. They organize public rehearsals to finance their activities and prepare for the coming carnival by sewing costumes, making floats, inventing new themes and organizing the percussionists and dancers so that the whole multi-media ensemble parades past the spectator in a harmonious configuration of colour, dance, song, rhythm and theme. Since the demise of the military regime, Samba School themes have emerged around the subject of torture, the abolition of slavery, and social injustice, including visions of a 'utopian' Brazil without external debt, social injustice and environmental degradation (Figure 9.10).

Figure 9.10 Despite the commercialization of the carnival parade, it can act as a vehicle of social criticism. This float represents the predicament of Brazil's poor — malnourished and surrounded by vultures.

The Schools also function as important neighbourhood organizations. They are present at birthdays, weddings, funerals and religious events celebrating the neighbourhood's patron saint. Recently, they have also set up workshops and Schools for children through which to transmit and maintain carnival traditions. The School thus sustains and reproduces a broad network of social relations and shared values. To belong to the 'world of samba' one must fully identify with its values and this requires a long apprenticeship. It is not necessary or sufficient to be just a proficient dancer or composer.

Since the 1930s the Samba Schools have changed considerably: they have grown in size and significance and acquired an official status as international tourist attractions. The organizational requirements and the need for capital investment in musical instruments has had a variety of consequences. The Schools are financed partly by the state tourism agency Riotour and partly by the income they acquire performing outside the carnival period. They are also supported by sponsorship from the 'magnates' of a profitable illegal lottery game known as *jogo do bicho* (the 'animal game') and money from drug dealers. In the absence of adequate housing and services, these sponsors often provide funds for nurseries and building materials. One result of this strategy of survival is that many Samba Schools are simultaneously connected to the illegal world of gambling and drugs and to the official world of the state.

The new pressures have also led to a rationalization of the Schools, introducing a greater division of labour and involving white professionals such as lawyers, accountants and administrators in positions of power and influence. As the competition is judged by officially-appointed judges that are drawn, in general, from the white middle-classes, some Schools appoint white professional artists to devise their costumes and select their parade theme. This has, to some extent, led to a reproduction of the social hierarchy of society at large within the Schools. Moreover, since the parade has become a nationally televised spectacle, it has also become a means of self-promotion for many of the white personalities of the media

élite who adorn the floats in positions of prominence. This is also the case for many samba composers within the Schools for whom the transmission of their music by the record industry is a way of escaping poverty. As one of the most popular televised spectacles, the parade generates a considerable revenue for television companies, advertisers and Riotour (Figure 9.11). In the struggle over contracts and the appropriation of profits, the Samba Schools have, on the whole, not been able to capitalize on the fruits of their parade; except during the mid-1980s when the radical League of Samba Schools obtained a 40% cut on the tickets for the parade and set up its own recording company.

These changes have also had repercussions within the network of social relations of the black community. As School composers have become professionalized and their work is tailored to a consumer market, samba has lost some of its improvisatory and collective character. In addition, the content of the theme songs has become more and more dissociated from the experience of the Samba School participants. Gradually, then, one can see how the specific music of a subordinate group in society has acquired new meaning. On the one hand, samba has become an exportable symbol of national identity. The value accorded to black music, however, is not reflected in an improvement of the socio-economic conditions of Brazil's black population.

Could it be argued that samba and the Samba Schools have become disconnected from their original roots in a 'culture of resistance'? Looking at the history of the Schools, could it be argued that their spirit of opposition has been absorbed by the hegemonic culture of white society as Brazil has industrialized? The answer to both questions is ambiguous: both 'yes' and 'no'. We have seen how the structure of the Samba Schools and the carnival parade have changed with the development of modern Brazil. In the absence of significant black representation within official political institutions, they remain as important civic organizations sustaining a black identity and memory. In order to change the social position of blacks and to undermine the still dominant ideology that whites are inherently superior, this

Figure 9.11   This image of a float with tropical fruit, including opened coconuts with straws, illustrates clearly how the Samba Schools have changed since the 1970s. The float reproduces the advertising image of Brazil as a tropical, 'exotic' paradise.

is an important precondition. Moreover, by virtue of their carnivalesque character, the Schools maintain a utopian image of a different world in which the prevalent social hierarchy has been dissolved or inverted. To what extent this fosters real social change, or merely allows society to continue as before after the tensions and frustrations it generates have been released during carnival, is a matter of continued and heated debate.

How do samba and carnival relate to industrialization? The following are not meant as definitive answers, but as food for thought.

- The emergence of a black subculture, and the manner in which it temporarily occupied an urban space physically and through the amplifying power of radio and the record industry, could be seen as a gesture through which a subordinate, marginalized group in society makes itself visible and audible, and affirms its identity.

- This attempt to occupy a 'cultural space' could, in turn, be seen as an attempt by the black population, deprived of the basic rights of citizenship — work, housing, services, education, political representation and cultural validation — to acquire a 'voice' in the newly formed republic. (Brazil's monarchy was abolished in 1889.)

- The fact that this identity and the 'right to a voice' were expressed primarily through dance and music reveals the way in which the language of the body and musical expression functioned as a means of resistance to the dehumanizing effects of slavery. Moreover, the fact that the content of samba lyrics frequently revolved around the rejection of work indicates that wage-labour offered the working classes (blacks, in particular) few opportunities for advancement or self-improvement through work. As described in earlier discussions of Brazilian models of development, industrialization has gone hand in hand with marked social inequalities. The Samba Schools could thus be seen as alternative 'civic organizations' through which a form of 'unofficial citizenship' has taken shape.

- Returning to the theoretical discussion at the beginning of this chapter, and at the risk of simplifying reality, it is possible to understand the emergence of the Samba Schools in terms of the three concepts of culture. They are artistic productions which arose out of the 'way of life' of a specific ethnic group. They also stand, to a greater or lesser extent, in an oppositional relationship to the hegemonic culture of white society; a society which knows how to partially absorb the oppositional characteristics of the Samba Schools.

Summary of Chapter 9

1 This chapter looks at cultural change and industrialization, both from a structural, societal level and from the perspective of certain social groups or agents.

2 At both these levels, culture is seen as a struggle for hegemony; the interaction between dominant and subordinate cultural forms.

3 In Brazil, the struggle for hegemony first crystallized in the period from the 1920s to the 1940s. It occurred both in the newly emerging notion of 'The Nation' through populism, and in the cultural expression of 'The People' through popular culture movements.

4 The populist alliance, in one form or another, continued right up to the military coup of 1964. At this point, the consensus over the direction and beneficiaries of development and industrialization collapsed.

5   After the 1964 coup, the popular culture movements were stamped out, as they were perceived as a political threat to the new social order and a block to Brazil's 'modernization'. The mass media, particularly television, were promoted by the military government in order to gain popular consent to the regime's new model of development. Highly selective material praising Brazil's economic development was broadcast. TV Globo was crucial in this and later manipulations of public opinion.

6   The struggle for hegemony can also be seen through the lens of individual or group experiences of migration and industrialization. The cultural impact of rural to urban migration is the transformation (but not complete loss) of an old 'way of life' intertwined with a new, urban 'way of life'. This synthesis of representations, images, beliefs and concepts is the means by which migrants experience and define themselves.

7   Such changes also manifest themselves through another notion of culture: artistic and intellectual products. Cultural expressions, such as poetry, are both part of, and independent of, social reality. The 'string literature' of the North East of Brazil is a good example of the mixture of fact and fiction, and shows how cultural values become transformed in an urban context but are still expressed in a form belonging to another cultural context.

8   The question of agency in the struggle for hegemony is shown in quite a different context: the Samba Schools of Rio de Janeiro. From their original role as a 'culture of resistance' for black Brazilians who were marginalized from white society (a process which dates back to slavery), the Samba Schools' spirit of opposition has, to some extent, been absorbed by the hegemonic culture. Nevertheless, Samba Schools remain important civic organizations which sustain a black memory and identity.

10

INDUSTRIALIZATION AND ENVIRONMENT

PAUL SMITH

"The 'environment' that is in the process of construction in less developed countries is separated from our own by underdevelopment. It is differently located, not simply in geographical terms, but in terms of its role in the development process. It follows that the 'environment' in less developed countries is an arena for different social aspirations and material struggles."

(Redclift, 1987)

Environmental issues are now high on the international political agenda. This increased concern about the environment has implications for development and industrialization throughout the world, and particularly in the less developed world. Discussion about global warming, deforestation and pollution of the oceans is affecting attitudes to economic growth and development at a local, national and international level. But taking effective political action to deal with these problems is not simple. Whose problems are they? Where does the responsibility for action rest? In the less developed countries (LDCs), the problems will not be perceived in the same way as they are perceived in the fully industrialized nations.

This chapter examines more than just the physical consequences of particular forms of development. As Redclift asserts, environmental problems are really development problems. So to understand environmental problems we have to look at the political and economic systems within which they occur.

There are clear implications here for the processes of economic development and industrialization throughout the developing world. Some people, who could be called environmental determinists, say that two hundred years of mindless capitalist expansion have brought us to the abyss of environmental ruin, and that the only way out is to seek radical alternatives to the economic growth model. In contrast, consider this quote from the World Commission on Environment and Development, established under the auspices of the United Nations in 1983 to take a global view of the relationship between economic growth and environmental impact:

"It is both futile and indeed an insult to the poor to tell them that they must remain in poverty to protect the environment."

(Brundtland, 1987)

The social processes which underlie political and economic processes also have to be appreciated and understood alongside the purely environmental. It is worthwhile emphasizing this point. It is easy to label people who write about the environment as 'environmentalists' and assume that they all prioritize the protection of the natural environment at the expense of human social and economic needs. In this chapter, we are considering the environment not as a separate issue, but within a wider social and economic context. To this end, the following questions are addressed.

Q How has environmental thinking developed in relation to development theory?

Q What is 'sustainable development' and what options do the LDCs have for industrialization?

Q How does the relationship between industrialization and the environment differ from one developing country to another? For example, what prospects do Thailand, India and Mexico each have of achieving sustainable development?

10.1 Environment and industry

Environment versus industrialization?

The concept of 'environment' now brings with it a whole range of images and connotations that come from the early days of the Industrial Revolution in Britain. From the early nineteenth century onwards, a rich and critical literature developed, presenting a variety of images of social deprivation alongside environmental pollution and degradation, brought about by the unbridled forces of industrial capitalism' (Figure 10.1). What much of the writings had in common was a dislike, ranging from muted distaste to outright condemnation of industrialism. By 'industrialism' they meant the wider social transformations associated with industrialization. Underlying the prose, however, was a diversity of political beliefs which ranged from romantic notions of returning to some sort of pre-industrial rural idyll, through the Utopian socialist visions of William Morris, to the revolutionary socialism of Marx and Engels.

The idealization of a pre-industrial order, where the emphasis is on the purely physical or ecological consequences of economic growth, evades fundamental questions about social and economic conditions. This is particularly relevant when we come to look at the LDCs. In Morris's writings we can see ample evidence of his desire to return to

Figure 10.1   Environmental impact at the heart of the Industrial Revolution in Britain: Coalbrookdale around 1830.

Industrialism: The social changes associated with the Industrial Revolution. Many 19th century writers saw industrialism as a disturbance of the 'natural order'. The Industrial Revolution changed fundamentally the means of production and the accompanying social and economic relationships. It also changed attitudes to the use of resources and the relationship between society and the environment.

a simple form of life, which find an echo in some contemporary 'green' literature. Yet he also left us with a rich legacy of ideas that are deserving of our serious attention today. His longstanding hatred of the utilitarian and imperialist values of capitalism led to his critique of the abstract idea of 'production'. Instead of the simple capitalist *quantum* of production, he began asking questions about what *kinds* of production. He

also demonstrated his awareness of Britain's imperialism abroad. He wrote:

> "Have nothing in your home which you do not either believe to be beautiful or know to be useful. …
>
> To further the spread of education in art, Englishmen in India are actively destroying the very sources of that education — jewellery, metalwork, pottery, calico printing, brocade weaving, carpets — all the famous and historical arts of the great peninsula have been thrust aside for the advantage of any paltry scrap of so-called commerce."
>
> (Morris, quoted in Thompson, 1976)

The essence of this argument finds a deal of relevance today. Rightly or wrongly Morris's ideas have tended to find support amongst the wealthier middle classes in Britain, perhaps as a way of coping with life in the late twentieth

Figure 10.2   Workers in a factory in Lusaka, loading cans of chemical waste onto a truck.

century. By contrast, the influence of Marx and Engels has been both dramatic and far reaching. Their late 20th century critics say that the ideas of Marx and Engels, by replacing one form of imperialism, industrial capitalism, with another, the conquest of Nature, have been responsible for the ruination of environments on a massive scale. Far from being 'anti-industrial' they saw industrialization as a progressive force, whose full realization to eradicate poverty was being impeded because of the struggle of class interests within capitalism (see Chapter 12 of *Allen & Thomas, 1992*).

The rhetoric of environmental conquest was all too readily translated into reality, as has become depressingly apparent now that the political barriers have been lowered in the USSR and in Eastern Europe. Yet, as we shall see later, contemporary Marxist argument has an important contribution to make to the debate about environment and development. Also, in what now seems a prophetic vein, Engels wrote in his *Dialectics of Nature* that we shall never understand the ethos of expansionism if we fail to remember that:

> "We ourselves are part of nature, and that what is involved in this mastery and conquest is going to have its effect on us. Let us not flatter ourselves overmuch on account of our human victories over Nature. For each such victory, Nature takes its revenge on us. We are reminded that we belong to Nature, and that all-over mastery of it consists in the fact that we have the advantage over all other creatures of being able to learn its laws and apply them correctly."

> (Engels, 1889; quoted in Williams, 1982)

Although this argument rests heavily upon the metaphor of conquest, it could equally be seen to reside in some contemporary ethic about sustainability. This serves to illustrate the value of delving, however briefly, into the history of ideas. There is nothing new about environmental concern. The predominant values that come through to current environmentalist thinking are those which tend to be highly critical of industrialism and industrialized societies.

Environment and industrialization?

The modern environmentalist movement can be said to have started in the late 1960s and early 1970s, with the formation of pressure groups like Friends of the Earth, which were openly committed to direct political involvement. Their message, while being an overtly political one, was scarcely new: that the only way to prevent environmental and ecological catastrophe was to change fundamentally the materialist and consumerist values of industrialized societies. Much of the expressed anxiety stressed the limits to the ability of the earth to sustain current (1970s) levels of economic and population growth, consumption of resources, and the destruction of whole ecosystems through industrial pollution and modern agricultural methods. (See Chapter 5 of *Allen & Thomas, 1992* for further explanation.)

There was a literary boom in 'doom and gloom' with titles like *The Population Bomb, How to be a Survivor* and *Blueprint for Survival* becoming bestsellers. (Figure 10.3 provides an indication of the shock tactics used.) Internationally, the predictions of impending crisis reached a peak in 1972 with two significant events: the publication of *The Limits to Growth* from the 'Club of Rome' (Meadows *et al.*, 1972), and the United Nations Conference on the Human Environment in Stockholm.

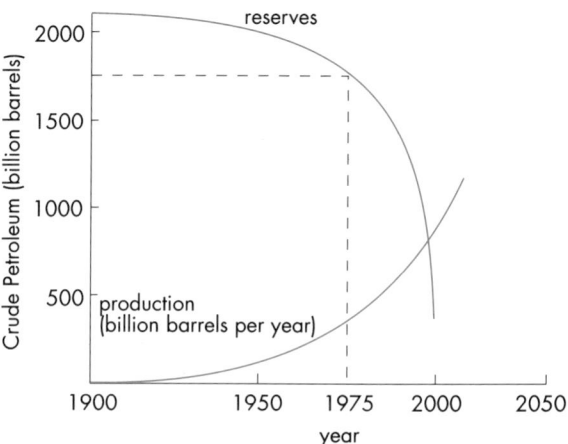

Figure 10.3   Predictions of world reserves of crude petroleum, assuming an exponentially increasing rate of consumption, according to Goldsmith et al., *1972.*

Limits to Growth used models of future resource use and population to foretell inevitable catastrophe by the year 2000 unless international action was taken immediately. The solution was seen in terms of achieving a stable world population and a steady state economy (in which growth was not the primary or stimulating ingredient). The Stockholm Conference was somewhat less alarmist. It placed more emphasis on inequalities between nations and set some important initiatives in motion (like the Law of the Seas Conferences). It is now regarded as a landmark for progress on environmental issues.

Several themes which come out of this brief examination of the history of modern environmentalist thought are pertinent to the relationship between the environment and development in the Third World. This is exemplified by two quotations from the writings of Raymond Williams.

> "We shall get nowhere in thinking about these problems [of industrial development and environmental impact] if we think that it is only the distinctive forms of modern industrial production that represent the problems of living well and sensibly on the earth."

> "Productive growth is not the abolition of poverty. What matters is the way production is organized, the way the products are distributed. It is also the way in which priorities between different forms of production are decided."

> (Williams, 1982)

This presents us with an alternative to, on the one hand, the depressing predictions of the 'ecodoomsters' and on the other, the technological over-optimism of the 'free marketeers' whose dominating ideology was in the ascendency during the 1980s.

Such ideas about how industrial development affects the environment do not tie in neatly with the different theories of economic development, which take different views of how industrial production is organized and controlled. Nevertheless, in unravelling the links between all of these it is useful to start with the two main approaches described in Chapters 5 and 6.

(i) *Structuralist* approaches emphasize:

> the need for transformation of economic and social structures;

> the importance of ownership and control of resources;

> the key role of industrialization.

(ii) *Neo-liberal* approaches emphasize the key role of markets over non-market (e.g. government) regulation.

However there is a third approach which appears to be more relevant to analysis of environment issues.

(iii) An explicitly *environmental* approach makes safeguarding the environment a priority, emphasizing such concepts as 'zero growth' option, and a steady-state economy. It is often associated with an 'appropriate technology' perspective emphasizing small scale and 'local' initiatives (possibly along the lines of E F Schumacher's *Small is Beautiful*, 1973).

The neo-liberal approach seems to represent the very antithesis of an explicitly environmentalist approach. After all, critiques of *laissez-faire* capitalism have provided the focus for argument for successive generations of the majority of environmental thinkers. Yet some of the most persuasive political and economic arguments, purportedly embracing a concern for environment, are emerging from neo-liberal approaches.

Another apparent contradiction arises with some of the more extreme environmentalist approaches. The political implications of attempting to implement the policies of the so-called 'deep ecologists' are such that the term 'ecofascism' has been used to describe them.

However, the structuralist approaches and the 'appropriate technology' environmentalist approach attempt to address the questions of economic growth, the way production is organized and the way products are distributed.

A common point of debate amongst all three approaches has been the notion of sustainable development.

10.2 Sustainable development

What does 'sustainable development' mean in terms of the relationship between industrialization and environment in the less developed world? Can it best be achieved by a neo-liberal approach or a structuralist approach? Or is it more appropriate to take an environmental approach with appropriate forms of technology and an emphasis on 'local' initiatives? Should we consider the environment *with* industrialization rather than the environment *versus* industrialization?

Towards sustainability

"Sustainable development is development that meets the needs of the present without compromising the ability of future generations to meet their own needs. It contains within it two principal concepts:

- *needs*, in particular those of the world's poor, to which over-riding priority should be given
- *limitations,* imposed by the state of technology and social organizations, on the environment's ability to meet present and future needs."

(Brundtland, 1987)

This definitive statement emerged from the United Nations World Commission on Environment and Development, chaired in the 1980s by the Prime Minister of Norway, Gro Harlem Brundtland. In fact, definitions of the concept have proliferated, leaving the sceptical observer to surmise that 'sustainable development' is merely a result of the latest political bandwagon. The richest nations are all trying to show concern for global environmental issues and to respond to what they perceive as the needs of the LDCs. However, the concept does deserve our serious consideration.

From the Brundtland Report definition we may deduce a number of serious concerns in relation to industry and environment in the less developed world:

- concern about the relationship between resource use, population growth and technological advancement
- concern about the production and distribution of industrial and energy resources amongst the less developed and more developed nations
- concern about uneven development, about the gross imbalances between the rich and poor nations
- implicit concern about economic dominance and ideological differences
- concern about environmental degradation and ecological destruction.

By focusing on human need and on development issues Brundtland appears to be offering a fundamental challenge to the materialist and consumerist values of the industrialized world (the North). The Report provides clear evidence for the links between poverty and environment in the LDCs. It sets out an agenda for action, particularly for the more developed nations. Yet for its critics, despite the considerable participation of many less developed nations in drawing it up, the Report represents the perspective of the North on what is best for the South, and it is full of contradictions.

A critical look at the findings of the Brundtland Report raises a whole series of questions which are not unique to the environmental aspects of development. Is economic growth synonymous with development? Is economic growth an adequate measure of development? What is it that is to be sustained; levels of production or levels of consumption? This last is a critical distinction. It is the patterns of consumption in the more developed world that makes development unsustainable on a global level. But the main focus for development is necessarily production. Can sustainable development really be concerned with meeting human needs, maintaining economic growth and conserving 'natural capital' at one and the same time?

The Brundtland Report goes into considerable detail over a range of issues, such as population, food, industrialization and urban growth. It explains the basis for concern, providing an agenda for achieving sustainable development, and proposing the institutional reforms that will be

Figure 10.4   Recycling is a routine activity in most of the Third World and a major source of informal employment: recycling shoes in Cairo, Egypt.

needed both nationally and internationally. (If you are interested in going into this in more depth, you should read the Report or at least the summary of it. See references at the end of this book.)

Certainly, the emphasis of Brundtland is environment *and* development, environment *with* industrialization, using appropriate technological means to achieve sustainable growth in both developed and developing countries. There is clearly an empathy with Williams' thinking here. But, perhaps inevitably, the World Commission did not, as Williams did, go on to argue how ecological, political and economic thought could, and should, come together in a new 'brand' of politics, underpinned by a progressive socialist commitment. The Brundtland Report is laced with references to the 'need for political will'. But it falls short in explaining how that is to be exercised and how the necessary radical reforms are to come about.

The entire credibility of the Report hinges on the premise that major economic growth can be achieved in ways that sustain and even enhance environmental capital. It argues that development, primarily through industrialization, is the best way of achieving population control, and that growing populations should be sustained at economic levels 'above the minimum' to satisfy fundamental needs, to improve the overall quality of life. This would mean an increase in consumption for many LDCs, but these cannot be of the order of those enjoyed at present in the industrially advanced nations. For all this to happen, two basic changes have to occur:

(i)   The nature of industrial development, specifically the forms of production and the use of resources, would have to change radically.

(ii) People in developed nations would have to lower significantly their use of resources.

It is easy to criticize Brundtland: it is optimistic, over ambitious, too far-reaching. Moreover it has been seen as a conscience-salving exercise for the rich nations. However, a good deal of the criticism has been of a subjective nature. What varying perspectives might the contrasting theoretical approaches considered in the previous section offer? The following brief analysis examines:

neo-liberal views (emphasizing the market)

a moderate *environmental* approach (stressing small-scale and local approaches rather than measures requiring strong central political intervention)

a *structuralist* perspective (emphasizing the unequal structural relationship between the North and South)

Contrasting approaches to sustainability

Neo-liberal views
For some neo-liberals, like Professor David Pearce of London University, the concept of sustainable development is a positive and optimistic one. Professor Pearce's report to the UK Department of the Environment in 1989 on the feasibility of achieving it, now in book form as *Blueprint for a Green Economy* has been welcomed in various quarters as 'providing an economics of hope for the world around us'. Whilst commending the Brundtland Report, Pearce says it does not define unambiguously what sustainable development is. Brundtland is critical of using market forces alone for achieving sustainability, but Pearce argues that sustainable development is a 'practical and feasible concept' precisely because of the market.

Pearce's argument rests on putting a value on the economic functions of the environment. Environmental problems are perceived as being essentially economic problems. 'They are manifestations of the failure of market systems to allocate resources efficiently', he points out. Everything can be given a *market value*, and environmental improvements can be seen as equivalent to economic improvements. Figure 10.5 illustrates the process in the form of a demand curve. The diagonal line shows the demand for the services of a natural environment. If a price were associated with demand, the lower the price the greater would be the demand. If there were no market and the price were zero the neo-liberal theory would suggest that too much (Q_0) of the environment would be used up. Thus, they argue, it is important to put a price on the en-vironment. The supply of environment is fixed, so Figure 10.5 has a vertical supply curve. Thus, if such a market in the environment existed, the price would settle at P^*, the equilibrium price, and the amount of environment used up would be Q^*.

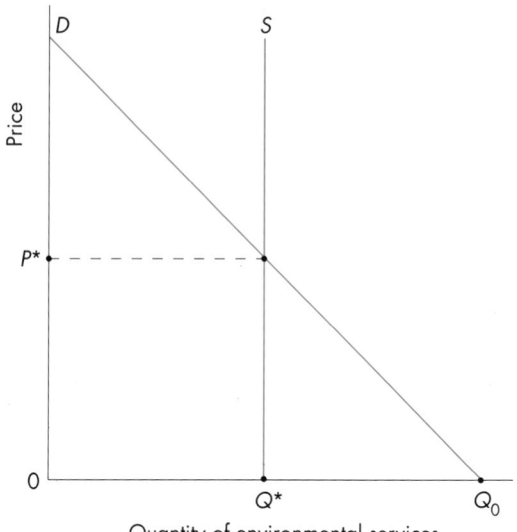

Figure 10.5 'Demand curve' for the natural environment.

Pearce recognizes that sustainable development must accept some trade-offs between narrowly construed economic growth and environmental quality, meaning that the economic value of environmental cost (and there usually is one) has to be understood.

In short, a neo-liberal interpretation of Brundtland is that environment and economics should be merged in decision-making, and *market incentives* employed. The 'polluter pays' principle and 'green' taxes are two examples of economic methods to encourage 'good environmental practice'. For an international environmental issue like global warming the neo-liberal would see market-based approaches as a necessary part of any attempt to reduce the impact of 'greenhouse gases', with the most attractive options involving the encouragement of energy efficiency.

Environmentalist approach

Moderate environmentalists have generally been more equivocal about the Brundtland Report and sustainability, welcoming some of its recommendations for local action and practical solutions in developing countries, but being very critical of the general impression that economic growth and environmental conservation are mutually compatible. The emphasis on the person rather than the product (echoing E F Schumacher's approach in *Small is Beautiful*) comes through in a good deal of the Brundtland rhetoric. But the potential contradictions between the local and the global in Brundtland are too glaringly obvious for most environmentalists. The Report urges us all 'to think globally but to act locally', but for many the Report's own thinking has not gone nearly far enough.

Those favouring more ecologically friendly solutions to the world's environmental problems have also been critical of the neo-liberal response, challenging the altogether simplistic proposition that you can put a realistic value on the environment and on environmental effects. How do we value the greenhouse effect? The consequences of such global environmental issues have not been foreseen due to lack of scientific knowledge, so how can the market allocate costs on the basis of information that does not even exist?

Some environmentalists have taken the argument further to link the questions of sustainability and continuing growth to the world's poor, and particularly to the developing nations. Their argument can be summed up in the comment from John Bowers of the British Association of Nature Conservationists:

> "If sustainability is to be accepted then the poor, both in the Third World and lower income groups in developed countries, must be protected. Substantial sacrifices will be required by the wealthy who consume the lion's share of the world's resources."
>
> (Bowers, 1990)

Structuralist perspective

The theme of inequality between North and South is expanded considerably within the structural approach. Structuralism is centrally concerned with the contradictions implicit in the Brundtland concept of sustainable development, imposed by the structural inequalities of the global economic system. Attention is focused, in particular, on the economic dependence of the less developed countries on the developed, and on the historical and social processes which have produced this. As a prominent commentator on these issues Michael Redclift explains: 'People in the South are being thrown against the contradictions of development in their struggle to survive' (1987). For writers like Redclift the Brundtland Report makes too many major assumptions about the ability of the capitalist system to accommodate the sort of changes required.

Clearly, this view is diametrically opposed to the neo-liberal arguments of people like David Pearce, with whom Redclift takes particular issue. Pearce's discussion of sustainable development makes no assumptions about who benefits or who loses, and fails to acknowledge that structural linkages among nations at different levels of development can result in a politically and culturally biased view of what is sustainable.

Pearce's approach may work for the industrially advanced countries, but it is wholly a perspective from the North. The core of the structuralist critique includes the issue of *equity* which Redclift sees as 'the driving force behind indiscriminate resource degradation in developing countries', but such considerations are not high on the neo-liberal agenda of looking primarily at total economic value.

Many structuralists, like many environmentalists, sympathize with Brundtland's aim of linking the environment with the needs of less developed countries, but challenge the fundamental assumption that sustainable development is achievable. Neo-liberals on the other hand, have generally embraced the concept of sustainability and made it their own. What does all this mean for the relationship between industrialization and environment in the less developed world? Is it realistic to talk in terms of progressing towards a sustainable future?

Comparing the three approaches

The position of the *neo-liberals* is that the system of industrial capitalism is sufficiently flexible and adaptable to allow sustainable development to be achieved globally, based upon market principles. For them capitalism has demonstrated its historical capacity to adapt to changing circumstances.

The *environmentally* oriented approach provides a varied mix. The argument for 'low input' technology and local initiatives is an attractive one, particularly for the less developed world; but the 'no growth' solution is not, neither is it politically acceptable. The implications for the former are unclear in political terms. How is change to occur? The appeals to 'populism', to local action and participation, sound encouraging, but how realistic are they in the political climate of the 'real' world?

The *structuralist* position is one of explaining the 'real' world situation in terms of structural economic dependency within a dominant global political economic context that is capitalist. Radical structural transformations are required if these inequalities are to be addressed and environmentally sound solutions found. However, the structuralist approach is limited by its generality.

A North and South issue?

Raymond Williams argues that what is crucially important for the developing nations is how decisions about prioritizing one form of production over another are taken. 'It is, then, the social and economic relations between people and classes', says Williams, 'which emerge from such decisions, which determine whether more production will reduce or eliminate poverty, or will simply create new kinds of poverty as well as new

kinds of damage and destruction [to the environment]'. The question of who decides and at what level such decisions are effectively taken becomes highly pertinent here.

We could argue that the way production and its priorities are organized at a national level creates the social relations which then determine how we distribute the production and how people actually live. The issue of national sovereignty may be significant. But in the industrialized nations of the West, the inherent capitalist priority of profit is the driving force of an international economic system that crosses national boundaries. The global economy crucially influences the relationship between the North and the South because it is dominated by the production and consumption interests of the industrially advanced nations.

This issue has been dealt with in *Allen & Thomas* (1992). Structuralism is a useful concept for exploring more specifically the links between industrialization in the less developed countries and environmental impact of industrialization. Industry is essential to developing countries if they are to widen their development base and meet the growing needs of their rapidly expanding populations. India, for example, is likely to have a population of around one thousand million by the year 2000. The Brundtland Report affirmed that 'all nations require and rightly aspire to efficient industrial bases to meet changing needs'.

Industry extracts minerals from the natural resource base, processes them and puts both products and pollution back into the environment. Whether or not profit is the motivating force, industries have seldom taken responsibility for the consequences of their actions, unless required to do so by law, and even then often only by lip service. If enforcement of national legislation is problematic within sovereign states, then how much more difficult is it in the international arena with the implementation of protocols and conventions? Some of the worst offenders are the transnational corporations (the TNCs). In 1984, a chemical leak from a Union Carbide pesticides factory in Bhopal India, killed more than 2 000 and maimed an estimated further 200 000.

Figure 10.6   Bhopal disaster, 1984.

Industrial production in the LDCs is diversifying and moving into more capital-intensive areas such as chemicals, machinery, metal products and equipment. In the mid-1980s the proportion of manufacturing value added (MVA) in gross domestic product (GDP) had increased to 19% (see Table 10.1). Heavy industries, traditionally the most polluting, had been growing in relation to light industries. Nonetheless the LDC share of world MVA had risen only from 10% to 13% between 1960 and 1985 (see Figure 1.3 in Chapter 1).

Energy consumption is also extremely uneven (see Table 10.2). The industrialized countries of North America, Western Europe and Japan used approximately half of the world's energy consumption in 1988, the centrally planned economies used about a third, and the less developed countries used a sixth (World Resources Institute, 1991).

The negative environmental impacts of industrial activity have long been recognized. But it was only in the late 1960s and early 1970s that

Table 10.1   Share of manufacturing value added in GDP, by economic grouping and income group (%)

	1960	1970	1980	1982
Developing Countries	14.2	16.6	19.0	19.0
Low income	11.2	13.8	15.0	15.0
Lower-middle income	11.0	13.5	16.4	16.6
Upper-middle income	19.4	21.6	24.1	23.3
High income	17.2	16.2	17.2	17.9
Developed Market Economies	25.6	28.3	27.9	27.1
Centrally Planned Economies (Estimated)	32.0	42.4	50.5	50.8

[Source: UNIDO, 1985]

Table 10.2 Global distribution of energy consumption in 1988

	% of world total consumption
North America	27.2
Western Europe	16.2
Centrally planned economies:	
USSR	17.3
China	9.0
Other	7.7
Asia and Australasia	12.3
Latin America	5.3
Middle East	2.4
Africa	2.6

[Original data source: *BP Statistical Review of World Energy*, 1989]

growing public awareness and concern, principally in the more developed countries, led to action by some governments and industry. Government regulatory measures and a number of economic instruments such as pollution charges and taxation, were considered; in line with the thinking of David Pearce and others who saw the market as a powerful instrument to achieve sustainability. But only a few governments actually introduced these measures. Industries also responded to some degree, principally in the more developed countries. Scandinavian and German companies, and a few US companies such as 3M, developed new processes designed to cut emissions, reduce pollution and avoid other adverse environmental impacts.

The good news, then, is that there have been achievements over the last two decades. Expenditure on pollution control measures has increased in some highly polluting industries such as steel, chemicals and energy production. Guidelines on safety, trade practices and technology transfer have been introduced, as have voluntary codes of practice. International industry associations, established to cooperate on improving industrial performance, has also facilitated pollution control. The Brundtland

Report is keen to emphasize that some firms, all former major polluters, that established teams to research and develop innovative technologies to meet new environmental standards 'are today [1987] among the most competitive in their fields, nationally and internationally'.

The bad news is that these improvements have been almost entirely limited to the industrially advanced nations, and even there many problems remain to be tackled and 'solved'. Along with competitiveness and innovation, energy efficiency, recycling and re-use have become the key themes for 'technologically aware' industrialists. Pollution control has become a thriving branch of industry in the developed countries. But polluting industries have sometimes been relocated to less developed countries.

Levels of air pollution in some 'Third World' cities have risen above anything witnessed in the industrial countries during the 1950s or 1960s. For example, peak levels of airborne particulates in Calcutta and Delhi, and of sulphur dioxide in Beijing, are several times greater than peak levels recorded in cities in developed countries (Table 10.3). Both types of pollutant are linked to inefficient burning of fossil fuels, with sulphur dioxide usually coming from coal in particular. It would be wrong to give the impression that air pollution is a problem in every Third World city. It is not, particularly where there is not a great deal of industry as in some African cities. Also, levels are seriously high in a number of developed countries; but conditions are clearly worse in cities like Beijing, Delhi, Manila and Bangkok. They are worse still in Mexico City, which is not recorded in Table 10.3, but is described later in this chapter.

Pollution problems that were once considered as 'local' are now global in scale, and as Brundtland solemnly reported:

> "Contamination of soils, ground-water, and people by agrochemicals is widening, and chemical pollution has spread to every corner of the planet. The incidence of major accidents involving toxic chemicals has grown. It is evident that measures to reduce, control and prevent industrial

Table 10.3 Peak air pollution levels in selected cities, 1982–1985 (in microgrammes per cubic metre)

	particulates	sulphur dioxide
Developed Countries		
Brussels (Belgium)	97	205
Frankfurt (Germany)	117	230
London (UK)	77	171
New York City (USA)	121	131
Warsaw (Poland)	248	205
Less Developed Countries		
Bangkok (Thailand)	741	48
Beijing (China)	307	625
Calcutta (India)	967	188
Delhi (India)	1062	197
Manila (Philippines)	579	198
São Paulo (Brazil)	338	173

[Source: World Resources Institute, 1989]

pollution will need to be greatly strengthened. If they are not, pollution damage to human health could become intolerable in certain cities, and threats to property and ecosystems will continue to grow."

(Brundtland, 1987)

Clearly, a heavy burden of responsibility continues to rest with the industrialized countries to 'clean up their act'. That they are making progress, as evidenced for example in the recent series of international climate conferences, may give some grounds for cautious optimism. But what of the responsibilities in the less developed world? To what extent does the structural interdependency between North and South provide industrializing countries with options or choices?

We should pause to take stock here of the various dimensions to this whole issue. There are a number of important considerations:

- For industrial development to be at all sustainable in the long term (discounting the 'no growth' scenario of some radical greens as being politically and economically unrealistic) there will have to be radical changes to the quality of that development.

- To accept the Brundtland concept of sustainability is not to suggest that industrialization has yet reached a quantitative limit, particularly in the LDCs;

- According to the UN Industrial Development Organization (UNIDO), world industrial output would have to increase by 260% for the consumption of manufactured goods in developing countries to reach current levels in the industrialized countries (based on 1987 figures).

- UNIDO also estimates anything from a five- to a ten-fold increase in world industrial output, depending when world population stabilizes 'sometime in the next century'. (UN projections range from 7.7 billion in 2060 to 14.2 billion in 2100.)

- Growth of this magnitude has the most serious implications for the future of the world's ecosystems, and its natural resource base.

We may rightly feel that any projections so far into the future should be treated with at least a modicum of circumspection. But, whichever way we approach the United Nations figures, there is cause for concern. Despite the growth of awareness of global environmental problems and the improvements referred to already, we are repeatedly being informed by a growing number of voices, including scientists, that the situation is deteriorating. There is a widening hole in the ozone layer over Antarctica. There are threats of global warming. There is widespread deforestation and desertification. And this is not just a concern being expressed by agitated 'Northern' voices. Note the following quote from a representative of a Brazilian ecology movement, presenting evidence to the Brundtland Commission:

> "Our ecological movement is not against industry, but we must think of the social function of industries and that pollution and progress are not the same thing. Pollution is not the synonym of progress and, therefore, the time has come for new development concepts to come up. Pollution should not be a synonym of progress because we know that pollution is controllable and when you do not control pollution you are transferring this pollution to the community of the whole."

> (Fabio Feldman, São Paulo, October 1985)

The reference to the 'social function of industries' brings us once more back to Williams' questions: what kinds of production; what priorities for production; and to a structuralist explanation. Do less developed countries have much of a choice? This is the subject of the next two sections, the second of which takes a more detailed look at three very different case studies from the less developed world.

What choices?

The United Nations' estimates to which reference has been made in the previous section make all kinds of assumptions about the ability or the 'freedom' of developing nations to choose their paths to further industrialization. For writers like Michael Redclift, quoted earlier, this is a blinkered approach which merely serves to underline the contradictions inherent in the concept of sustainable development.

Using structuralist theories, it is possible to predict a situation in which the shortage of key commodities leads to the more developed world exerting the strong pressure to secure their supplies; political pressure, economic pressure, and in the extreme, military pressure. Just such a situation existed in 1991 in the Middle East in relation to oil. And it is equally feasible that similar scenarios could occur in the future in other parts of the developing world. Raymond Williams has expressed it thus:

> "We can see the possibility of recruiting wide areas of public opinion to cast as 'enemies' the poor countries which have been assigned the role of supplying the raw materials, the oil, the whole range of basic commodities, at prices which are convenient to the functioning, in received terms, of the older industrial economies."

> (Williams, 1982)

Events at the Uruguay round of GATT negotiations (see Chapter 2) appear to support the structuralist argument that LDCs are assigned the dependent role. A widely expressed view, particularly from Third World commentators, is that the main priority of the industrialized nations in the Uruguay Round was:

> "... to extend their control over the global economy. In the past this was achieved through a mixture of colonialism and threats of military intervention. Today it is hoped that GATT and the threat of retaliation will serve the same purpose."

> (Raghavan, 1990)

One particular argument being advanced is that GATT could advance TNC domination of the world economy to a 'point of no return'. Raghavan talks in terms of a world divided between the 'knowledge-rich' and the 'knowledge-poor' where the latter are 'permanently blocked from acquiring the knowledge and capacity to be rich'. His argument continues:

> "In economic and social terms, Third World countries could be said to be on the point of being rolled back to the colonial era. Third World governments would not only be

unable to act to advance the economic well-being of their peoples, but would be obliged to protect the interests of TNCs and foreign enterprises against their own peoples."

(Raghavan, 1990)

One structuralist view is that, far from environmental considerations leading to a more equal use of resources for development, there will be increased inequality and constrained development in LDCs.

To be aware of these arguments is to demonstrate the complexity of the issues under discussion, and yet we should not leave the question of the United Nations' projections there. The UN made the point that 'industrialization has yet to reach a quantitative limit, particularly in the developing countries'. Yet material limits there have to be. If we consider that the United States currently (in 1991) uses something like 370 times as much energy per capita as Sri Lanka, then it seems very unlikely that the ecological balance of the planet could sustain developing countries using similar levels.

In short, this means that the less developed world cannot follow the development path of the more developed. Nor can the industrialized nations continue along this same path without changing their habits.

What propositions might we consider that would see all nations moving, if not along the same path, at least in the same direction? Such propositions might include:

- a realignment of political and economic blocs that does not adversely affect the LDCs

- a serious commitment on the part of the more developed nations and the World's financial institutions to review and to amend radically current positions on debt and policies for structural adjustment

- a serious commitment by the industrialized nations to achieve the goals of sustainable development sooner rather than later

- the continuing development of new technologies that avoid the most dire environmental consequences, and their export through technology transfer to the LDCs without strings attached

- an end to 'ecological imperialism' like calls to 'internationalize' Amazonia.

Given such an hypothetical context, what theoretical choices might exist for developing countries in their desire to industrialize without causing major environmental damage? A range of possible themes that are practicable could be considered here:

- the promises and risks of new technologies;

- the establishment of internationally agreed environmental standards and incentives to help achieve them;

- dealing with industrial hazards;

- the disposal of hazardous waste;

- strengthening international efforts to assist developing countries to develop safer technology.

Before taking a brief look at the first and last of these possibilities, we should be clear about the political economic context within which such initiatives might occur.

We have been considering contrasting perspectives of sustainable development: *neo-liberal* market-led, *environment*-oriented (emphasizing 'local' action), and *structuralist*. It should be evident from the foregoing discussion that the structuralist explanation of unequal nations at different stages of development is powerful, particularly in terms of its critique of market-led development processes. It highlights the essential contradictions within the concept of sustainable development, which purports to promote radical change yet derives from an ideology dominated by market economics.

Herein lies both the strength and the weakness of structuralist explanations. For sustainable development is, for many, about achieving practical results on the ground. Maneka Gandhi, Indian Junior Environment Minister 1990–1991, said 'it means just clean water, clean air and a rational land use. That's all sustainable development is about'. The first inference is that issues of sustainable development may appear to involve meeting simple environmental needs in many LDCs: such as water, land and housing. The meaning of environment in particular circumstances can be broader than the issues of humanly produced waste, hazard and pollution. But the second inference is that although sustainable development appears technically feasible and relatively simple it does not happen 'just like that'. Just because those advocating sustainable development can effectively argue that global resources are available to meet the basic human needs of the world's population, it does not mean that changes will occur without dramatic structural transformations.

New technologies and international cooperation

As has already been demonstrated in the industrially advanced world, new technologies can offer great opportunities for improving productivity, health and the overall quality of life, whilst at the same time minimizing risk to the environment. Significant advances have been made in Scandinavia, Germany, and in the most progressive industries in the highest per capita energy consuming nation of all, the USA. The 3M (Minnesota, Mining and Manufacturing) Company has for more than a decade reoriented its whole productive process to be 'environmentally friendly', including reduction of waste and built in product recyclability. Developments in information technology and the introduction of new materials can contribute towards energy and resource efficiency.

In the field of biotechnology, developments in genetic engineering could have major implications for the environment. Energy derived from plants, new high-yield crop varieties, and integrated pest management are three major areas of predicted improvements. It is also being confidently forecast that biotechnology could yield cleaner, more efficient alternatives to a whole range of industrial processes and polluting products, and make a major contribution to the problem of hazardous waste disposal through

the advancement of new techniques to treat solid and liquid wastes.

Clearly, new energy-efficient technologies, promising reduced risks to the environment, are capable of promoting sustainable forms of development in the industrialized North. But what are the prospects for the less developed world? The 'green revolution' and the provision of new seeds became the domain of the huge transnational chemical industries. The chemical companies have been concerned with reaping the benefits from developing and controlling a limited number of crop varieties, often requiring large inputs of specific fertilizers and pesticides, which they also produce. Such dependency scarcely enhances either the chances or the choices for the LDCs with agriculture-based economies to achieve sustainability.

The green revolution may have had a significant impact upon productive output in many developing countries, but not without a considerable environmental cost. The necessary research into new techniques and production processes, to promote 'environmental compatibility' and minimize the risk element, is both costly and time consuming. Can the less developed world afford either in its struggle to industrialize?

Those industries which are fastest growing in developing countries are pollution-intensive and based on exploiting natural resources. Many developing countries do not possess either the technical or the institutional capacity for making the most of imported or new technologies. These have to be bought in from outside. However, lack of capital means that new industry may only be started with aid or commercial loans, or from investment from the transnational corporations.

The international economic system holds few favours for governments in the South. As you read in Chapter 2 the running up of large external debts, high interest rates, and the inequitable trade situation which sees less developed countries receiving less than a fair market price for their commodities, means that allocating scarce financial resources on environmental protection gets a very low priority. Yet the industrialized world is busily drawing up the guidelines which stress that 'nations have to bear the costs of any inappropriate industrialization' (Brundtland, 1987).

This is a cleft stick for the LDCs. In a world of rapid technological change they have neither the resources nor the time to prevent or remedy environmental damage. The existing technology is 'dirty'. It is heavily polluting and energy consuming. New technology is expensive and comes with strings attached. We might argue, from the relative luxury of our 'northern' observation points, that governments must tighten their existing environmental legislation, although even here there are no guarantees that this would be consistently enforced.

A burden of responsibility certainly rests with the governments of the LDCs; but arguably a far greater burden resides with the governments of the richest nations and with the transnational corporations (TNCs). Less developed countries will continue to have a very restricted range of options without substantial assistance from the international community, in financial, technical and institutional terms. The TNCs have a major responsibility to 'smooth the path to industrialization in the nations in which they operate', according to Brundtland. How optimistic can we afford to be that either of these essential undertakings will occur at a significant level before the turn of the century?

10.3 Industrialization and development: contrasting cases

In the following case studies we will take a brief look at the challenges of industrialization and development which are being faced in three contrasting Third World areas, each at a different level and stage of development. Thailand is a rapidly industrializing country on the Pacific rim, facing severe environmental problems. Haryana State in India has a local initiative for promoting energy efficiency and the use of renewable resources, as a counterbalance to the huge Narmada Valley Project. In Mexico City there is a seemingly intractable problem of balancing the demand for continued industrial expansion with the provision of environmental safeguards.

Thailand

Between 1960 and 1990 Thailand's GDP expanded more than eighteenfold, with a buoyant 7.5% average annual growth rate throughout that period. According to Bank of Thailand forecasts, the Thai economy was set to expand by a further 9.7% at the start of the 1990s, with indicators suggesting continued high growth in virtually every sector. Trade has played a central role. Export volume expanded by 34% in 1987, which has since led to a further major increase in investment. The capital city, Bangkok, has witnessed explosive growth, from a modest city of some 450 000 people at the end of the Second World War, to something over 8 million according to 1989 estimates.

Thailand has achieved such remarkable sustained growth because of a consistent record of macro-economic stability, and an enduring commitment to undertake structural economic reforms, encouraged by the World Bank. The substantial input of foreign capital, including aid, to boost development in Thailand is certainly creating wealth. But a significant proportion goes abroad again in the form of export capital, especially on debt repayments, and as profits to the transnational corporations.

Problems of rapid growth
The paradox is that such economic dynamism coexists with severe economic, social and environmental problems. Although economic growth has undoubtedly reduced poverty, severe imbalances in the distribution of wealth have applied relentless pressure on natural resources and on an inadequate infrastructure.

Is sustainable development an achievable goal in Thailand, or is growth being achieved at a price? Thai financial institutions continue to paint an optimistic picture for the 1990s, claiming that Thailand is now Asia's top performing economy, and even the world's fastest growing economy. However, the labour force remains largely rural-based, with two-thirds of the population (in 1989) of almost 54 million still engaged primarily in agricultural activities.

Despite industrial expansion, Thailand is still heavily dependent on the natural resources that continue to make an important contribution to the country's GDP. Even so, the share (by value) of agricultural products in Thailand's exports fell from 48% in 1981 to 34% in 1986, while the share of manufactured products increased from 35% to 55% over the same period.

There is certainly a recognition by a concerned minority in Thailand of the need for policies directed towards sustainability and conservation. Equally there is an uneasy acceptance that many economic development projects have paid too little attention to the long-term sustainability of their natural resource base; that laws and regulations have been weighted in favour of the

Figure 10.8   Impact of industrialization and urbanization on the poor, a Bangkok slum.

unscrupulous, rather than the conscientious; and that a fair distribution of the wealth derived from Thailand's natural resources and industrial progress is as distant a prospect as ever.

Pollution in Bangkok

The most potent images of rapid growth are to be found in Bangkok itself. As industrialization has continued apace, the economic relations of the country have become progressively oriented towards the capital city, to the extent that over 75% of Thailand's factories dealing with hazardous chemicals are now located within Bangkok's hinterland. The growth of private transport has been equally phenomenal, and the city is fast becoming choked with traffic (Figure 10.7).

Like all burgeoning Third World cities Bangkok has its shanty towns, with their associated problems of sanitation, health and securing a fresh water supply (Figure 10.8). Water is a crucial issue. So much of it is being pumped out of the underground aquifers that the city is literally sinking by up to 100 mm a year. The authorities have a major task ahead in prioritizing expenditure to deal with this and other pressing matters of infrastructure, like public transport and essential services.

Living in Bangkok is becoming more and more environmentally hazardous. Air and water quality are deteriorating. Every year there is

Figure 10.7   Urban congestion in Bangkok, Thailand, 1989.

serious flooding, exacerbated by the logging of forests in the north. The disposal of waste, industrial and domestic, an ever present headache, is getting worse. The problems are the hallmarks of four decades of rapid uncontrolled and largely unplanned growth. As in all developing cities, the urban underclasses are suffering the most and carry the least political clout, but the problems are beginning to affect everyone. Here is an extract taken from a letter written by one concerned woman in Bangkok:

"It seems not enough to learn from other countries' experiences; we have to be an NIC and learn the lesson first hand. Unfortunately, by the time we learn that being an NIC is not to the advantage of Thailand, which is basically an agricultural country, it will be too late. Once fertile farmlands have been turned into factory sites, beaches and forest reserves have become tourist resorts, paralysed traffic has become a way of life, the air has become heavy with industrial smoke in Bangkok, and there would be more natural disasters to contend with as nature takes her revenge on us."

(*The Bangkok Post*, 26 November, 1989)

Plans for sustainable development

The Thai government has a long-term plan to develop the country's eastern seaboard to take some of the pressure off Bangkok and its hinterland. There are also policies in the process of implementation for rural development to open up the interior of Thailand. To concerned citizens the official response is that growth is essential as the only solution to poverty, and that increased awareness on environmental issues will ensure that Thailand will not make the same mistakes as the industrialized nations. One particular safeguard being stressed is the incorporation of 'state of the art' technologies into the forefront of the development process, supported by loans and the transfer of technology from the West.

Dr Dhira Phantumvanit, one of the country's foremost environmentalists, argued in 1987 that 'Despite its acknowledged problems, Thailand has a real opportunity to pioneer in an emerging field of sustainable development. Much of the groundwork has been laid, even though the legal and administrative framework cannot yet exploit the full potential of the investments already made.' There is certainly a sense amongst leading politicians and economists that Thailand can 'contain growth' and steer a course towards sustainability.

There is a powerful argument that economic growth and industrialization are essential to eradicate poverty in the developing world. This is a cornerstone of the Brundtland Report. However, the free-market-based approach embraced by Thailand through her strong ties with the more developed countries of the West is hardly likely to produce an equitable distribution of resources internally, and the price being paid in environmental terms is considerable.

India

The environment and development problems facing India are of a different order. The population is expected to reach one billion by the year 2000. In 1991 the UN estimated that more than a third of the population was below what is in any case a very low poverty line. (See Chapters 1–3 of *Allen & Thomas, 1992* for definitions of poverty.) India has made great strides to industrialize, and to initiate major economic development schemes through a rolling programme of five-year development plans. However more and more Indians are questioning the whole approach to the process of development, specifically the scale of projects and to who actually benefits from them.

Narmada Valley

At the forefront of controversy has been the Narmada River scheme, which in the 1990s is set to become the world's largest hydro-electric power and irrigation complex (Figure 10.9). The project involves the building of 30 major dams, 135 medium-sized dams, and 3 000 small dams, over a period of fifty years. It is designed to irrigate some 20 000 square kilometres in the drought-prone states of Gujarat and Madhya Pradesh, provide drinking water for the whole region, and generate 500 megawatts of electricity. It represents the archetypal 'grand

Figure 10.9   The fertile plain of the Narmada River basin: a geological fault ensures soil retains productivity whether rains are heavy or light. All will be submerged by the Sardar Sarowar reservoir.

development scheme', and much of the estimated costs of around US$40 billion will be met by the World Bank.

The Narmada Valley project has also produced India's first nationwide environmental protest movement, bringing together campaigners for peasants' rights, fishermen, the urban poor and other groups. The protesters see the scheme as being an environmental catastrophe, a 'technological dinosaur' and an example of great social injustice. For the dams, when completed, will displace more than 200 000 people, submerge 2 000 square kilometres of fertile land, and 1 500 square kilometres of forest.

The essence of their argument is that environmental damage would be minimized with hundreds of local irrigation projects, which could do the same job (although not provide the electricity) at a fraction of the cost. In this they have the support of a number of prominent politicians, including Maneka Gandhi. Poor farmers and agriculture in general will lose out, because the whole scheme will benefit more intensive farming methods, encouraging those who are already prosperous to grow more cash crops, leaving peasants upstream with even less water.

Just such a process has been typical of large scale development schemes all over the developing world. What purports to be development for everyone in fact can benefit only those who are already wealthy and the developers themselves. It is, in effect, a classic example of 'top-down' thinking, the imposition of grandiose ideas from above.

Haryana State

At the other end of the spectrum, in terms of the scale of development and the politics involved, comes an example of a sustainable energy project in Haryana State to the north west of New Delhi. It was initiated on an experimental basis in 1984 by the Tata Energy Research Institute (TERI) in Delhi, an organization that is mostly funded by the Tata Industrial Group, one of the largest corporations in India. The aim has been to demonstrate the practical achievements of their work on local renewable sources of energy. The project has centred on one village, Dhanawas, which has about 300 inhabitants. The long-term objective is to spread the ideas to other villages in the state.

Participation by the villagers is a cornerstone of the initiative, in what is clearly a 'bottom-up' process. All work has been undertaken in complete cooperation with the village council, with the equitable concept of the 'common property resource' as a lynchpin of resource management and use policies. There has been to date (1991) no costs borne directly by the inhabitants, modest funding coming jointly from TERI, the Indian government and the FAO.

The principal features of the project have been:

- The establishment of an 18 acre plantation on what were very poor saline soils supporting only scrub vegetation. The policy is for long-term improvement of soil quality, using hardy nitrogen-fixing species like acacia and mesquat

which can be used as a source of much needed fuelwood on a sustainable basis. All the trees are held as a common property resource.

- The development of a number of bio-gas makers, which use a mixture of cow dung and water. The capacity of each unit is 2 cubic metres per day, which is sufficient for about five hours cooking on modern cookstoves or ten hours of lighting. The plan is to introduce enough units to make the village self-sufficient in renewable sources of fuel, reducing the consumption of fuel wood in conventional cookstoves (Figure 10.10).

Figure 10.10   Sustainable energy sources in Dhanawas, Haryana State, India, 1990. (Top) Mustard stalks. (Bottom) Cow dung.

- The building of a gasifier, which uses a mixture of shredded mustard stalks, cow dung and water in the form of small pellets and converts them into gas. The equipment is capable of generating the equivalent of five kilowatts of electricity with an 80/20 gas/diesel mix, enough power to provide lighting for the whole village.

- The use of solar powered water heaters.

Essentially the project concerns the use of intermediate technology to promote the efficient use of renewables, thus cutting the cost of conventional fuel consumption in rural areas. It is not being suggested that such projects can solve the problems of energy use in the cities. A central problem is that Haryana State is amongst the most agriculturally productive states in India, and the inhabitants of Dhanawas have been willing and able to participate because their village is relatively well off. Poorer villages have other priorities, like access to safe water and income generation.

Nevertheless, the TERI project does demonstrate what can be achieved locally with a small budget, and with the political cooperation of the government. At the same time such initiatives are taking place within a context of continuing pressure for economic growth nationally, as the Narmada project illustrates. In India, it is a question of striving to achieve a balance between huge, national multimillion-dollar projects and small-scale local schemes, with the emphasis not necessarily on the former.

Mexico City

The environmentally and socially damaging effects of industrialization, combined with high rates of population and rapid urban growth, are starkly illustrated in Mexico City. Of all major cities in the less developed world, Mexico City must surely face the greatest environmental and social problems. In Bangkok we saw the adverse consequences of rapid growth and development in a country with a continuously high rate of economic growth, striving to achieve NIC status. In Mexico City we see the impact on urbanization processes of a rapidly rising population; a combination of high natural increase and continuing migration from rural areas.

Figure 10.11   Pollution in Mexico City

Population and poverty

Mexico City's 1991 population of over 19 million is expected to rise to 25 million by the year 2000, according to UN predictions. Even though the pace of demographic growth is slowing a little, to many who live in the city and to many more outside observers, the problems appear insurmountable.

Mexico City's inhabitants also have to contend with the natural hazard of living in an earthquake-prone area. Records indicate that the city has been struck 122 times since 1460. The latest serious tremor in 1985 caused widespread death and destruction. Estimates of the total number of fatalities have varied from 10 000 to as many as 60 000. Over 45 000 homes were destroyed or severely damaged. Schools serving some 40 000 pupils were devastated and an estimated 40% of the city's hospital beds were put out of action.

Floods are also a recurrent threat, as in Bangkok. But it is on the human side, in the social, economic, political and technical processes that contribute to urbanization, that Mexico City attracts the greatest attention as an 'urban nightmare'. Environmental disaster may be waiting in the wings in Bangkok, but it has arguably already assumed centre stage in Mexico City.

A description of the social deprivation and environmental degradation in Mexico City is a catalogue of some of the worst ills of the 'Third World' city. Housing conditions are poor; 40% of families live at densities of more than two per room, and 25% live in a 'house' with only one room. Sanitation is substandard and waste disposal deficient, posing major health and pollution problems. Road traffic (there are now over 2.75 million vehicles in the city) is causing very serious congestion and air pollution, with smogs a frequent occurrence during the dry half of the year. Most significantly, Mexico City's industrial concentration of oil refineries, power stations and cement works adds considerably to the pollution and environmental hazards.

The task facing the city's urban managers is formidable and, perhaps not surprisingly, much criticism is focused on government for incompetence and corruption. But some observers contend that, with more than five million being added to the city's population between 1980 and 1990, the local authorities and government agencies have accomplished a great deal in terms of increasing the number of homes with piped water and mains drainage, improving public transport and building new roads.

Politics and pollution

Nevertheless, the crucial problems of ensuring continuous supplies of safe water and of progressively reducing air pollution levels remain unresolved, and appear indeed to border on the insoluble. Even an efficient city administration, able to lay its hands on the requisite funds, would have its work cut out to clean up the polluted skies. For here we encounter an all too familiar story, that of political conflict surrounding the control of pollution, and specifically the 'dirty' industrial processes which give rise to it.

There are two principal sources of air pollution: motor vehicles and heavy industry. Attempts to control the pollution caused by vehicles would be vigorously opposed by the motor industry. (It is the considerable political lobbying pressure of the motor industry in the industrially advanced nations, particularly the USA, that is hampering attempts to reach international agreement on how to tackle global warming.) They would also be opposed by those in government concerned with stimulating economic growth. For it has been the rapid growth of the motor vehicle industry during the past two decades that has contributed significantly to increasing Mexico's GNP.

Efforts to impose controls on the major industrial polluters, who now contribute around 30% of the total air pollution, will also be bitterly contested. If legislation is introduced on the 'polluter pays' principle and production costs rise (as they inevitably would), these will be passed on to the consumer, thus fuelling inflation.

Mexico City appears to be facing insoluble problems because of rapid growth and increasing industrial concentration. Successive goverments have all pursued the goal of urban and industrial deconcentration. They have set up rural-based commissions to stimulate agricultural development in the regions. They have also attempted to woo industry away from the city, offering tax incentives to companies willing to locate outside the metropolitan area. Well over 100 new industrial estates have been established throughout the country. But in practice, these schemes have had only limited success, as more and more activity has continued to locate in Mexico City's hinterland. As in Bangkok, but on a far larger scale, we see the conflict between much-needed economic growth and equally essential environmental safeguards.

10.4 Sustainable industrial futures?

One of the principal lessons from the three case studies is that there are no simple explanations about environmental impact and deterioration in the less developed world. We cannot talk in terms of a single cause and effect, but only of multiple causes with a variety of effects. It is misguided to see all problems in terms of inappropriate development and industrialization emanating from the industrially advanced nations. Governments in the LDCs have to shoulder a share of the responsibility. The problem, as this chapter has sought to demonstrate, is that they are most often presented with very limited choices.

The case studies demonstrate the challenges which developing nations face in trying to strike a balance between the need to industrialize and the increasing pressures from the international community to 'safeguard' the environment. Their options are often heavily constrained. From whatever perspective we choose to explore these issues, whether it be neo-liberal, structural or environment-centred, the problems remain complex. There are always gaps (and sometimes yawning gulfs) between the rhetoric or theory and the reality, particularly the political economic reality.

Neo-liberal ideology
It is worth questioning the conventional wisdom that global environmental problems can be resolved within a dominant neo-liberal ideology

of development, and that the capitalist system is sufficiently flexible to deal with environmental problems. Even so, neo-liberals such as Pearce have worked out practical proposals based on prices, which aim for sustainable development.

Structuralist framework
Within the structuralist framework, the key is to acknowledge the need for structural change to reduce inequalities between nations. The Brundtland Report, like the Brandt Report mentioned in Chapter 5, can be read as a proposal to deal with inequalities between North and South, recognizing their mutual interests. The framework of welfare-based capitalism could adapt to the requirements of an economically and environmentally sustainable system. This would mean acknowledging and coping with the contradictions inherent in the concept of sustainable development. And this is something that neither the more radical structuralists nor the radical 'deep' environmentalists are prepared to do.

Radical structuralists appear to be strong on explanation and weak on practicality. The Marxist approach in particular offers a challenging and relevant analysis of the fundamental aspects of economic dependency in global development. The 'environment' is not seen in isolation as some kind of 'fetish'. People, poverty and inequality are placed above the issues of the market place.

Environmentally centred approach
The followers of writers like E F Schumacher emphasise the need for 'local' action and low-impact technology within an environmentally-centred approach. Such an approach has appeal. The case study of Dhanawas in India pointed up the significance of participation and 'bottom-up' initiatives. But is 'local' a realistic overriding context for tackling global environmental problems? Where is the political and economic realism?

'Sustainable development is ultimately a local activity', writes Lloyd Timberlake (1988); 'governments do not do development, people do'. One may be cautiously optimistic about the movement (politically) of people to bring about change, but a lot has to happen. Habits of production and consumption in the industrialized

North have got to change, and sooner rather than later. National aspirations and goals must be seen in a far wider, global context. The industrialized nations have got to clear up their own mess before expecting less developed countries to do likewise.

Third World views

In all of this discussion, the view from the less developed world can easily be submerged. Many Third World critics continue to argue that the West has an immense historical debt to pay. The consequences of following the 'conventional path' of economic development over 200 years of history has been disabling and dependency-creating for much of the developing world. These are manifested in rising debt, in structural adjustment programmes, in trade protectionist policies. The role of science and technology is seen by many not as 'liberator' but as 'destroyer'. They point, in particular, to the huge annual expenditure on armaments. The end to the Cold War offered a chink of light that funds might be diverted away from military expenditure into a 'peace dividend'. But sceptics remain unconvinced, as there are still numerous wars being fought in various parts of the world.

Many questions about 'the environment' remain unanswered for the citizen of a less developed country, who does not have enough to eat and has no permanent place to live.

Summary of Chapter 10

There is now widespread international concern about the environmental damage caused by industrialization. But industrialization seems the only way out of poverty for developing countries.

Three different approaches to this problem can be identified:

1 Neo-liberals maintain that 'free-market' mechanisms can work to safeguard the environment, if the environment is given a monetary value.

2 Structuralists maintain that economic and social structures, especially the ownership and control of resources, needs to change if we are to safeguard the environment while developing industry.

3 Environmentalists emphasise small-scale and local initiatives, and some advocate a 'zero-growth' option for international economic policies.

In the 1980s, the UN adopted a policy of 'sustainable development' which does not fall neatly into any of these categories. In 1987, the Brundtland Report *Our Common Future* provided evidence for links between poverty and environmental damage in developing countries, and set out an agenda for action.

Brief case studies emphasized these points.

- Thailand is a newly industrializing country in which the government is struggling with urban pollution and deforestation.
- In India, the huge Narmada Valley dam project has been criticized for its environmental impact. But in Haryana State an experimental renewable energy project illustrates an 'intermediate technology' solution.

- Mexico City is the world's largest and fastest growing city. Its environmental and social problems seem insurmountable. It also suffers regularly from earthquakes and floods. Government attempts at deconcentrating industry have had limited success.

LDC governments have very few options open to them in trying to achieve sustainable industrial development. New technologies may help. But the industrialized nations will have to take a lead in safeguarding the environment worldwide while supporting development in the Third World.

11

CONCLUSIONS

DAVID WIELD, HAZEL JOHNSON AND TOM HEWITT

This book has focused on industrialization and its relationship to economic, social and cultural development. It began by examining the changing international circumstances that have shaped economic development strategies since the 1950s and how international conditions have influenced global industrialization.

Two case studies of Brazil and South Korea gave a detailed view of how industrialization can occur, as well as its problems and effects. These case studies were also used to assess the relevance and usefulness of two important theoretical perspectives, structuralism and neo-liberalism, in interpreting the conditions for, and implications of, industrialization. The explanatory power of each theory varied between the two cases and between historical periods.

But the theories were not so good at explaining some crucial elements of both processes and effects of industrialization. When we focused on the technological, environmental, social and cultural processes associated with industrialization, it highlighted some of the shortcomings of macroeconomic theories of industrial development. It also gave new insights into the dynamics and impact of industrialization in specific areas: on the environment, on people's lives and livelihoods and on technological learning.

11.1 Some key themes

The Introduction to this book stated that an assessment of industrialization depended on the criteria used to measure the process. The aim of Chapters 1–10 was to give you a broad analysis, to enable you to choose your own criteria and make your own assessment of industrialization. Here are a few of the key themes.

The global dimension

The period after the Second World War until the early 1970s was characterized by rapid global expansion of output and trade. This was followed by global economic recession. In the last two decades the room for manoeuvre of less developed countries has narrowed considerably. Nonetheless, we have seen that some developing countries have been able to develop their economies rapidly even within such global restrictions.

The two cases of Brazil and South Korea can be used to map a path through the economic history of the twentieth century. During the first major recession of the century, in the 1920s and 1930s, the Brazilian state used its powers and room for manoeuvre to 'swim against the global tide' and make a once and for all change, from an economy driven by coffee production for export, to a more diversified and industrial one. From the 1940s to the 1970s further industrialization grew from this base so that Brazil became one of the ten biggest industrial nations. But from the mid-1970s growth has slowed. South Korea, like Brazil, industrialized rapidly since the second world war, but has also been able to prosper during the current world recession, as Brazil did in the previous one. In fact, South Korea's economy has gone from strength to strength in the last two decades of global recession.

Neo-liberal and structuralist perspectives are both useful in helping to understand that internally and externally oriented industrialization policies have been important for each country's development.

From the 1960s in South Korea, and to some extent from the 1970s in Brazil, there emerged a historical trend towards a more externally oriented approach. International banks and foreign companies were pushing less investment into developing countries. This dramatically affected most of these countries, including Brazil, and put further pressure on them to expand export trade.

Thus, studying the global context of industrialization in the 1970s and 1980s shows that it is extremely difficult, if not impossible, for industrialization to be carried out independently of world economic conditions. This is not the age for internally oriented development, isolated from the global economy. The pressure to be competitive in international markets has pushed such attempts to the sidelines.

The state and industrial policy

A crucial question is the role of the state in industrialization: should it intervene or not; and if so, how? The book has examined the debates between the import-substituting and export-oriented industrialization policies. Import substitution is associated with greater state intervention; export orientation with less state intervention. We found, as with the theories, that they are not mutually exclusive. In practice, experiences of industrialization have been mixtures of the two: in different combinations, in different places and at different times.

Even though we have shown the broad constraints of the neo-liberal approach, there has been an unmistakable tendency in recent years for state intervention to give way to markets. This has occurred across the board, but the neo-liberal prescriptions appear to be less painful when applied to a strong economy like South Korea than to a weakening one dealing with short term crisis management (such as in Brazil in the 1980s). Both Brazil and South Korea have been moving towards less state intervention after an extended period of direct state involvement in industrialization. Perhaps the crucial differences between the two cases are:

(i) The state in South Korea took a more strategic stance towards industry, directing investment through incentives to the private sector, while the Brazilian state has been more directly involved in production itself, through state-owned monopolies. In addition, South Korean industrialization has been based on building national capacity through local private firms, whereas Brazil has been much more reliant on foreign capital.

(ii) Although indebted following the Korean war, the South Korean economy was able to pay off its foreign loans. So it could weather the world recession of the 1970s and 1980s. As a result, it was easier for the state to take a more 'hands-off' approach and leave the economy to the already strong private sector. In Brazil, by contrast, the

Figure 11.1.

accumulated burden of indebtedness has made any change fraught with difficulty.

The limits of macro-economic theories of development

The use of the two theoretical perspectives chosen has allowed us to delve quite deeply into two very complex industrialization processes. We have also introduced core elements of industrialization processes that such theories address in a relatively limited way.

For example, the chapter on gender described how women have been sometimes been marginalized from organized industrial work, as in Latin America in the 1950s and 1960s. At other times women have been targeted for certain types of employment, as in the labour-intensive garment and electronics industries in South East Asia since the 1970s. That chapter discussed some of the limits of gender-based perspectives as well as showing the dangers of theoretical frameworks that ignored gender. One example was the problems associated with seeing industrialization as a linear process with an inexorable tendency to larger-scale, higher-productivity industry leading to the death of pre-industrial and non-factory production. Studying gender relations made it much easier to see that non-factory and informal production is a part (sometimes an expanding part) of the industrialization process of nations and not a pre-industrial relic on its way out.

Industrialization and urban livelihoods

A closer view of specific aspects of industrialization such as those presented in Chapters 7–10 reveals that not all nations, and still less all citizens, benefit equally from industrialization. Even when industrialization is considered successful by some measures, many individuals and groups are excluded from that success. Indeed, a high social cost has invariably been associated with certain phases of industrialization.

Our attention to those who provide the labour for industrialization — manual and skilled workers, women and men, managers, technicians and scientists — has been limited. Yet the national and international effects of industrialization are critical for rural and urban livelihoods. For example, the Introduction to this book said that industrialization 'enables an increasing range and quality of goods to be produced and is a major source of employment'. But the range and quality of goods

Figure 11.2   An urban product of rapid industrialization in Brazil: a favela in Rio de Janeiro.

resulting from industrialization will not necessarily be directed to the needs of the many low-income earners in the urban and rural areas of the Third World. In addition, while industries in both formal and informal sectors provide jobs, they also provide a huge variety of working conditions and wage levels, some of which are the basis of increasing income generation and others of which are extremely exploitative. Also, as we have seen, working conditions for women can be very different from those for men.

But those working in formal and informal sector industries are not just victims (as well as beneficiaries) of industrialization. They do resist, organize and seek to change conditions of work, and they affect the types and directions of industrial expansion and contraction. But we should remember that change is not automatic and that those who choose to confront orthodoxies can be in great danger. Members of the Brazilian movement for land have suffered violence and death, as have demonstrators against authoritarianism in South Korea. The livelihoods of urban workers and the urban poor are thus affected by complex social relations in households and businesses, as well as by the 'abstract' interaction of the demand for and supply of labour and goods in the industrialization process.

In summary, the four themes we have highlighted are:

- the importance of the international economy in the industrialization of individual countries

- the contested role of the state in industrialization

- the limits of theory

- industrialization and urban livelihoods.

11.2   Other experiences of industrialization

Although the interests of this book have ranged widely, there remain many gaps. For example, little has been said concerning socialist experi-

ences of industrialization, or the diverse experiences of other late industrializers. Nor have we discussed what room for manoeuvre exists for small and medium sized countries with weaker economies or how industrialization is linked to agricultural development? We can only give a taste of the issues involved, but enough to point out that debate on industrialization is by no means exhausted.

Socialist experiences of industrialization

Socialism has been an important influence on industrialization and development. Not least because there have been no successful socialist revolutions in societies where capitalism has been most developed. So socialist industrialization models arise from policies and practices in less developed countries. Economically, socialist development has meant state ownership of all major enterprises, linked to central planning of the relationship between enterprises. Socialism has also centrally included state control over investment, trade, labour markets, and strong state intervention in agriculture and in relationships between industry and agriculture, town and country (*Allen & Thomas, 1992,* Chapter 12).

The Soviet model of industrialization became the key alternative model to capitalist development; a model of rapid state-oriented industrialization, through state control of the economy and accumulation. The state owned and invested in large scale industry and industrialized agriculture. Although there have been changes over time, overall, the Soviet industrialization model had four key characteristics relevant for the concerns of this book.

First, it was a strongly inward-oriented industrialization: national state production for national needs. The Soviet Union faced hostility from the whole of the rest of the world until the 1940s, and from most of it even after that.

Second, it involved extensive use of a rich resource base. Some argue that this resource base allowed extensive (and wasteful) use of natural resources (and destruction of the environment) rather than more intensive and productive use of them.

Third, it was a faster industrialization process than had ever been seen before. Harsh and wasteful as it was, it did enable the Soviet economy to withstand the military onslaught of Nazi Germany.

Fourth, after the Second World War the Soviet model was attractive to many newly independent countries and to national leaders of movements for independence, and influenced structuralist ideas.

The Soviet experience thus provides a model of rapid large scale industrialization alternative to capitalism, achieved through extensive and centralized state economic control and planning. But, just as we have demonstrated in the book that capitalist industrialization processes are extremely diverse, so there is not just a single model of socialist industrialization. Though based on the Soviet model, the eastern European experiences exhibited strong diversity, and included different types of economic organization and market reform from the 1960s. Vietnam, Cuba, and North Korea (White, 1983) also developed differently, though all within a strongly centrally planned, state controlled economy.

Why did the Soviet economy and society gradually move to an irrecoverable crisis from the mid-1970s? One argument is that although central planning allowed massive initial mobilization of new resources and people for 'extensive industrialization', it was less able to build on that industrialization to improve quality and productivity through the creative and flexible use of skilled labour. Then, with increasing globalization of technologically sophisticated industry, the relatively closed nature of the Soviet economy became less able to take up new technologies.

The Chinese industrialization model is the other classic case of socialist industrialization although it differed significantly from the Soviet experience. The Chinese economy in 1949 had much less industrial development than the Russian one in 1917. The Chinese revolution had been fought primarily in rural areas with peasant support, rather than in cities through workers strikes. The revolution included a strongly nationalistic dimension, arising from anti-Japanese, anti-colonial occupation, and anti-British and French domination of Chinese trade, including opium. Before coming to power, the Chinese leadership had spent a long period (since 1933) in 'liberated areas'. The sum total of these differences was to make it extremely difficult for the Chinese to carry through a similar process of industrialization to that which had occurred in the USSR. The Chinese party arose out of, was dependent for its support on, and was based in rural society. Further, rural society and the countryside carried even more weight in terms of population and contribution to the economy in China than in the USSR in the 1920s. Industrialization based upon the break-up of rural society was not a feasible project in China.

One trend arising from these constraints was not to rely solely on large scale industrialization as the motor of socialist economic development. Mao Tse Tung emphasized the need to encourage agri-

Figure 11.3   A Russian poster: 'Without heavy industry we cannot construct any industry at all'.

culture and light industry, and to 'walk on two legs'. One leg was based on local initiative, labour-intensive, decentralized and 'self-reliant'. The other was advanced and large-scale (starting with technologies imported from the USSR in the early 1950s). 'Walking on two legs' was a policy to lower the divisions and inequalities between town and country.

There would be significant industrialization of rural areas and strong reliance on popular mobilization to make up for lack of financial resources to buy sophisticated technologies. After the death of Mao in 1976 the emphasis on popular mobilization diminished and market reforms were begun. The balance moved towards technological modernization using foreign (this time Western and Japanese) technology. There was a resultant growth spurt which turned into high inflation, a fragmented economy, and which led to the political crisis of the late 1980s.

But the earlier period of trying to combine different scales of production and different types of

Figure 11.4   China 'walking on two legs'.

organization, not relying on foreign, advanced technologies, integrating town and country, industrialization for peasants and not just workers, and national and local self reliance, has also been extremely influential in some countries of the Third World.

Other rapid industrializers

Brazil and South Korea are two examples of what have become known as newly industrializing countries (NICs) or 'semi-industrialized' countries. Defined either in terms of a strategy of export-oriented industry or simply in terms of a threshold of the share of manufacturing in GDP, the countries usually included as NICs are: Hong Kong, Singapore, South Korea, Taiwan, Brazil, Mexico, Argentina, India, Egypt, Turkey, Malaysia, the Philippines, Thailand and Indonesia.

Summary data on some of these countries are shown in Table 11.1.

Some of the countries listed above have been defined as 'first-tier' NICs and some as 'second-tier' NICs. The second tier NICs are principally in South East Asia: Thailand, Malaysia, Indonesia, and the Philippines. These began to industrialize rapidly in the 1960s and 1970s following the examples of first-tier NICs such as South Korea and Taiwan.

Malaysia

Malaysia which, in the early 1990s, was undergoing rapid structural transformation with some economic success is a typical example from the second-tier NICs. British colonizers made no attempt to industrialize Malaysia and so at independence in 1950, Malaysia was a late starter. Through the 1950s and then more intensively in the 1960s, import substitution policies for manufacturing were encouraged. Protectionism played a key role in this.

While manufacturing was built up over these decades, protectionism created certain problems (Edwards, 1990):

- The tariff structure gave no incentive for firms to seek out imports.

Table 11.1 Economic characteristics of selected NICs in the early 1980s

Country	% Manufacturing in national income	% Manufactures in exports	% Annual growth in manufacturing (1975 prices)	
			1963–73	1973–81
India	17.2	65.3	3.7	5.1
Egypt	17.3	44.1	3.3	8.2
Malaysia	18.4	47.4	9.1	9.2
Turkey	18.6	55.7	9.9	3.4
Mexico	23.5	32.2	8.9	6.9
Philippines	25.7	55.0	6.5	6.6
Argentina	25.8	57.8	6.5	–0.8
Singapore	27.6	79.9	18.0	10.0
Brazil	28.2	70.9	9.7	6.2
Hong Kong	30.8	97.0	12.3	12.3
South Korea	33.8	93.2	20.4	13.4
Developed economies*	27.3	84.7	6.1	1.6

* Simple average for Canada, Federal Republic of Germany, Japan, UK and USA.
[Data source: Weiss, 1990].

- Protectionism favoured the assembly of final consumer goods which created a reliance on the import of intermediate goods.

- Most of the industries were foreign-owned resulting in large remittances out of the country.

So, during the 1970s, Malaysia moved towards export-oriented industry. Free trade zones were set up for this purpose. Although manufacturing (and exports) expanded rapidly, another set of problems directly related to the export-oriented strategy emerged:

- There was still little net foreign exchange saving to reinvest in the Malaysian economy.

- Industrial wages were low (to attract foreign capital) and working conditions in the export factories were appalling.

- There was little technology transfer to the rest of Malaysian industry.

In short, the free trade zones were little more than foreign enclaves with little or no linkage with the rest of the economy. To remedy this, at the start of the 1980s, there was another change of direction towards more heavy industry (e.g. steel and machinery). This involved state investment and was a return to import substitution. Financing this phase incurred substantial debts from external borrowing. To service these debts, emphasis was once again placed on export industries.

As this thumbnail sketch illustrates, Malaysia's industrialization has been rapid. In itself, such a rapid transformation of the economy has meant an upheaval of the country's social fabric. Such rapid change could also result in continued instability: booms and slumps in rapid succession.

Manufacturing output in the 1980s was growing at rates approaching South Korea and at a similar level to Brazil during the 'economic miracle' years previously. But these data hide a recession in the mid-1980s and are no guarantee that growth will continue through the 1990s.

Over the last three decades, Malaysia has tried various industrialization strategies: ISI, EOI and heavy industrialization. It has increasingly fallen under the region's dominant power, Japan, as well as the first tier NICs South Korea, Taiwan, Hong Kong and Singapore. This dynamic economic environment has had a positive influence on Malaysia's industrialization.

Smaller economies

But what of those countries which fall outside any clear regional sphere of influence? What are the possibilities for smaller, economically weaker nations, with their relatively limited room for manoeuvre and their increasing debt burdens? In particular, sub-Saharan Africa since the mid-1980s has been projected as a 'hopeless' case for development. And indeed, over the period 1980–89, GDP per capita for sub-Saharan Africa dropped by 1.2%. At the same time they have faced increasing pressure to instigate neo-liberal structural adjustment programmes, to the extent that most foreign government to government aid has depended on signing such programmes. Industrial development in sub-Saharan Africa has brought very mixed results.

Zimbabwe

An example of a country that performed reasonably well in the 1980s without structural adjustment was Zimbabwe. As colonial Rhodesia, Zimbabwe had significant industrial growth during the Second World War, when there was import substitution industrialization to produce goods that were previously imported. There was a further import substitution surge in 1966–80, the period of the white settlers' unilateral declaration of independence (UDI), under pressure of economic sanctions. From 1966 to 1974 annual growth of manufacturing reached 9.6% per annum (Wield, 1981). Colonial Rhodesia is thus a classic case where industry was strongly internally ori-

ented, specifically to the white settler consumer market. The state operated strong control, directly owning some major industries, investing in infrastructure, and operating import tariff protection.

The crisis and collapse of the UDI regime brought severe decline in industrial production (25%) between 1974 and 1978. Given this crisis and the strongly internally oriented economy facing the outwardly oriented 1980s, Zimbabwe has performed relatively well, with one of the highest growth rates in Africa, about 4% annually. The government retained protective barriers and tight trade and foreign exchange controls. Industrial output grew by over a third, diversified and now brings in significant export earnings. Zimbabwe has, therefore, followed a path to industrialization which has tried to stem pressures to liberalize and structurally adjust. However, this has meant that it lost IMF support from 1984 in a dispute over foreign exchange and the World Bank refused to extend a loan fund for export promotion in 1987 because Zimbabwe would not agree to 'new stringent IMF-type macro economic policy preconditions' requiring trade liberalization (Stoneman, 1990).

> "Zimbabwean policy-makers, however, have a reasonable understanding of the sources of growth in the NICs, and reject the free-market interpretation of the World Bank. And plainly they have an ambition to make of Zimbabwe 'an African NIC', despite its manifest range of disadvantages ..."
>
> (Stoneman, 1990, p.6)

The argument is that Zimbabwe's industrial base is not yet strong enough for a major policy change towards strongly neo-liberal policies and that other countries, like Brazil and South Korea, needed a much longer period of relative protection before being strong enough to expand with increased external orientation.

This argument about Zimbabwe is based partly on the idea of a 'special case'. That Zimbabwe should not be lumped with African worst cases, like Ghana and Uganda, that have accepted structural adjustment packages and thus been given inflows of loans. In this book we have argued that each case of industrialization should be treated as a specific case and Zimbabwe is a special situation of relative success. Still, in the gloom surrounding African industrialization and development it is important to note that ten or so sub-Saharan countries of Africa had manufacturing growth rates of over 3% per year through the 1980s. What of the other 30? The arguments below are those usually given for their problems, some would say crises:

(i) There is an over-reliance on ISI policies, without regard to the huge productivity increases that would be needed to justify large investments on larger-scale factories. The weaker links between different units in the economy meant that large fractions of industrial inputs had to be imported with foreign exchange costs.

(ii) Technology capability build-up is weak. Technology capability is, in many cases, seen as just requiring technology transfer of the factory from foreign countries and getting it to work in its new environment. The broader problems of technological capability that we detailed in Chapter 7, like the need for explicit policies on production-based innovation and on education and training for all the workforce (not just the elite part), were less easy to implement.

(iii) Overall, the external environment for investment in the 1980s has been bad. There has been very little foreign investment over the recent period.

Links between agriculture and industry

Whatever the strategy, industrialization cannot be pursued without reference to agricultural development. What are the links between agriculture and industry, and how do they affect urban and rural livelihoods? As we have seen, industrialization has been a global but very uneven phenomenon in the Third World. Some countries, such as Brazil, have had an industrial base for decades; others have very little industry at all. Thus there are very different distributions of economic activity, jobs and incomes between agricultural and industrial sectors and different

Figure 11.5.

degrees of linkage between agriculture and industry.

Agriculture obviously provides food for growing urban populations. Even where there are substantial food imports, the commercialization of food production for urban markets is widespread. However, the increasing demand for commercialized food raises questions about what foods are produced and how, and about who benefits. While there is large-scale food production for national consumption in many Third World economies, much locally consumed food is produced by small farms with little land, using mainly family or other unpaid labour and experiencing low levels of productivity and remuneration.

In addition to food, agriculture provides raw materials as industrial inputs, earns foreign exchange through agricultural exports which can be channelled into industrial investment, requires industrial inputs (machines, fertilizers), creates infrastructural linkages such as roads and transport which also require industrial inputs, and is itself a part of the industrialization process through processing and transforming crops and livestock. So when we were considering the question of 'what is meant by industrial production?', in the Introduction to this book, industrialized agriculture would obviously be included in, or have links to, the subsectors of food products, drink and tobacco, textiles, wood production and furniture, paper and printing. Some agricultural production could be characterized as industrial production in terms of its large scale, complex techniques and machinery, linkages with other sectors, complex divisions of labour, diverse skills and the use of technology rather than people to supply energy. Examples might be fruit production and packaging or sugar plantations and processing plants. However there are many more limits on changing organization and technology in agriculture than in industry (see *Allen & Thomas, 1992*, Chapter 20).

While there are many important links between the development of industry and agriculture, one of the most fundamental is labour. The process of commercialization in agriculture to meet national urban and industrial demand as well as increase exports and foreign trade involves many changes in social relations. One frequent effect of commercialization is increasing concentration of land for some producers, and growing landlessness or diminishing access to land for others. The growth of rural wage labour is not necessarily met by equivalent demand in agriculture and, given low productivities for many small producers, rural incomes are often very low. Thus excess rural labour forces have met industrial demand for labour but have also swelled the ranks of urban under-employed and unemployed.

It is therefore important to realize that industrialization is only part of the picture of Third World development. In fact, industrialization and agricultural development are intimately connected. The creation of adequate livelihoods in both country and town involves complex and integrated development strategies, from above and below.

Some of these issues are taken up in detail in the third volume in this series (Bernstein *et al.*, 1992).

11.3 The future of industrialization

What is the future of industrialization in the 1990s? In the Introduction to this book, we suggested that industrialization could be looked at in two ways: as a way of producing things and as a total process of industrialization. Both these elements appear to be changing rapidly. Let's look first at the organization of industry itself and those who work in it. The 1980s have brought the rise of a new theory of industrial organization. The theory begins from the belief that that the 'old orthodoxy' of large scale, assembly line, highly concentrated, vertically integrated enterprises (a description both for Fordist capitalist enterprises and for centrally owned and controlled enterprises in socialist countries), is untenable and changing. Those who make this kind of argument make the following points. Increasingly, more specialized (niche) markets are growing with more sophisticated customers who value quality, design, more environmentally sound products;

thus quality over quantity and choice over uniformity. Firms, instead of striving to be the most efficient at producing lots of the same things cheaper than anyone else, need to be aware of market trends and be flexible enough to change production at short notice. New microelectronic technologies allow more of this flexibility. For example, in Chapter 1 the example was given of the car industry where it is possible to produce a number of different models on the same production line. Such specialization, it is argued, is based on a division of labour requiring much closer integration between different firms, for example between suppliers and producers. There is thus more opportunity for small and medium firms to compete with large ones at lower scale of production. And the lower scale production would be more humane and less alienated.

Such a 'post-Fordist' future appears to have ambiguous consequences for the Third World. On the one hand, there is the possibility that lower scales of production will create opportunities for Third World producers. Within production organization there is the possibility that work would be more humanized, with better control of work at shop floor level.

On the other hand, there is the possibility that the need for increased integration in production means that subcontractors could no longer operate at long distances from major production units, and

that work organization, in becoming more flexible, might also become more intensive. Thus, one future scenario is an optimistic one, involving a more pleasant creative work environment, flexible hours, more environmentally sound products, a more equal workforce with a 'culture' of harmony. Another scenario would involve a part-time workforce, intensification of work, where flexibility means also no unions or social welfare.

At a global level too, there are big changes afoot in this process of industrialization. The beginning of the 1990s has heralded massive changes. The collapse of the 'second world' has brought with it the fall of centralized command-style industrialization models. Indeed, in some countries of Eastern Europe the loss of faith in state control has reached the point where calls for liberalization of the economy drown any worries that production could be decimated if they were implemented.

But does the demise of the USSR mean that there is no counter to overwhelming US power in the world? The global pre-eminence of the USA is reminiscent of *pax Britannica* in the latter part of the nineteenth century. On the one hand, the USA as a nation that seemingly can dictate the direction of global policies giving much less room for political independence of Third World countries. This has been associated in international politics with a relative increase in power of the World Bank and the IMF and a relative decrease in

Figure 11.6.

power of third world nations within the United Nations. On the other hand, there is the relative economic decline of the United States in comparison to Japan and Europe:

"…the evidence is substantial that the competitiveness of the American economy is eroding, and manufacturing is taking the brunt of the downward shift … Measured in each of seven ways — by unprecedented trade deficits in manufactured goods; by declining shares of world markets for exports; by lagging rates of productivity increases; by eroding profit margins; by declining real wages; by the increasing price elasticities of imports; and by an eroding position in world high technology markets — American [meaning USA's] industry confronts a severe problem of competitiveness, which it has never known before … Clearly something is very wrong … Can Americans make semiconductors or hubcaps better than the Japanese if most of our production equipment has to come from Japan?"

(Cohen & Zysman, 1987).

Is the strategic triumph of the USA over the USSR the beginning of the end for the 'US Empire'? One lesson of Britain's relative economic decline is that it has lasted for over a century already and Britain is still a major military power if not an economic one. Thus, one irony is that the USA is seemingly in a completely dominant position politically at a time when there is, inside the USA, a serious worry about the economic future of the nation as the world's greatest economic power. Another conundrum is that neo-liberalism continues its domination as an economic theory into the 1990s at the same time as the European Community and Japanese governments invest heavily in the industries and technologies of the future, including less polluting ones. And finally, markets are increasingly freed in a period of continued concentration and globalization of industrial ownership so that the concentration in some key industries (like aerospace, computing and cars) is such that just a few companies control a majority of markets world-wide.

Given the challenges from Europe and Japan, how will the US fare in the coming years. One answer for the 1990s might be the USA as completely dominant militarily but decreasingly dominant economically; neo-liberalism continuing its dominance but new perspectives coming from European and Japanese attempts to continue economic growth with increasingly resource and environmental constraints; of growing own-

Figure 11.7.

ership concentration in multinational corporations decreasingly owned and focused in the USA.

What does this mean for the 'South'? In this book we have mapped industrial development in relatively industrialized parts of the 'South', referred to other groups of nations trying to catch the NICs, and mentioned those that have had problems keeping up with the industrial bandwagon in the 1980s recession. Even here we have seen that some have managed to continue to produce more goods for their populations, even though others have faced serious crises in the world 'slump'.

One thing is clear. If the conflict or relationship between East and West (until the 1980s) and, subsequently, between the US, Europe and Japan is one between equals, the North–South divide is not a divide between equals. The history of destabilization of alternative development models in the South by the North, of racism and of destruction continues unabated.

The World Bank concludes its *World Development Report 1991* by saying:

> "There is more agreement today than at any time in recent history about what needs to be done [about development] and how to do it. What remains is to put these ideas into practice everywhere"
>
> (World Bank, 1991, p.157).

Certainly old-style industrialization looks less viable for the 1990s. But in our view, this does not mean that the neo-liberal agenda is the only way forward. For example, perhaps the future is in looking for strategies that do not mean building up every industry, where economies of scale are not the most important investment criteria, where the difference between heavy and light industry decreases, even where the difference industry-services collapses. What is important is to note that there is a choice and that directions are not pre-ordained.

References

Agarwala, R.(1983) *Price Distortions and Growth in Developing Countries*, World Bank Staff Paper 575, World Bank, Washington.

Allen, T. & Thomas, A. (1992) *Poverty and Development in the 1990s*, Oxford University Press/The Open University, Oxford (Book 1 of this series).

Allsopp, C. J. & Joshi, V. (1986) 'The Assessment: the international debt crisis', *Oxford Review of Economic Policy*, 2 (1), pp.1–33.

Amado, J. (1945) *The Violent Land*, Knopf, New York.

Amado, J. (1984) *Jubiaba*, Avon, New York.

Amado, J. (1988) *Captains of the Sand*, Avon, New York.

Amsden, A. (1989) *Asia's next giant: South Korea and late industrialization*, Oxford University Press, New York and Oxford.

Asian Development Bank (1990) *Asian Development Outlook*, Manila, Philippines.

Bacha, E. (1976), 'Issues and evidence on recent Brazilian economic growth', *Development Discussion Paper* No.12, Harvard Institute for International Development, Harvard.

Baer, W. (1965), 'The inflation controversy in Latin America: a survey' *Latin American Research Review*, 2(2).

Balassa, B. & Associates (1982) *Development Strategies in Semi-Industrialized Countries*, Johns Hopkins University Press, Baltimore.

Balassa, B., Bueno, G., Kuczynski, P. & Simonsen, M. (1986) *Toward Renewed Economic Growth in Latin America*, Institute for International Economics, Washington.

Ban, S.H., Moon, P.Y. & Perkins, D.H. (1980) *Rural Development*, Harvard University Press, Harvard.

Beenstock, M. (1984) *The World Economy in Transition*, Allen and Unwin, London.

Bell, M. (1982) *Technical Change in Infant Industries: a review of the empirical evidence*, Science Policy Research Unit, University of Sussex, Brighton.

Bello, W. (1990) *Brave new Third World: strategies for survival in the global economy*, Earthscan, London.

Benería, L. & Roldán, M. (1987) *The Crossroads of Class and Gender: industrial homework, subcontracting and household dynamics in Mexico City*, University of Chicago Press, Chicago.

Berg, M. (1985) *The Age of Manufactures*, Fontana, London.

Berger, M. (1989) 'Introduction' in Berger, M. & Buvinic, M., *Women's Ventures; Assistance to the Informal Sector in Latin America*, Kumarian Press, West Hartford.

Bernstein, H., Crow, B. & Johnson, H. (1992) *Rural Livelihoods: crises and responses*, Oxford University Press/The Open University, Oxford (Book 3 of this series).

Bernstein, H. (1971) 'Modernization theory: a sociological study of development', *Journal of Development Studies*, 7(2), pp.141–160.

Bornschier, V. & Chase-Dunn, C. (1985) *Transnational Corporations and Underdevelopment*, Praeger, New York.

Boserup, E. (1987) *Women's Role in Economic Development*, Gower Press, Aldershot.

Bradford, C. (1987) 'Trade and structural change: NICs and the next tier NICs as transitional economies', *World Development*, 15(3).

Brandt, W. *et al.* (1980) *North-South: a programme for survival*, Independent Commission on International Development Issues (The Brandt Report), Pan Books, London.

Brundtland *et al.* (1987) *Our Common Future*, World Commission on Environment and Development (The Brundtland Report), Oxford University Press, London.

Carvalho, R. de Q. (1991) 'Why the market reserve is not enough: the diffusion of industrial automation technology in Brazilian process industries and its policy implications', in Schmitz, H. & Cassiolato, J. (eds), *Hi-Tech For Industrial Development: lessons from the Brazilian experience in electronics and automation*, Routledge, London.

Cassiolato, J.E. (1991) 'The user–producer connection in high-tech: a case-study of banking automation in Brazil', in Schmitz, H. & Cassiolato, J. (eds): *Hi-Tech For Industrial Development: lessons from the Brazilian experience in electronics and automation*, Routledge, London.

Chenery, H., Robinson, S. & Syrquin, M. (eds.) (1986) *Industrialization and Growth: a comparative study*, Oxford University Press, Oxford.

Cline, W. (1982) 'Can the East Asian model of development be generalized?', *World Development*, 10(2).

Cline, W. R. (1984) *International Debt: systemic risk and policy response*, Institute for International Economics, Washington D.C.

Cohen, S.S. & Zysman, J. (1987) *Manufacturing Matters*, Basic Books, New York.

Cumings, B. (1981) *The Origins of the Korean War*, Princeton University Press, New Jersey.

Datta-Chaudhuri, M. K. (1981) 'Industrialization and foreign trade: the development experiences of South Korea and the Philippines' in Lee, E. (ed.), *Export-led Industrialization and Development*, ILO, Geneva.

de Andrade, M. (1984) *Macunaíma*, Quartet, London.

de Andrade, O. (1979) *Seraphim Grosse Pointe*, Nefertiti Press, Paris.

Dicken, P. (1986) *Global Shift: industrial change in a turbulent world*, Harper and Row, London.

Dornbusch, R. & Park, Y. (1987) 'Korean growth policy', *Brookings Papers on Economic Activity*, 2.

Dosi, G. (1988) 'The nature of the innovation process' in Dosi, G., Freeman, C., Nelson, R., Silverberg, G. & Soete, L. (eds) *Technical Change and Economic Theory*, Pinter, London.

Drèze, J. & Sen, A. (1989) *Hunger and Public Action*, Oxford University Press, New York.

Eaton, J & Gersovitz, M. (1981) 'Debt with potential repudiation: theoretical and empirical analysis', *Review of Economic Studies*, 48, pp.289–309.

Edwards, C. (1990) *Malaysia's Industrialisation: what next?* Unpublished working paper, University of East Anglia, Norwich.

Elson, D. (1991) (ed.) Male Bias in the Development Process, Manchester University Press, Manchester.

Emmanuel, A. (1972) *Unequal Exchange: a study of the imperialism of trade*, New Left Books, London.

Evans, P. (1979) *Dependent development: the alliance of multinational, state and local capital in Brazil*, Princeton University Press, New Jersey.

Evenson, R. & Ranis, G. (1990) *Science and Technology: lessons for development policy*, Intermediate Technology Publications, London.

Fishlow, A. (1985) 'The state of Latin American economics', in *Economic and Social Progress in Latin America*, Inter-American Development Bank, Washington.

Frank, C.R, Kim, K.S. & Westphal, L. (1975) *Foreign Trade Regimes and Economic Development*, National Bureau of Economic Research, New York.

Fransman, M. & King, K. (eds) (1984) *Technological Capability in the Third World*, Macmillan, London & Basingstoke.

Freeman, C. (1990) Unpublished data presented at IDS workshop, 'Hitech for industrial development', Institute of Development Studies, University of Sussex, 20–22 June.

Freire, P. (1972) *The Pedagogy of the Oppressed*, Penguin, Harmondsworth.

Freyre G. (1933) *Casa Grande é Senzala*, Liceros Do Brasil, Lisbon; Putnam, E. (tr.) (1986) English translation *The Masters and the Slaves: a study in the development of Brazilian civilization*, University of California Press.

Frischtak, C. (1986) *The informatics sector in Brazil: policies, institutions and the performance of the computer industry*, Industrial Strategy and Policy Division, World Bank, Washington.

Fröbel, F., Heinrichs, J. & Kreye, O. (1980) *The New International Division of Labour*, Cambridge University Press, Cambridge.

Fröbel, F., Heinrichs, J. & Kreye, O. (1986) *Umbruch in der Weltwirtschaft*, Rowohlt, Hamburg.

Furtado, C. (1976) Economic *Development of Latin America: historical background and contemporary problems*, Macedo, S. (Tr), 2nd edition, Cambridge University Press, Cambridge.

Gerhart, J. D. (1989) Foreword to 'Beyond survival: expanding income opportunities for women in developing countries', Special Issue of *World Development*, 17(7).

Gibson, H. D. (1989) *The Eurocurrency markets, Domestic Financial Policy and International Instability*, Macmillan, London.

Glucksman, M. (1990) *Women Assemble: women workers and the new industries in inter-war Britain*, Routledge Kegan Paul, London.

Goldsmith, E. *et al.* (1972) *A Blueprint for Survival*, Tom Stacey, London.

Gordon, D. (1988) 'The global economy: new edifice or crumbling foundations?', *New Left Review*, 168 (March), pp.24–65.

Gramsci, A. (1971) *Selections from the Prison Notebooks*, Hoare, Q. & Smith, G.N. (trans. & eds), Lawrence & Wishart, London.

Greenaway, D. (1983) *International Trade Policy: From Tariffs to the New Protectionism*, Macmillan, London.

Grieco, J. (1984): *Between Dependency and Autonomy: India's experience with the international computer industry*, University of California Press, California.

Guimaraës, C. & Amaral, R. (1988) 'Brazilian television: a rapid conversion to a new order', in Fox, E. (ed.) *Media and Politics in Latin America*, Sage Publications.

Guttentag, J. M. & Herring R. J. (1986) 'Disaster myopia in international banking', *Princeton Essays in International Finance*, 164.

Gwynne, R. (1990) *New Horizons?: Third World industrialization in an international framework*, Longman, Harlow.

Hall, S. (1981) *Notes on Deconstructing the Popular in People's History and Socialist Theory*, Samuel, R. (ed.), Routledge.

Halliday, J. & Cumings, B. (1988) *Korea: the unknown war*, Pantheon.

Hamilton, C. (1986) *Capitalist Industrialization in Korea*, Westview Press, Boulder and London.

Harris, L. (1988) 'Financial reform and economic growth; a new interpretation of South Korea's experience', in Harris, L. (ed) *New Perspectives on the Financial System*, Croom Helm, London.

Harris, N. (1986), *The end of the Third World: newly industrializing countries and the decline of an ideology*, Penguin, Harmondsworth.

Heeks, R. (1991) 'State policy, liberalization and the development of the Indian software industry', PhD thesis, Open University.

Hirschman, A. (1981) 'The rise and decline of development economics' in Gerrsovitz, M., Diaz-Alejandro, C., Ranis, G. & Rosenzweig, M.R.(eds) *The Theory and Experience of Economic Development*, Allen and Unwin, London.

Humphrey & Wield (1983) 'Industrialization and energy in Brazil' , Case Study 6 in the Open University course *U204 Third World Studies,* Open University, Milton Keynes.

Humphrey, J. (1982) *Capitalist Control and Workers' Struggle in the Brazilian Auto Industry*, Princeton University Press, New Jersey.

Humphrey, J. (1987) *Gender and Work In the Third World: Sexual Divisions in Brazilian Industry,* Tavistock, London.

Ianni, O. (1971) *O Colapso do Populismo*, Civilização, Rio de Janeiro.

ILO (1988), *Bridging the Gap: Four Newly Industrializing Countries and the Changing International Division of Labour*, International Labour Office, Geneva.

ILO (1988a) *Year Book of Labour Statistics 1986*, International Labour Office, Geneva.

ILO (1990) *Year Book of Labour Statistics, Retrospective edition on Population Censuses, 1945–89*, International Labour Office, Geneva.

Jenkins, R. (1987) *Transnational Corporations and Uneven Development*, Methuen, London.

Joekes, S. (1987) *Women In the World Economy,* Oxford University Press, Oxford.

Kaplinsky, R. (1984) 'The international context of industrialization in the coming decade', *Journal of Development Studies*, 21(1).

Kaplinsky, R. (1984a) 'Trade in technology — who, what, where and when?' in Fransman, M. & King, K. (eds) *Technological Capability in the Third World*, Macmillan, London & Basingstoke.

Kaplinsky, R. (1988) *Industrial Restructuring in LDCS: the role of information Technology,* Institute of Development Studies, Brighton.

Killick, T. (ed) (1984) *The Quest for Economic Stabilisation*, Gower, London.

Kim, J. (1975) *Divided Korea: the politics of development 1945–72*, East Asia Research Centre, Harvard University Press, Cambridge, Mass.

Kim, Y. (1991) 'Women, home-based work and questions of organising: the case of South Korea', Paper presented at the International Workshop on Women Organising in the Process of Industrialisation, Institute of Social Studies, The Hague, April 1991.

Kitching, G. (1982) *Development and Underdevelopment in Historical Perspective: populism, nationalism and industrialisation,* Routledge, London.

Kline, S. J. (1989) *Innovation Styles in Japan and the United States: cultural bases; implications for competitiveness,* Report INN-3B, December, Stanford University.

Krueger, A. (1974) 'The Political Economy of the Rent-Seeking Society', *The American Economic Review,* 34(3).

Krueger, A. (1978) *Liberalization Attempts and Consequences*, Ballinger Publishing Company for National Bureau of Economic Research, Cambridge, Mass.

Kumar, K. (1978) *Prophecy and Progress,* Penguin, Harmondsworth.

Kuznets, P. (1977) *Economic Growth and Structure in the Republic of Korea*, Yale University Press, New Haven.

Lal, D. (1983) *The Poverty of 'Development Economics'*, Institute of Economic Affairs, Hobart Paperback 16, London.

Landes, D. (1969) *The Unbound Prometheus*, Cambridge University Press, London.

Lee, E. (1979) 'Egalitarian peasant farming and rural development; the case of South Korea', *World Development,* 7 (4/5), pp.493–517.

Lessard, D. R. & Williamson, J. (1987) Capital Flight and Third World Debt, Institute for International Economics, Washington D.C.

Lever, H. & Huhne, C. (1985) *Debt and Danger: the world financial crisis*, Penguin, London.

Lim, L. (1990) 'Women's work in export factories: the politics of a cause' in Tinker, I. (ed.) *Persistent Inequalities: women and world development*, Oxford University Press, Oxford.

Little, I. M. D. (1981) 'The experience and causes of rapid labour-intensive development in Korea, Taiwan Province, Hong Kong and Singapore and the possibilities of emulation', in Lee, E. (ed.), *Export-led Industrialization and Development,* International Labour Office, Geneva.

Little, I. M. D. (1982) *Economic Development: theory, policy and international relations*, Basic Books, New York.

Luedde-Neurath, R. (1984) 'State intervention and foreign direct investment in South Korea', *IDS Bulletin*, 15 (2), p.23.

Luedde-Neurath, R. (1988) 'State Intervention and Export-oriented Development in South Korea', in White, G. (ed.), *Developmental States in East Asia*, Macmillan/Institute of Development Studies, Basingstoke.

Marcel, M . & Palma, G. (1987) *The Debt Crisis: the Third World and British banks*, Fabian Research Series, 350.

Marx, K. (1973) *Grundrisse,* Penguin, Harmondsworth.

Marx, K. (1888) 'Theses on Feuerbach' in Marx, K. & Engels, F., *The German Ideology*, Student Edition 1974, Arthur, C.J. (ed.) , Lawrence and Wishart, London.

Max Nettlau archives (1913) International Institute, Amsterdam.

Meadows, D. *et al.*(1972) *The Limits to Growth*, Earth Island, London.

Meier, G. (1984) *Emerging from Poverty: The Economics that Really Matters,* Oxford University Press, Oxford.

Milner, C. (ed) (1990) *Export Promotion Strategies; theory and evidence from developing countries,* Harvester Wheatsheaf, New York and London.

Mitter, S. (1986) *Common Fate, Common Bond: women in the global economy*, Pluto Press, London.

Mitter, S. (1989) *The Role of Women in Industrial Development*, UNIDO, Vienna.

Mody, A. (1987) *Information Industries: the changing role of newly industrializing Countries. Technology and Government Policy in Telecommunications and computers,* Brookings Institute, Washington D.C.

Moser, C. (1989) 'The impact of recession and structural adjustment policies at the micro-level: low income women and their households in Guayaquil, Ecuador', *Invisible Adjustment*, 2, UNICEF.

O'Connor, D.C. (1985) 'The Computer Industry in the Third World: Policy Options and Constraints', *World Development*, 13(3).

OECD (1984) *Investing in Free Export Processing Zones*, Development Centre Studies, OECD, Paris.

OECD (1988) *The Newly Industrializing Countries : Challenge and Opportunity for OECD Industries*, OECD, Paris.

Ogle, G. (1990) *South Korea: dissent within the economic miracle*, Zed Books, London and New Jersey.

Oxfam (1981) *Brazil — a mask called progress*, an Oxfam report by Neil Macdonald, Oxfam, Oxford.

Pearson, R. (1991) 'Male bias and women's work in Mexico's border industries', in Elson, D. (1991) (ed.) *Male Bias in the Development Process,* Manchester University Press, Manchester.

Pearce, D. *et al*. (1989) *Blueprint for a Green Economy*, Earthscan, London.

Phantumvanit, D. (1987) *Thailand: natural resource profile,* Oxford University Press, Oxford.

Phillips, A. & Taylor, B. (1980) 'Sex and skill: notes towards a feminist economics', *Feminist Review*, 6.

Phongpaichit, P. (1988) 'Two roads to the factory: industrialisation strategies and women's employment in South East Asia' in Agarwal, B. (ed.) *Structures of Patriarchy: the State, the Community and the Household,* Zed Press, London.

Pinchbeck, I. (1981) *Women Workers and the Industrial Revolution 1750–1850,* Virago Press, London.

Pineda Ofreneo, R. (1984) 'Subcontracting in export-oriented industries: the impact on Filipino women', in Norland, I. *et al.* (eds) *Industrialisation and the Labour Process in South East Asia*, Institute of Cultural Sociology, University of Copenhagen, Denmark.

Raghavan, C. (1990) 'Recolonization: GATT in its historical context', *The Ecologist,* 20 (6) pp.205–207.

Ramos, G. (1961) *Barren Lives*, Texas University Press.

Redclift, M. (1987) *Sustainable Development: exploring the contradictions*, Methuen, London.

Rego, J L do (1966) *Plantation Boy*, Knopf, New York.

Ribeiro, M.V., Alencar, C. & Ceccon, C. (1991) B*razil Vivo 2: A República*, Vozes, 2nd edition, Petrópolis, Brazil.

Riedel, J. (1988) 'Economic development in East Asia: doing what comes naturally?' in Hughes, H. (ed.), *Achieving Industrialization in East Asia*, Cambridge University Press.

Rostow, W.W. (1960) *The Stages of Economic Growth: a non-communist manifesto*, Cambridge University Press.

Sachs, J. (1985) 'External debt and macroeconomic performance in Latin America and East Asia', *Brookings Papers on Economic Activity*, 2, pp.523–564.

Saffioti, H. (1978), *Women in Class Society*, Monthly Review Press, New York and London.

Scammel, W. M. (1975) *International Monetary Policy: Bretton Woods and After*, Macmillan, London.

Schmitz, H. & Cassiolato, J. (eds) (1991) *Hi-Tech For Industrial Development: lessons from the Brazilian experience in electronics and automation*, Routledge, London.

Schmitz, H. (1982) *Manufacturing in the Backyard*, Pinter, London.

Schmitz, H. (1989) *Flexible Specialisation — a new paradigm of small-scale industrialisation?*, IDS Discussion Paper 261, Institute of Development Studies, Brighton.

Schumacher, E. (1973) *Small is Beautiful*, Abacus, London.

Seers, D. (1963) 'The limitations of the special case', *Bulletin of the Oxford Institute of Economics and Statistics*, 25(2).

Sen, A.K. (1983) 'Development: which way now?', *Economic Journal*, 93 (Dec.).

Sharpston, M. (1976) 'International subcontracting', *World Development*, 4(4).

Sheahan, J. (1987) *Patterns of Development in Latin America: poverty, repression and economic strategy*, Princeton University Press, New Jersey.

Simão, A. (1966) *Sindicato e Estado*, Dominus Editora, São Paulo.

Singer, H. (1988) 'The World Development Report 1987 on the blessings of 'outward orientation': a necessary correction', *Journal of Development Studies*, January 1988.

Singer, H. (1989), 'Lessons of post-war development experience: 1945–88' Discussion Paper no 260, April, Institute of Development Studies, University of Sussex, Brighton.

Singer, P. (1976) 'Evolução da Economia Brasileira: 1955-1975', *Estudos CEBRAP*, 17, São Paulo.

Singh, A. (1977) 'UK industry and the world economy: a case of de-industrialisation?', *Cambridge Journal of Economics*, 1.

Skidmore, T. (1988) *The Politics of Military Rule in Brazil 1964-1985*, OUP, New York.

Sklair, L. (1989) *Assembling for Development: the maquila industry in Mexico and the USA*, Unwin Hyman, Boston and London.

Spraos, J. (1984) 'IMF conditionality – a better way', *Banca Nazionale del Lavoro Quarterly Review*, 157, pp.411–421.

Standing, G. (1989) 'Global feminization through flexible labour', *World Development*, 1(7).

Stanyer, P. & Whitley, J. (1981) 'Financing world payments imbalances', *Bank of England Quarterly Bulletin*, 21(2), pp.187–199.

Stewart, F. & Sengupta, A. (1982) *International Financial Cooperation: a framework for change*, Pinter, London.

Stoneman, C. (1990), 'Policy reform or industrialisation? The choice for Zimbabwe' Paper presented to conference on 'The impact of policy reform or trade and industrial performance in developing countries', University of Bradford, 21–22 June.

Suzigan, W. (1989) Unpublished paper 'Condicionantes e princípios básicos de uma estratégia industrial Brasileira para a década de noventa', University of Campiuas, Brazil.

Tew, B. (1977) *The Evolution of the International Monetary System: 1945–77*, Hutchins, London.

Thompson, E. P. (1976) *William Morris*, Pantheon Press, London.

Tigre, P. B. (1986) 'Perspectivas da indústria Brasileira de computadores na segunda metade do anos 80' Instituto de Economica Industrial, Universidade Federal do Rio de Janeiro (IEI/UFRJ).

Timberlake, L. (1988) 'The Brundtland Report: an opportunity for NGOs?' Conference speech, International Institute for Environment and Development, Brussels.

Todaro, M.P. (1981) *Economic Development in the Third World*, 2nd edn, Longman, New York and London.

Tsiang, S. & Wu, R-I. (1985) 'Foreign trade and investment as boosters of take-off: the experience of the four Asian NICs' in Galenson, W. (ed.), *Foreign Trade and Investment: Economic Development in the Newly Industrializing Asian Countries*, The University of Wisconsin Press, Madison.

Tyler, W.G. (1981) *The Brazilian Industrial Economy*, Lexington Books, Lexington, Mass.

UN (1987) *International Statistics Yearbook*, United Nations, New York.

UNCTAD (1988), United Nations Conference on Trade and Development, New York.

UNCTC (1985) *Transnational Corporations and International Trade: selected issues*, United Nations Center for Transnational Corporations, New York.

UNCTC (1988) *Transnational Corporations in World Development*, United Nations Center for Transnational Corporations, New York.

UNDP (1990) *Human Development Report 1990*, Oxford University Press, Oxford.

UNIDO (1985) *World Industry — a statistical review*, United Nations Industrial Development Organization, Vienna.

UNIDO (1986) *Industry and Development: Global Report 1986*, United Nations Industrial Development Organization, Vienna.

UNIDO (1990) *Industry and Development: Global Report, 1989/90,* United Nations Industrial Development Organization, Vienna.

Vaitsos, C. (1974) *Inter-Country Income Distribution and Transnational Enterprises*, Clarendon Press, Oxford.

Van Liemt, G. (1988) *'Bridging the Gap; four newly industrializing countries and the division of labour,* International Labour Office, Geneva,.

Wade, R.(1983) 'South Korea's agricultural development; the myth of the passive state', *Pacific Viewpoint*, 24(1); also in Wade, R. (1990) *Governing the Market*, Princeton University Press, New Jersey.

Weiss, J. (1990) *Industry in Developing Countries: theory, policy and evidence,* Routledge, London and New York.

Wells, J. (1986) 'Latin America: Can't Pay...Won't Pay', *Marxism Today*, August, pp.16–22.

Westphal, L. E., Yung, W. R. & Pursell, G. (1984) 'Sources of technological capability in South Korea' in Fransman, M. & King, K. (eds) *Technological capability in the Third World*, Macmillan, London & Basingstoke.

White, G. (1983), 'Chinese Development Strategy after Mao' in White, G., Murray, R. & White, C., *Revolutionary Socialist Development in the Third World*, Wheatsheaf, Brighton.

Wield, D.(1981), 'Manufacturing Industry' in Stoneman, C., *Zimbabwe's Inheritance*, MacMillan, Basingstoke.

Williams, (1981) *Culture*, Fontana, London.

Williams, R. (1982) *Socialism and Ecology*, SERA Publications, London.

Wolf, D.L. (1991) 'Daughters, decisions and domination: an empirical and conceptual critique of household strategies', *Development and Change*, 21, pp.43–47.

World Bank (1983) *World Development Report 1983*, Oxford University Press, Oxford.

World Bank (1986) *World Development Report 1986*, Oxford University Press, Oxford.

World Bank (1987) *World Development Report 1987*, Oxford University Press, Oxford.

World Bank (1988) World Develop*ment Report 1988*, Oxford University Press, Oxford.

World Bank (1989) *World Development Report 1989,* Oxford University Press, Oxford.

World Bank (1990) *World Development Report 1990*, Oxford University Press, Oxford.

World Bank (1990a) *World Debt Tables,* World Bank, Washington D.C.

World Bank (1991), *World Development Report 1991*, Oxford University Press, Oxford.

World Resources Institute (1989) *World Resources 1988–89*, Basic Books, New York.

World Resources Institute (1991) *World Resources 1990–91,* Basic Books, New York.

Yeager, L. B. (1976) *International Monetary Relations: history, theory and policy,* 2nd edition, Harper and Row, New York.

Young, K., Wolkowitz, C. & McCullagh, R. (eds) (1984) *Of Marriage and the Market*, Routledge Kegan Paul, London.

Yusuf, S. & Peters, R. K. (1985) *Capital Accumulation and Economic Growth: the Korean paradigm*, World Bank Staff Working Paper 712, World Bank, Washington, D.C.

Index compiled by Kate Legon

Acknowledgements

Grateful acknowledgement is made to the following sources for permission to reproduce material in this book:

Text

Box 3.2: adapted from World Bank (1990), *World Development Report,* © The World Bank; *Box 3.6:* MacDonald N. (1991), *Brazil: A Mask Called Progress,* Oxfam; *Box 6.1:* The World Bank (1987), *World Development Report,* © The World Bank; *Chapter 8:* Pongpaichit P. (1988), 'Two roads to the factory: industrialization strategies and women's employment in South East Asia', in Agarwal B. (ed), *Structures of Patriarchy, the State, the Community and the Household,* Zed Books Ltd; *Chapter 9:* Almeida J.G., *A Vida Do Nordestino Que VE1 OP/S,* Ed,Cordel, São Paulo.

Tables

Table 6.4: adapted from Agarwala R. (1983), 'Price distortions and growth', *World Bank Staff Working Papers,* © The World Bank; *Table 7.1:* adapted from Schmitz H. and Cassiolato J. (1991), *Hi-Tech for Industrial Development: Lessons from the Brazilian Experience in Electronics and Automation,* 1st ed, Routledge; *Table 10.3:* World Resources Institute (1989), *World Resources 1988-89,* 1st ed, Basic Books Inc.

Diagrams

Figure 1.6: Figure from *Global Shift* by Peter Dickens. Copyright © 1986 by Peter Dickens. Reprinted by permission of Harper Collins Publishers; *Figure 1.11:* adapted from the World Bank (1987), *World Development Report,* © The World Bank; *Figure 6.4:* Michaely M., Papageorgiou D. & Choksi A.M.. (1991), *Liberalizing Foreign Trade: Volume 7, Lessons of Experience in the Developing World,* © The World Bank; *Figures 6.5 & 6.6:* adapted from The World Bank (1987), *World Development Report,* © The World Bank; *Figure 10.5:* Pearce D., Maruandya A. & Barbier E. (1989), *Blueprint for A Green Economy,* Earthscan Publications.

Photographs and cartoons

Part 1 title page: Tom Hanley; *Part 2 Title page:* Andes Press Agency; *Figures 1(a), (b):* Sue Cunningham; *Figure 1(c):* Tom Hanley; *Figure 1(d):* Centre for World Development Education / World Bank / J.R. Nonato; *Figure 1(e):* Hutchison Library; *Figure 2:* Dr John Humphrey; *Figure 1.4:* Ron Giling / Panos Pictures; *Figure 1.5:* Tom Hanley; *Figure 1.7:* Ford of Britain; *Figure 1.8:* Vauxhall Motors Ltd, Luton; *Figure 1.9: The Times of India; Figure 1.13:* Jenny Matthews / Format; *Figure 1.14:* Tom Hanley; *Figure 2.1:* © Times Newspapers Ltd, 1982; *Figures 2.3 & 2.9:* Raul Ampuero; *Figure 2.6:* Leo Rosenthal / Pix; Figure 2.7: Cartoon by David Low, reproduced by permission of *New Statesman & Society; Figure 2.8:* © Universal Press Syndicate 1983; *Figure 2.10:* Jenny Matthews / Format; *Figure 2.12:* Julio Etchart; *Figures 3.3, 3.6, 3.13, 3.15 & 3.16:* Claudius Ceccon; from Ribeiro, M.V., Alencar, C., Ceccon, C. (1991), *Brasil Vivo,* Vozes; *Figure 3.4:* Topham; *Figure 3.5:* Brazilian Embassy; *Figure 3.7:* Hutchison Library, photo by Jesco Von Puttkamer; *Figures 3.9 & 3.12:* Julio Etchart; *Figure 3.11:* Agencia o Globo; *Figure 3.14:* Panos Pictures, © Susan Cunningham; *Figure 4.4:* Embassy of the Republic of Korea, London; *Figure 4.5 (top):* The Hulton-Deutsch Collection; *Figure 4.5 (bottom):* Korean National Tourism Corporation; *Figure 4.6:* A Handbook of Korea (1988), 7th ed, Seoul International Publishing House; *Figure 4.7:* The Hulton-Deutsch Collection, photographer: Bert Hardy; *Figures 4.8, 4.10, 4.12, 4.13, 4.14:* Tom Hanley; Figure 4.15: Panos Pictures, © photo Heldur Jaan Netocny; *Figure 5.1:* Popperfoto; *Figure 5.2:* Liba Taylor / Panos; *Figures 5.3, 5.4 & 5.9:* from Regan, C., Sinclair, S. & Turner, M. (1988) *Thin Black Lines* Development Education Centre, Birmingham; *Figure 5.5 (left):* Hutchison Library; *Figure 5.5 (right):* Ron Giling / Panos Pictures; *Figure 5.6:* ODI (1988), *ODI Briefing Paper - Commodity Prices - Investing In Decline,* © Overseas Development Institute, London; *Figure 5.7:* John Humphrey; *Figure 5.10:* Andy Hall / Select; Figure 5.11: Centre for World

Development Education / World Bank; Figure 5.12: Associated Press Photo; Figure 5.14: World Bank (1987), *World Development Report*, © The World Bank; *Figure 5.15: New Internationalist*, No 222, August 1991; Figure 5.16: Michael Pickstock / Panos Pictures; *Figure 6.1 (top):* Associated Press / Topham; *Figure 6.1 (bottom):* Associated Press. Photo; Figure 6.2 (top): Hutchison Library; *Figures 6.2 (bottom), 6.7 (bottom), 6.8 (left) & 6.11:* Tom Hanley; *Figures 6.3 & 6.8 (right):* Sue Cunningham; *Figure 6.7 (top):* Hutchison Library; *Figure 6.9:* Centre for World Development Education / World Bank / J.R. Nonato; *Figure 6.12:* Tom Hewitt; *Figure 6.13:* Batellier J.F. (1984), *Is Anybody Out There?* Free Association Books; *Figure 6.14:* Diego Goldberg / Camera Press; *Figure 7.1:* Compix; *Figures 7.2 & 7.8:* Tom Hewitt; *Figure 7.3:* Julio Etchart; *Figures 7.4 & 7.9:* Ron Giling / Panos Pictures; *Figure 7.5:* Tropix / J Schmid; *Figure 7.6 (top):* Cooper & Hammond / Panos Pictures; *Figure 7.6 (bottom):* Intermediate Technology; *Figure 7.7:* Reprinted by permission from *Nature*, Vol 275, copyright © 1978 Macmillan Magazines Ltd; *Figure 7.10:* David Spark; *Figure 8.1:* Ron Giling / Still Pictures; *Figure 8.2:* Centre for World Development Education / World Bank; *Figures 8.3, 8.5(a), & 8.5(b):* Tom Hanley; *Figure 8.4:* ILO; *Figure 8.6:* Sean Sprague / Panos Pictures; *Figure 8.7:* Sue Darlow / Format; *Figure 9.3:* J. Barros, Editions Cordel, São Paulo; *Figure 9.8:* Rugendas, M. (1853) *Maderische Reise in Brasilien*, Zentralbibliotek, Zurich; *Figure 9.9:* from postcard published by the South Bank Centre, London, 1989, original painting in Museu Nacional de Belas Artes, Rio de Janeiro; *Figures 9.10 & 9.11:* Sue Cunningham Photographic; *Figure 10.1:* National Museum for Science and Technology; Figure 10.2: Ron Giling / Still Pictures; *Figure 10.4:* Oxfam; *Figure 10.6:* Sight Savers / Associated Press Photo; *Figures 10.7, 10.8 & 10.10:* Paul Smith; *Figure 10.9:* Susan Griggs Agency, © David Beatty; *Figure 10.11:* Mark Edwards / Still Pictures; *Figures 11.1 & 11.7:* from Regan, C., Sinclair, S. & Turner, M. (1988) *Thin Black Lines* Development Education Centre, Birmingham; *Figure 11.2:* Hutchison Library, © Michael MacIntyre; *Figure 11.3:* Aurora Press; *Figure 11.4:* Richard and Sally Greenhill; *Figure 11.5:* from *New Internationalist*, October 1991; *Figure 11.6;* from *Times Higher Education Supplement*, 4 Oct. 1991.

Editors' acknowledgements

The editors with to acknowledge the valuable contributions made to this book by Chris Edwards, Rhys Jenkins and Ruth Pearson of the University of East Anglia, and by Heather Gibson and Euclid Tsakolotos of the University of Kent.

List of acronyms, abbreviations and organizations

CACEX	the trade department of the Bank of Brazil
COMECON	Council for Mutual Economic Assistance (economic association of Soviet-bloc countries)
CPE	centrally planned economy
CUT	*Central Unica dos Trabalhadores*, a Brazilian trade union organization formed in the 1970s
CVRD	the Brazilian state-owned mining company
DC	developed country
DFI	direct foreign investment
EAP	economically active population
ECLA	Economic Commission for Latin America (United Nations)
EEC	European Economic Community
EOI	export-oriented industrialization
EPZ	export processing zone
FAO	Food and Agriculture Organization (United Nations)
FTZ	free trade zone
GATT	General Agreement on Tariffs and Trade
GDP	gross domestic product
GNP	gross national product
ILO	International Labour Office (United Nations)
IMF	International Monetary Fund
ISI	import-substitution industrialization
KDP	Korean Democratic Party
LDC	less developed country
LIBOR	London interbank offered rate (a market interest rate for loans to developing countries)
MFZ	Manaus Free Zone (Brazil)
MNC	multinational corporations
MVA	manufacturing value added
NIC	newly industrializing country
OECD	Organization for Economic Co-operation and Development
OPEC	Organization of Petroleum Exporting Countries
PDS	the political party of the military in Brazil
POSC	Pohan Iron and Steel Company (Korea)
PT	*Partido Trabalhista* (Workers' Party), a Brazilian political party
TERI	Tata Energy Research Institute (India)
TNC	transnational corporation
UDI	unilateral declaration of independence (Zimbabwe)
UDR	'Democratic Rural Union', a Brazilian landowners' organization
UN	United Nations
UNCTAD	United Nations Conference on Trade and Development
UNCTC	United Nations Center for Transnational Corporations
UNDP	United Nations Development Programme
UNIDO	United Nations Industrial Development Organization

Index